子連れ狼

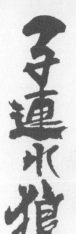

LONE
WOLF

AND
CUB

story
KAZUO KOIKE

art
GOSEKI KOJIMA

DARK HORSE COMICS

translation
DANA LEWIS

lettering & retouch
DIGITAL CHAMELEON

cover illustration
BILL SIENKIEWICZ

publisher
MIKE RICHARDSON

editor
TIM ERVIN-GORE

assistant editor
JEREMY BARLOW

consulting editor
TOREN SMITH for **STUDIO PROTEUS**

book design
DARIN FABRICK

art director
MARK COX

Published by Dark Horse Comics, Inc., in association
with MegaHouse and Koike Shoin Publishing Company.

Dark Horse Comics, Inc.
10956 SE Main Street, Milwaukie, OR 97222
www.darkhorse.com

First edition: February 2002
ISBN: 1-56971-590-4

1 3 5 7 9 10 8 6 4 2

Printed in Canada

To find a comics shop in your area, call the
Comic Shop Locator Service toll-free at 1-888-266-4226.

TWILIGHT OF THE KUROKUWA

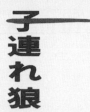

子連れ狼

By KAZUO KOIKE
& GOSEKI KOJIMA

VOLUME
18

A NOTE TO READERS

Lone Wolf and Cub is famous for its carefully researched re-creation of Edo-Period Japan. To preserve the flavor of the work, we have chosen to retain many Edo-Period terms that have no direct equivalents in English. Japanese is written in a mix of Chinese ideograms and a syllabic writing system, resulting in numerous synonyms. In the glossary, you may encounter words with multiple meanings. These are words written with Chinese ideograms that are pronounced the same but carry different meanings. A Japanese reader seeing the different ideograms would know instantly which meaning it is, but these synonyms can cause confusion when Japanese is spelled out in our alphabet. *O-yurushi o* (please forgive us)!

LONE WOLF AND CUB

子連れ狼

TABLE OF CONTENTS

the eighty-eighth

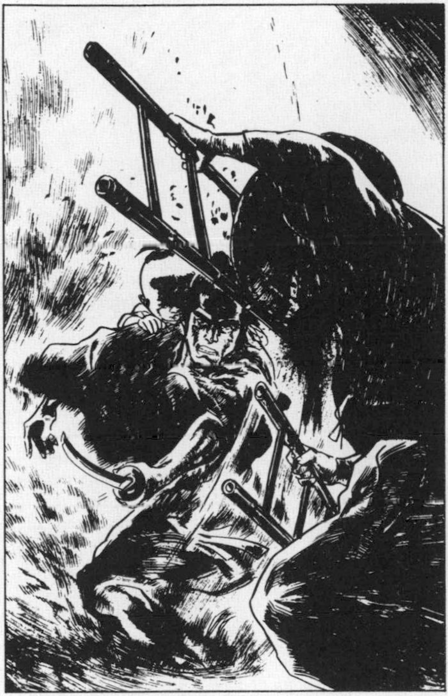

Firewatchers of the Black Gate

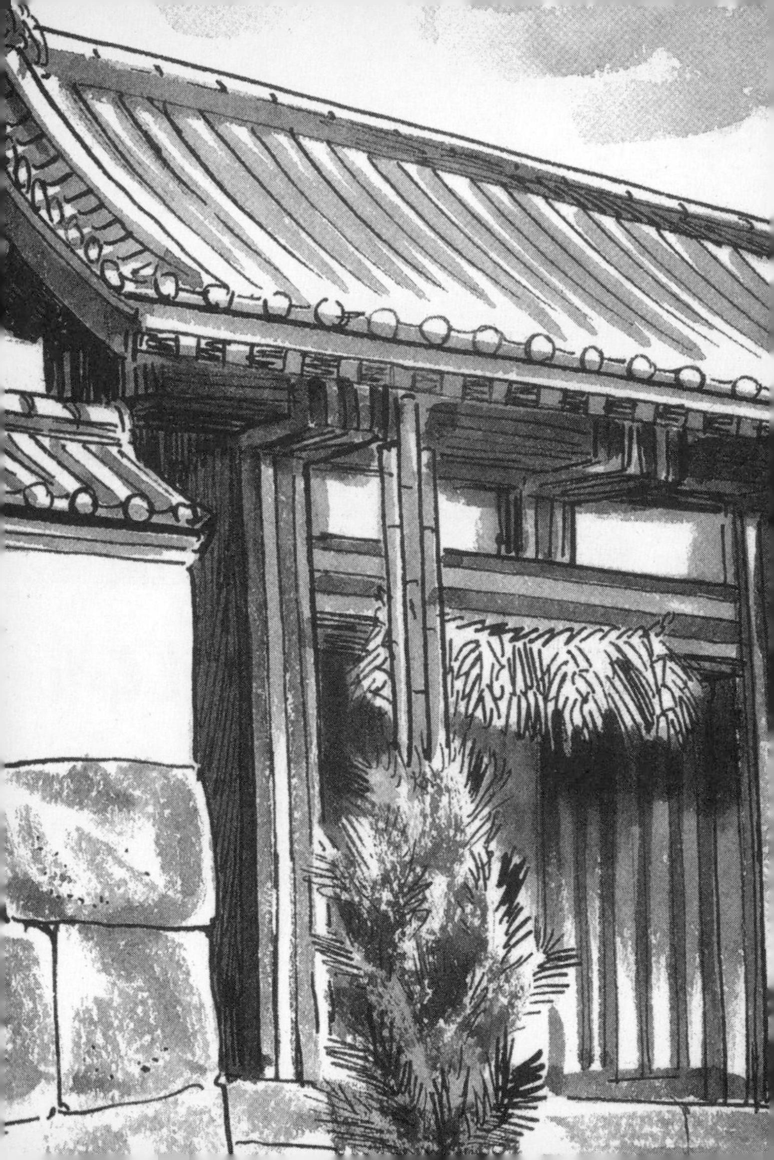

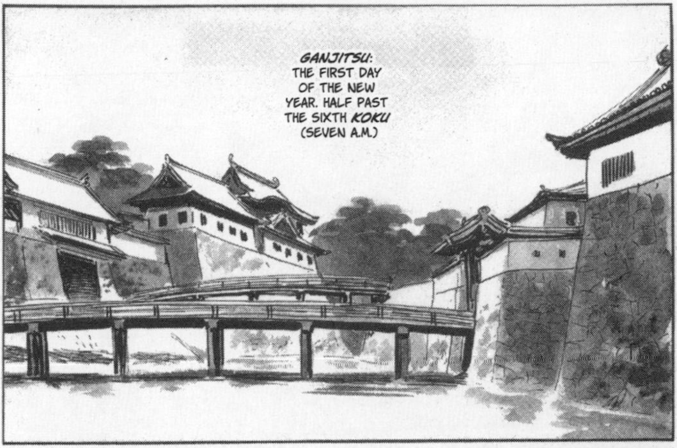
GANJITSU: THE FIRST DAY OF THE NEW YEAR. HALF PAST THE SIXTH KOKU (SEVEN A.M.)

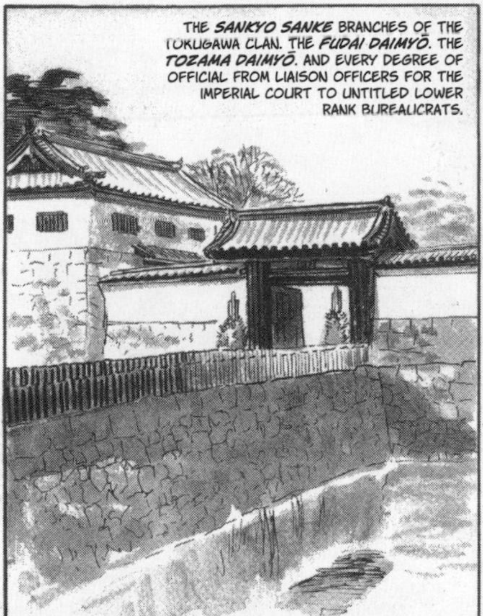
THE SANKYO SANKE BRANCHES OF THE TOKUGAWA CLAN. THE FUDAI DAIMYŌ. THE TOZAMA DAIMYŌ. AND EVERY DEGREE OF OFFICIAL FROM LIAISON OFFICERS FOR THE IMPERIAL COURT TO UNTITLED LOWER RANK BUREAUCRATS.

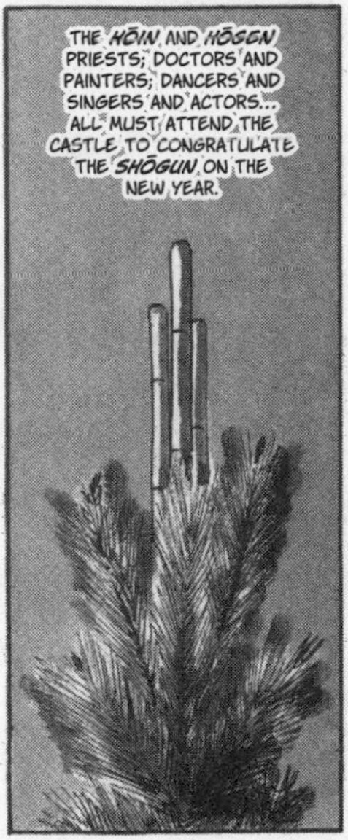
THE HŌIN AND HŌSEN PRIESTS; DOCTORS AND PAINTERS; DANCERS AND SINGERS AND ACTORS... ALL MUST ATTEND THE CASTLE TO CONGRATULATE THE SHŌGUN ON THE NEW YEAR.

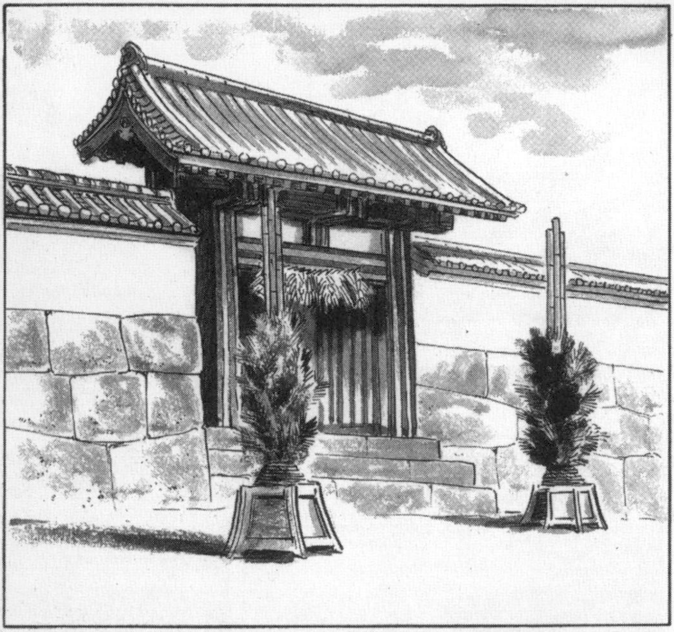

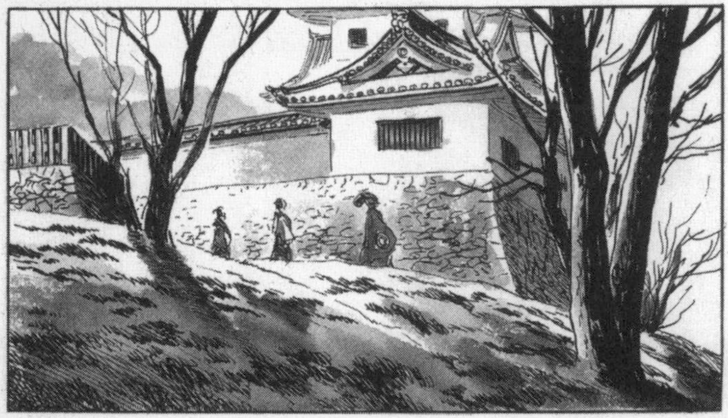

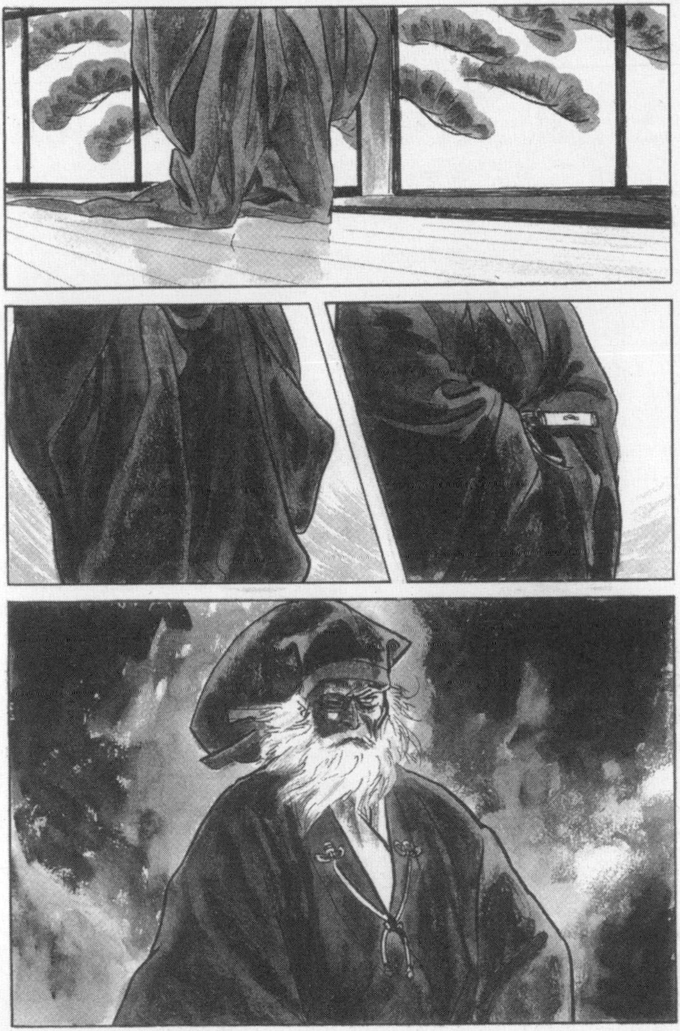

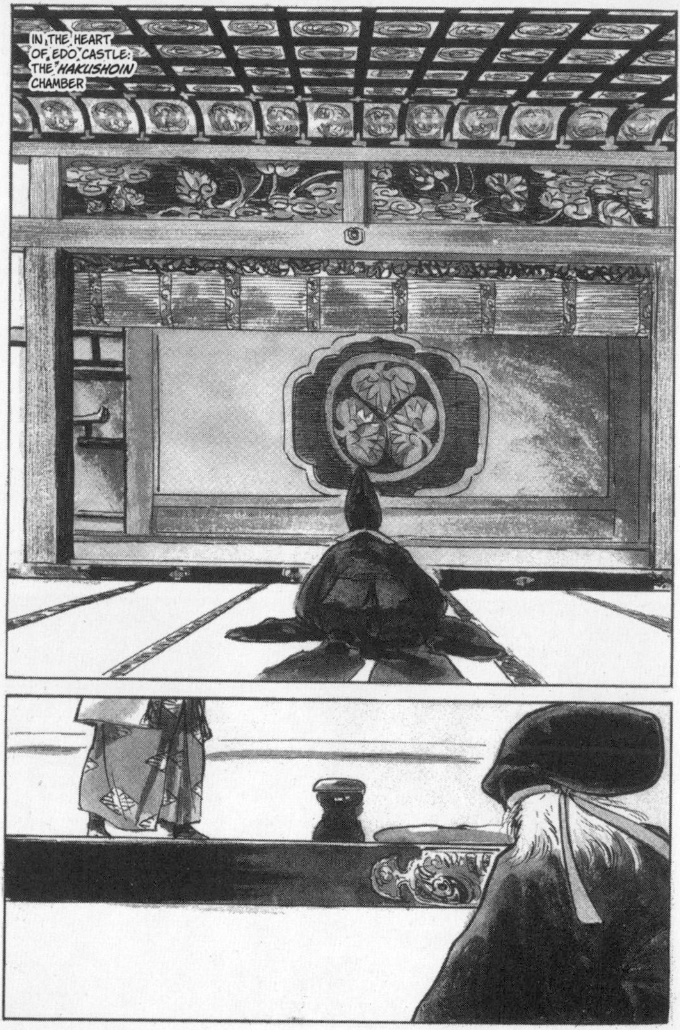
IN THE HEART OF EDO CASTLE: THE HAKUSHOIN CHAMBER

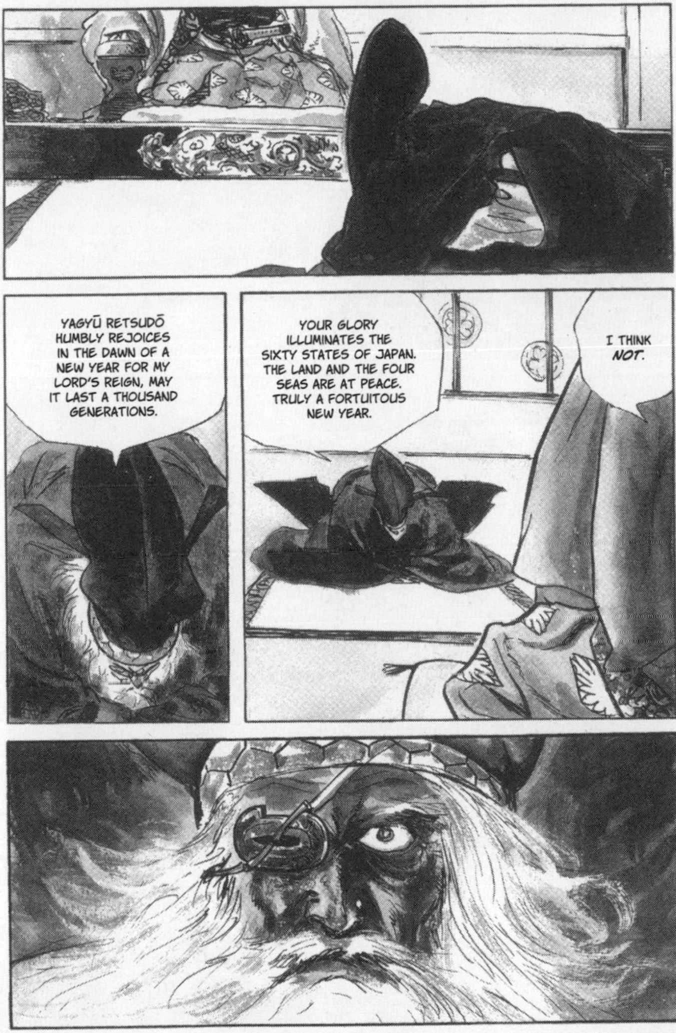
YAGYŪ RETSUDŌ HUMBLY REJOICES IN THE DAWN OF A NEW YEAR FOR MY LORD'S REIGN, MAY IT LAST A THOUSAND GENERATIONS.
YOUR GLORY ILLUMINATES THE SIXTY STATES OF JAPAN. THE LAND AND THE FOUR SEAS ARE AT PEACE. TRULY A FORTUITOUS NEW YEAR.
I THINK *NOT*.

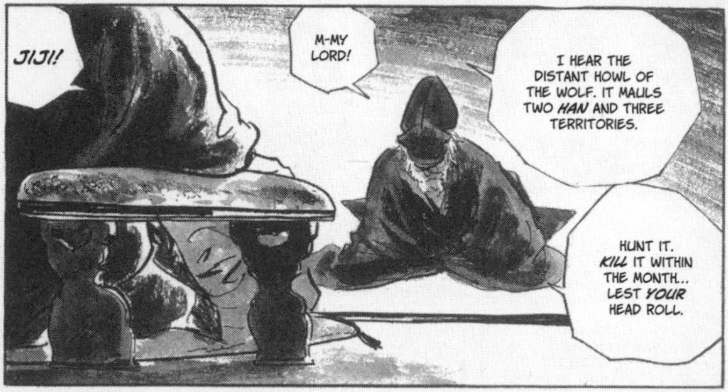
I HEAR THE DISTANT HOWL OF THE WOLF. IT MAULS TWO *HAN* AND THREE TERRITORIES.
HUNT IT. *KILL* IT WITHIN THE MONTH... LEST *YOUR* HEAD ROLL.
M-MY LORD!
JIJI!

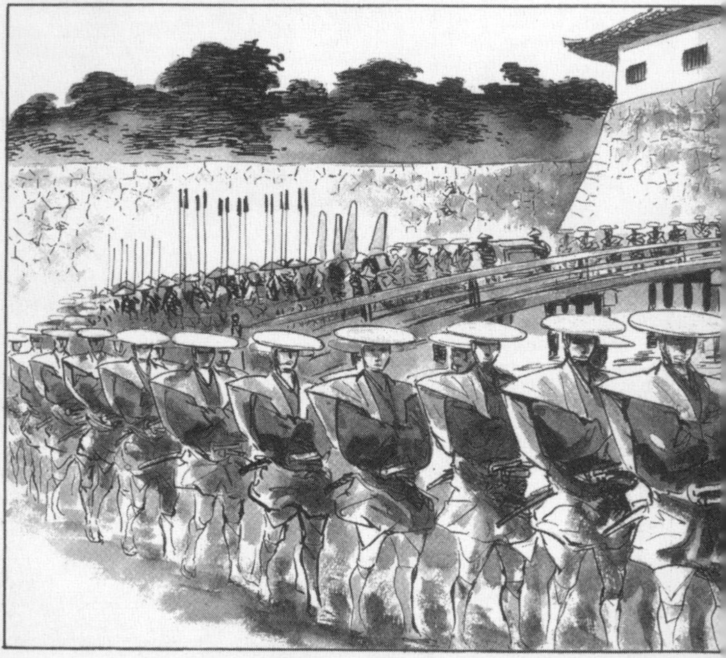

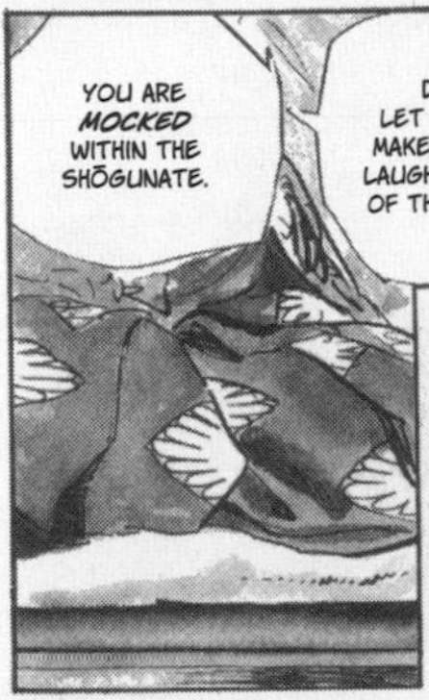
YOU ARE MOCKED WITHIN THE SHŌGUNATE.
DON'T LET HATRED MAKE YOU THE LAUGHINGSTOCK OF THE EMPIRE.
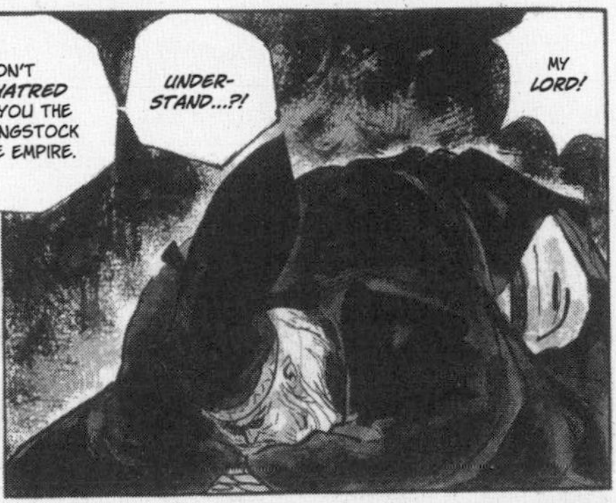
UNDER-STAND...?!
MY LORD!
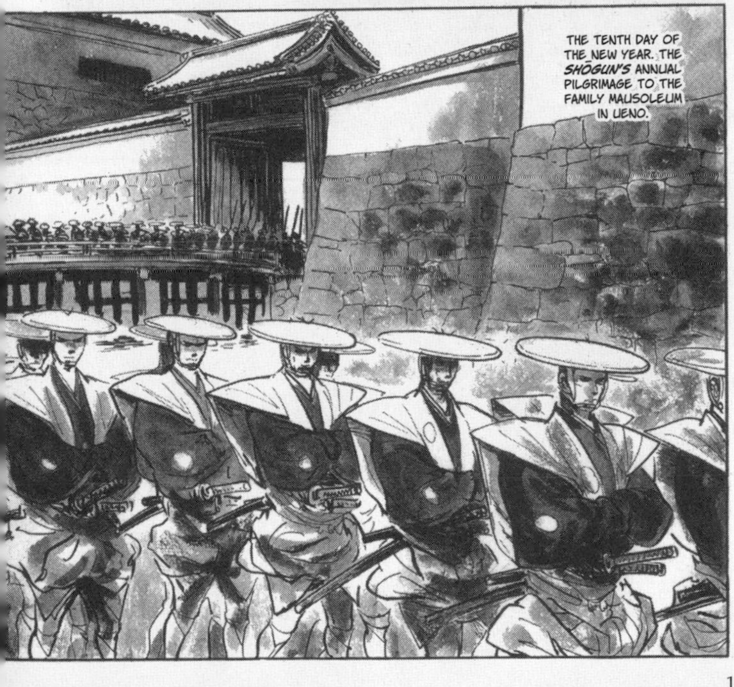
THE TENTH DAY OF THE NEW YEAR. THE SHŌGUN'S ANNUAL PILGRIMAGE TO THE FAMILY MAUSOLEUM IN UENO.

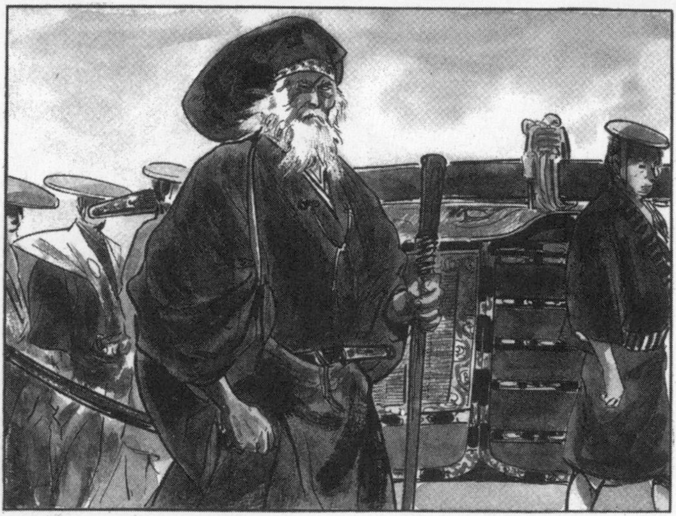

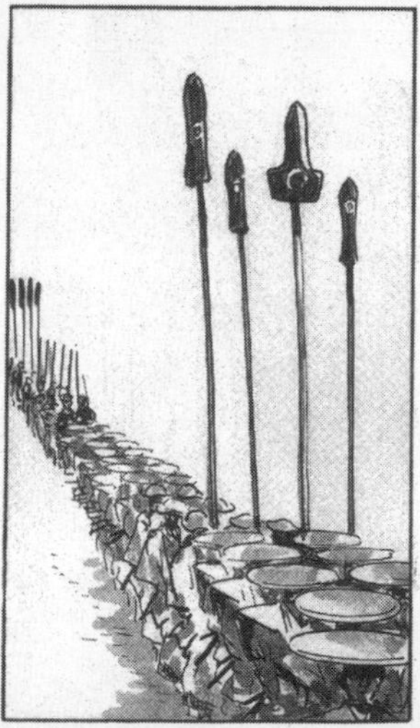

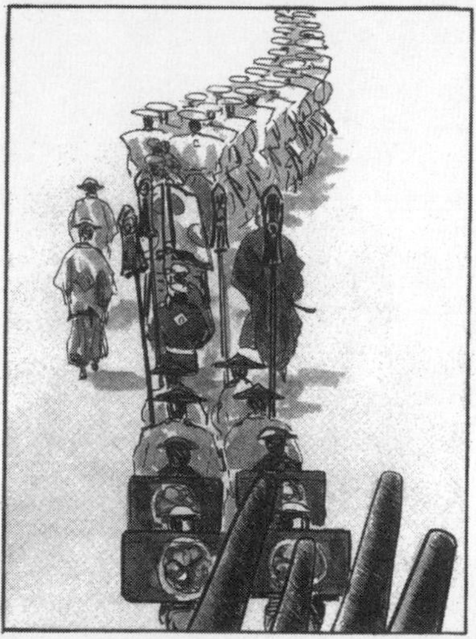

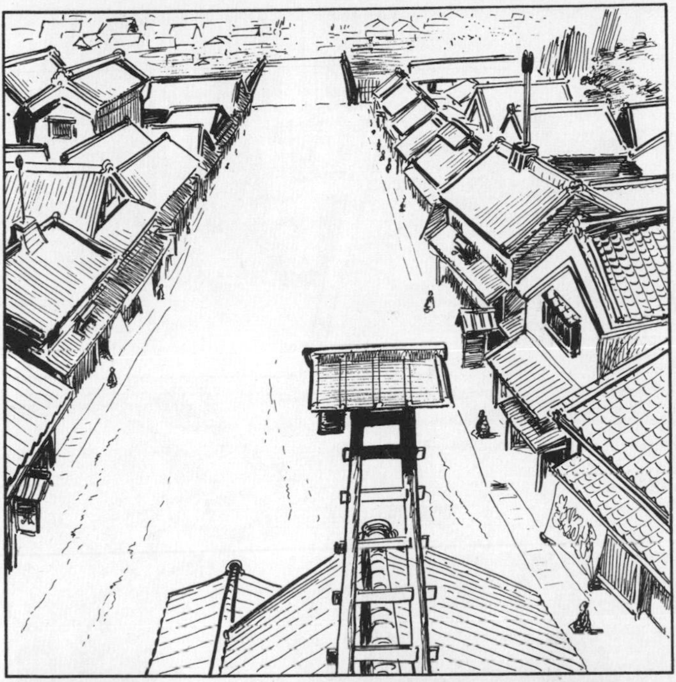

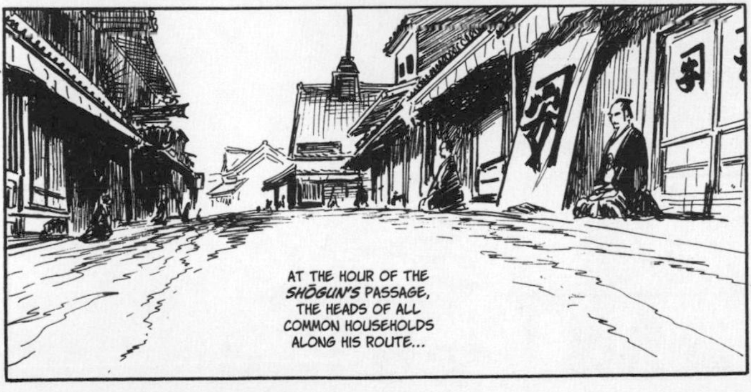
AT THE HOUR OF THE
SHŌGUN'S PASSAGE,
THE HEADS OF ALL
COMMON HOUSEHOLDS
ALONG HIS ROUTE...

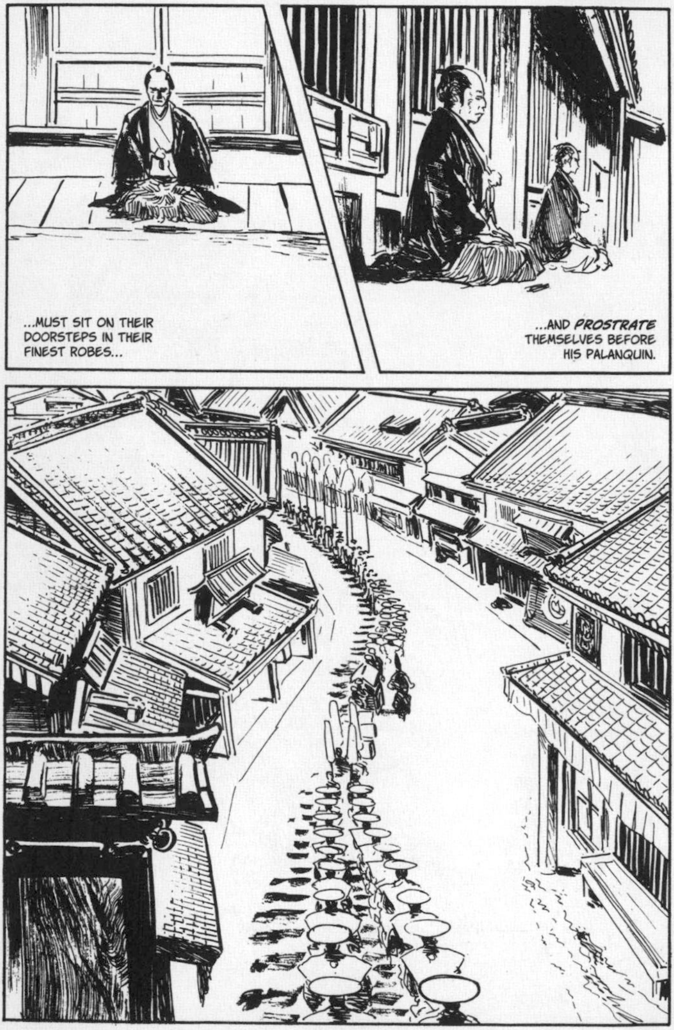
...MUST SIT ON THEIR DOORSTEPS IN THEIR FINEST ROBES...
...AND PROSTRATE THEMSELVES BEFORE HIS PALANQUIN.

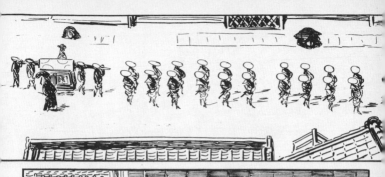

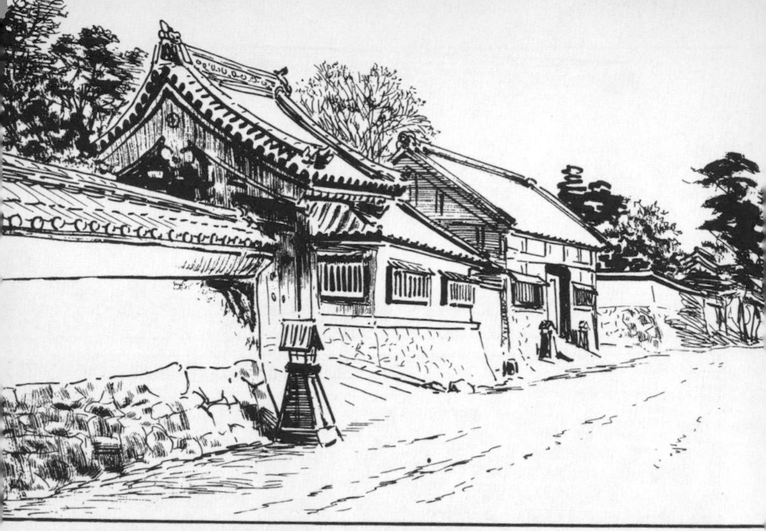

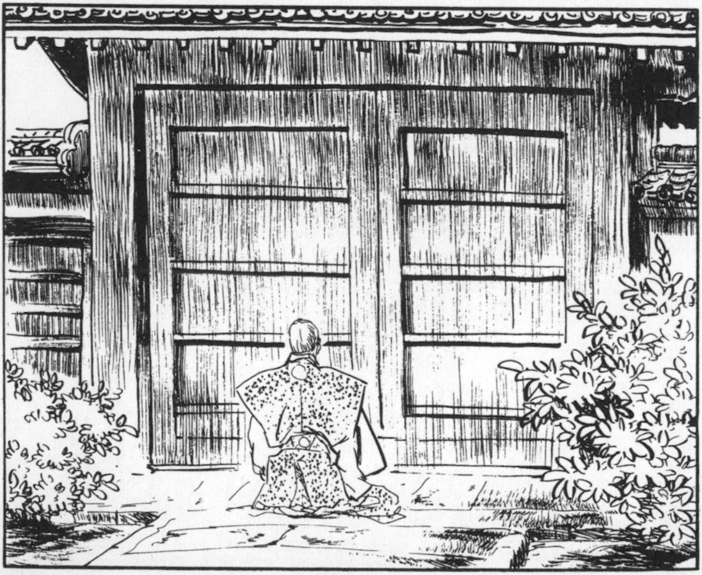

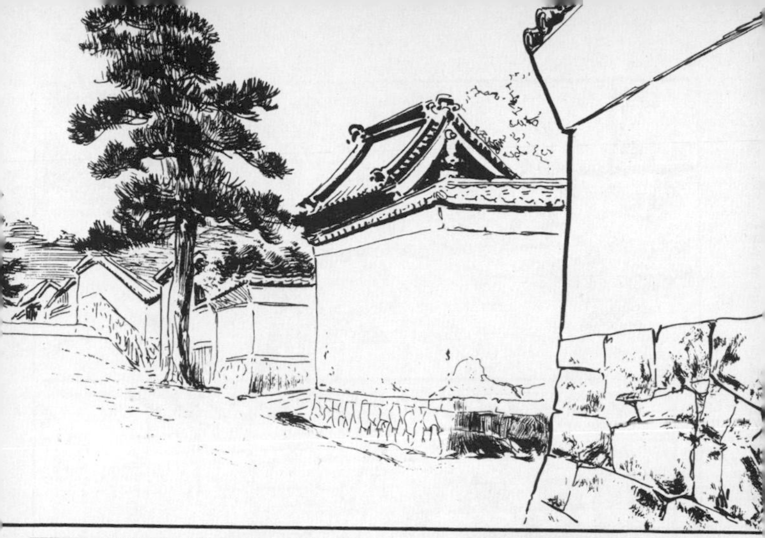

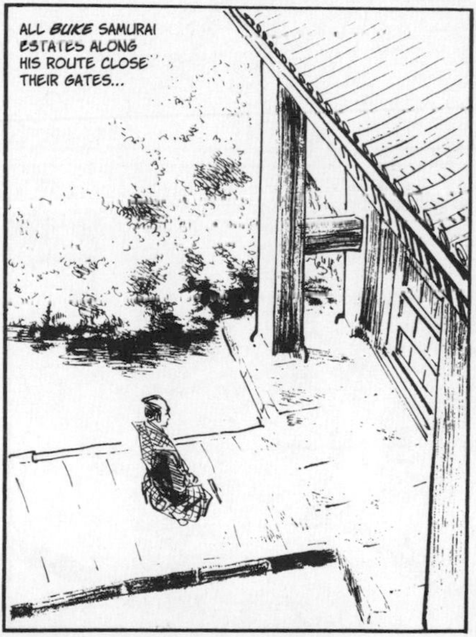
ALL *BUKE* SAMURAI ESTATES ALONG HIS ROUTE CLOSE THEIR GATES...

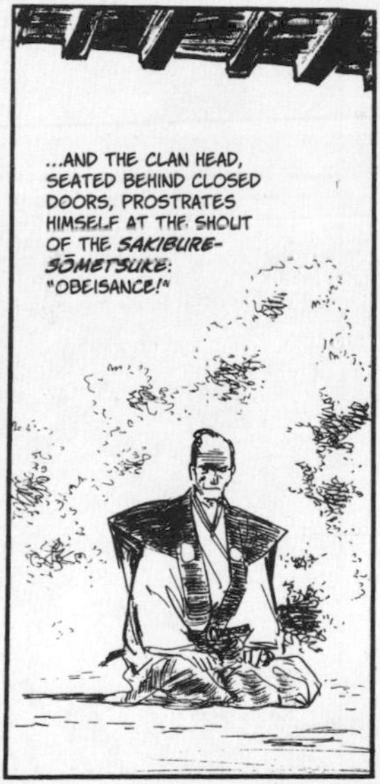
...AND THE CLAN HEAD, SEATED BEHIND CLOSED DOORS, PROSTRATES HIMSELF AT THE SHOUT OF THE *SAKIBURE-SŌMETSUKE*: "OBEISANCE!"

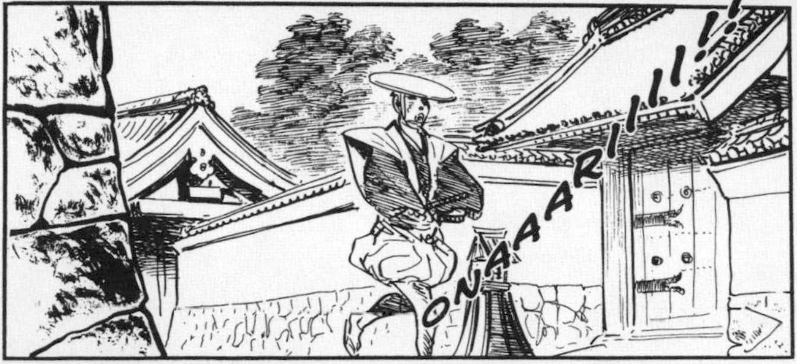
ONAAARI!!!!!!

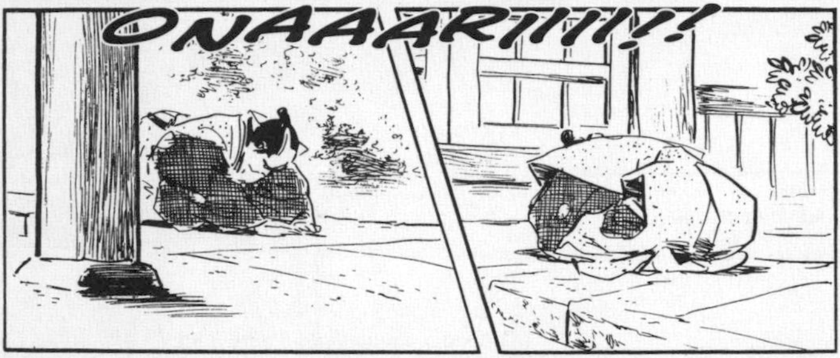
ONAAARIIII!!

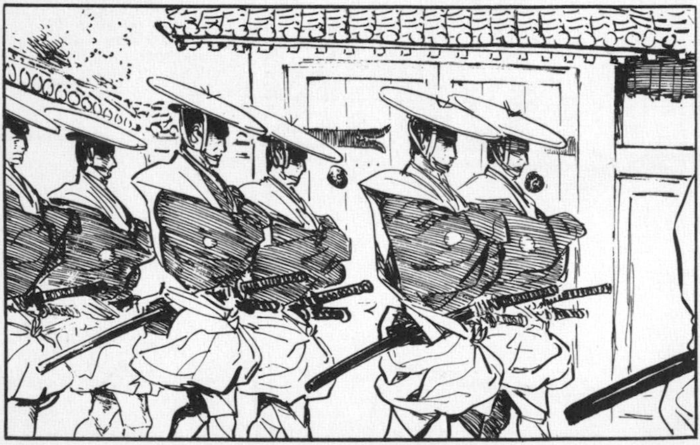

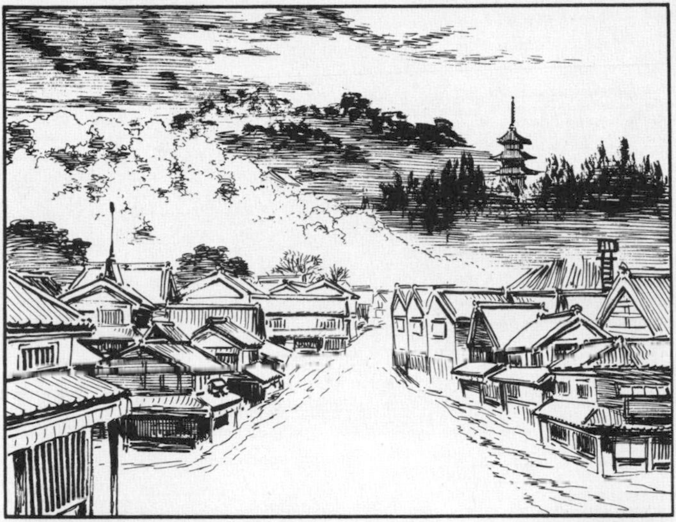

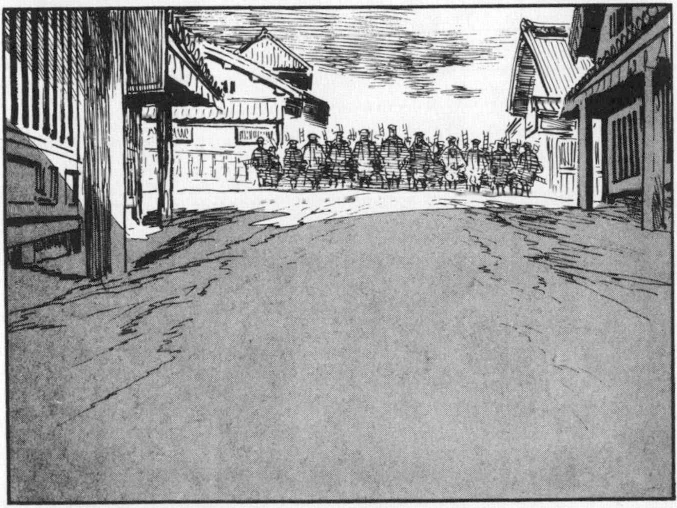

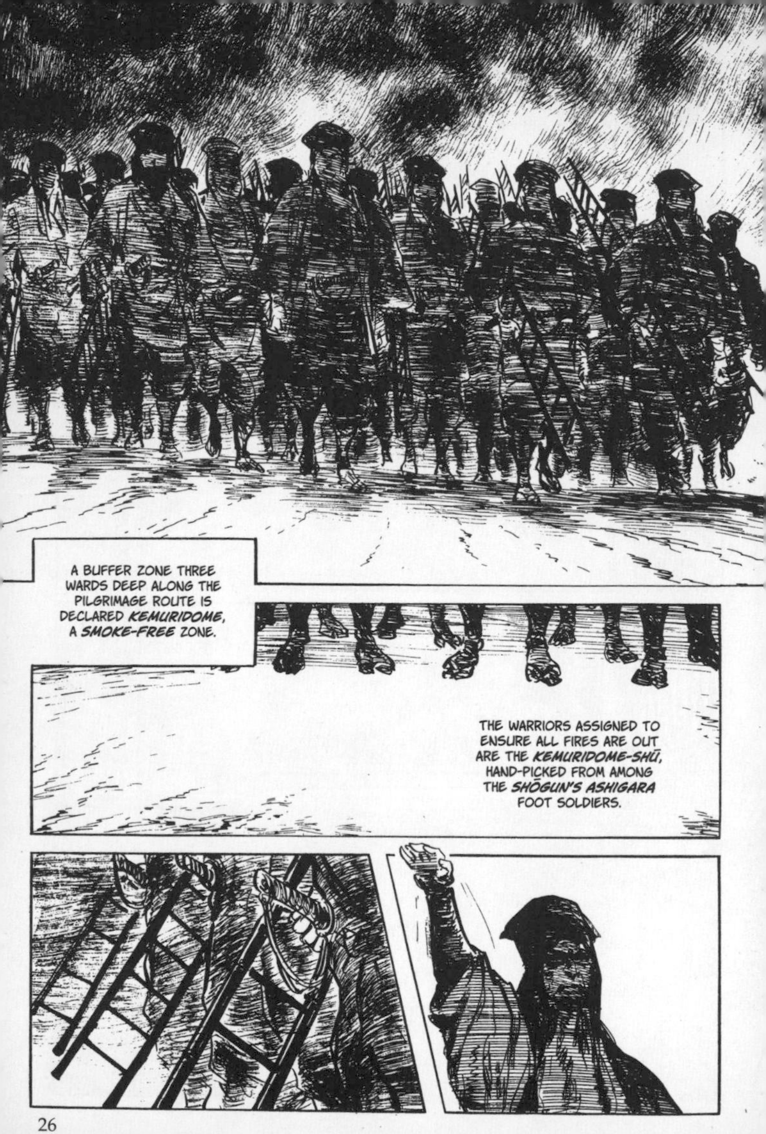
A BUFFER ZONE THREE WARDS DEEP ALONG THE PILGRIMAGE ROUTE IS DECLARED *KEMURIDOME*, A *SMOKE-FREE* ZONE.
THE WARRIORS ASSIGNED TO ENSURE ALL FIRES ARE OUT ARE THE *KEMURIDOME-SHŪ*, HAND-PICKED FROM AMONG THE *SHŌGUN'S ASHIGARA* FOOT SOLDIERS.

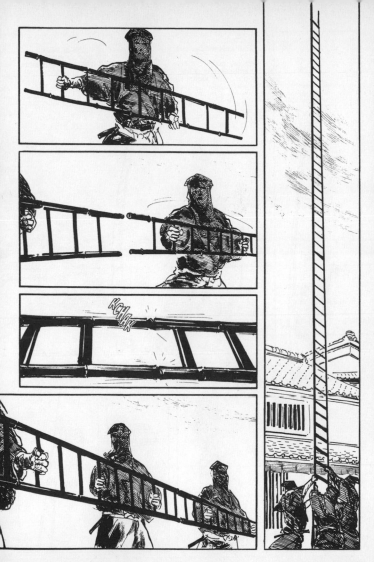

KCHAK

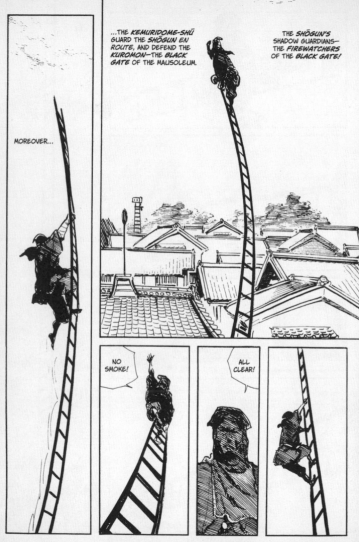

...THE *KEMURIDOME-SHŪ* GUARD THE *SHŌGUN* EN ROUTE, AND DEFEND THE *KUROMON*—THE *BLACK GATE* OF THE MAUSOLEUM.

THE *SHŌGUN'S* SHADOW GUARDIANS— THE *FIREWATCHERS* OF THE *BLACK GATE!*

MOREOVER...

NO SMOKE!

ALL CLEAR!

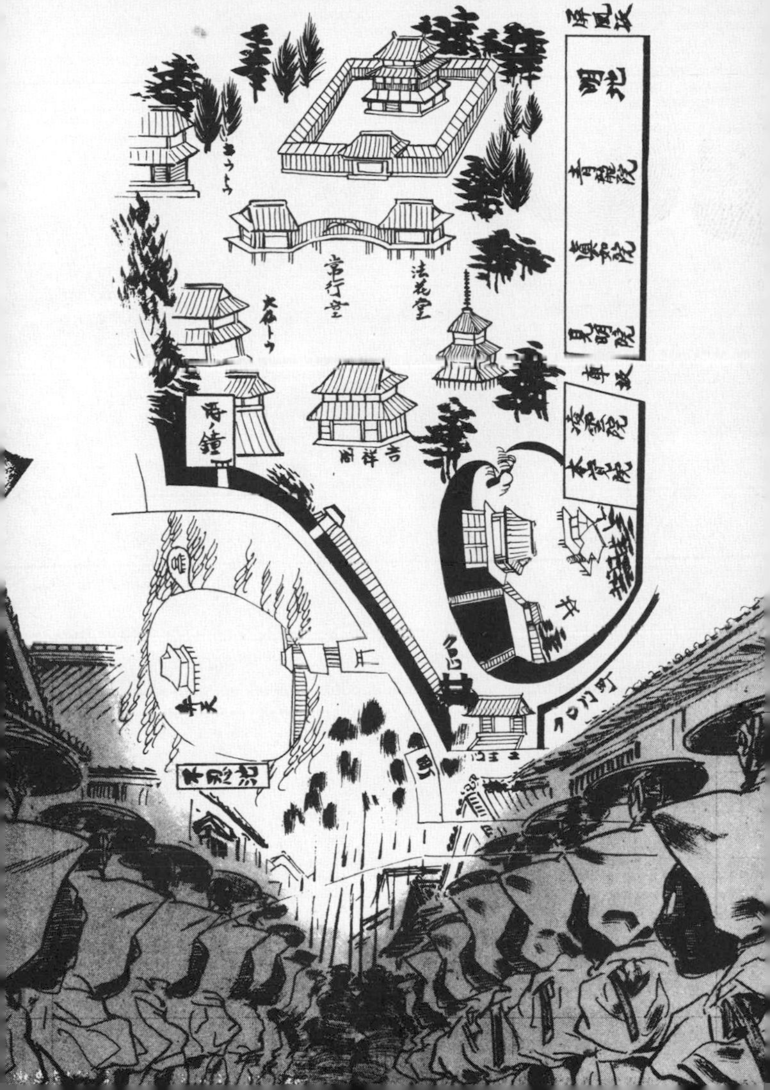
屏風坂
真如院
見明院
車坂
凌雲院
春性院
常行堂
法花堂
大石トウ
時ノ鐘
吉祥閣

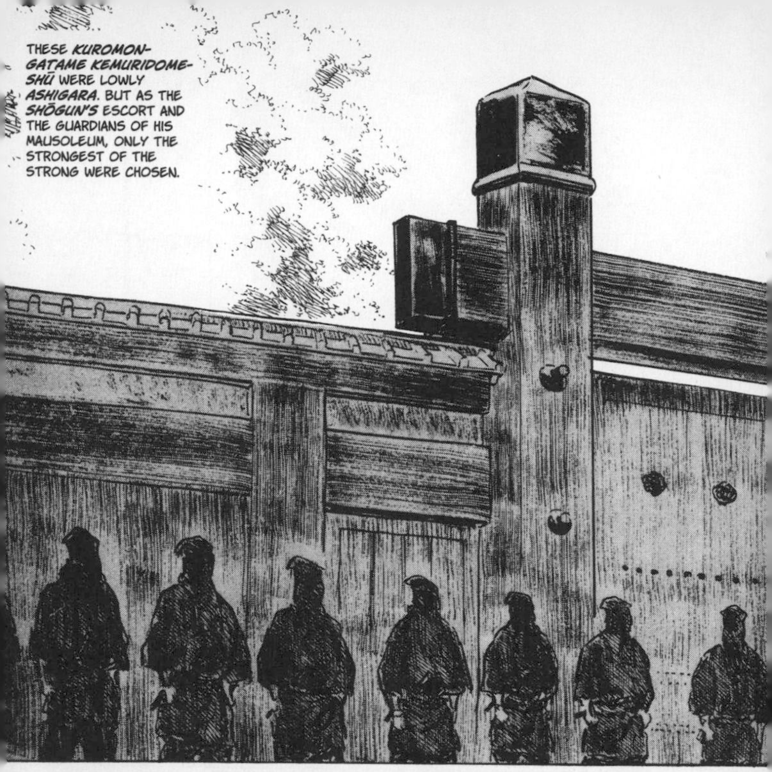
THESE *KUROMON-GATAME KEMURIDOME-SHŪ* WERE LOWLY *ASHIGARA*. BUT AS THE *SHŌGUN'S* ESCORT AND THE GUARDIANS OF HIS MAUSOLEUM, ONLY THE STRONGEST OF THE STRONG WERE CHOSEN.
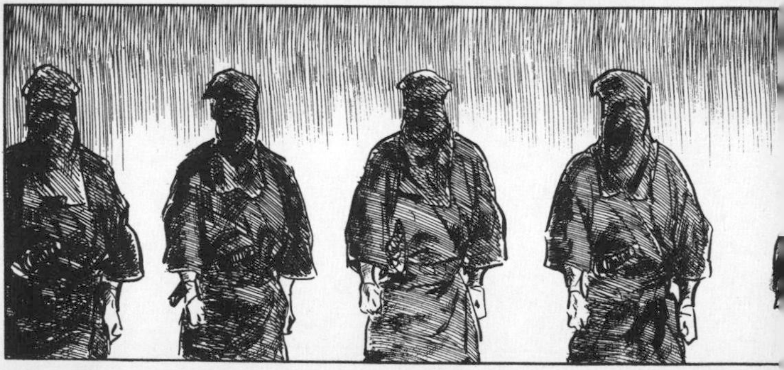

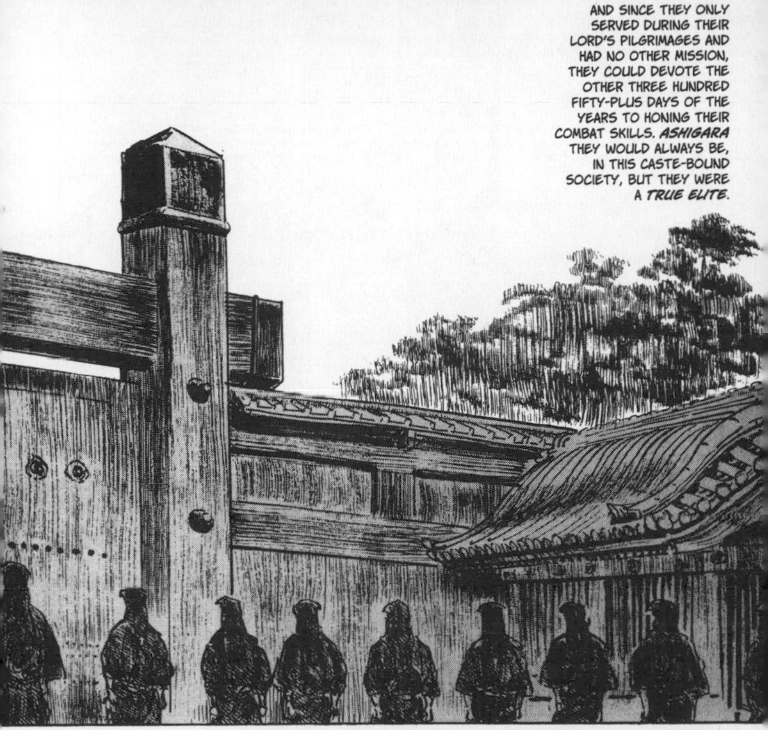
AND SINCE THEY ONLY SERVED DURING THEIR LORD'S PILGRIMAGES AND HAD NO OTHER MISSION, THEY COULD DEVOTE THE OTHER THREE HUNDRED FIFTY-PLUS DAYS OF THE YEARS TO HONING THEIR COMBAT SKILLS. *ASHIGARA* THEY WOULD ALWAYS BE, IN THIS CASTE-BOUND SOCIETY, BUT THEY WERE A *TRUE ELITE*.

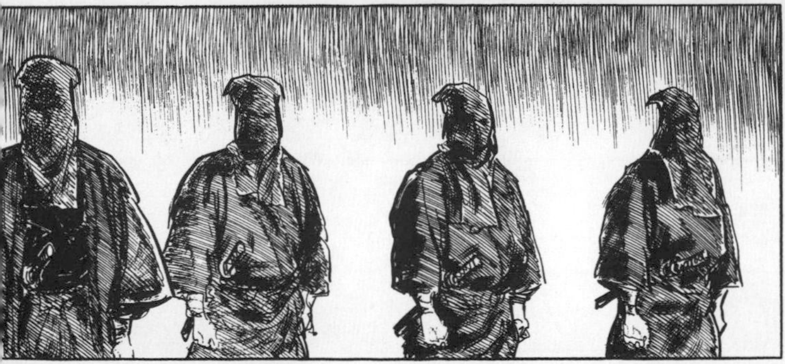

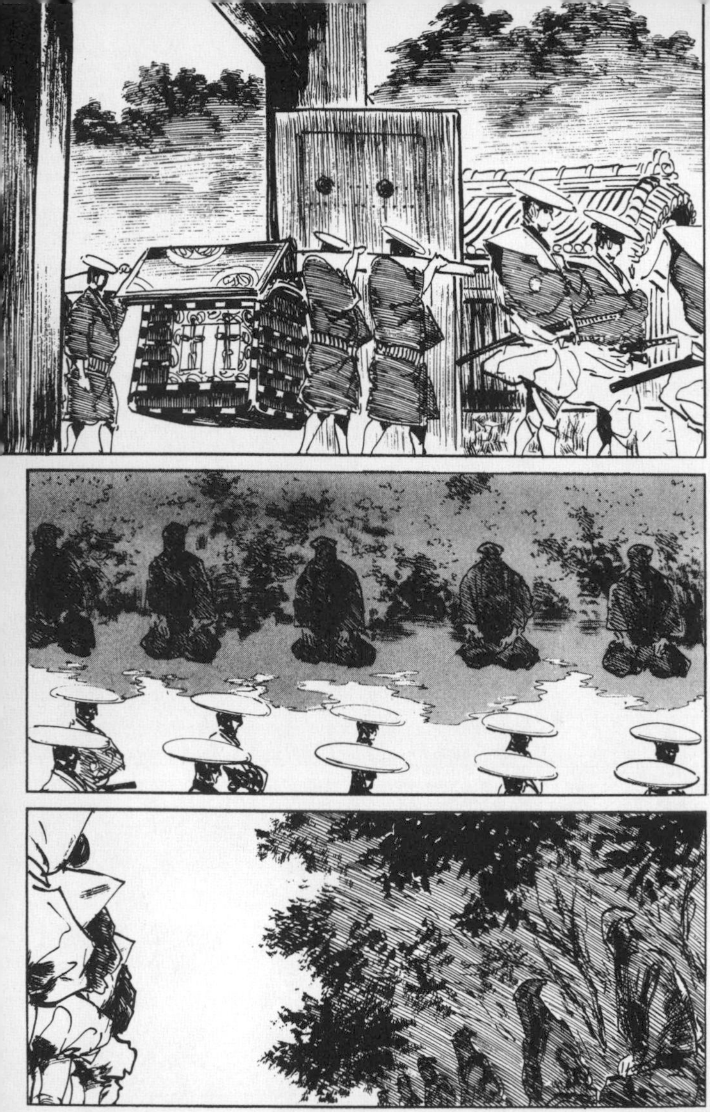

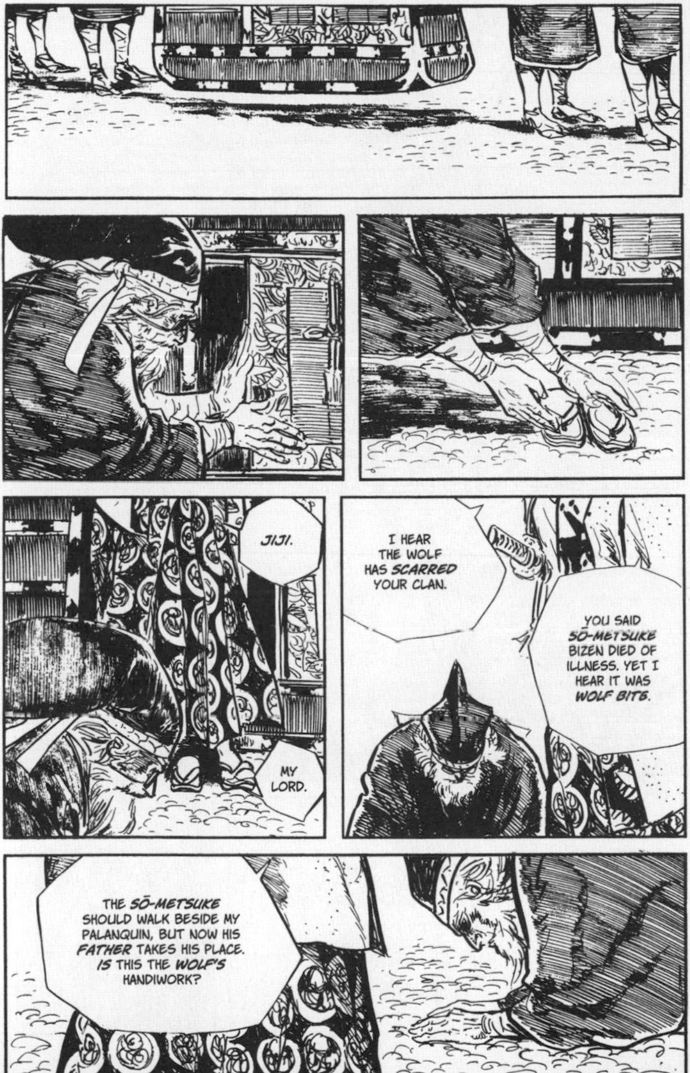
JIJI.
MY LORD.
I HEAR THE WOLF HAS SCARRED YOUR CLAN.
YOU SAID SŌ-METSUKE BIZEN DIED OF ILLNESS. YET I HEAR IT WAS WOLF BITE.
THE SŌ-METSUKE SHOULD WALK BESIDE MY PALANQUIN, BUT NOW HIS FATHER TAKES HIS PLACE. IS THIS THE WOLF'S HANDIWORK?

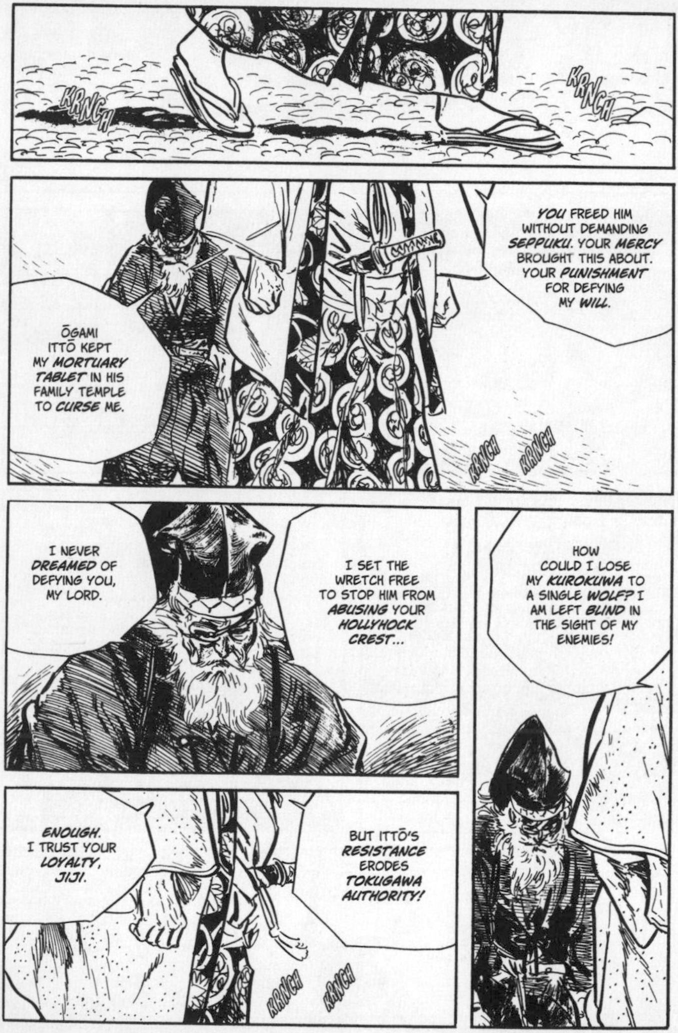
KRNCH
KRNCH
ŌGAMI ITTŌ KEPT MY *MORTUARY TABLET* IN HIS FAMILY TEMPLE TO *CURSE* ME.
YOU FREED HIM WITHOUT DEMANDING *SEPPUKU*. YOUR *MERCY* BROUGHT THIS ABOUT. YOUR *PUNISHMENT* FOR DEFYING MY *WILL*.
KRNCH
KRNCH
I NEVER *DREAMED* OF DEFYING YOU, MY LORD.
I SET THE WRETCH FREE TO STOP HIM FROM *ABUSING* YOUR *HOLLYHOCK CREST*...
ENOUGH. I TRUST YOUR *LOYALTY, JIJI.*
BUT ITTŌ'S *RESISTANCE* ERODES *TOKUGAWA AUTHORITY!*
KRNCH
KRNCH
HOW COULD I LOSE MY *KUROKUWA* TO A SINGLE *WOLF?* I AM LEFT *BLIND* IN THE SIGHT OF MY ENEMIES!

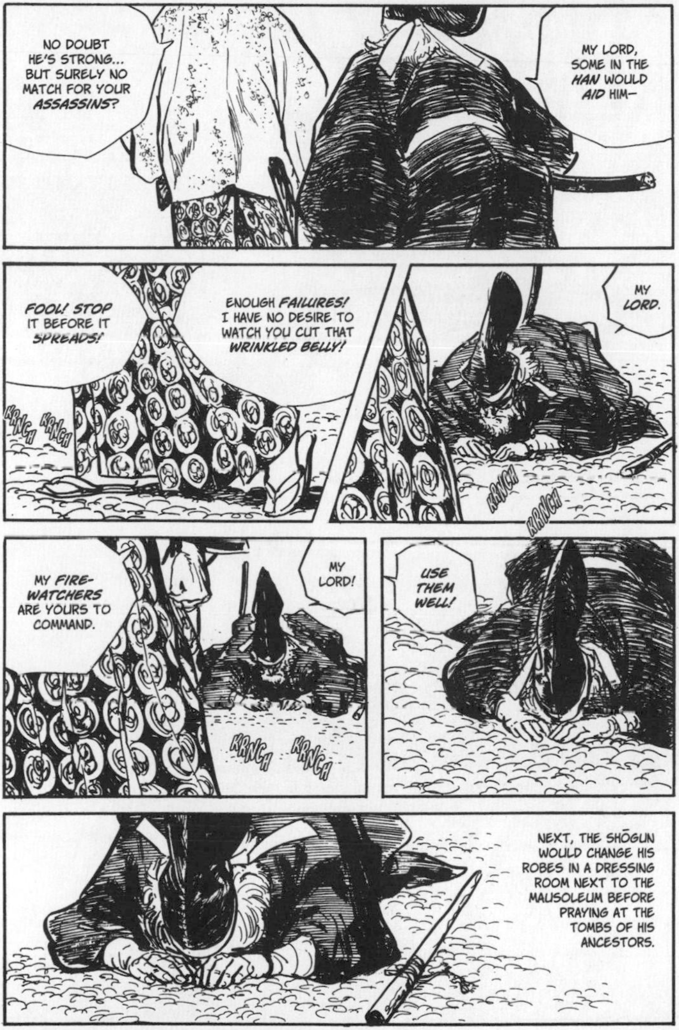
NO DOUBT HE'S STRONG... BUT SURELY NO MATCH FOR YOUR *ASSASSINS*?
MY LORD, SOME IN THE *HAN* WOULD *AID* HIM—
FOOL! STOP IT BEFORE IT *SPREADS!*
ENOUGH *FAILURES!* I HAVE NO DESIRE TO WATCH YOU CUT THAT *WRINKLED BELLY!*
KRNCH KRNCH
MY *LORD.*
KRNCH KRNCH
MY *FIRE-WATCHERS* ARE YOURS TO COMMAND.
MY LORD!
KRNCH KRNCH
USE THEM WELL!
NEXT, THE SHŌGUN WOULD CHANGE HIS ROBES IN A DRESSING ROOM NEXT TO THE MAUSOLEUM BEFORE PRAYING AT THE TOMBS OF HIS ANCESTORS.

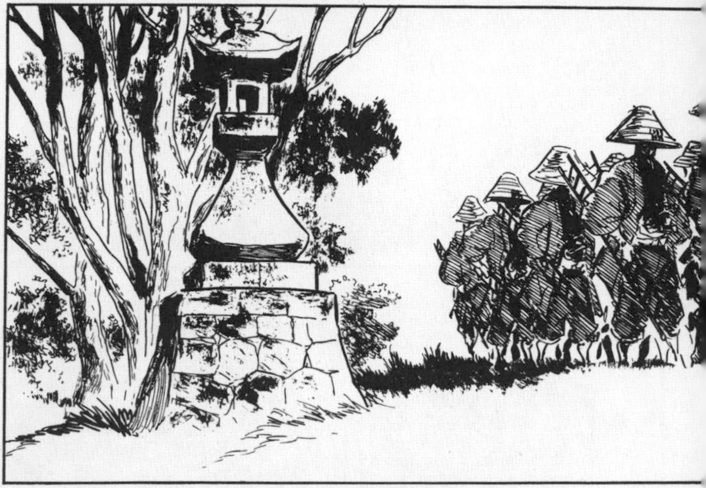
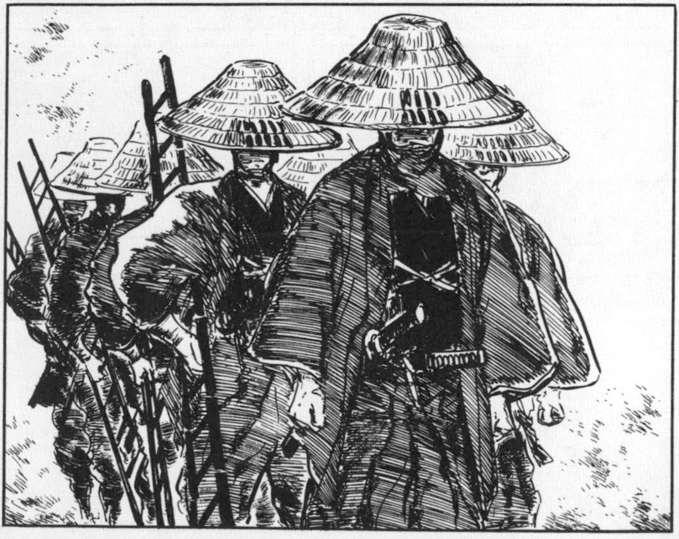

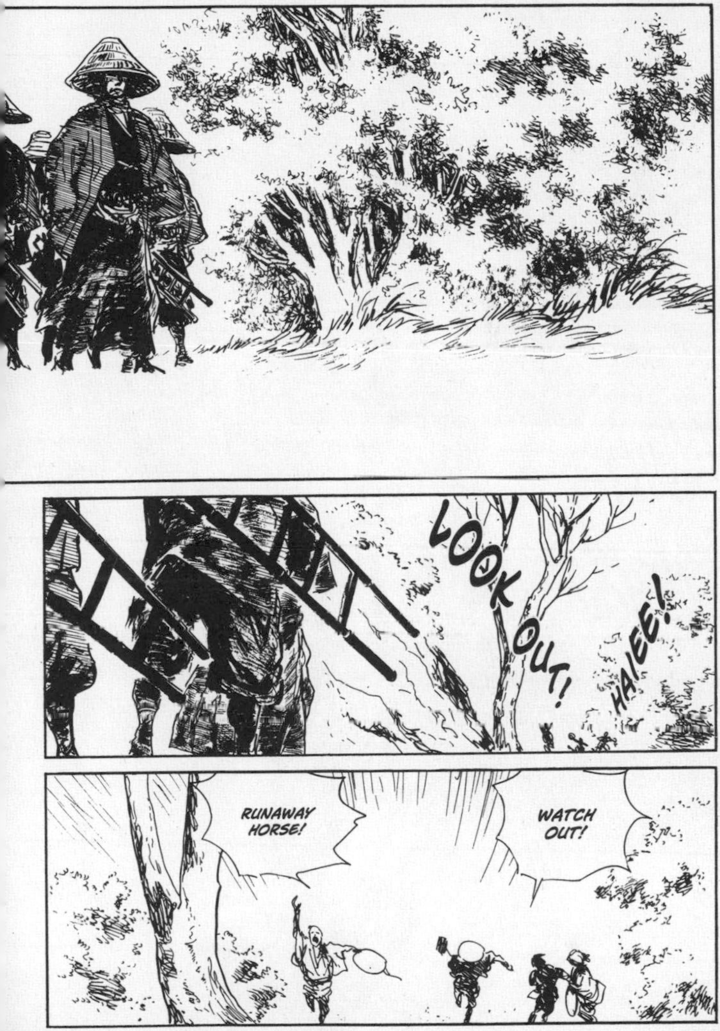
LOOK OUT!
HAIEE!
WATCH OUT!
RUNAWAY HORSE!

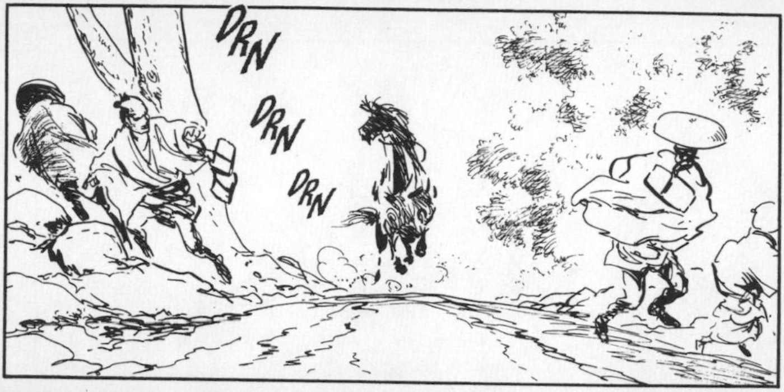
DRN
DRN
DRN
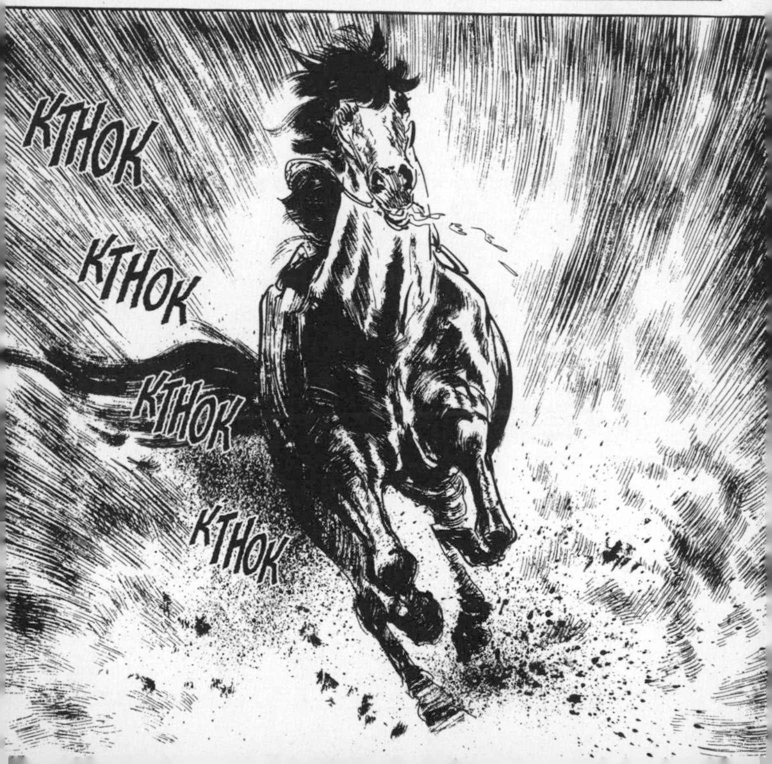
KTHOK
KTHOK
KTHOK
KTHOK

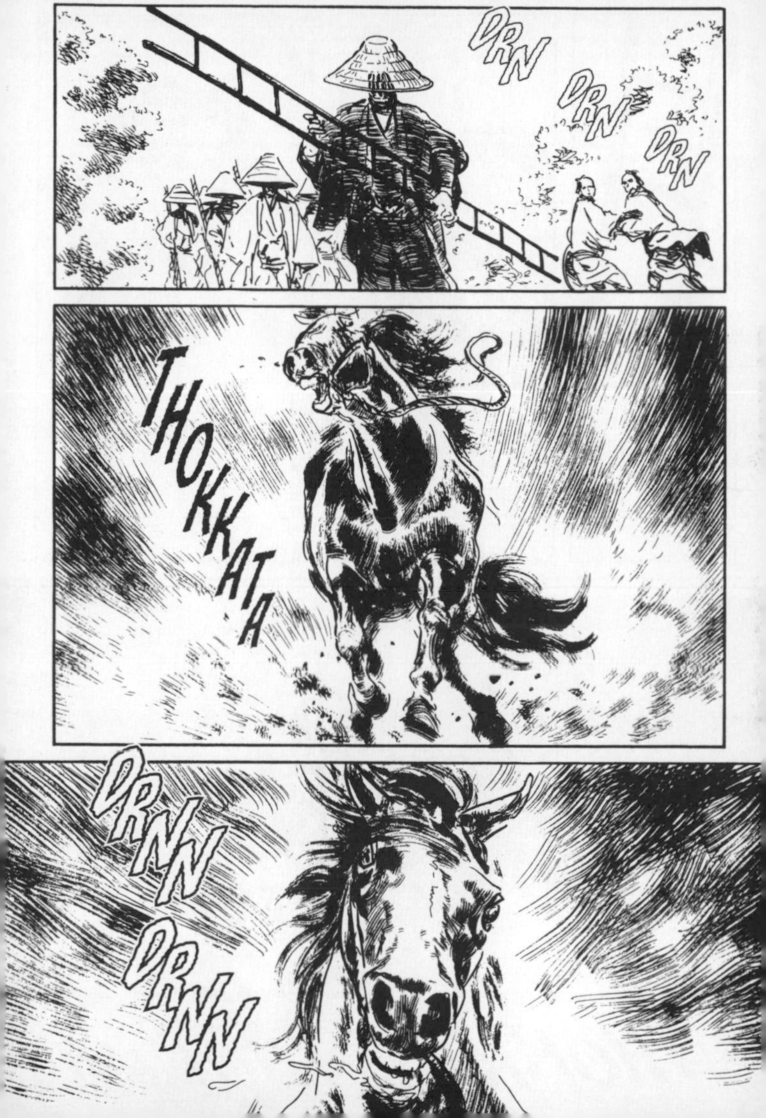
ORN
ORN
ORN
THOKKATA
ORNN
ORNN

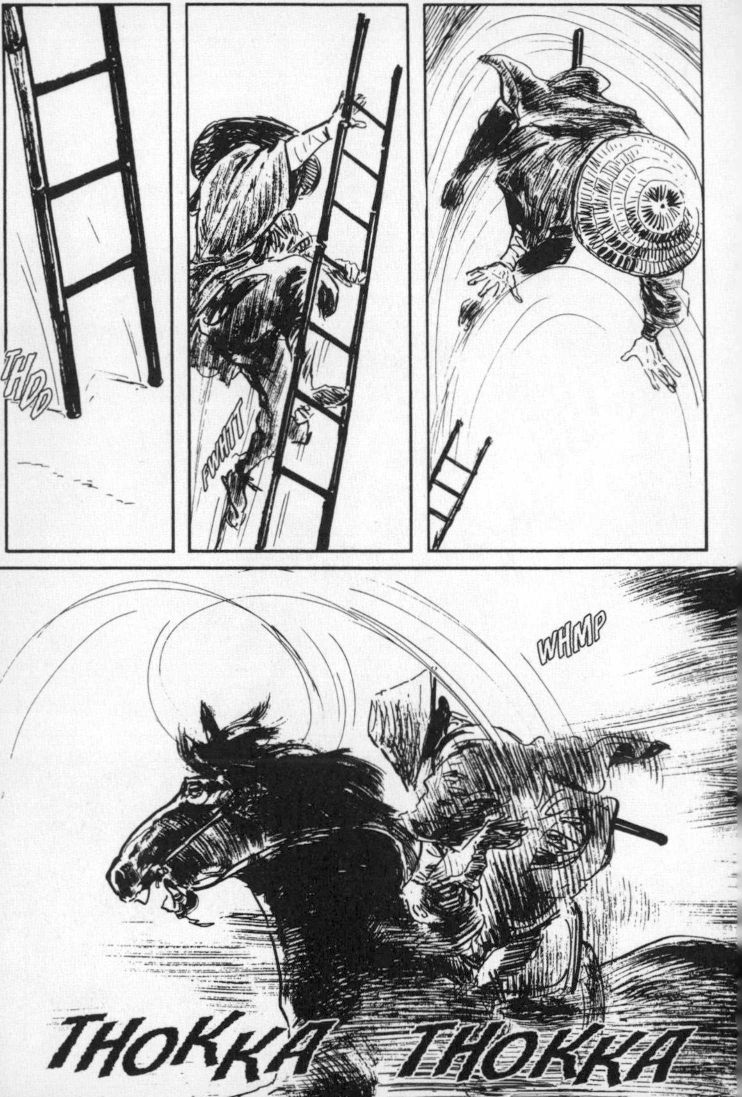
FWHTT
THDD
WHMP
THOKKA THOKKA

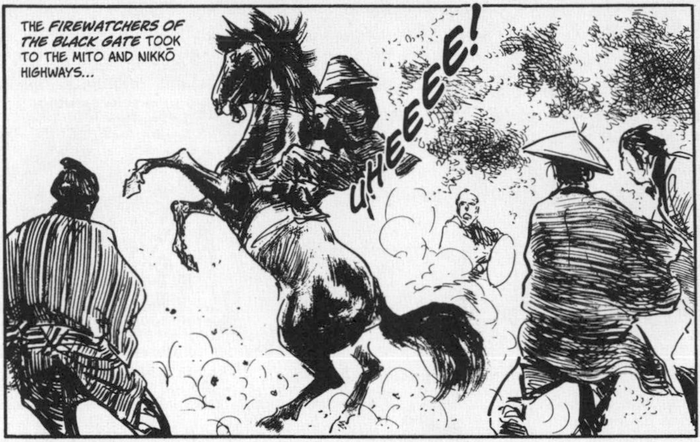
THE *FIREWATCHERS OF THE BLACK GATE* TOOK TO THE MITO AND NIKKŌ HIGHWAYS...
UHEEEEE!

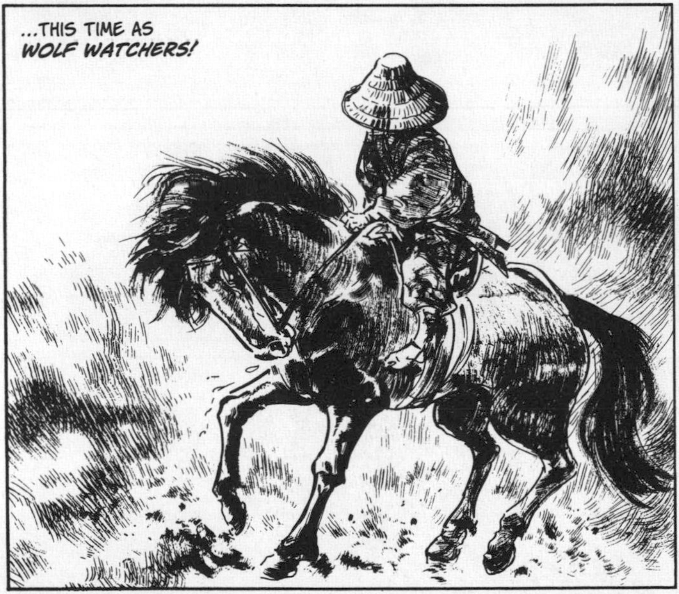
...THIS TIME AS *WOLF WATCHERS!*

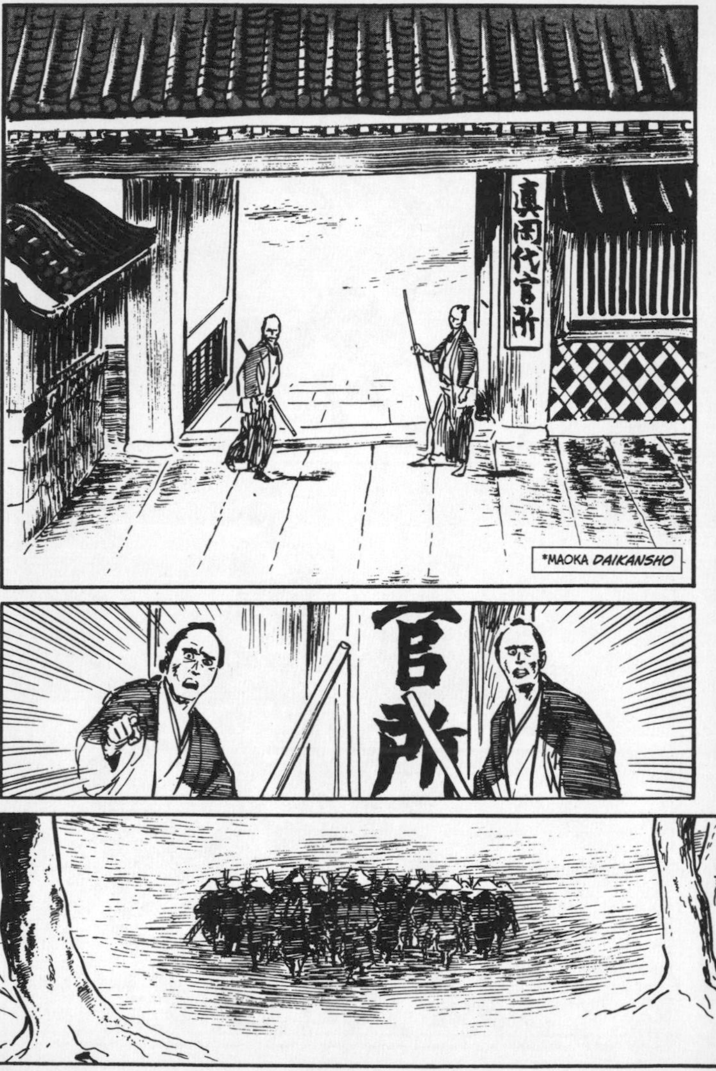
真岡代官所
*MAOKA DAIKANSHO
官所

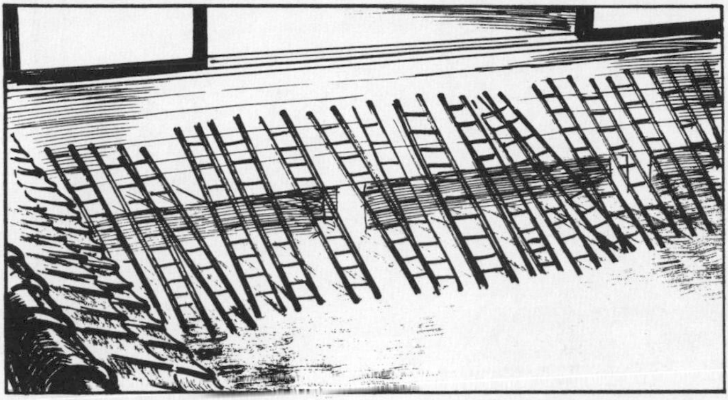
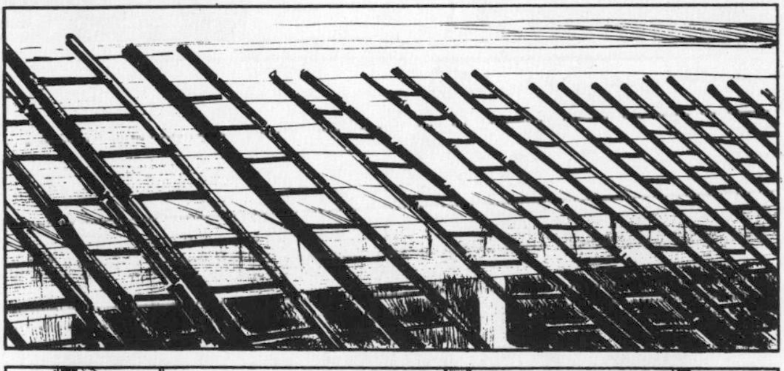
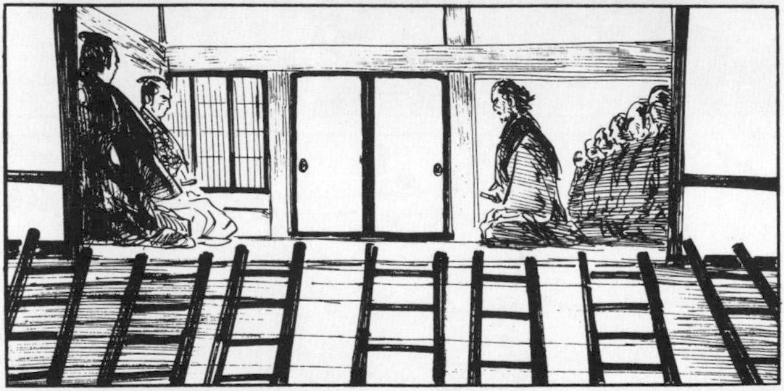

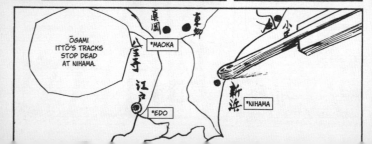

ŌGAMI ITTŌ'S TRACKS STOP DEAD AT NIHAMA.

*MAOKA

*EDO

*NIHAMA

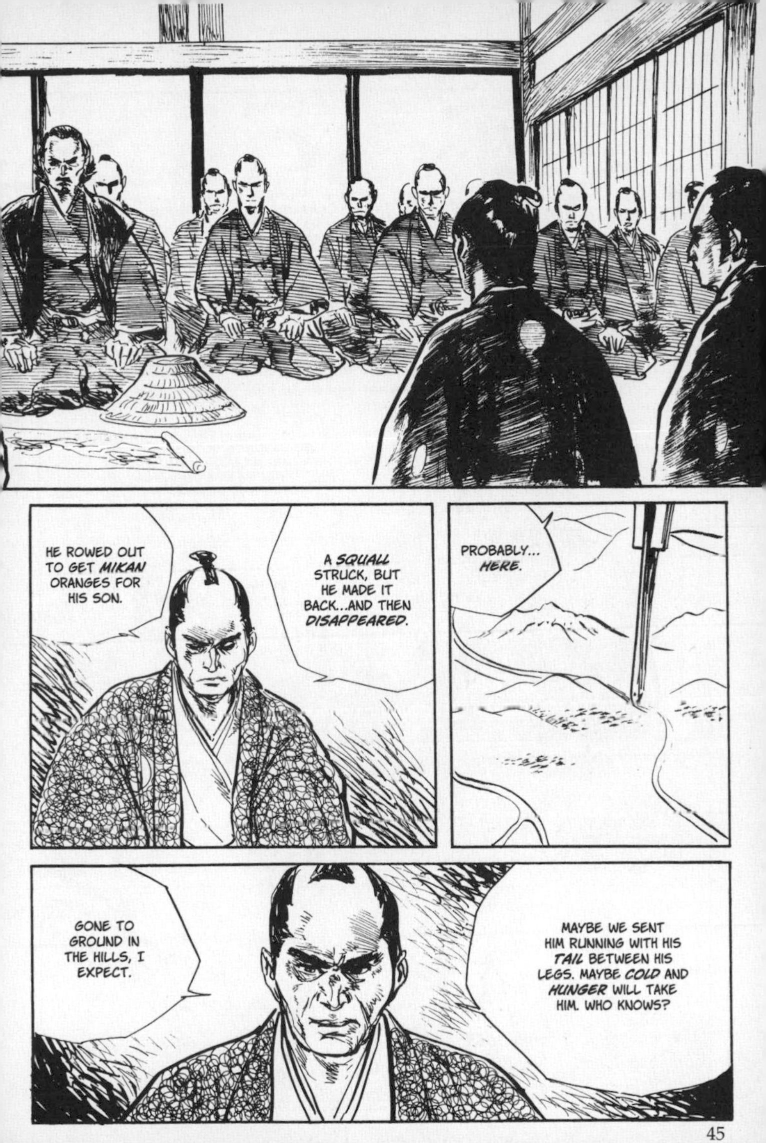
HE ROWED OUT TO GET *MIKAN* ORANGES FOR HIS SON.
A *SQUALL* STRUCK, BUT HE MADE IT BACK...AND THEN *DISAPPEARED*.
PROBABLY... *HERE*.
GONE TO GROUND IN THE HILLS, I EXPECT.
MAYBE WE SENT HIM RUNNING WITH HIS *TAIL* BETWEEN HIS LEGS. MAYBE *COLD* AND *HUNGER* WILL TAKE HIM. WHO KNOWS?

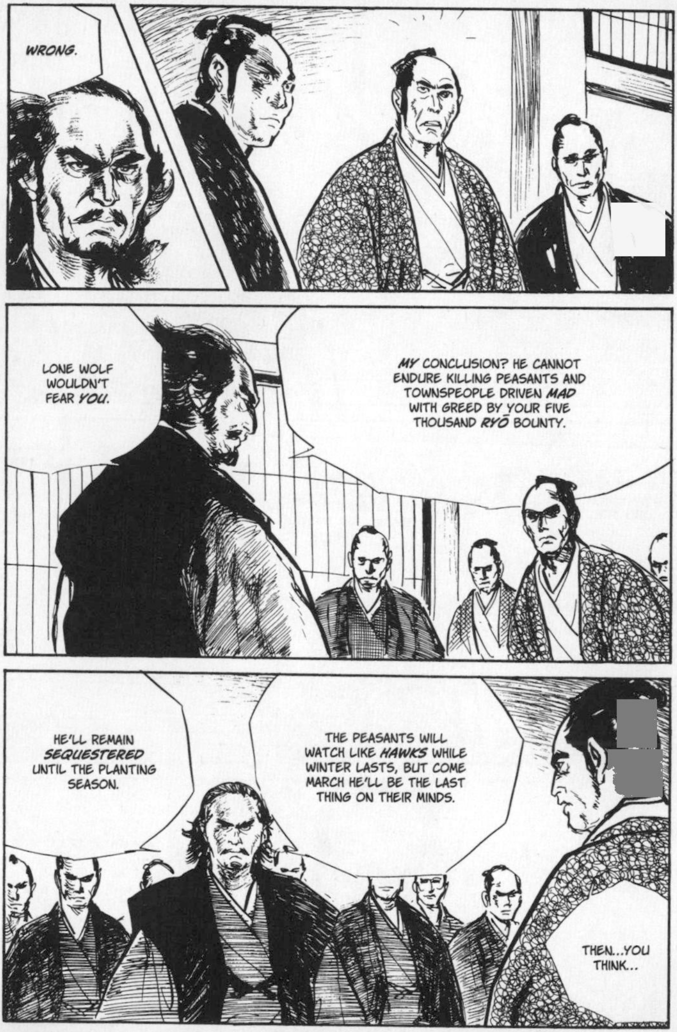
WRONG.
LONE WOLF WOULDN'T FEAR *YOU*.
MY CONCLUSION? HE CANNOT ENDURE KILLING PEASANTS AND TOWNSPEOPLE DRIVEN *MAD* WITH GREED BY YOUR FIVE THOUSAND *RYŌ* BOUNTY.
HE'LL REMAIN *SEQUESTERED* UNTIL THE PLANTING SEASON.
THE PEASANTS WILL WATCH LIKE *HAWKS* WHILE WINTER LASTS, BUT COME MARCH HE'LL BE THE LAST THING ON THEIR MINDS.
THEN...YOU THINK...

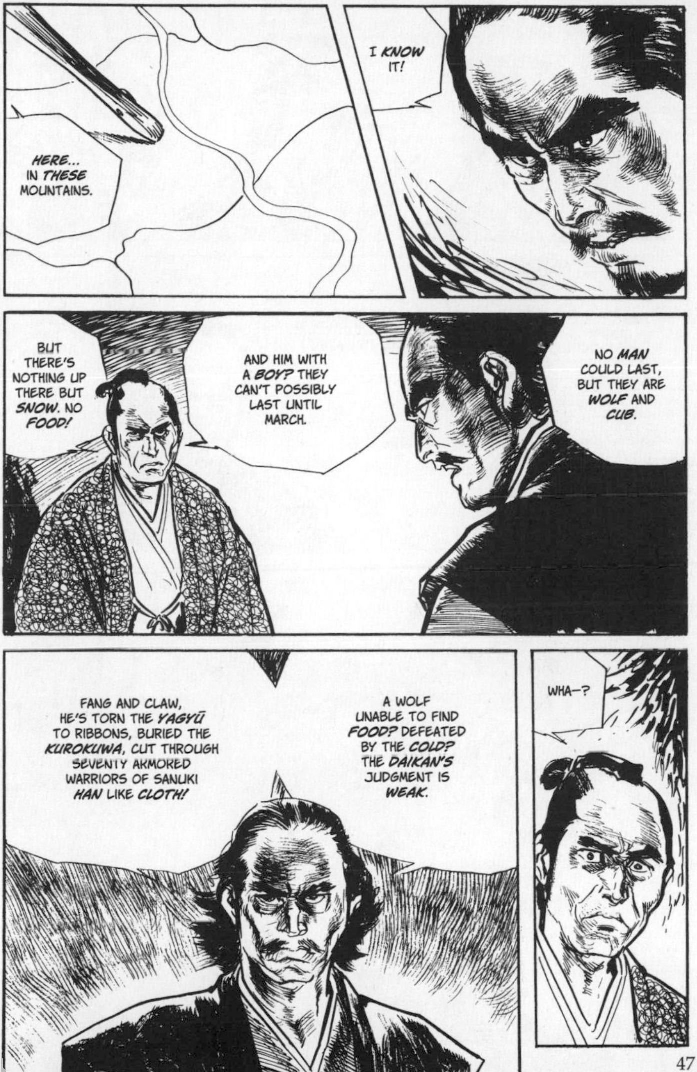
HERE... IN *THESE* MOUNTAINS.
I *KNOW* IT!
BUT THERE'S NOTHING UP THERE BUT *SNOW*. NO *FOOD!*
AND HIM WITH A *BOY?* THEY CAN'T POSSIBLY LAST UNTIL MARCH.
NO *MAN* COULD LAST, BUT THEY ARE *WOLF* AND *CUB*.
FANG AND CLAW, HE'S TORN THE *YAGYŪ* TO RIBBONS, BURIED THE *KUROKUWA*, CUT THROUGH SEVENTY ARMORED WARRIORS OF SANUKI *HAN* LIKE *CLOTH!*
A WOLF UNABLE TO FIND *FOOD?* DEFEATED BY THE *COLD?* THE *DAIKAN'S* JUDGMENT IS *WEAK*.
WHA–?

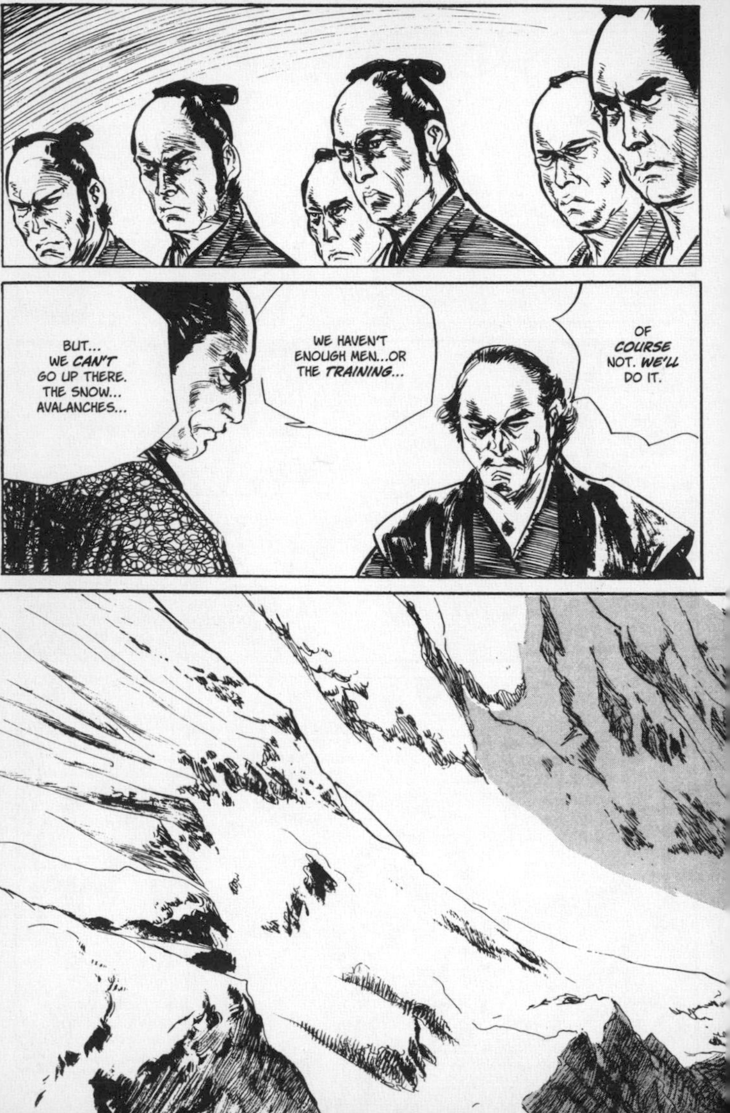
BUT... WE CAN'T GO UP THERE. THE SNOW... AVALANCHES...
WE HAVEN'T ENOUGH MEN...OR THE TRAINING...
OF COURSE NOT. WE'LL DO IT.

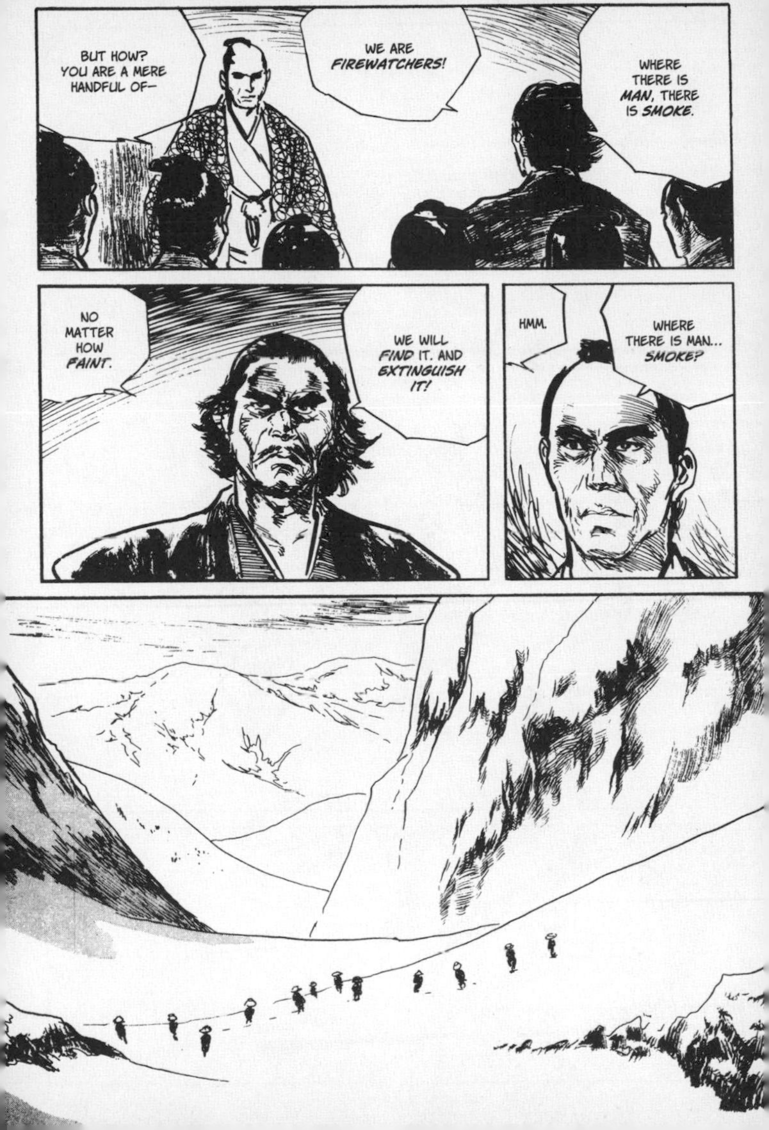
BUT HOW? YOU ARE A MERE HANDFUL OF—
WE ARE *FIREWATCHERS!*
WHERE THERE IS *MAN*, THERE IS *SMOKE*.
NO MATTER HOW *FAINT*.
WE WILL *FIND* IT. AND *EXTINGUISH* IT!
HMM.
WHERE THERE IS MAN... *SMOKE?*

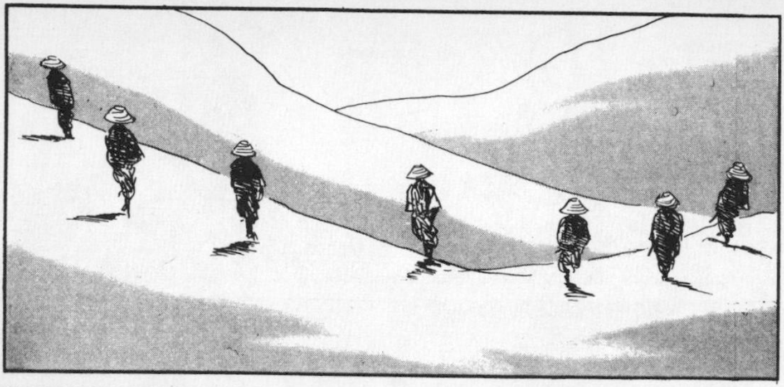
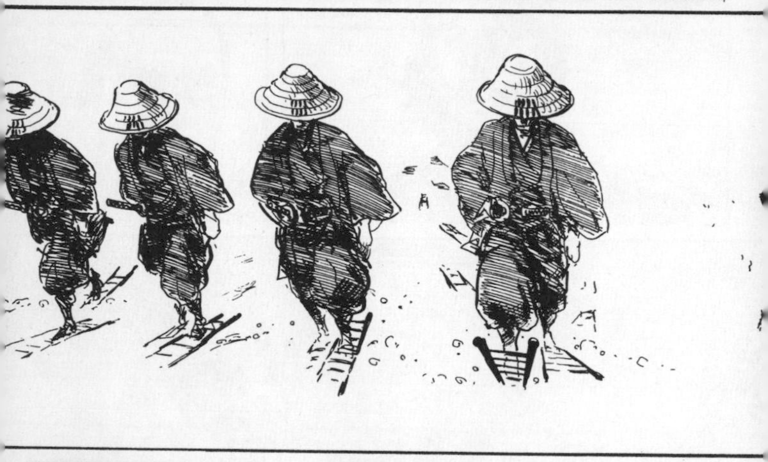
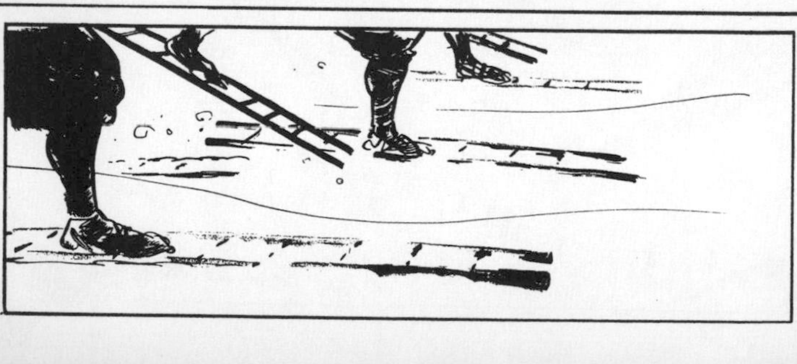

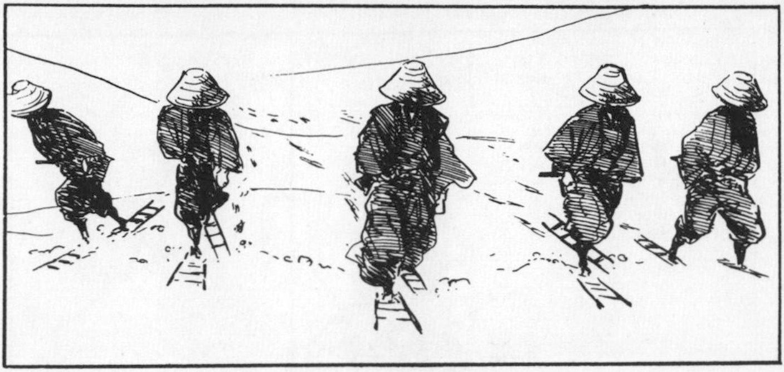
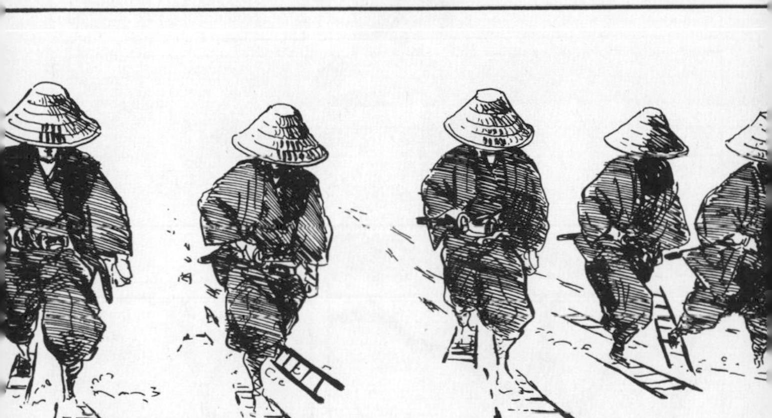
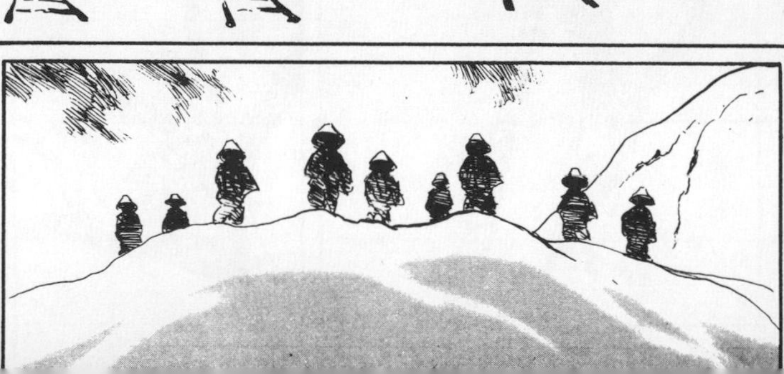

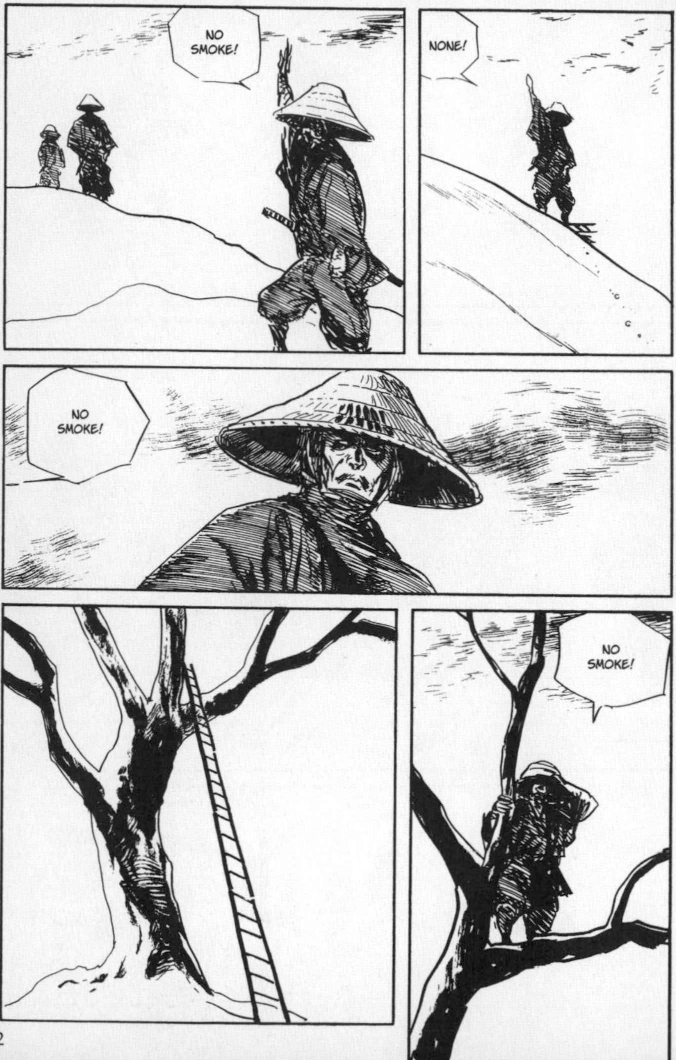
NO SMOKE!
NONE!
NO SMOKE!
NO SMOKE!

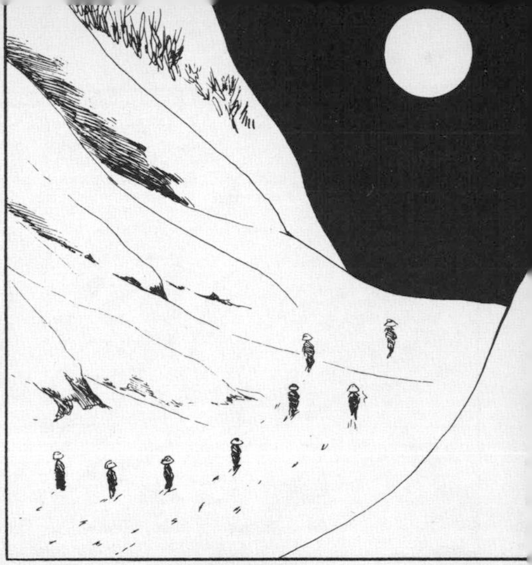

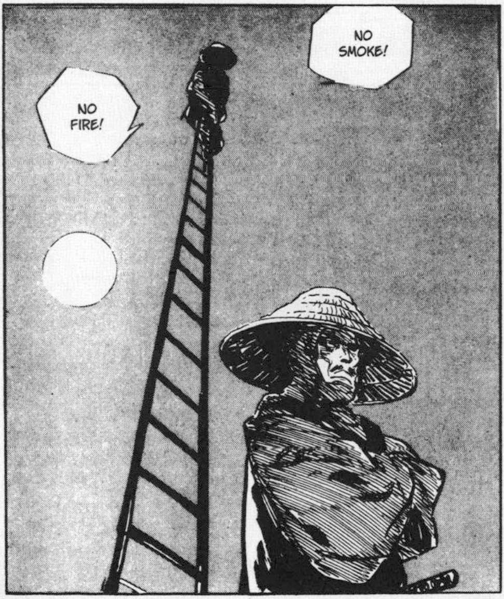
NO SMOKE!
NO FIRE!

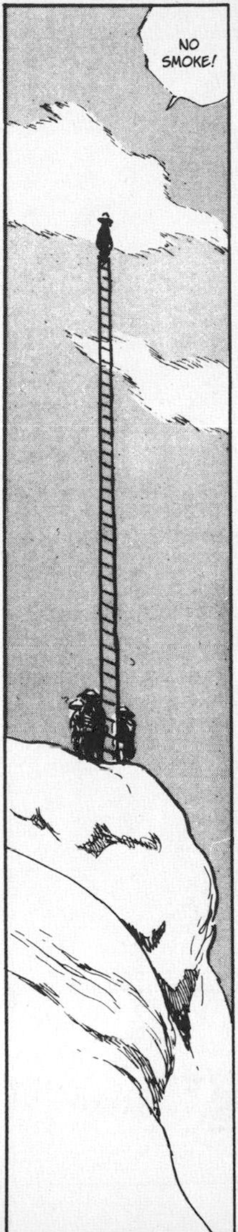
NO SMOKE!

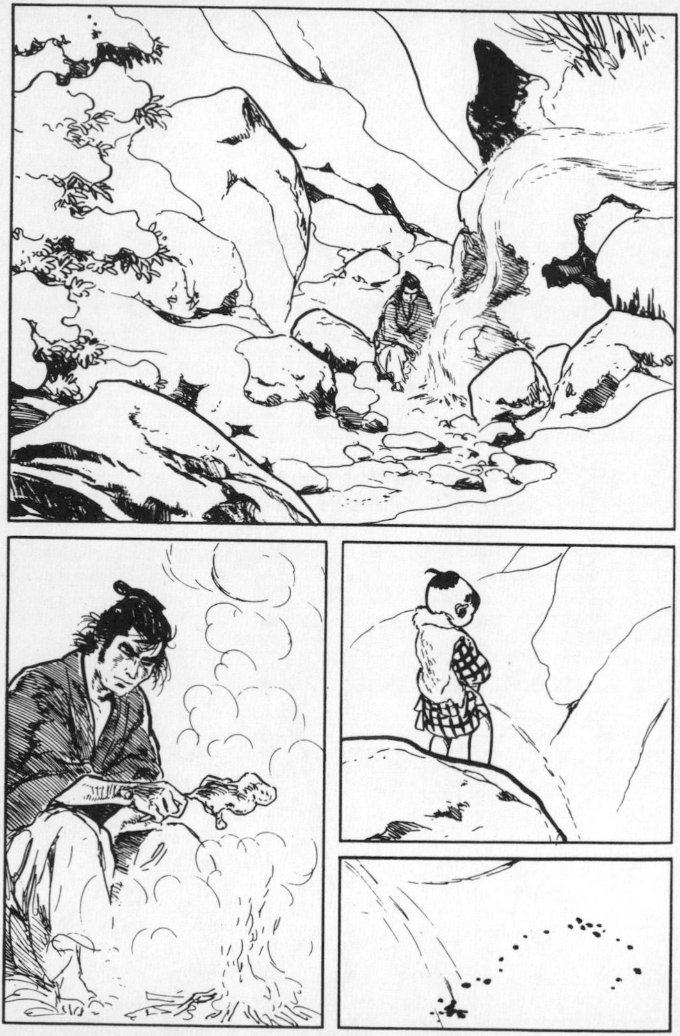

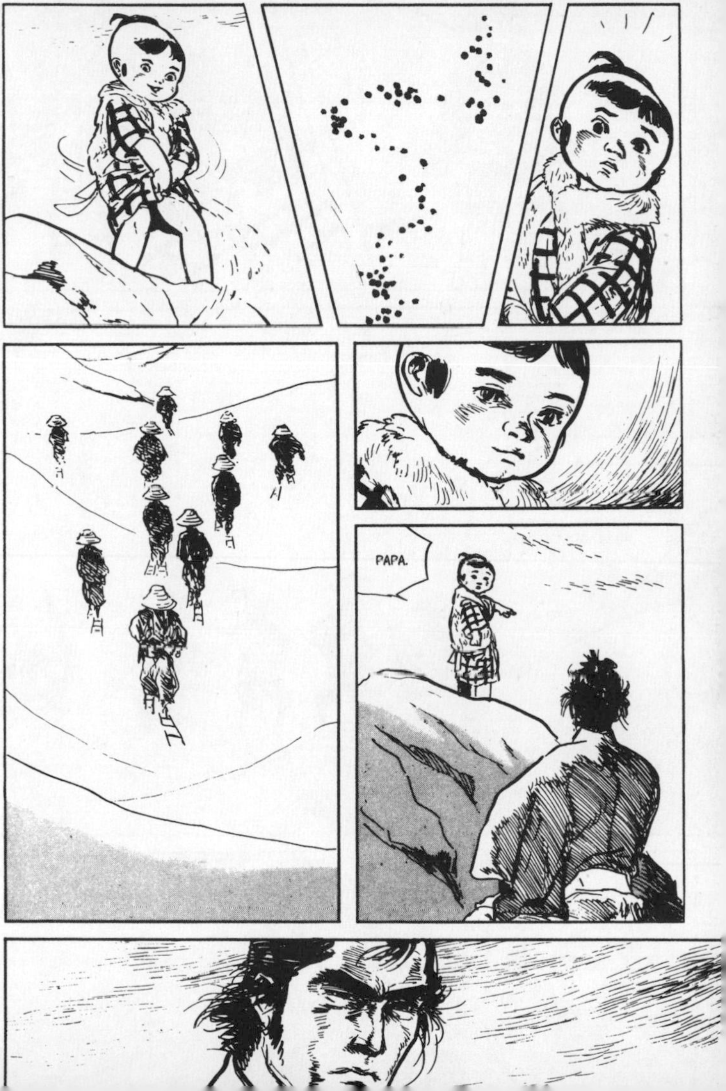
PAPA.

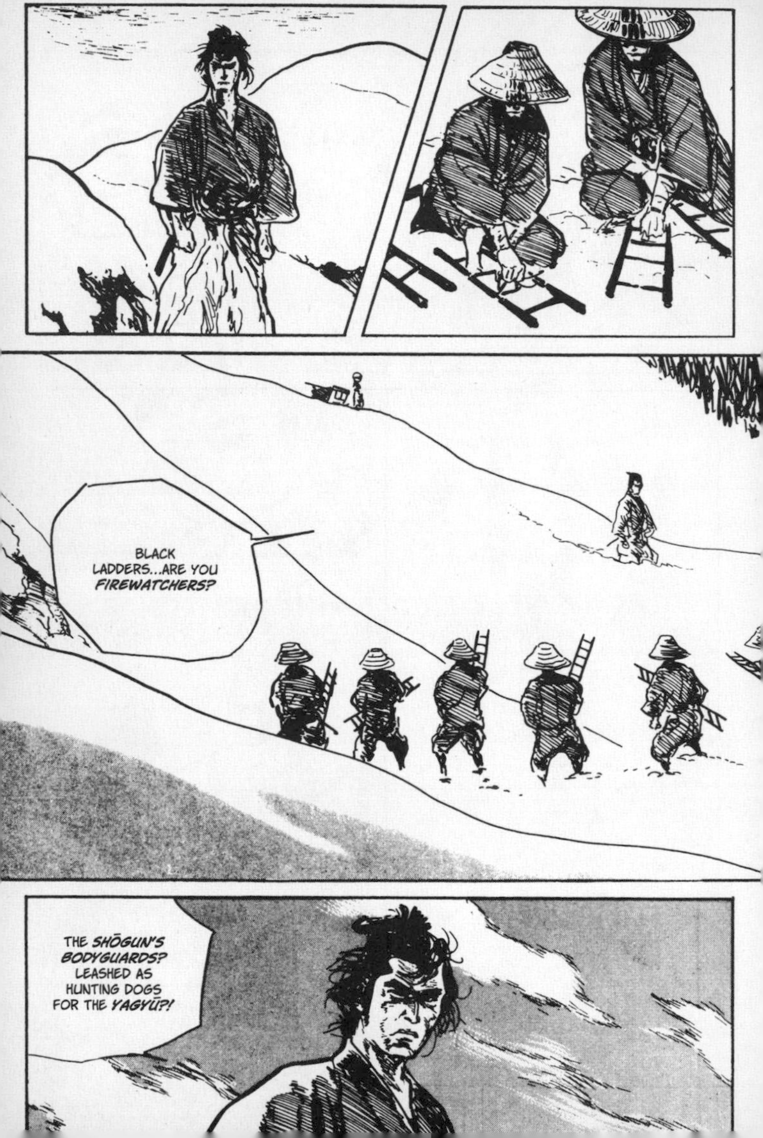
BLACK LADDERS...ARE YOU *FIREWATCHERS?*
THE *SHŌGUN'S BODYGUARDS?* LEASHED AS HUNTING DOGS FOR THE *YAGYŪ?!*

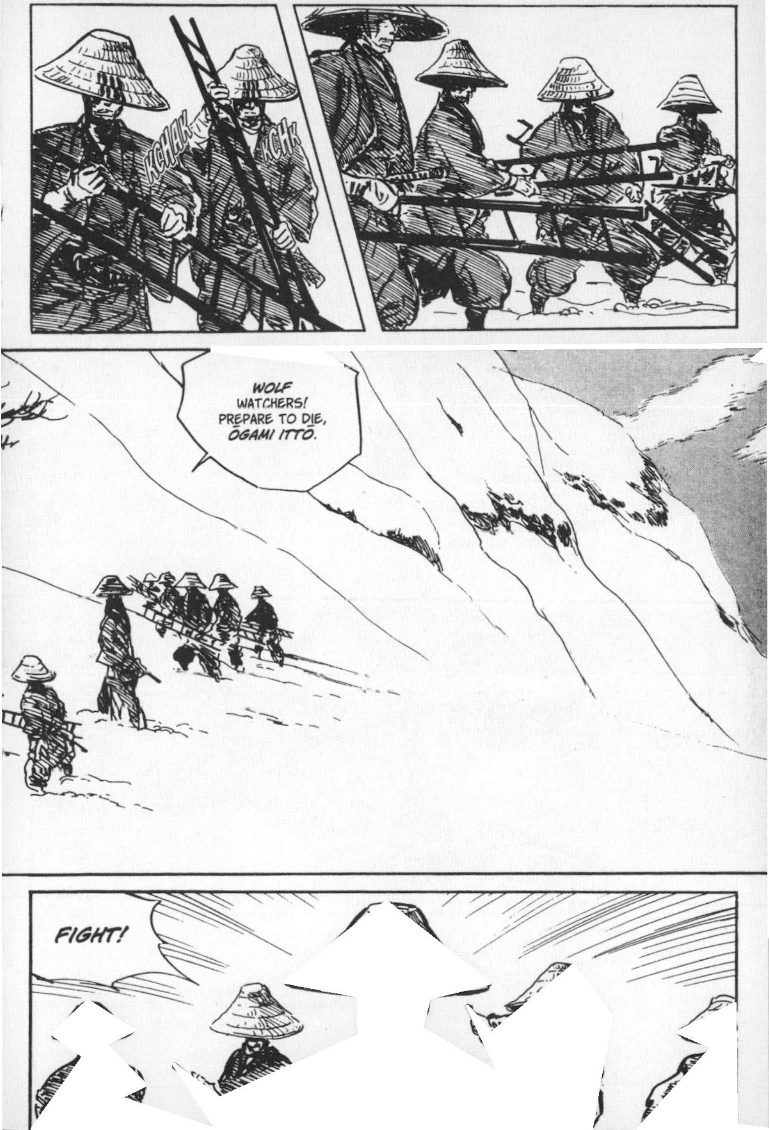
KCHK
KCHAK
WOLF WATCHERS! PREPARE TO DIE, ŌGAMI ITTŌ.
FIGHT!

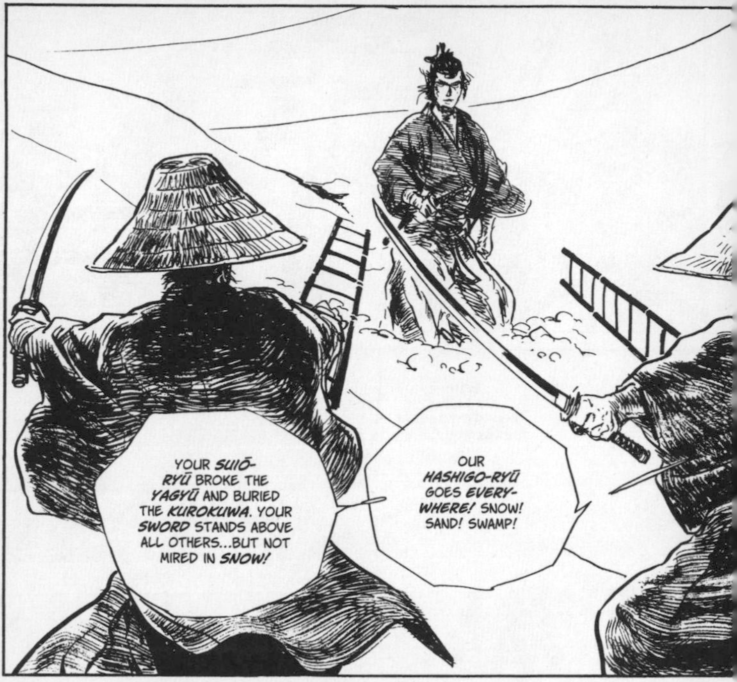
YOUR *SUIŌ-RYŪ* BROKE THE *YAGYŪ* AND BURIED THE *KUROKUWA*. YOUR *SWORD* STANDS ABOVE ALL OTHERS...BUT NOT MIRED IN *SNOW!*
OUR *HASHIGO-RYŪ* GOES *EVERYWHERE!* SNOW! SAND! SWAMP!

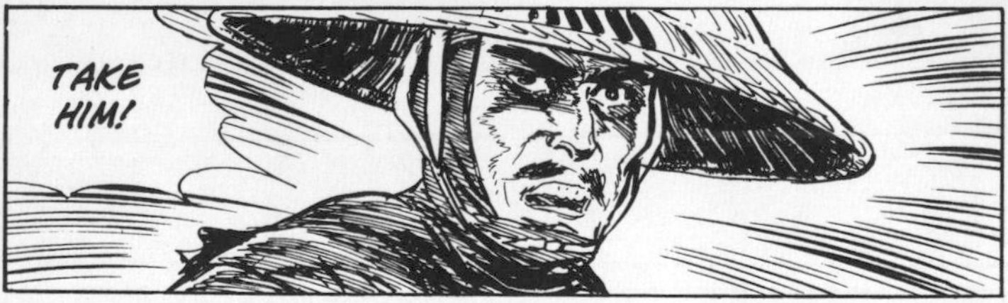
TAKE HIM!

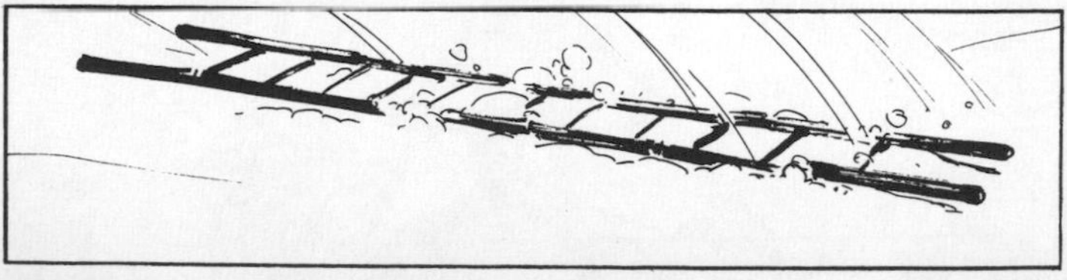

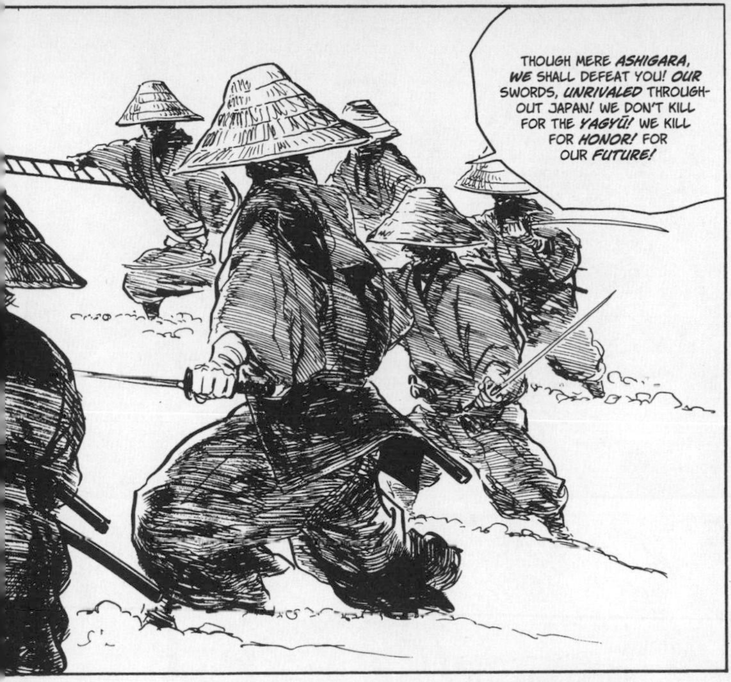
THOUGH MERE ASHIGARA, WE SHALL DEFEAT YOU! OUR SWORDS, UNRIVALED THROUGHOUT JAPAN! WE DON'T KILL FOR THE YAGYŪ! WE KILL FOR HONOR! FOR OUR FUTURE!
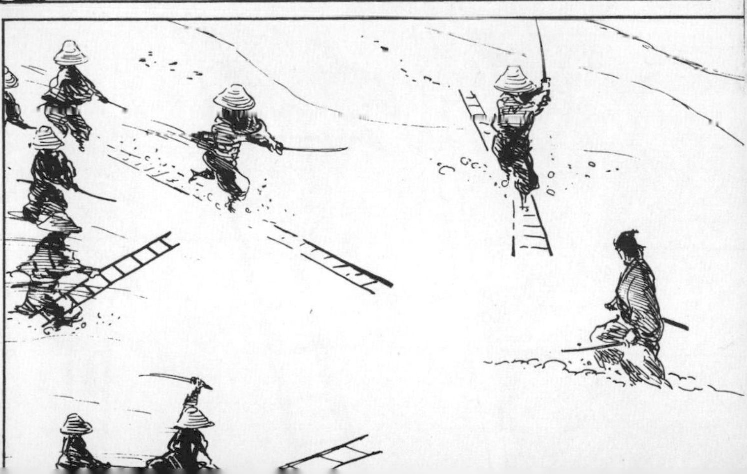

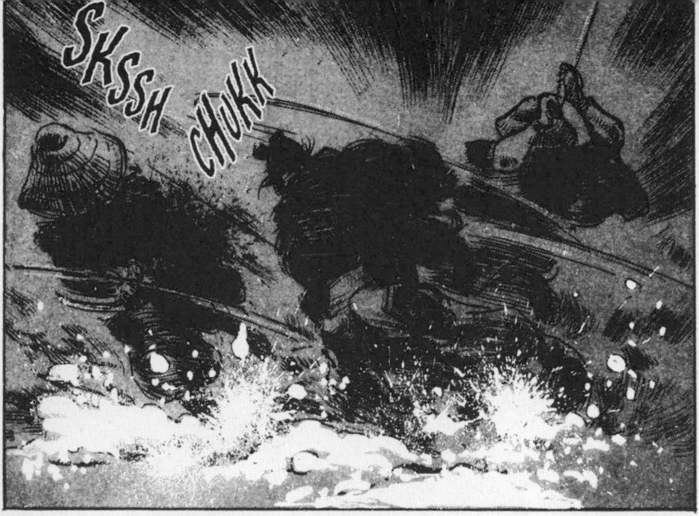
SKSSH
CHUKK
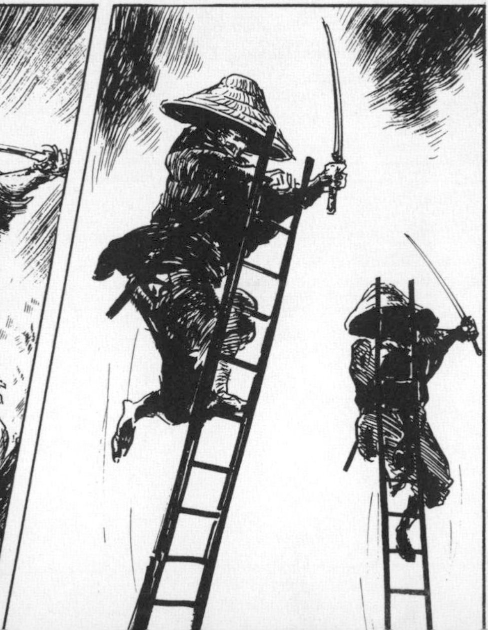
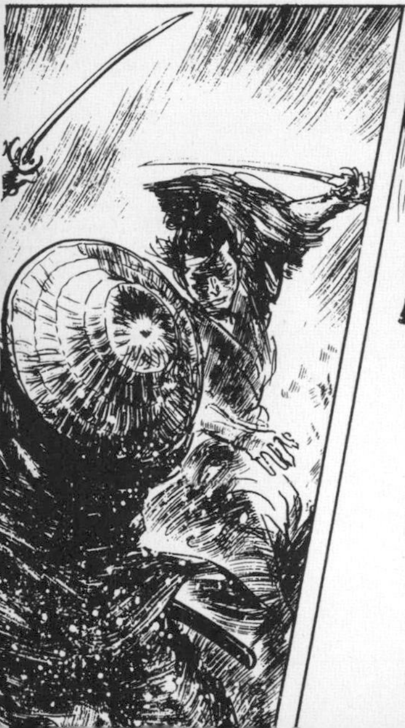

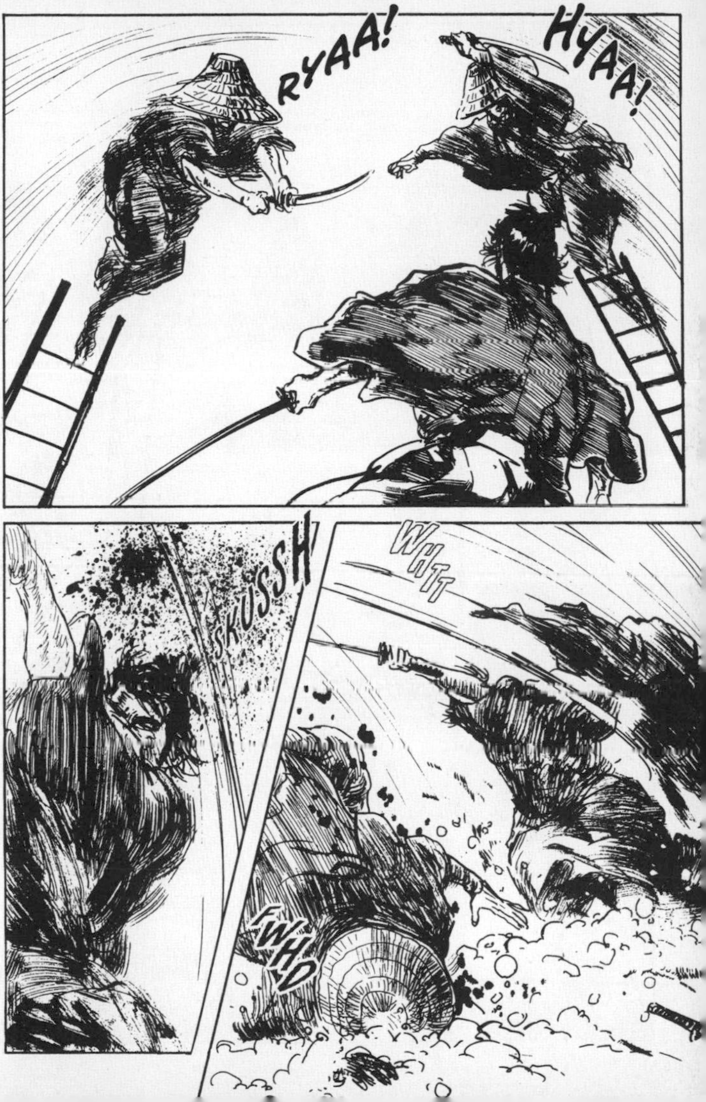
HYAAA!
RYAA!
WHTT
FWHD
SKUSSH

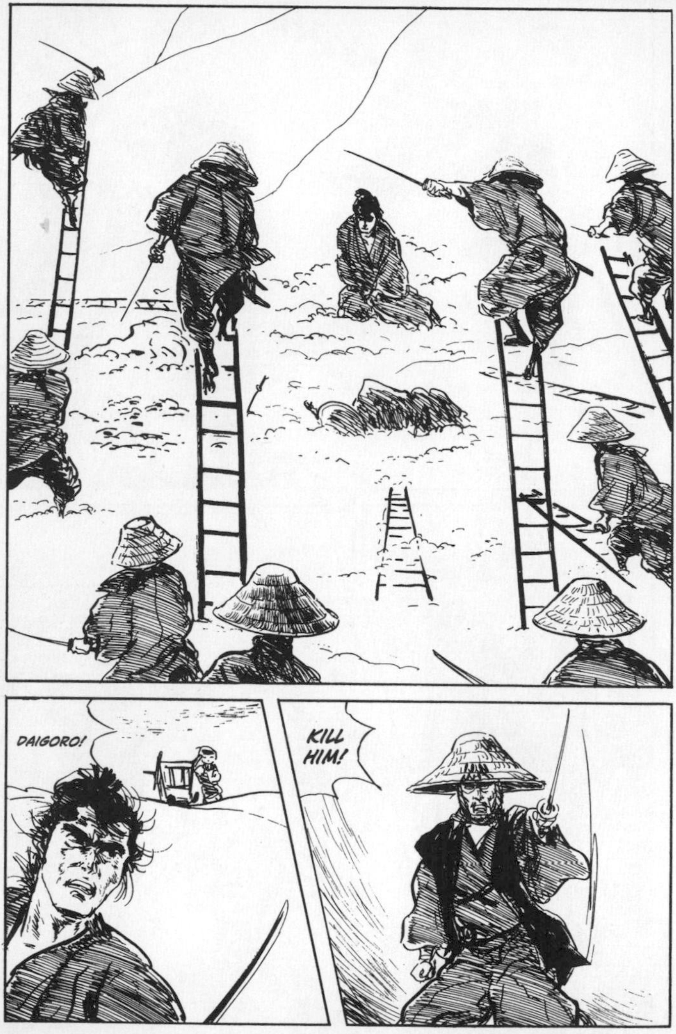
KILL HIM!
DAIGORO!

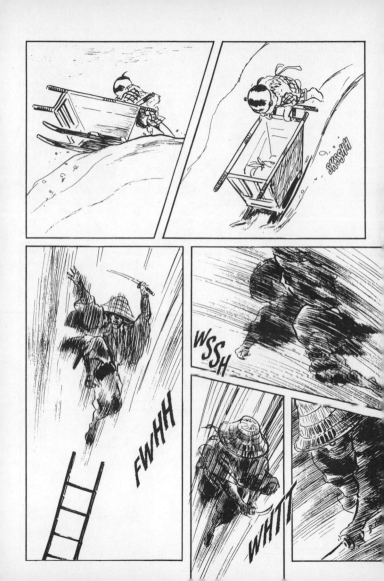

HISSSS

WSSH

FWHH

WHTT

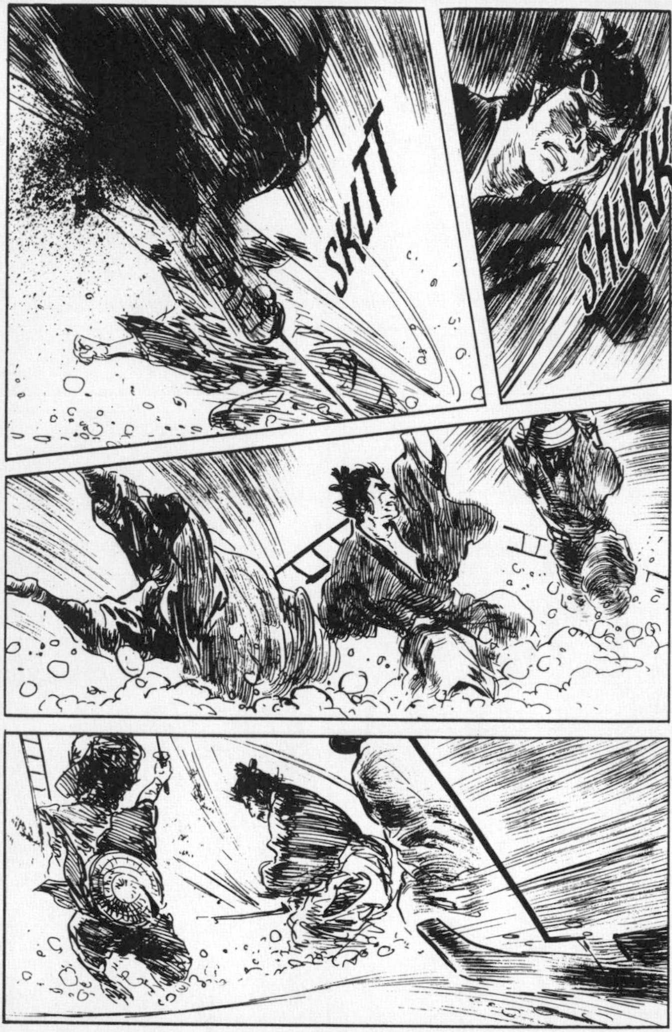
SHUKK
SKLTT

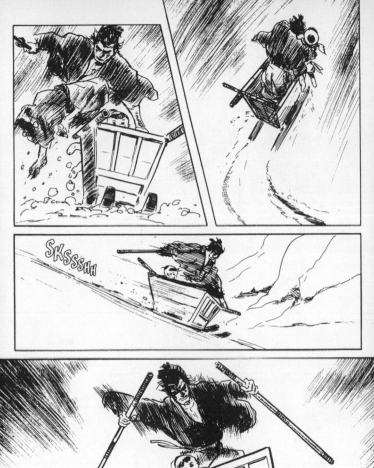

SKSSSHH

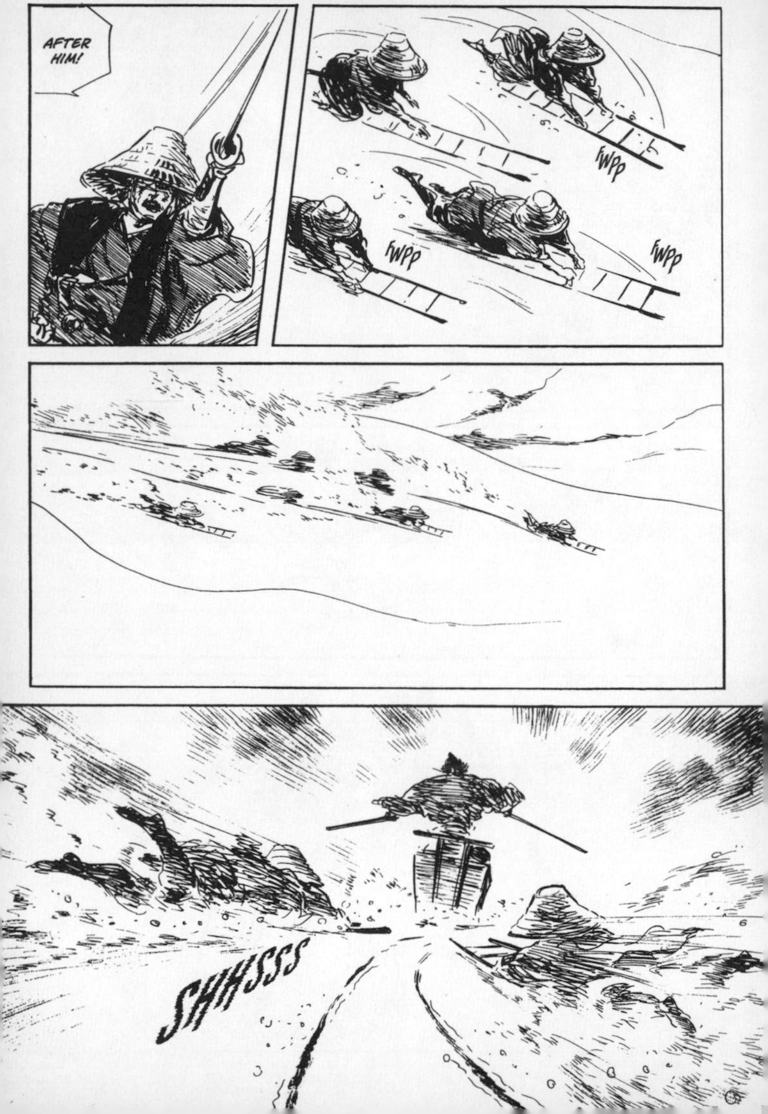
AFTER HIM!
FWPP
FWPP
FWPP
SHHSSS

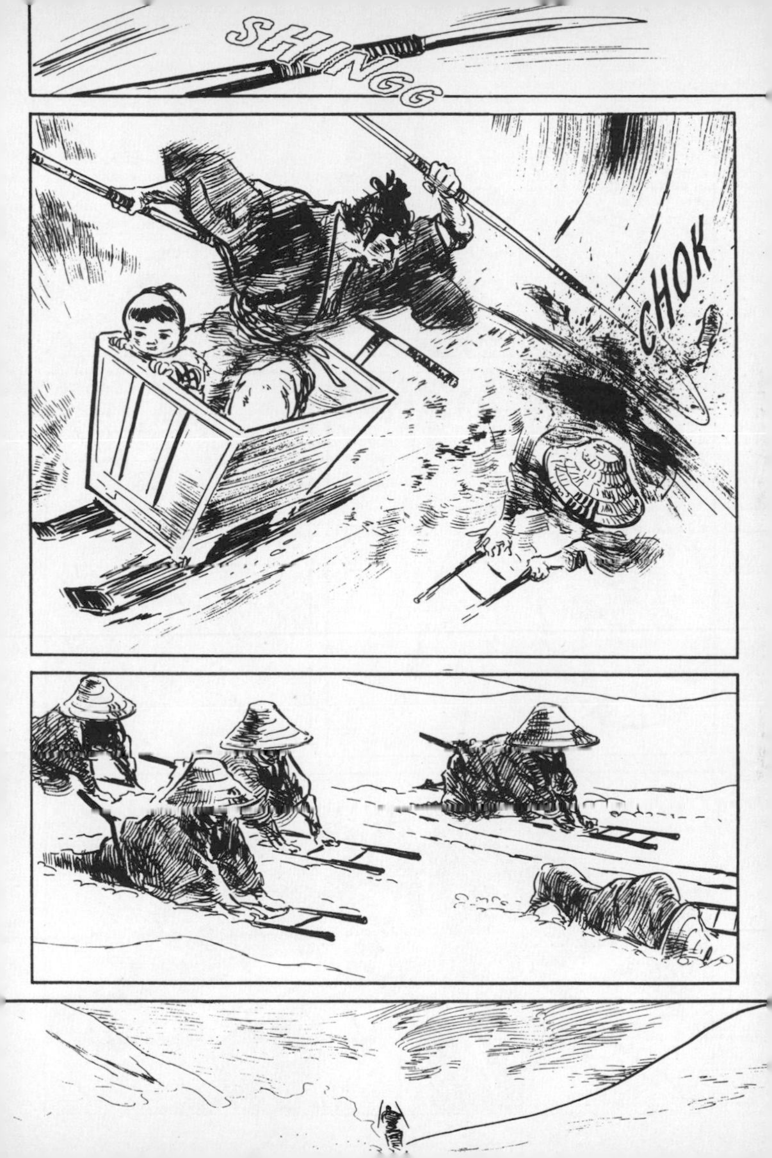
SHINGG
CHOK

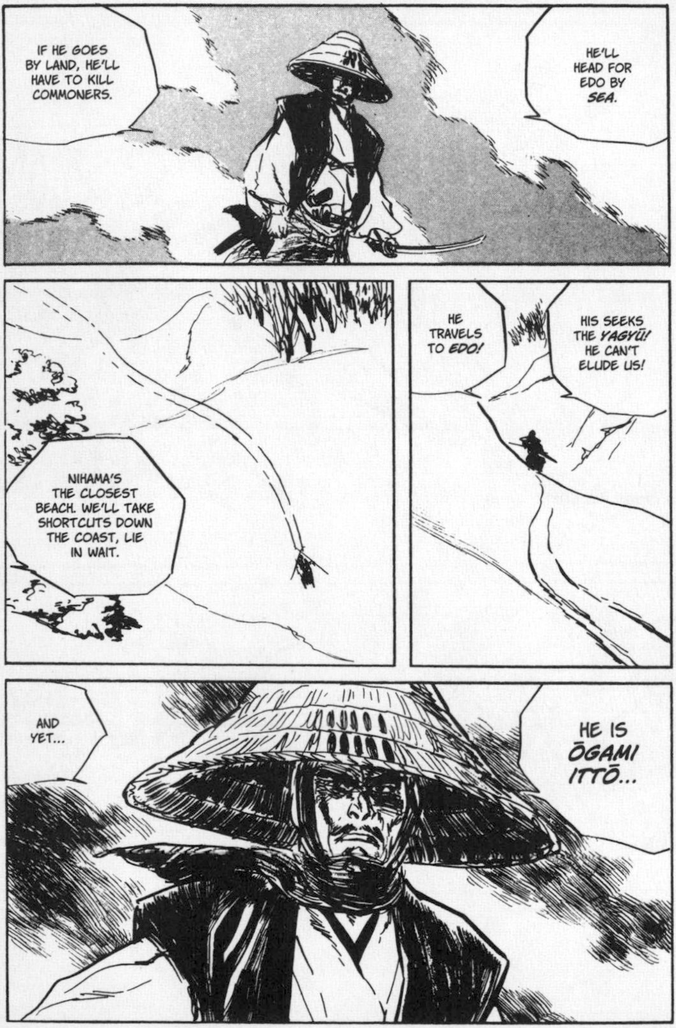
HE'LL HEAD FOR EDO BY *SEA*.
IF HE GOES BY LAND, HE'LL HAVE TO KILL COMMONERS.
HIS SEEKS THE *YAGYŪ!* HE CAN'T ELUDE US!
HE TRAVELS TO *EDO!*
NIHAMA'S THE CLOSEST BEACH. WE'LL TAKE SHORTCUTS DOWN THE COAST, LIE IN WAIT.
HE IS *ŌGAMI ITTŌ...*
AND YET...

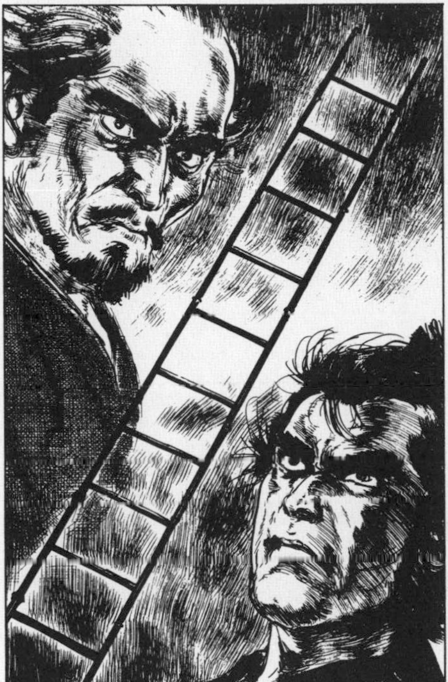

the eighty-ninth

The Immortal Fire Watchers

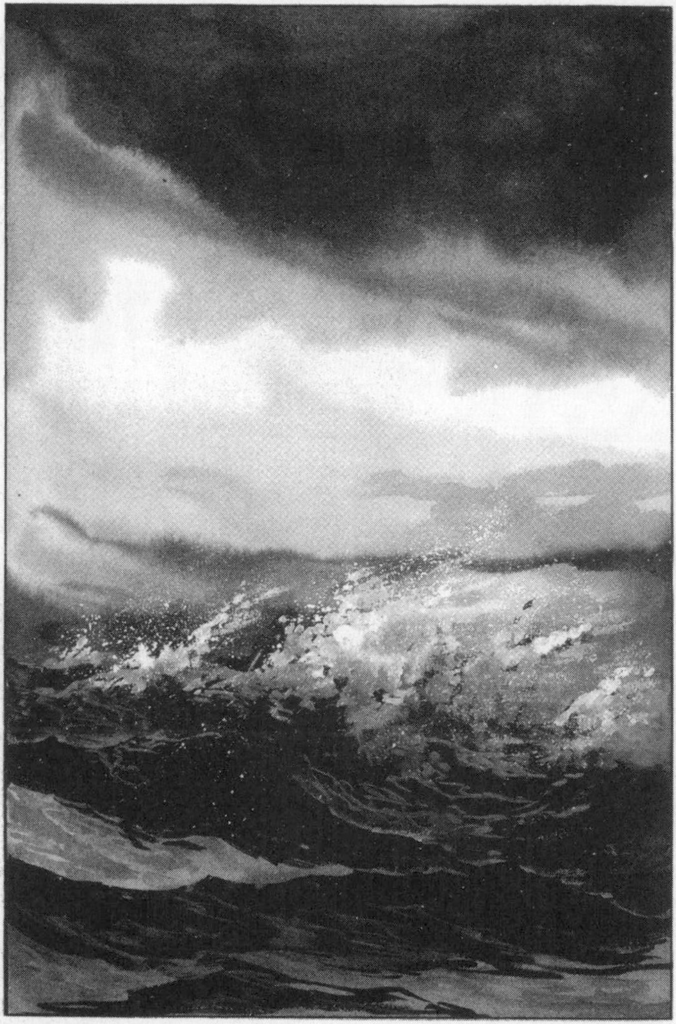

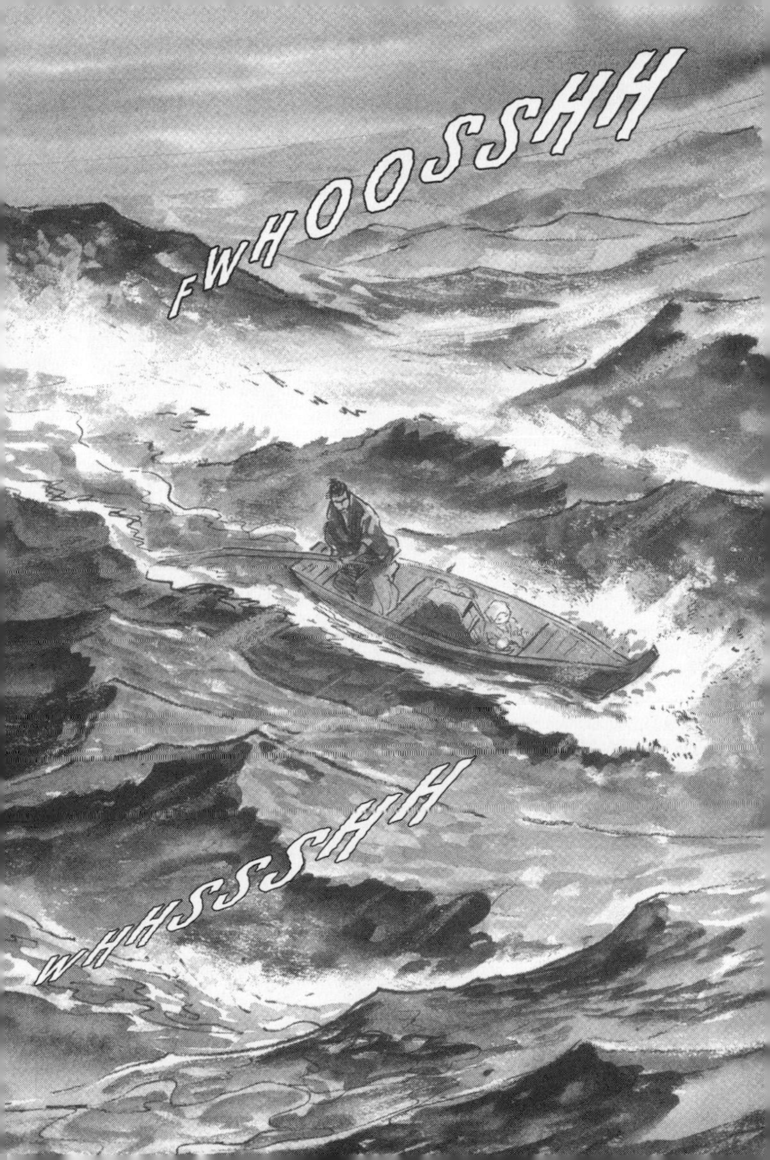
FWHOOSSHH
WHSSSSHH

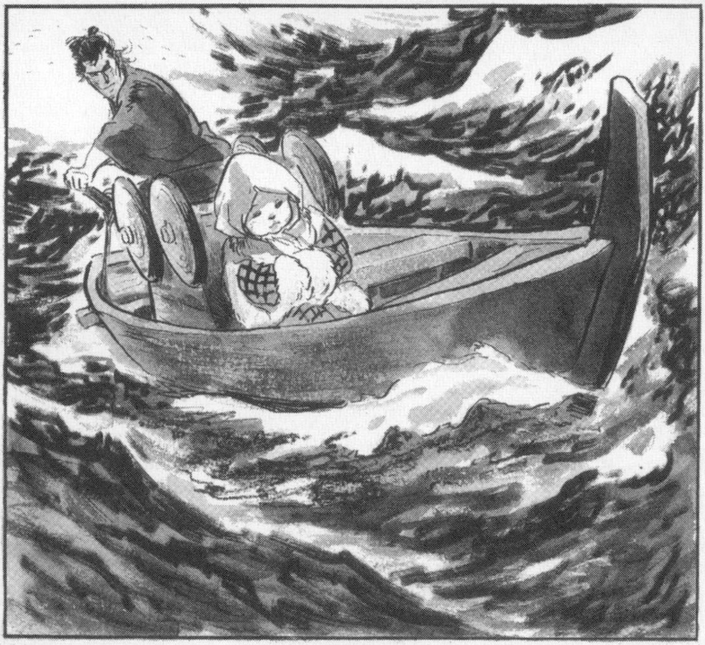

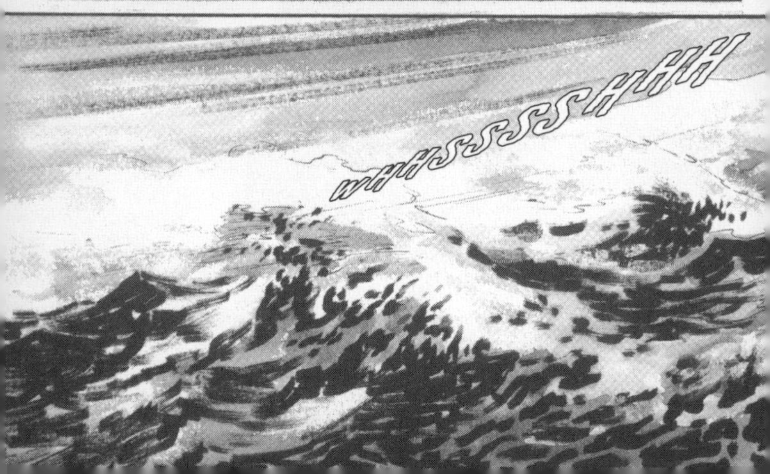
WHHSSSSSHHH

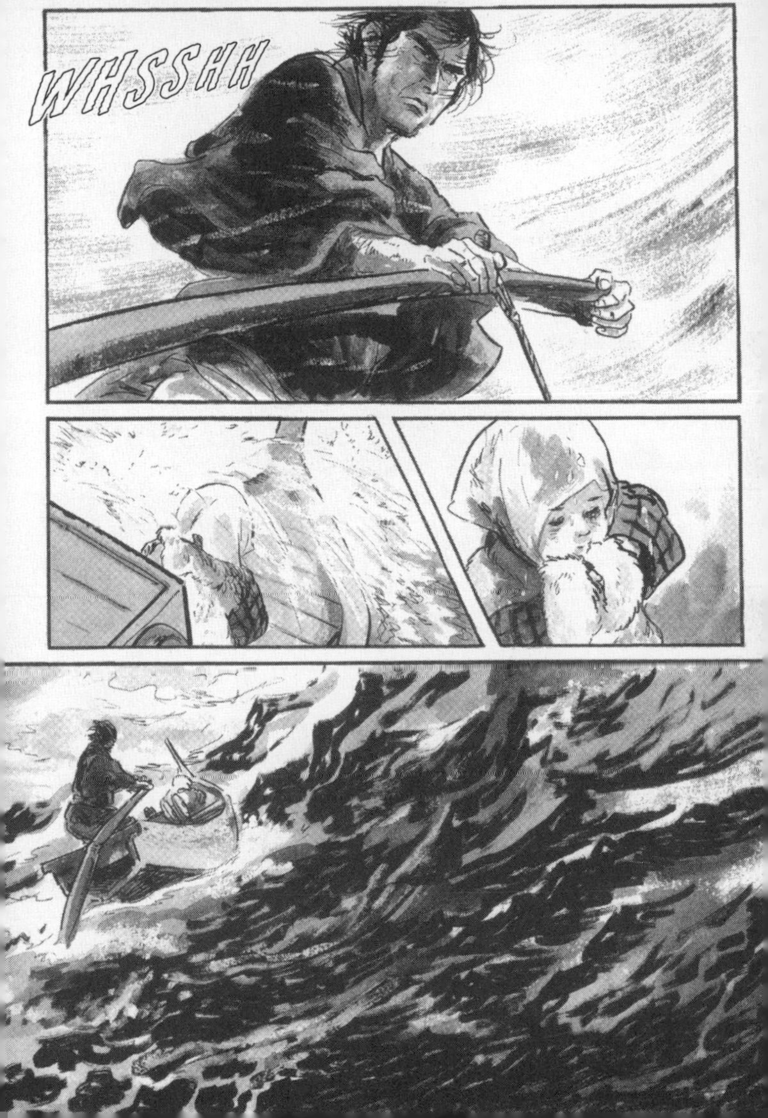
WHSSHH

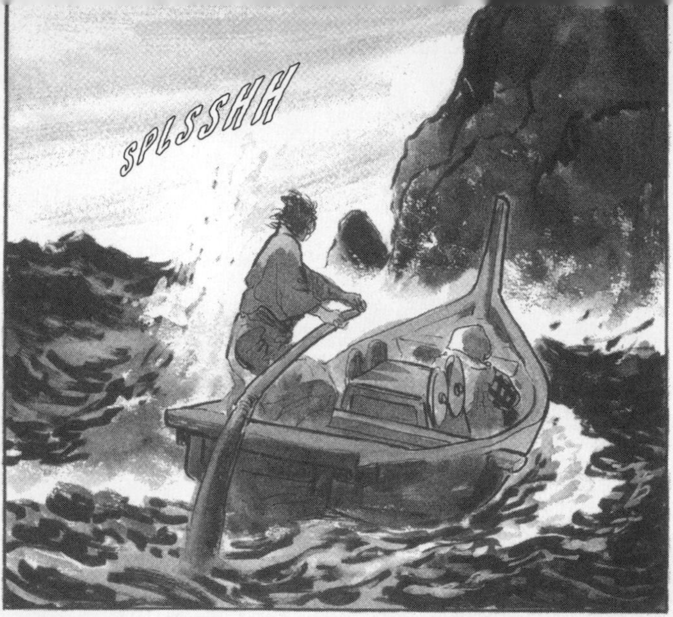
SPLSSHH
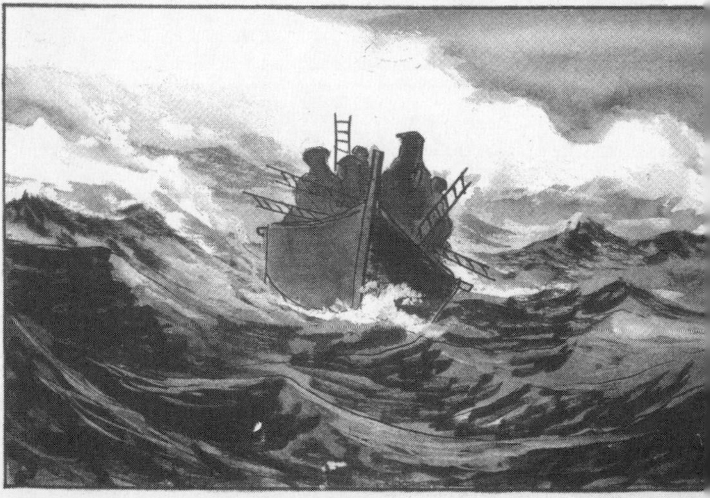

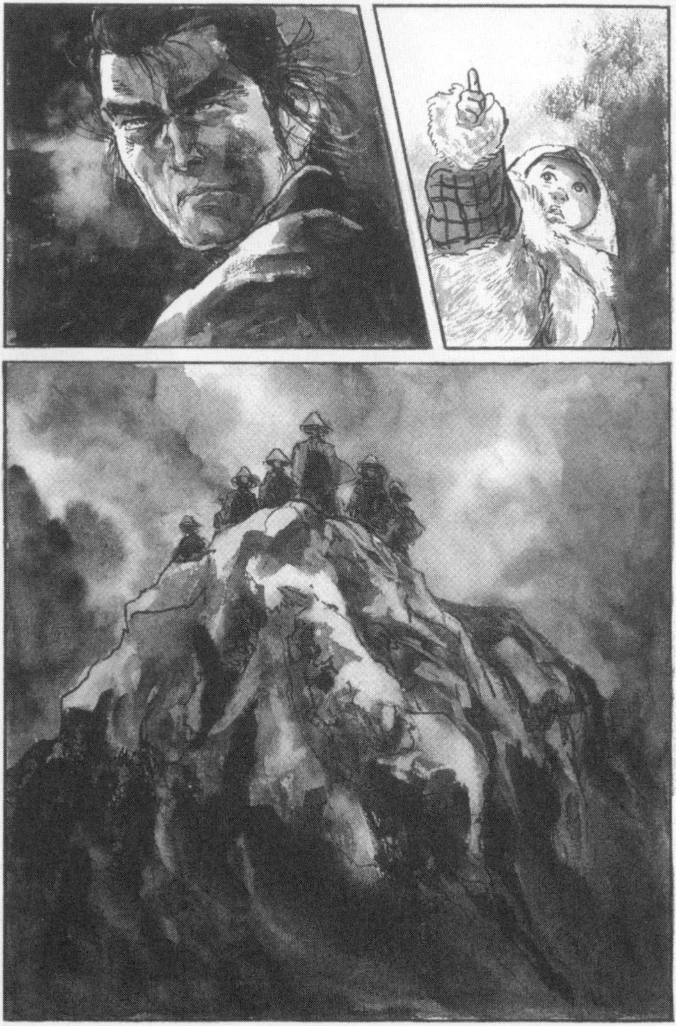

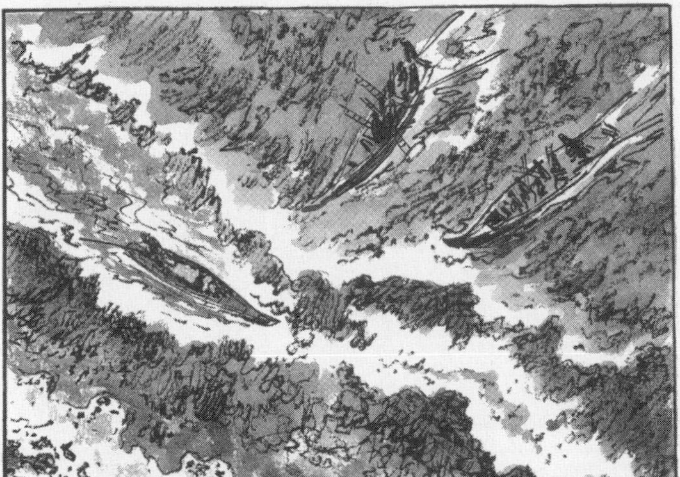
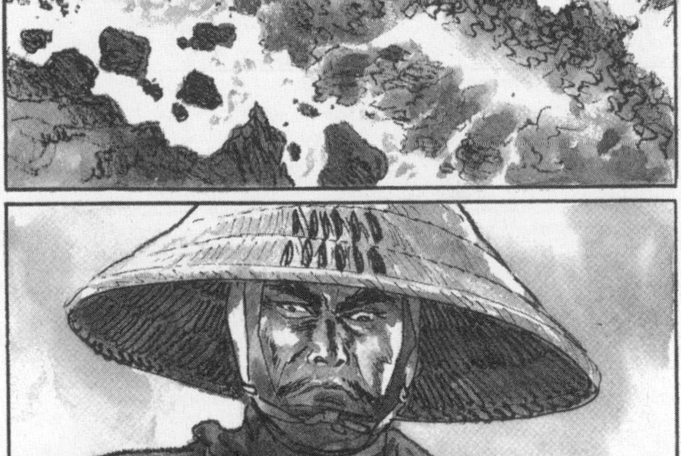

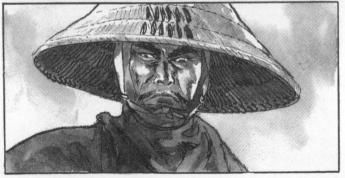

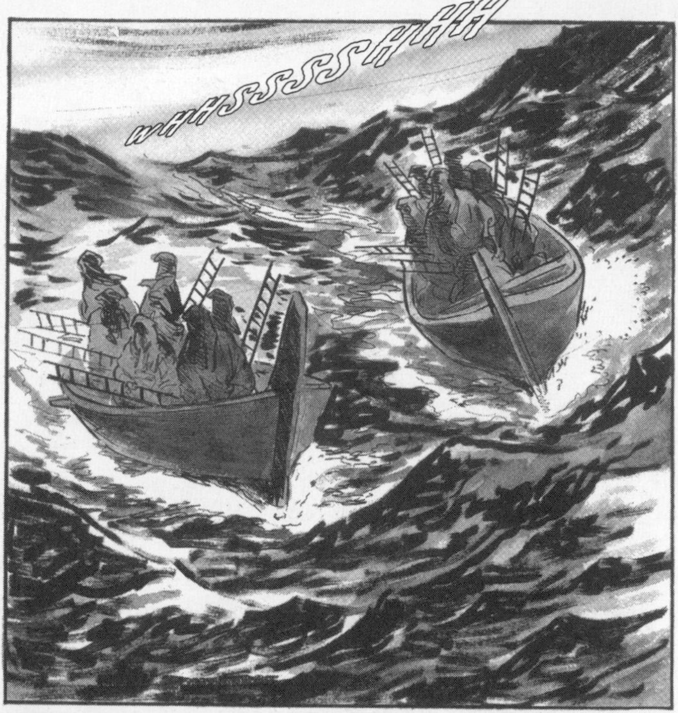
WHHSSSSSSHHH
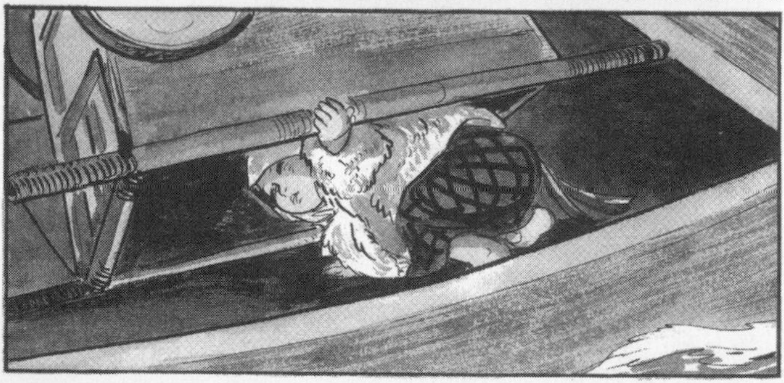

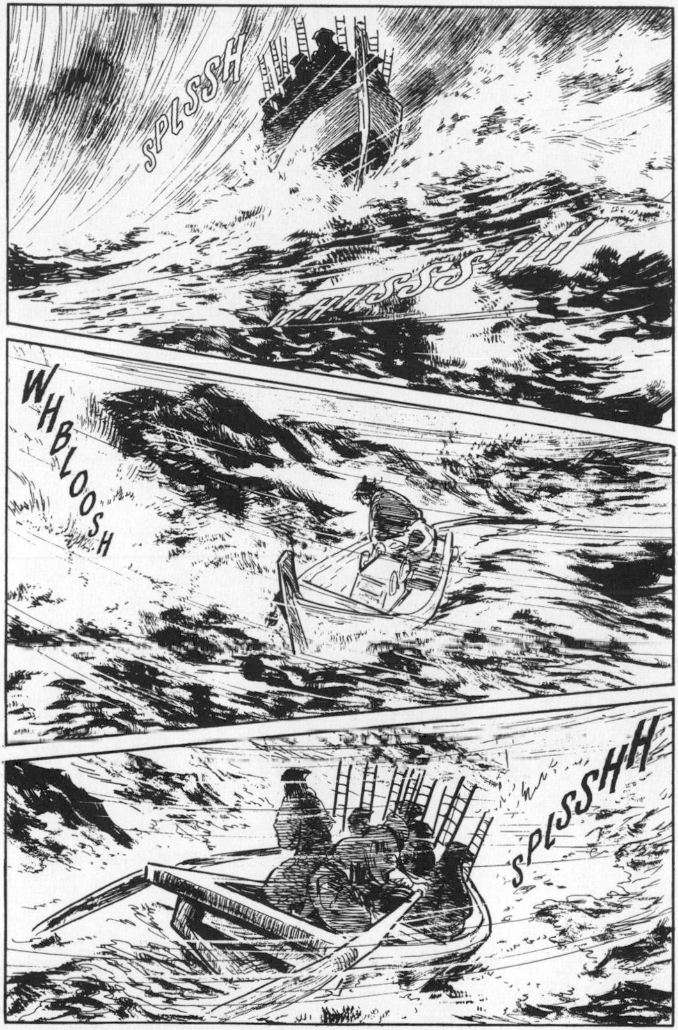
SPLSSH
WHSSSHH
WHBLOOSH
SPLSSHH

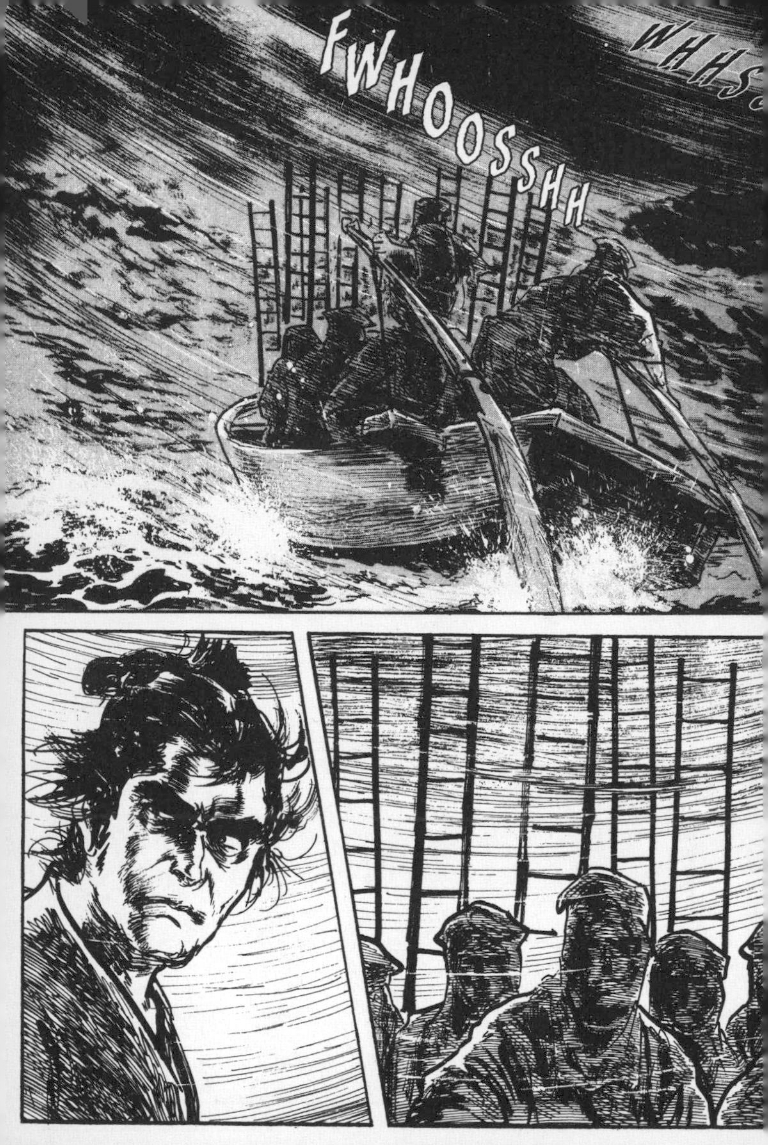

WHHS
FWHOOSSHH

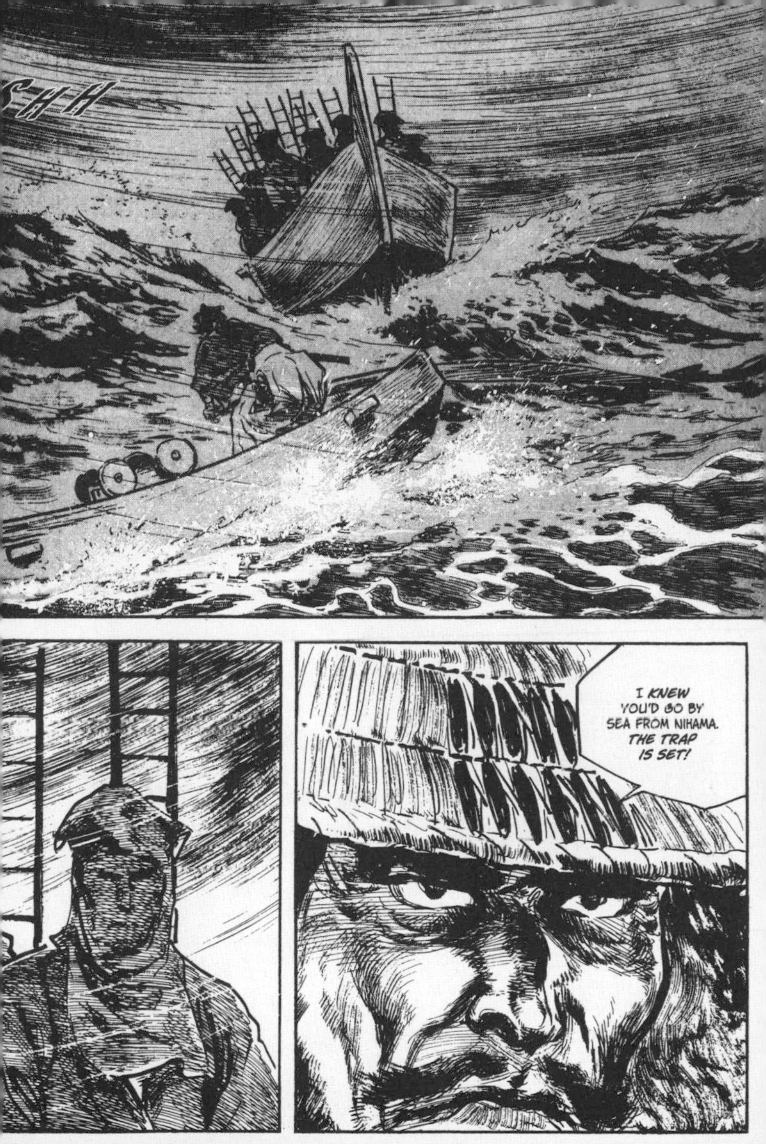
SHH
I KNEW YOU'D GO BY SEA FROM NIHAMA. THE TRAP IS SET!

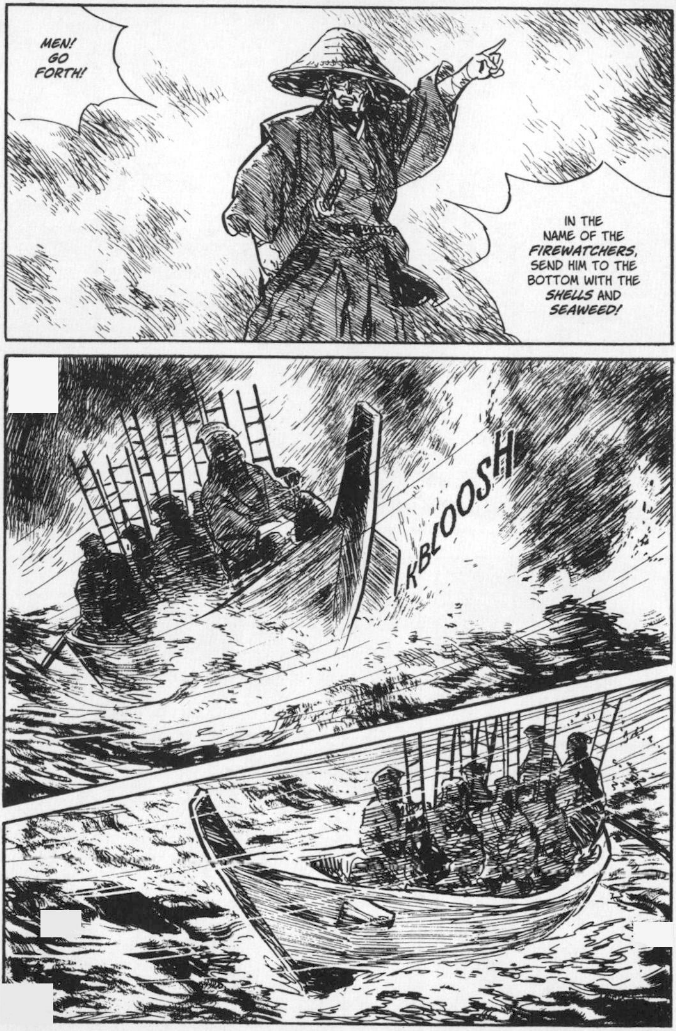
MEN! GO FORTH!
IN THE NAME OF THE FIREWATCHERS, SEND HIM TO THE BOTTOM WITH THE SHELLS AND SEAWEED!
KBLOOSH

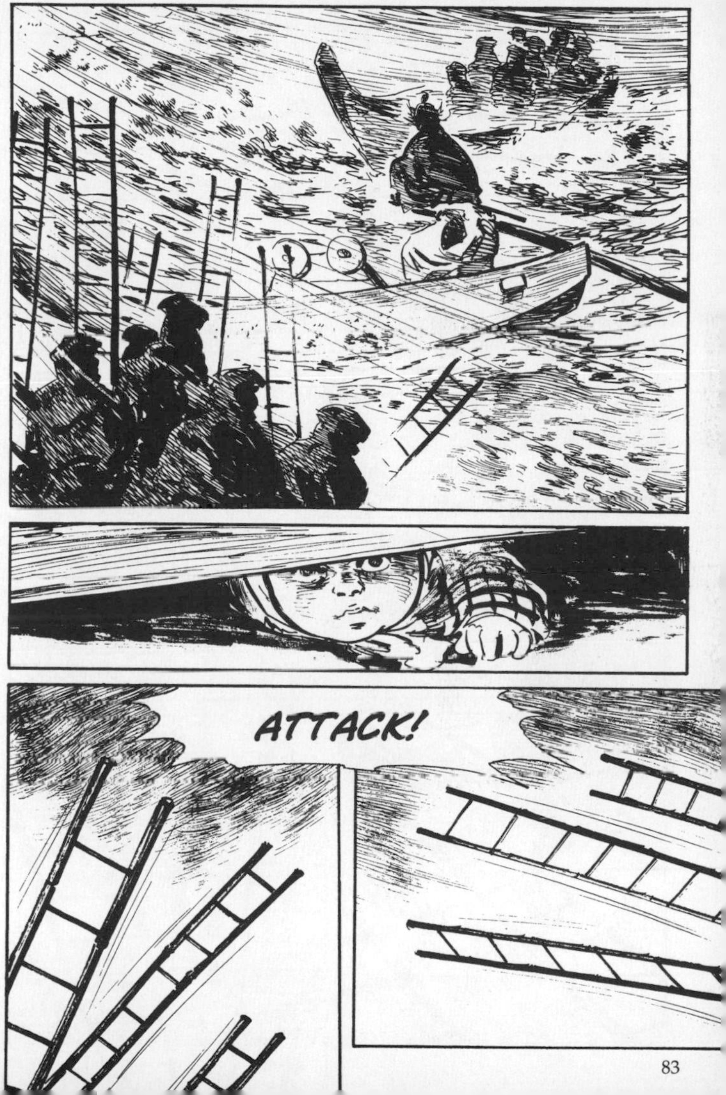
ATTACK!

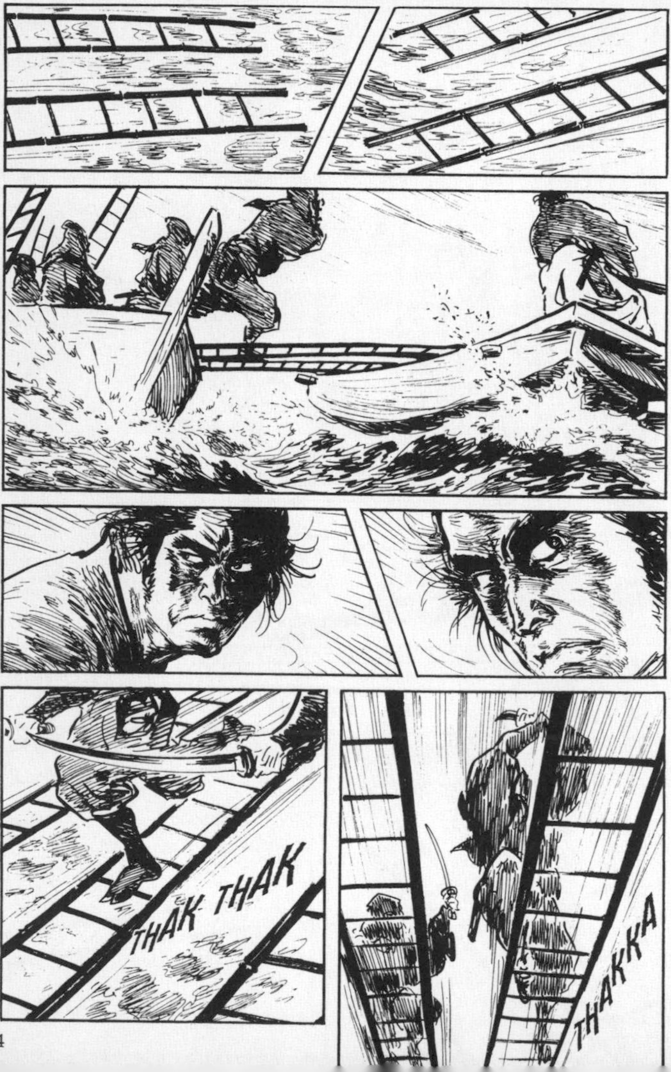
THAKKA
THAK THAK

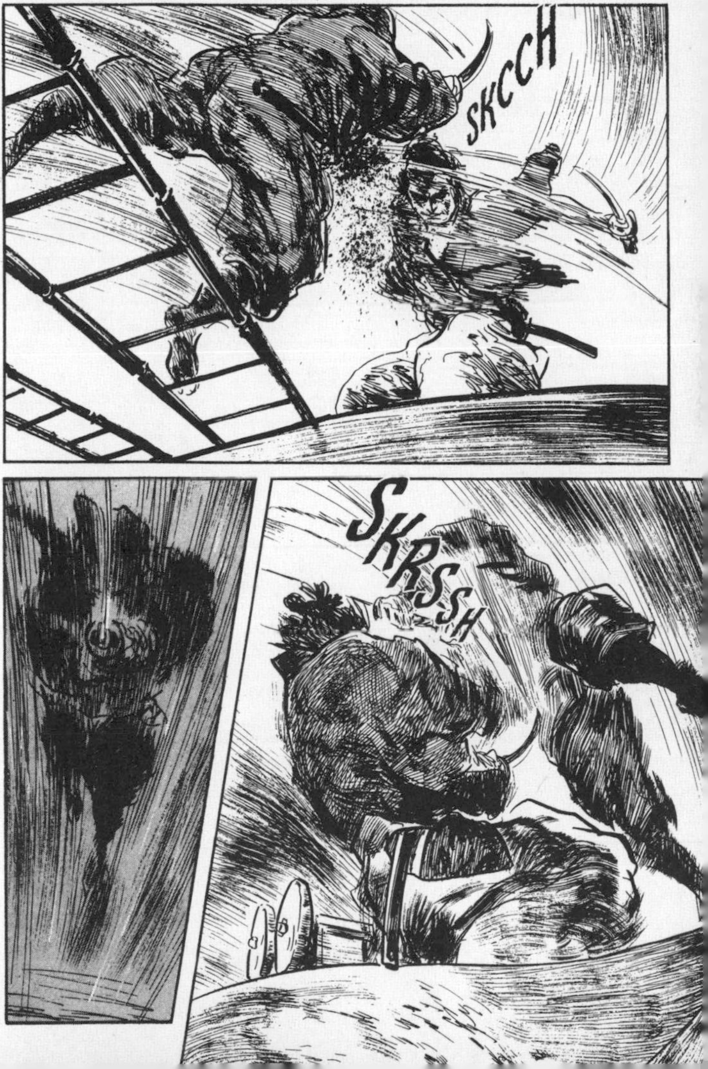
SKCCH
SKRSSH

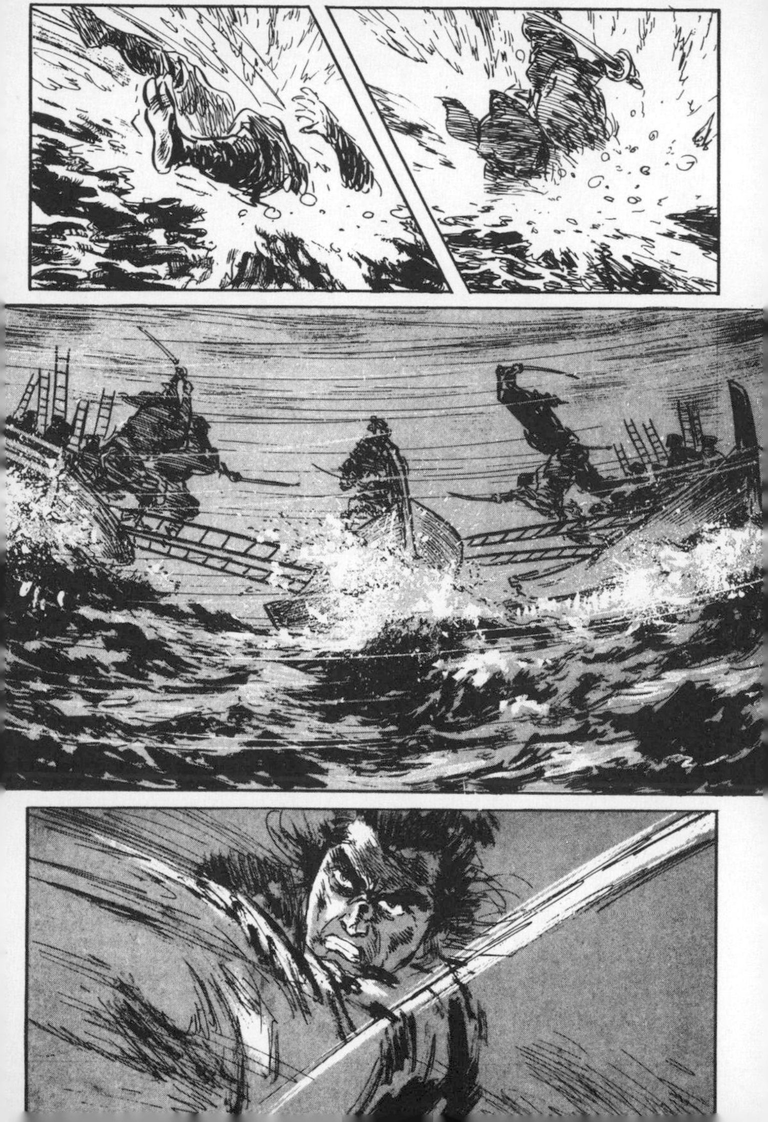

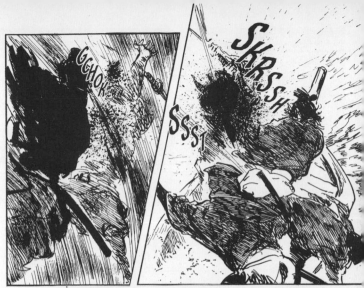

GGHOK

SKRSSH

SSSi

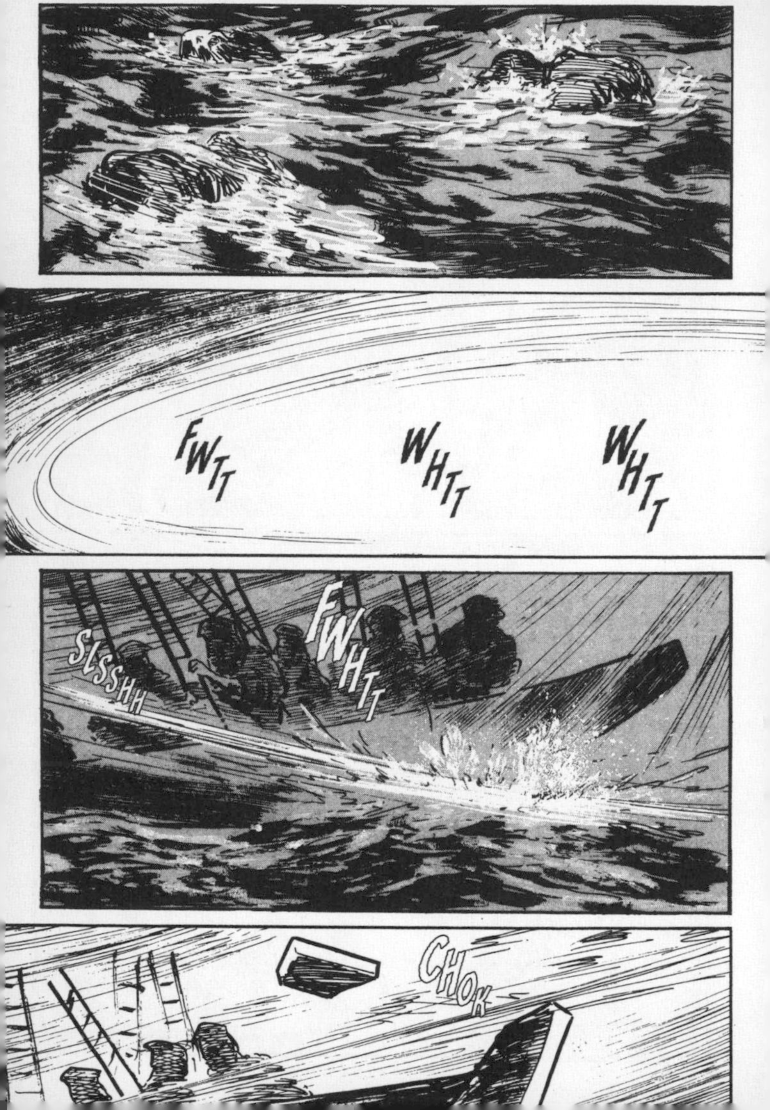
WHTT
WHTT
FWTT
FWHTT
SLSSHH
CHOK

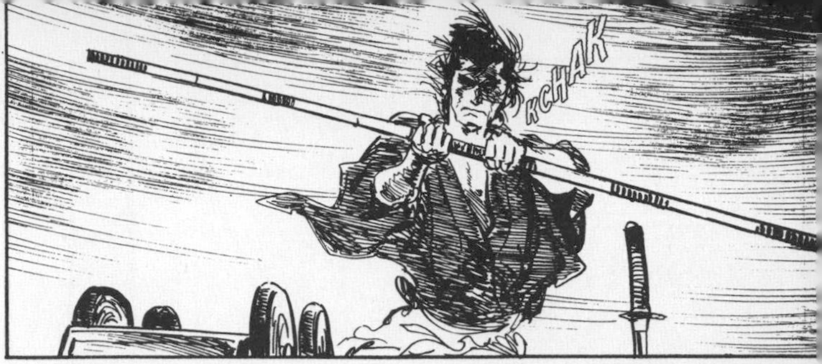
KCHAK
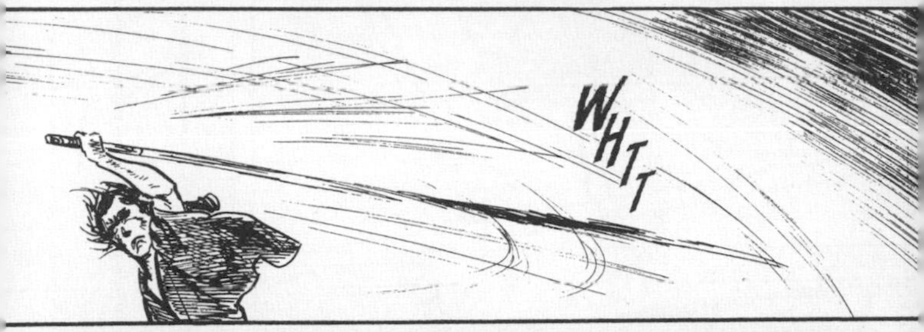
WHTT
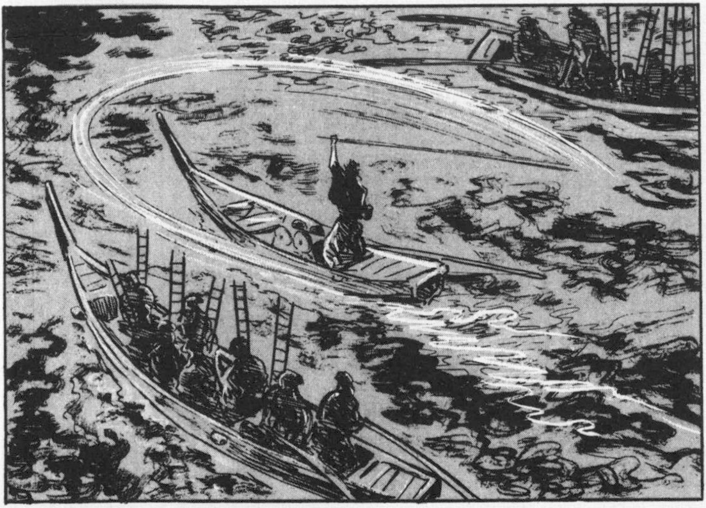

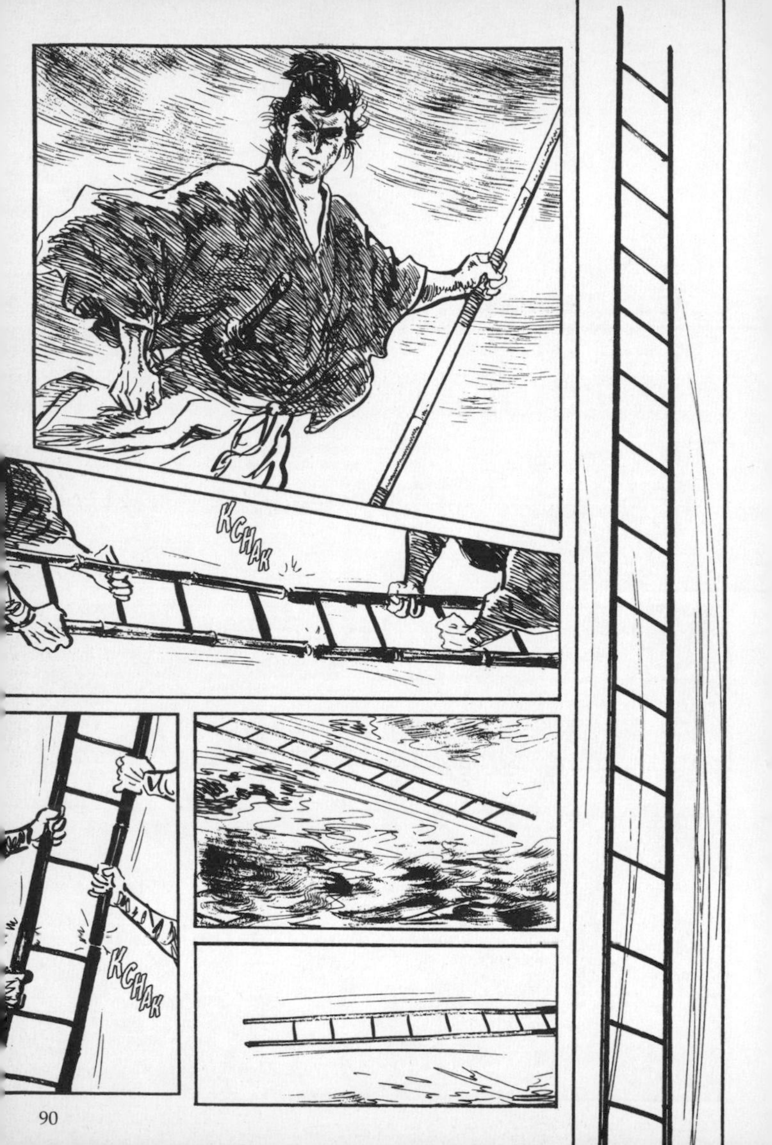
KCHAK
KCHAK

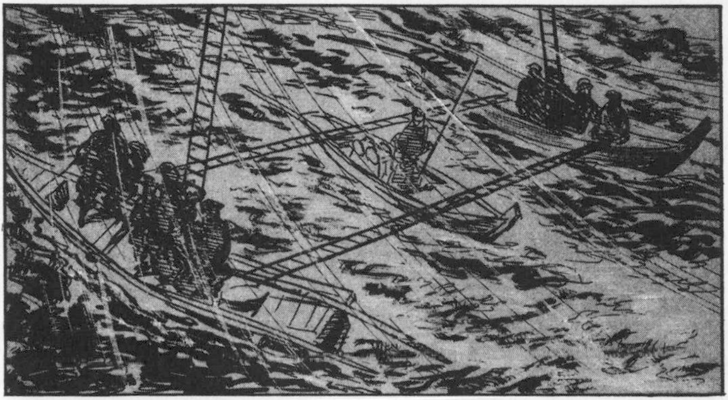
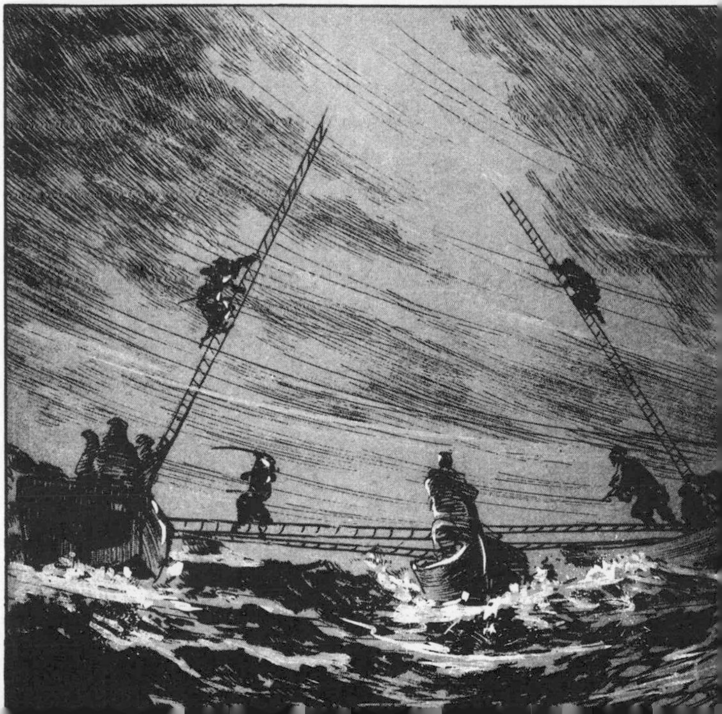

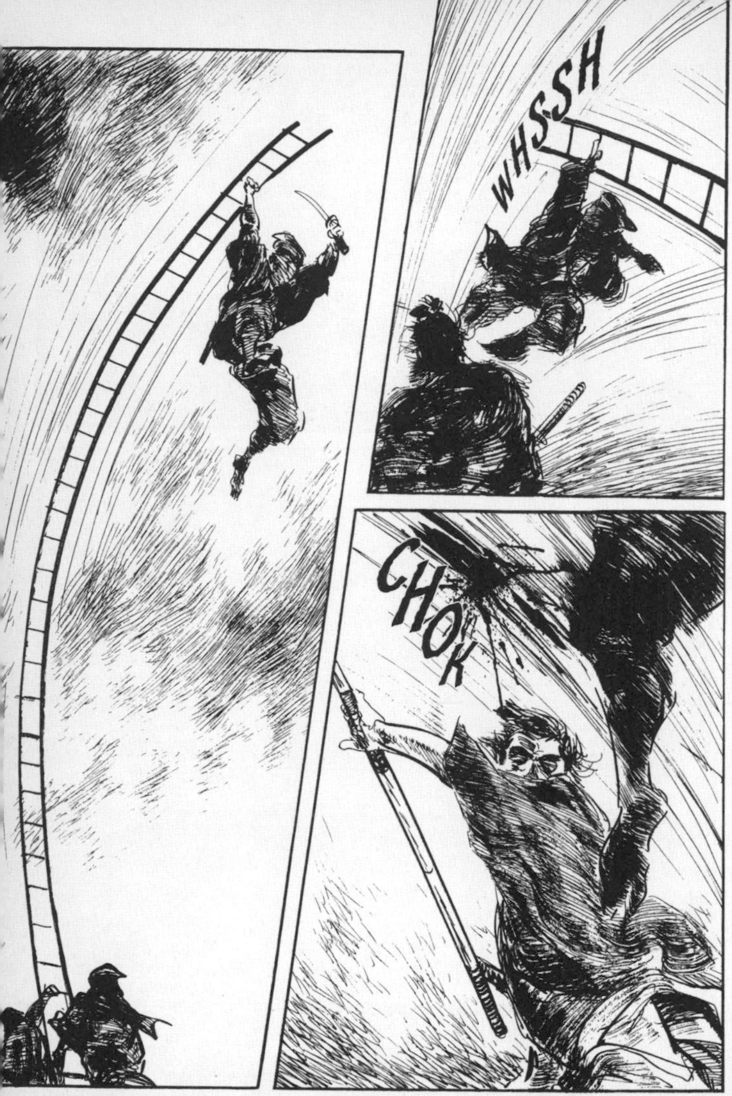
WHSSH
CHOK

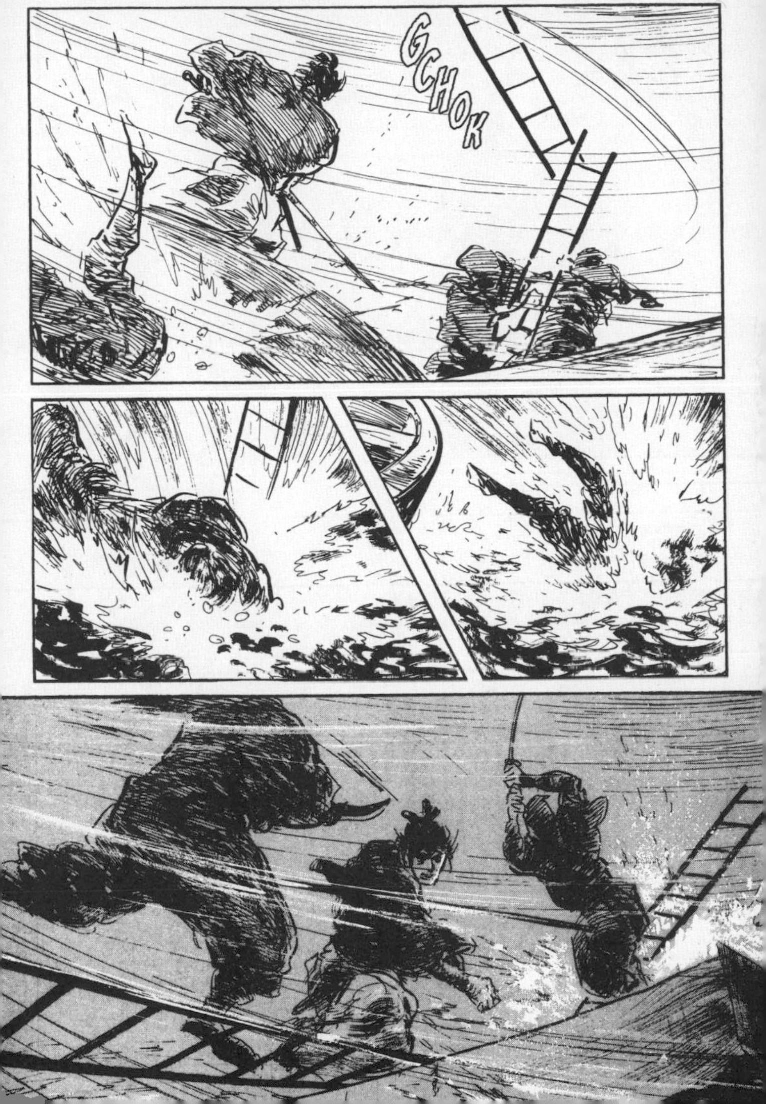
GCHOK

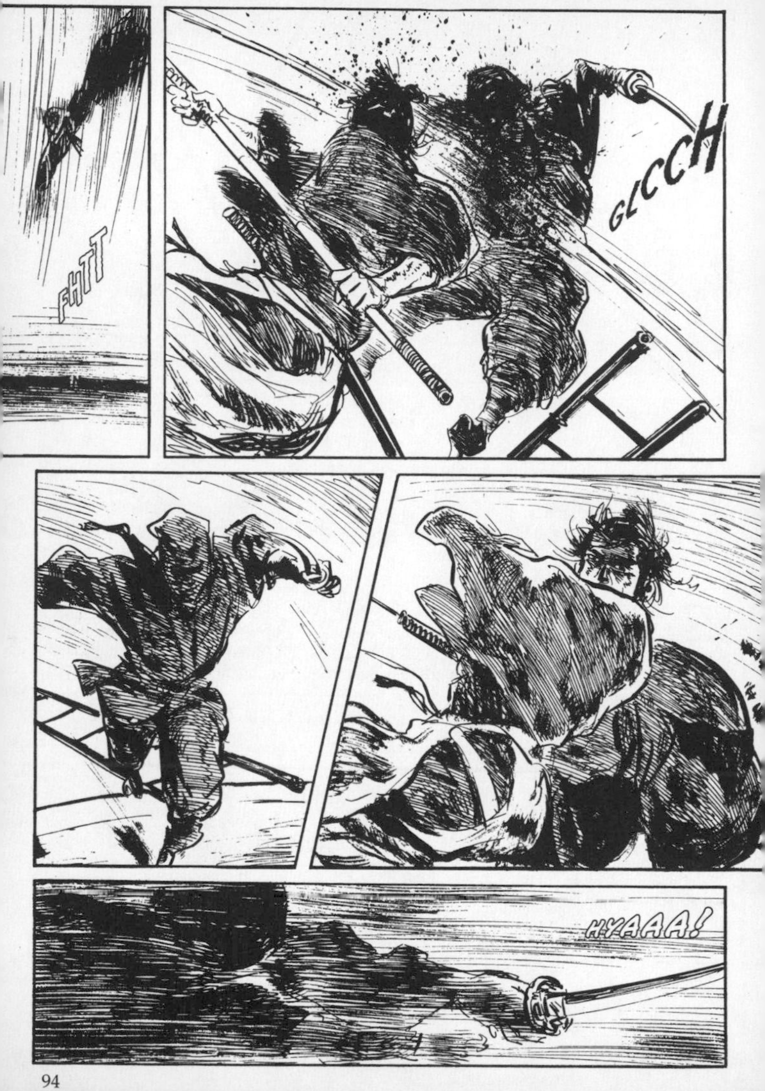
GLCCH
FHTT
HYAAA!

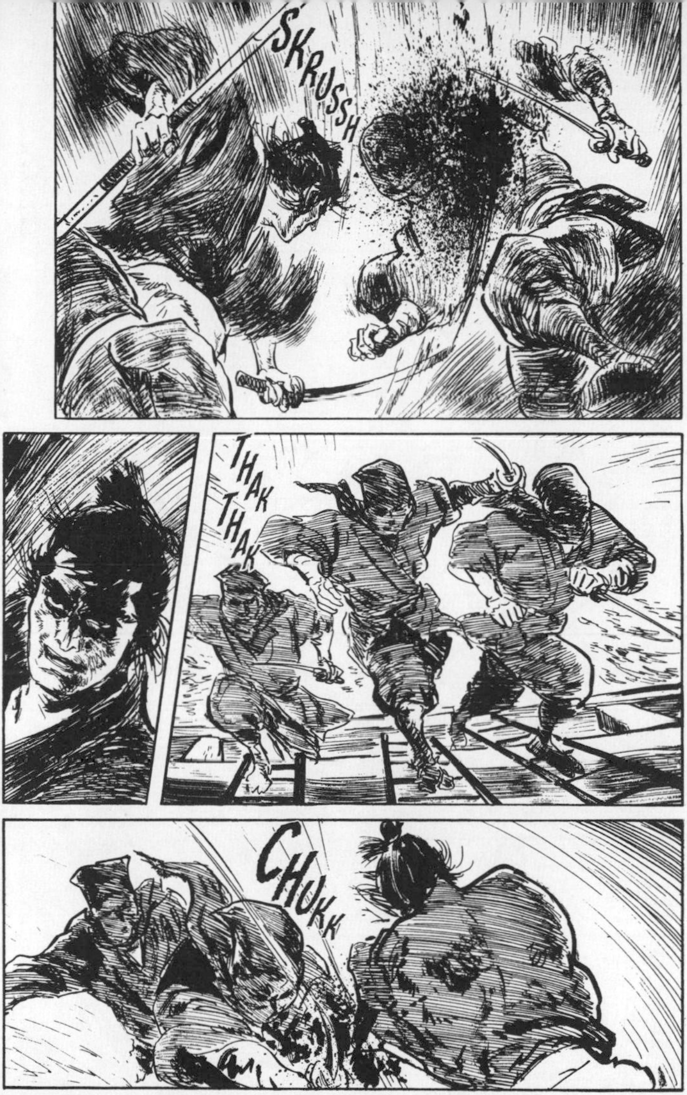
SKRUSSH
THAK THAK THAK
CHUKK

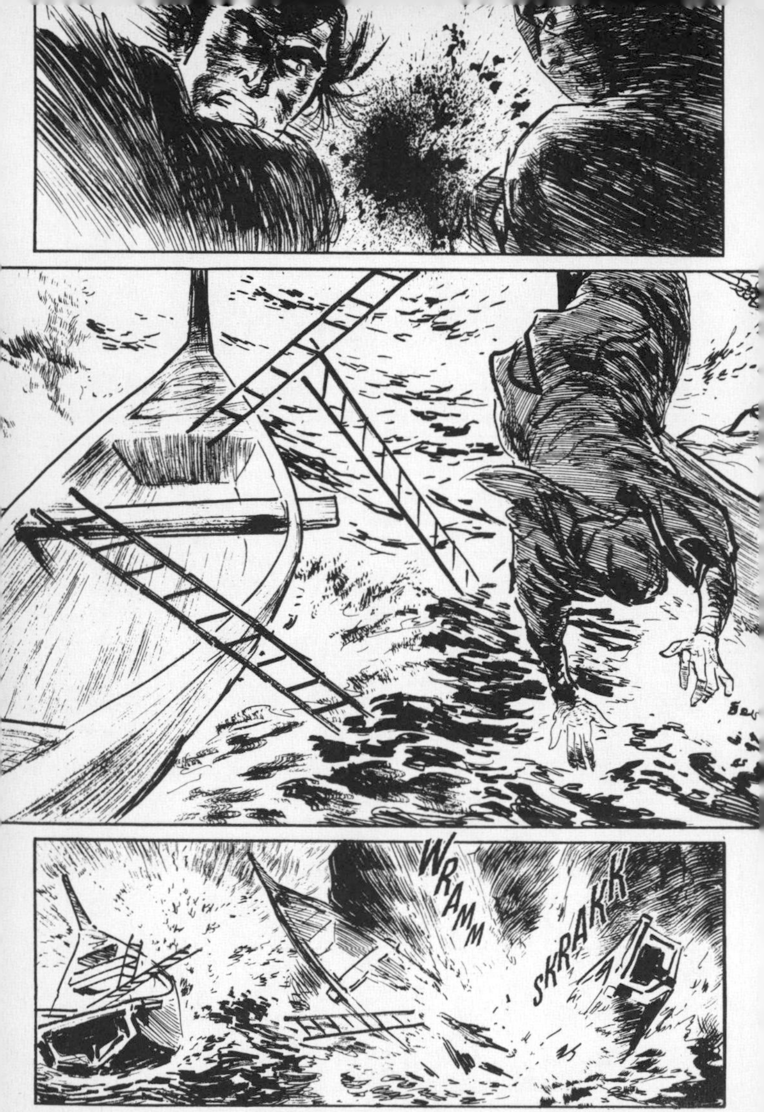
WRAMM
SKRAKK

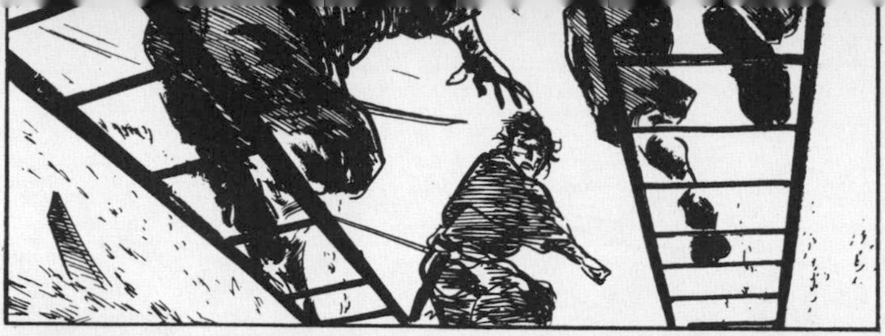
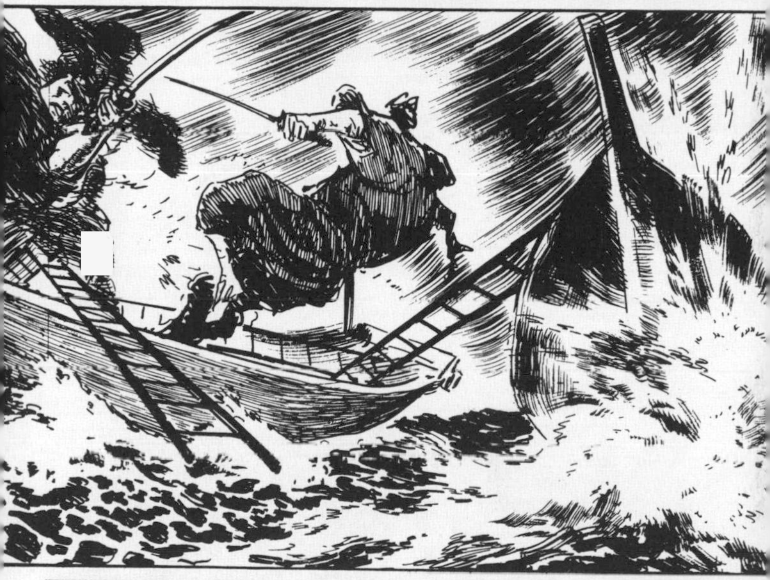
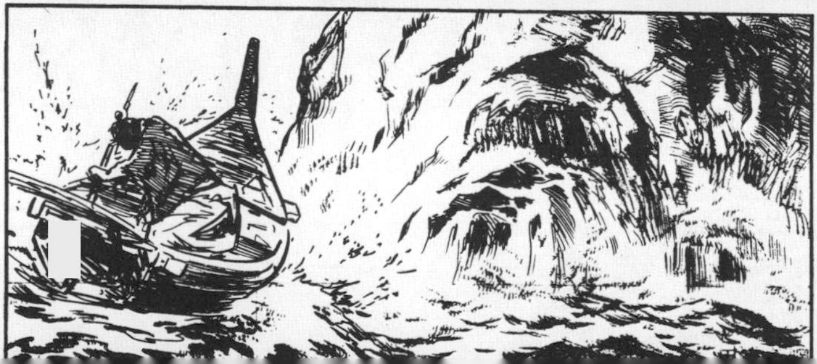

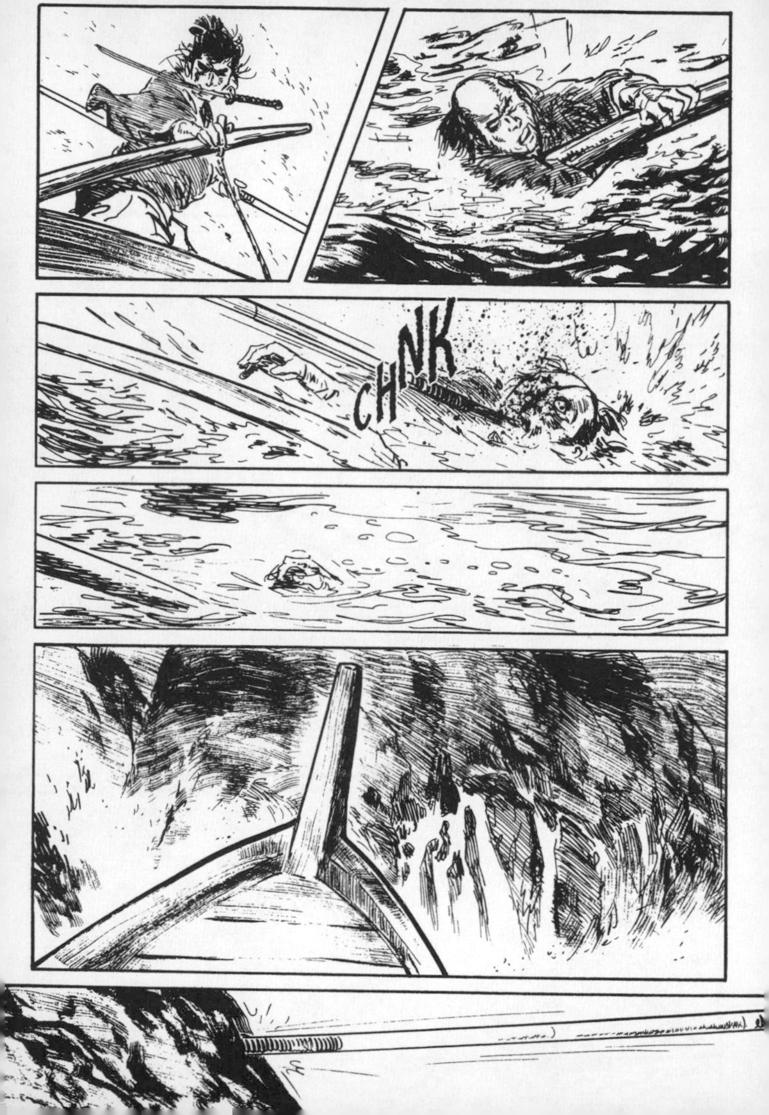
CHNK

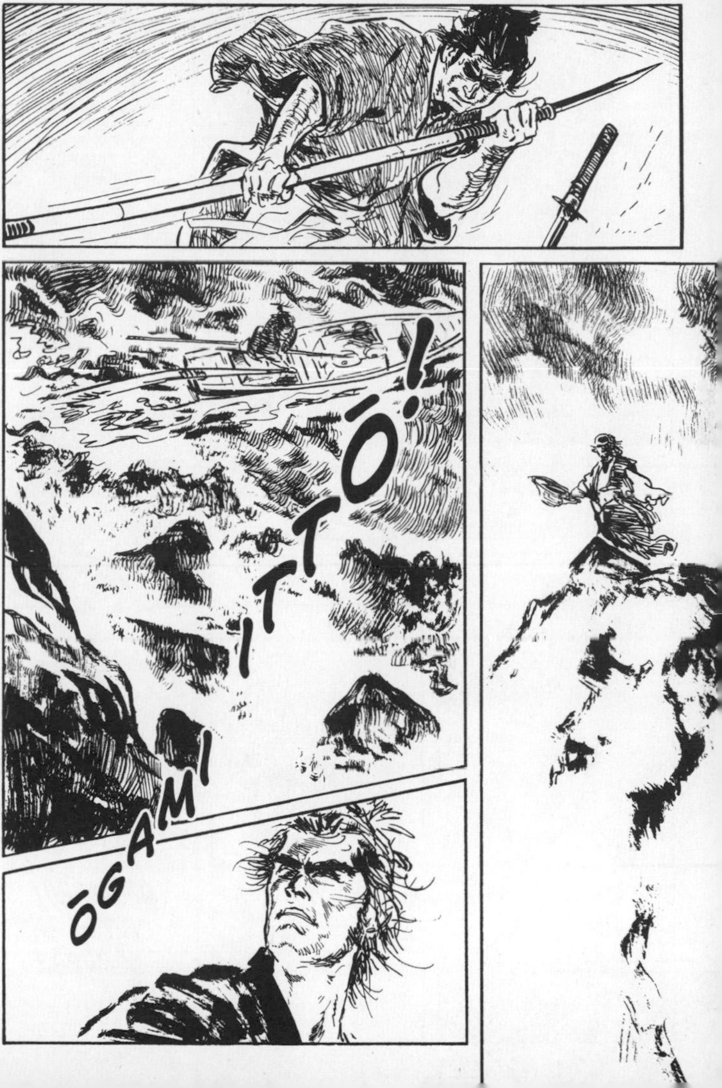
ŌGAMI ITTŌ!

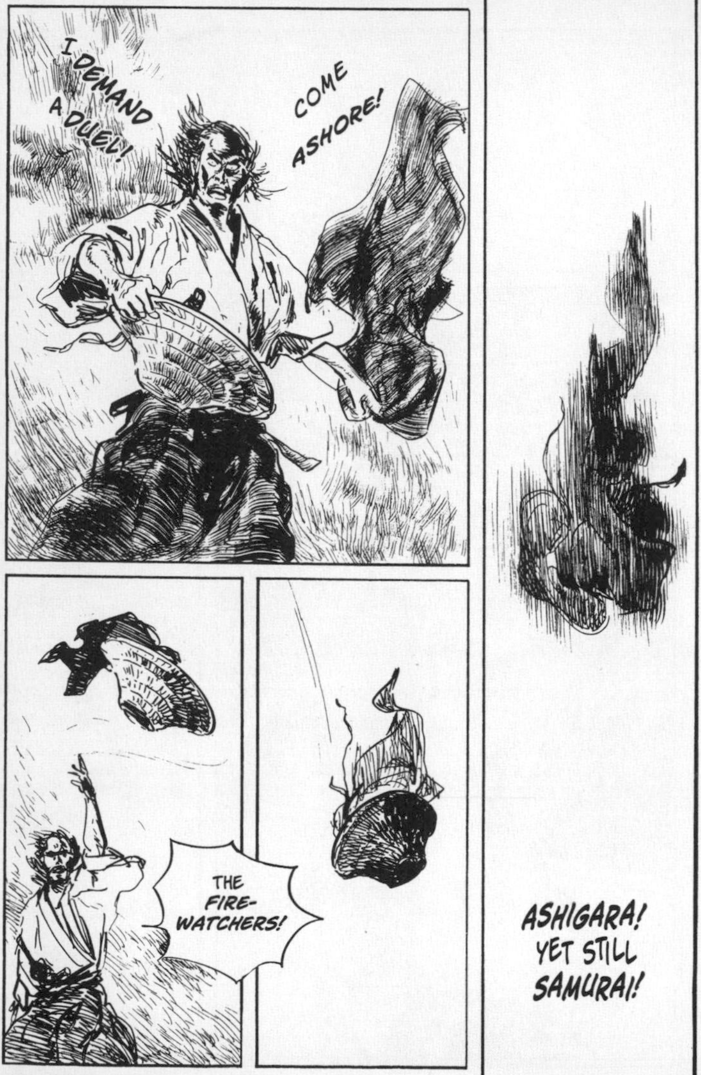
I DEMAND A DUEL!
COME ASHORE!
THE FIRE-WATCHERS!
ASHIGARA! YET STILL SAMURAI!

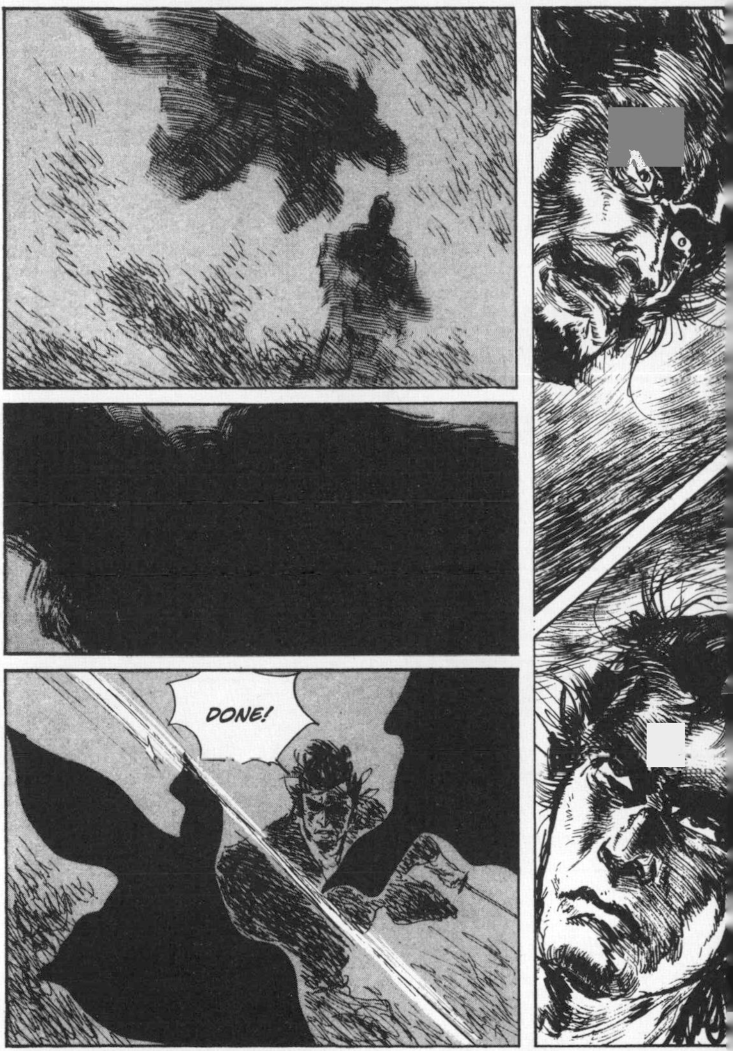
DONE!

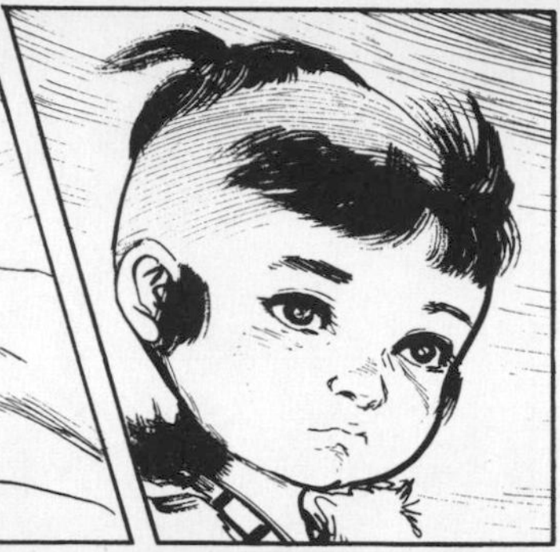
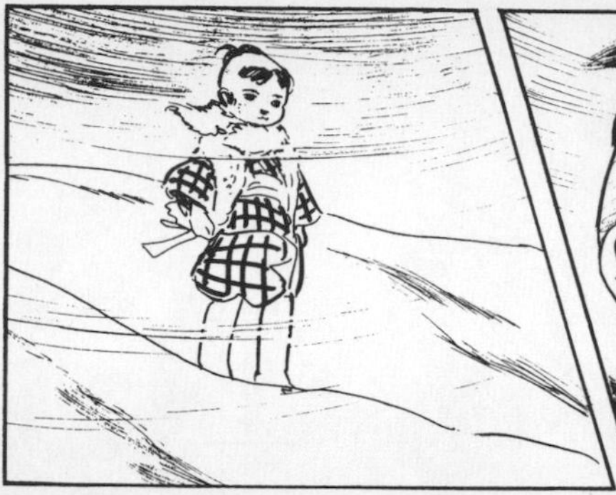
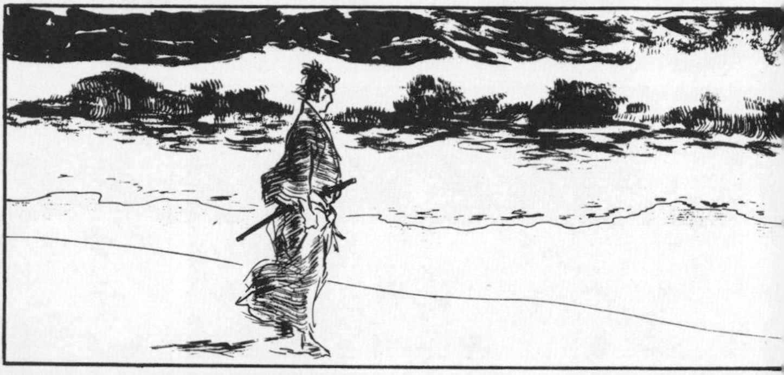
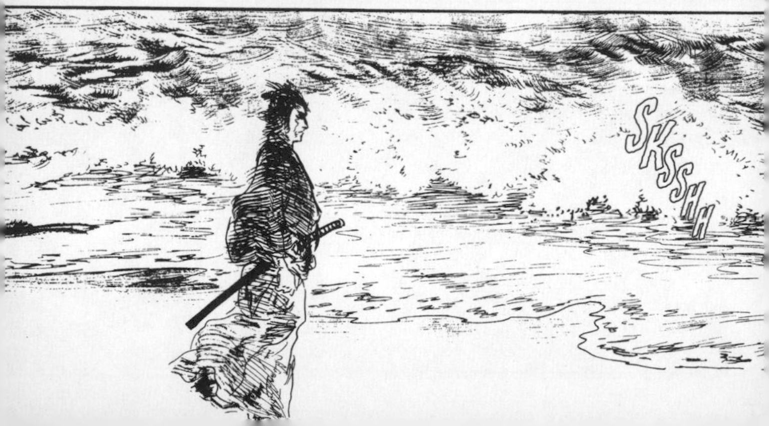
SKSSHH

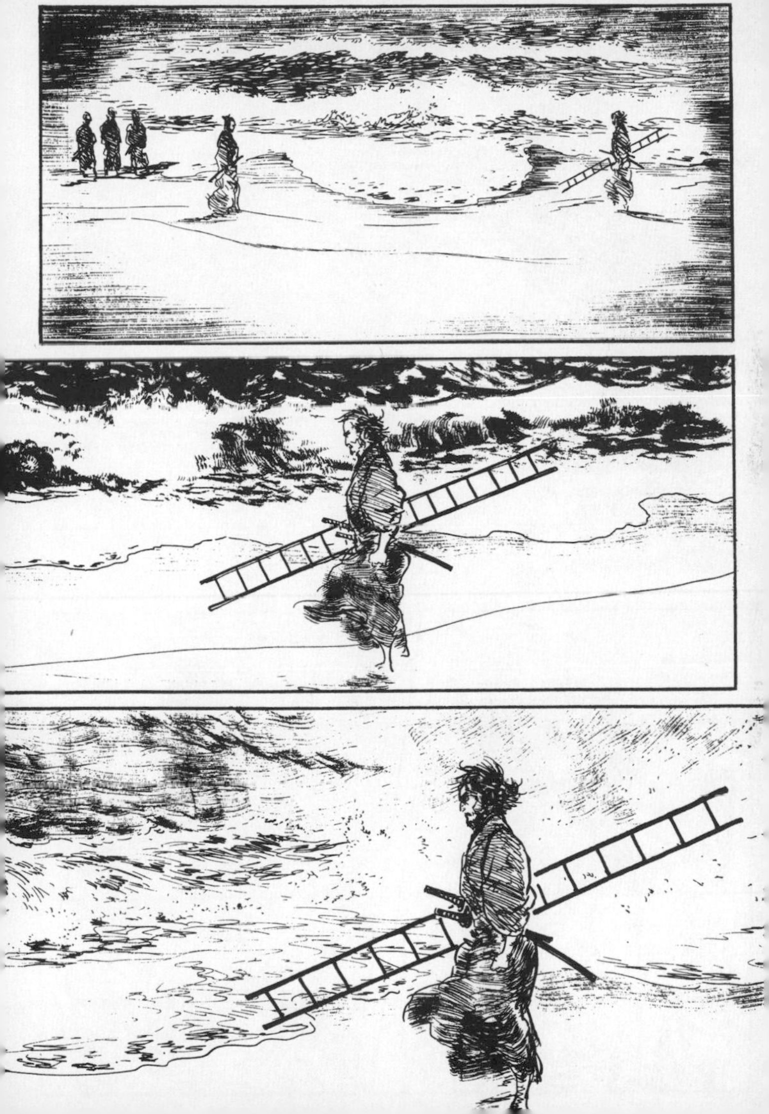

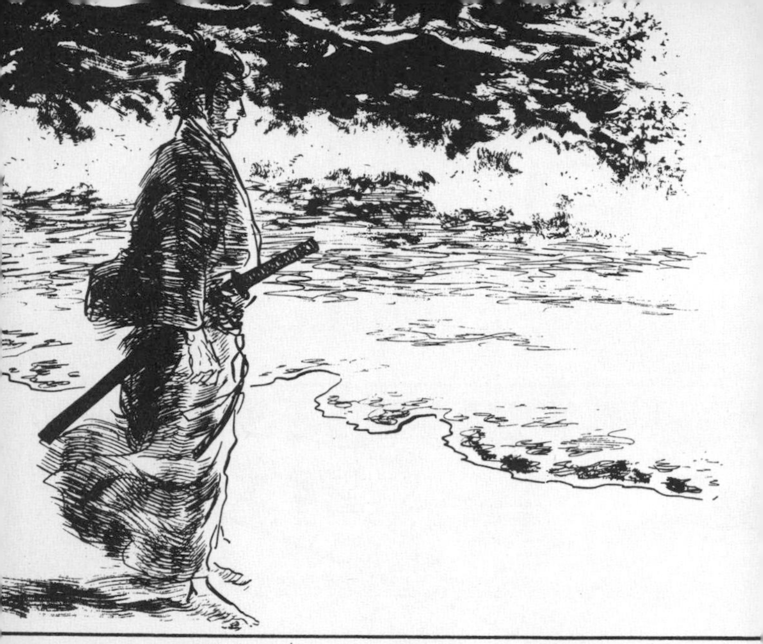

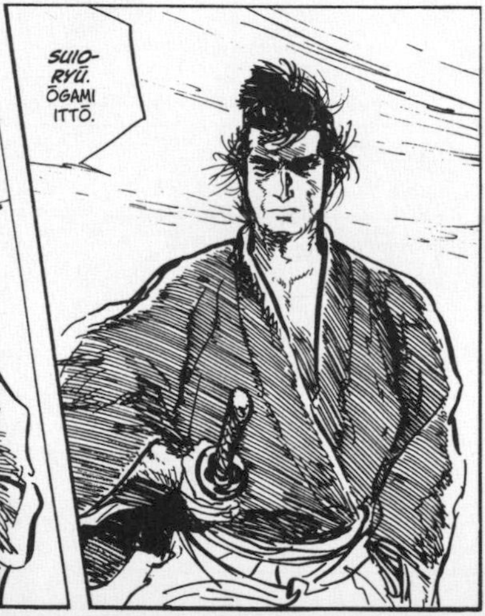
SUIO-RYŪ. ŌGAMI ITTŌ.

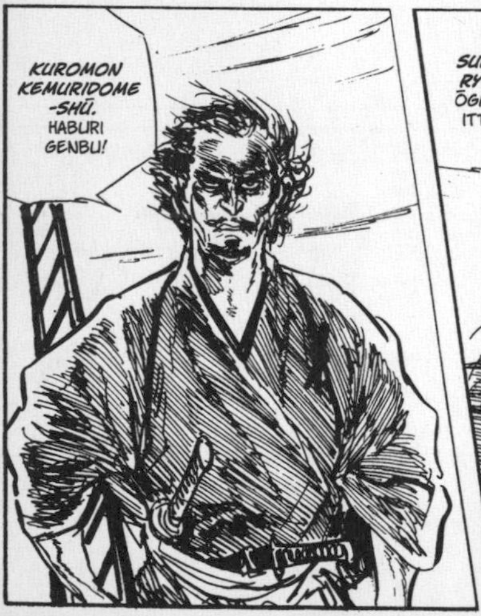
KUROMON KEMURIDOME-SHŪ. HABURI GENBU!

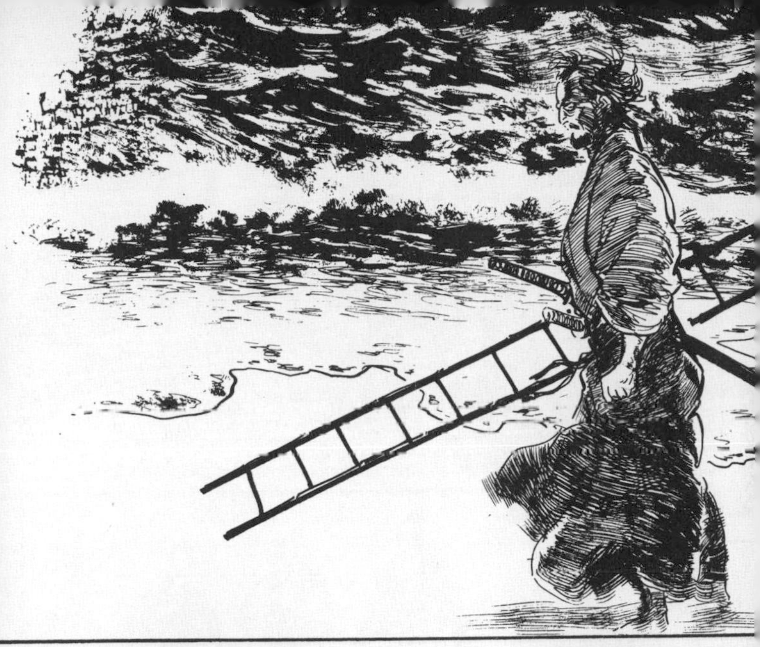

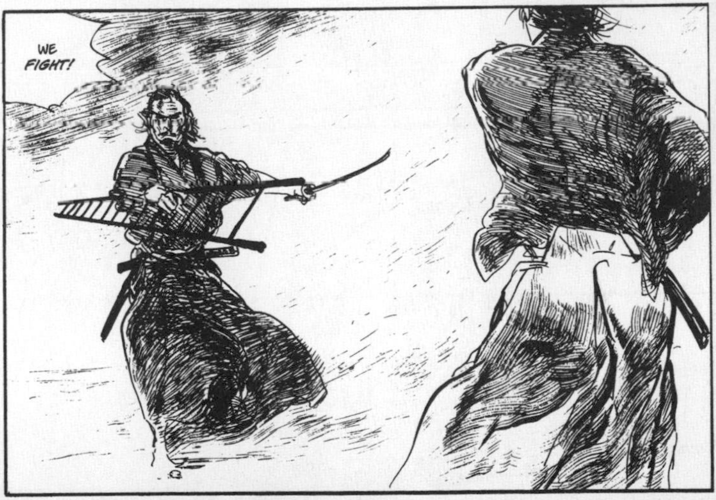
WE FIGHT!

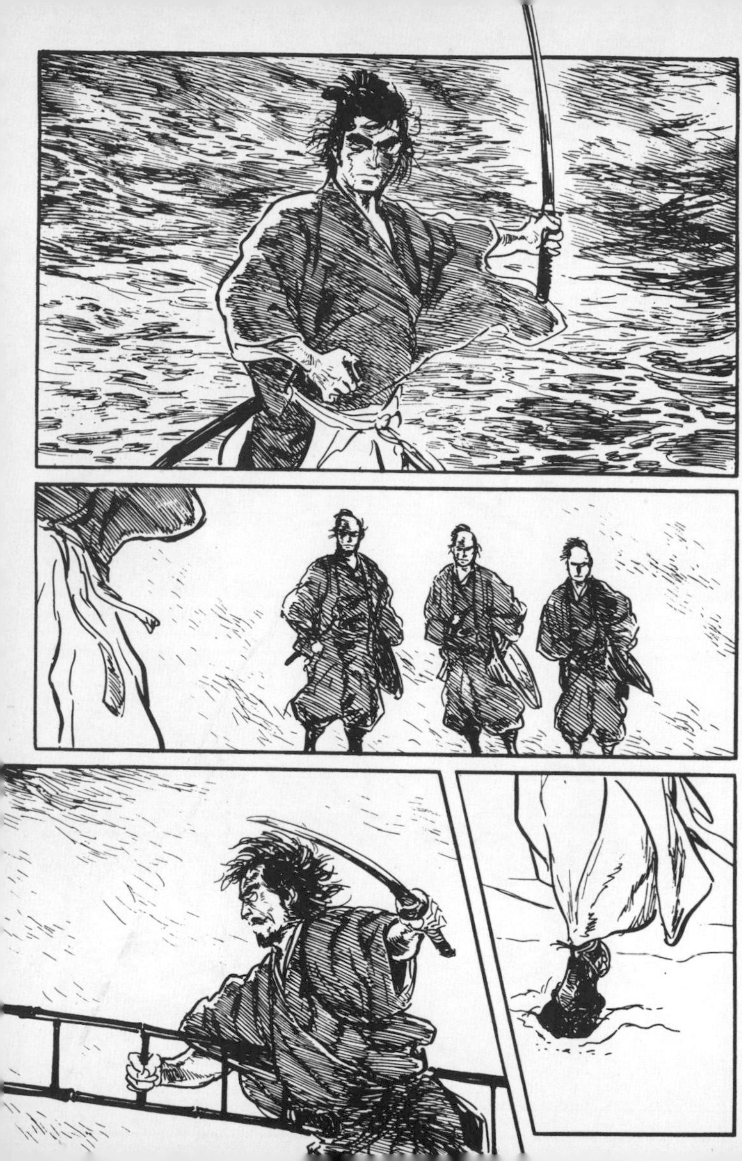

SKSSH

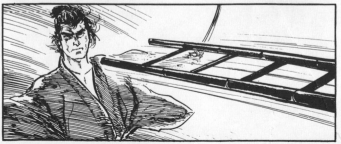

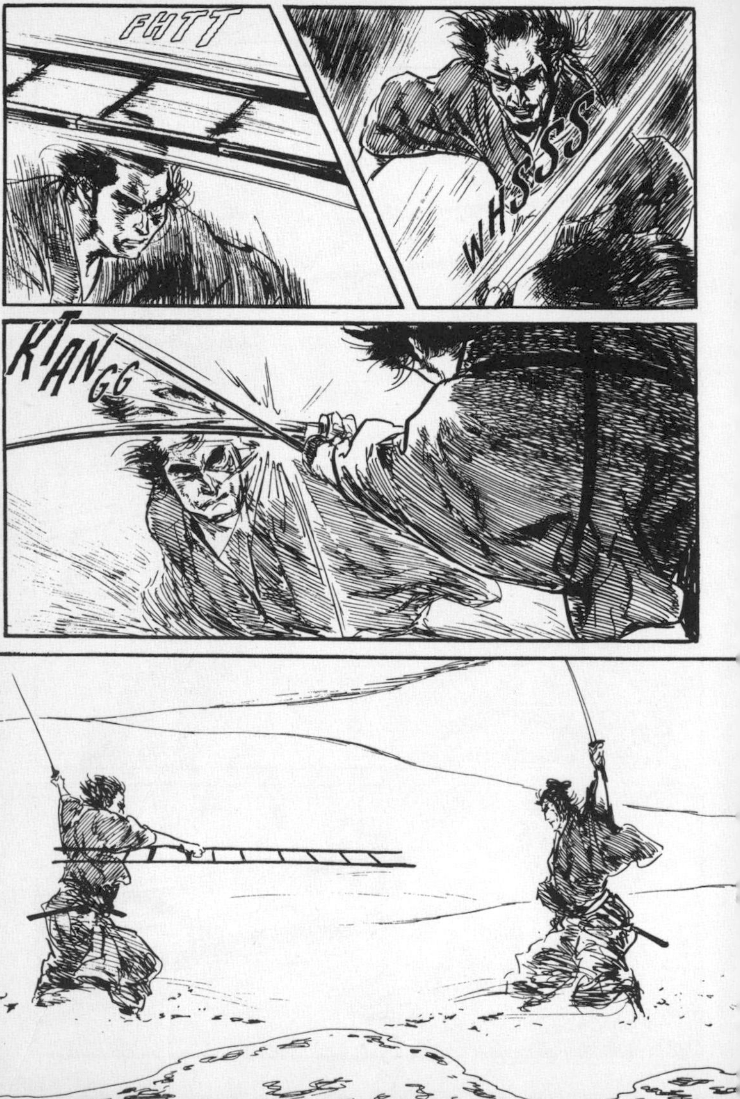
WHSSSS
FHTT
KTANGG

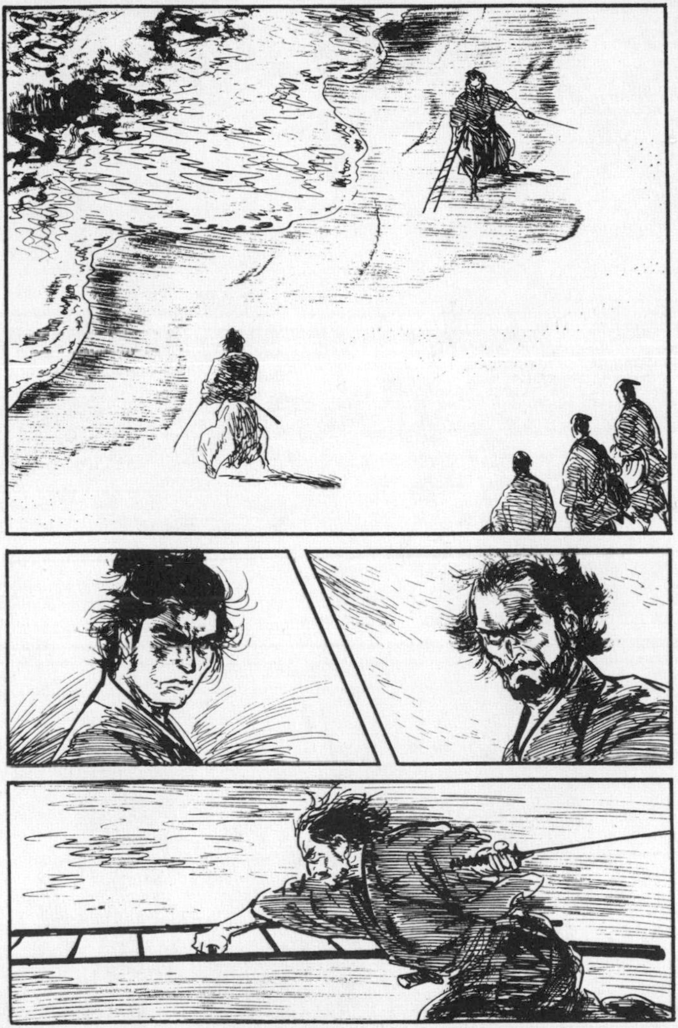

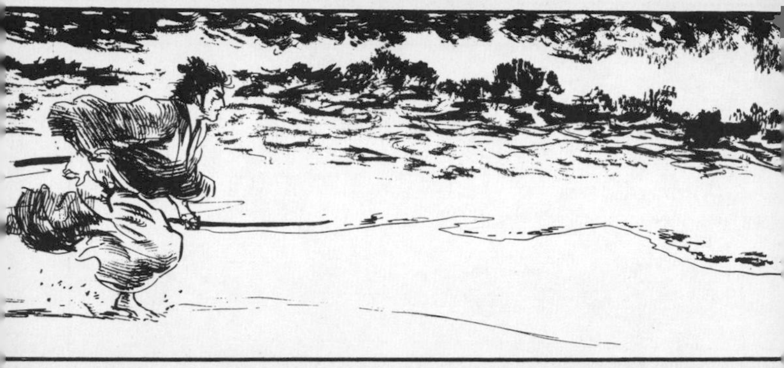

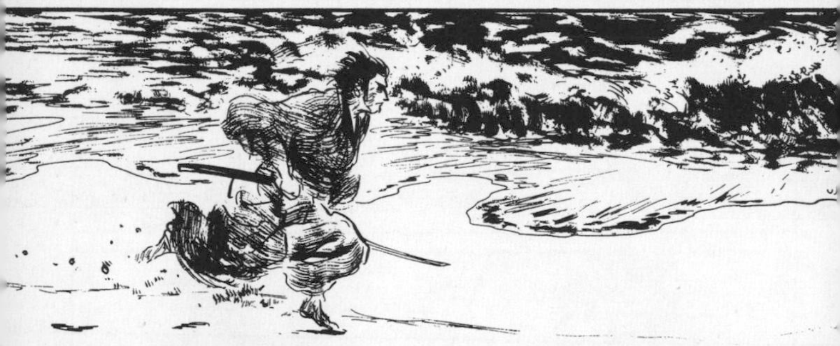

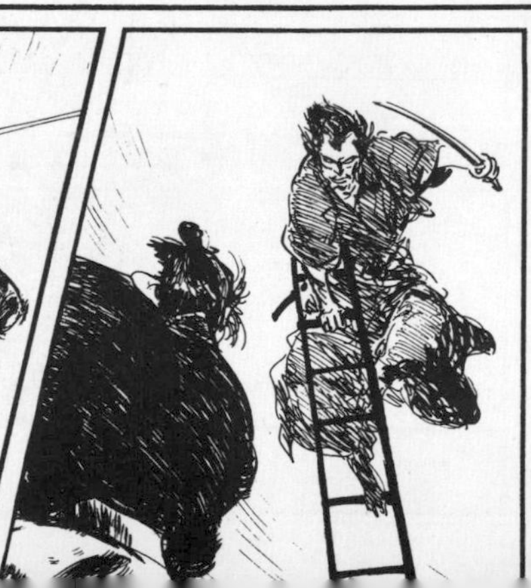

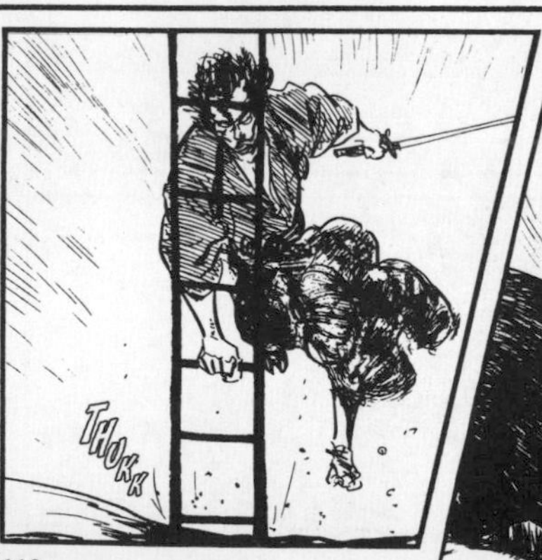
THUKK

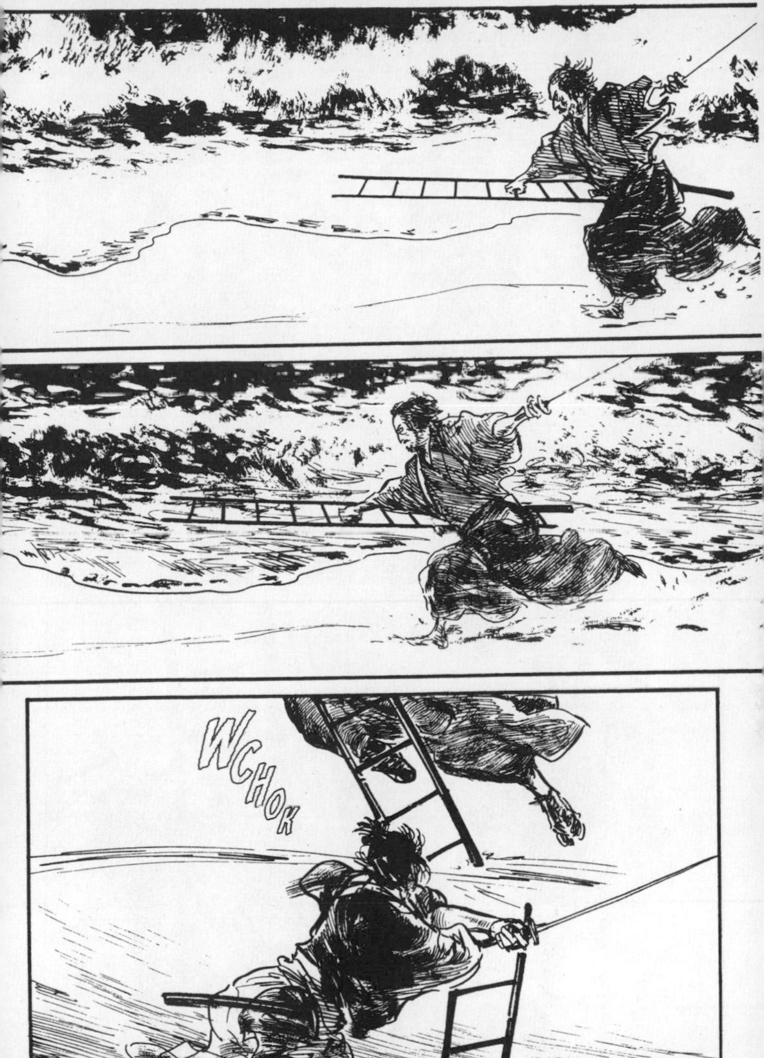
WCHOK

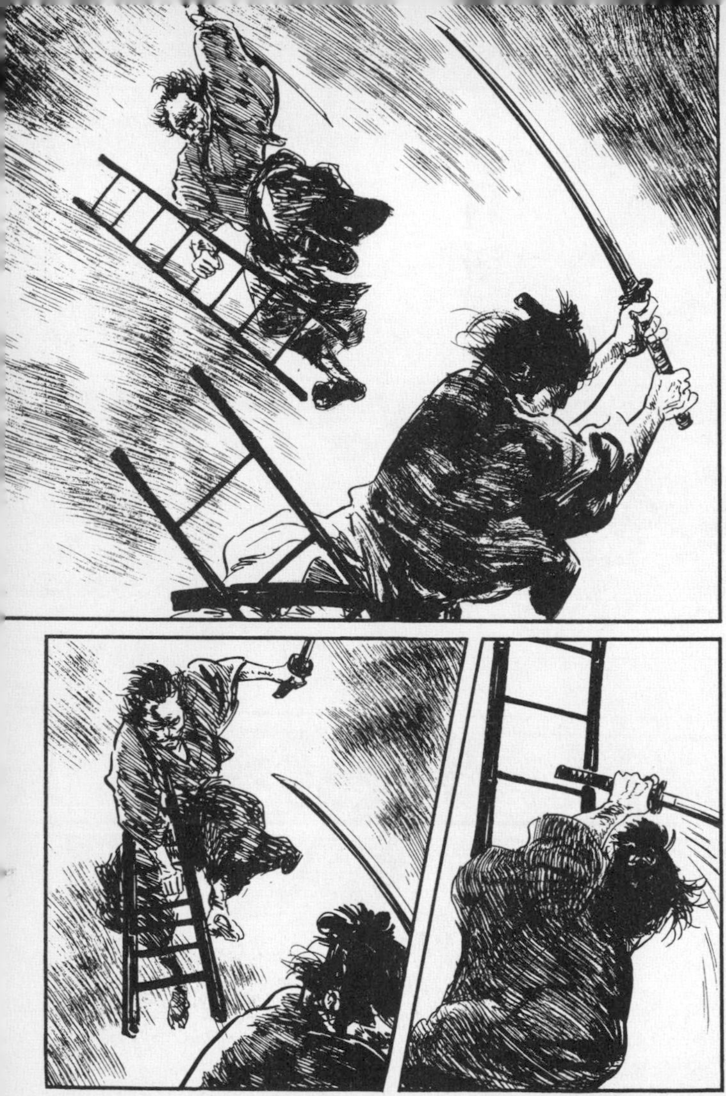

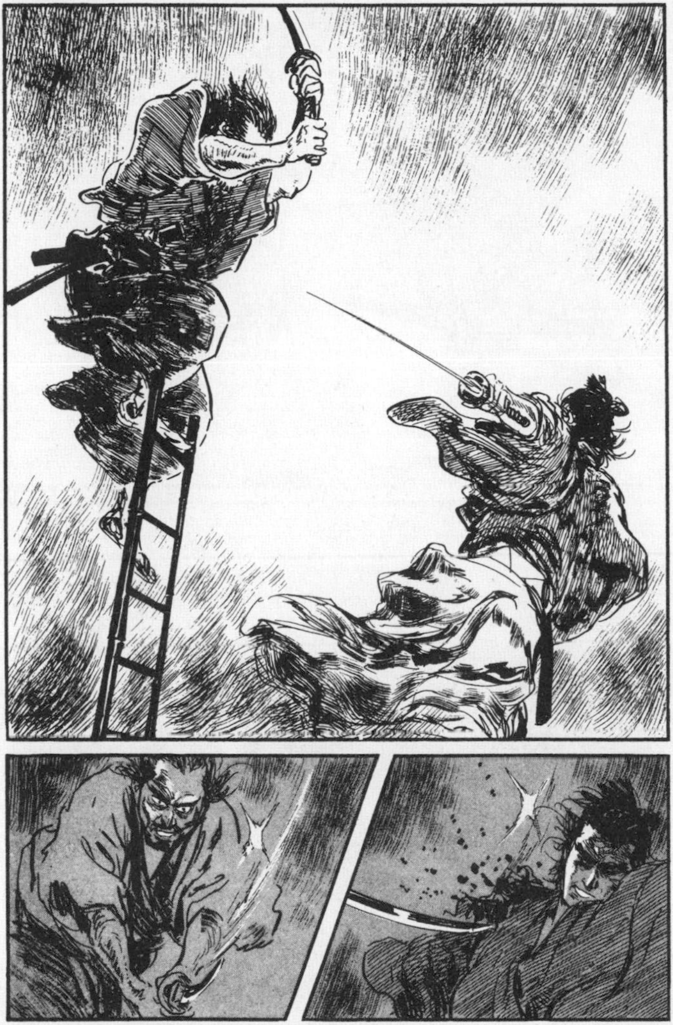

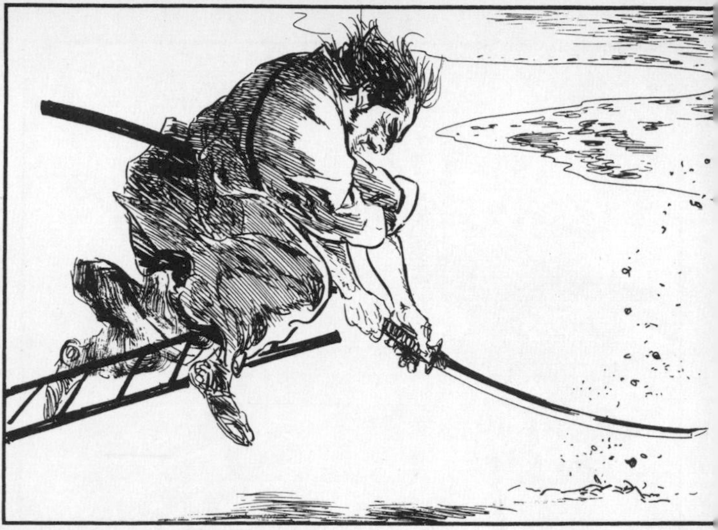
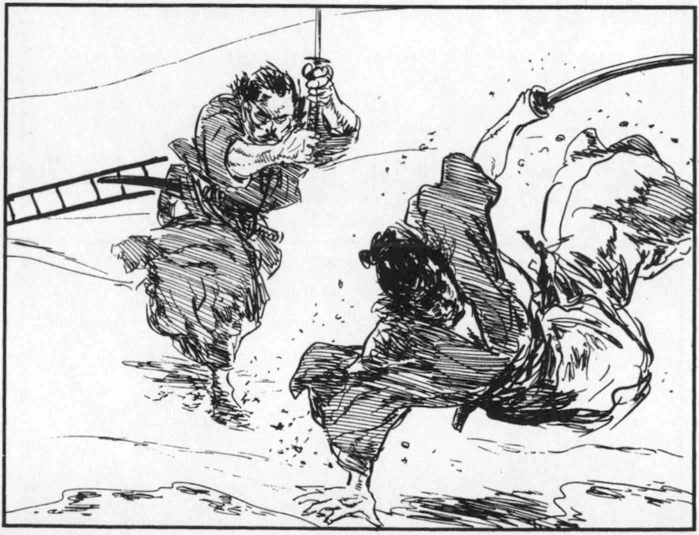

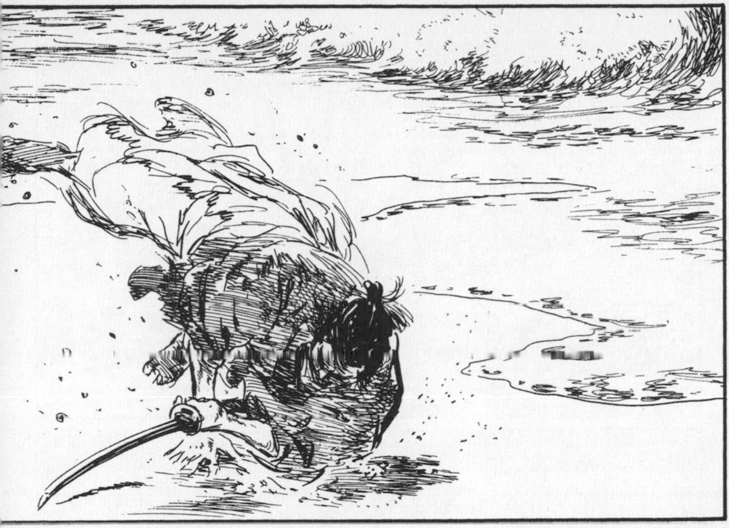

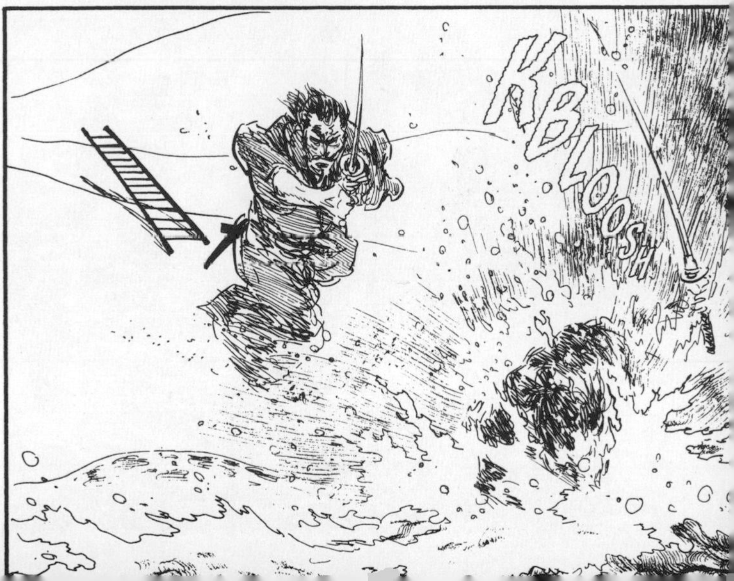
K'BLOOSH

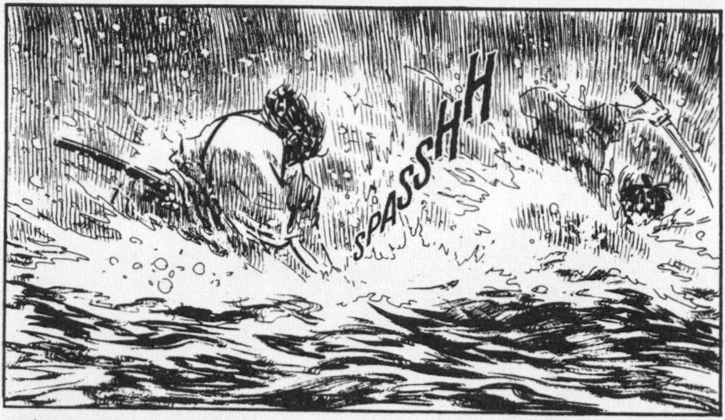
SPASSHH

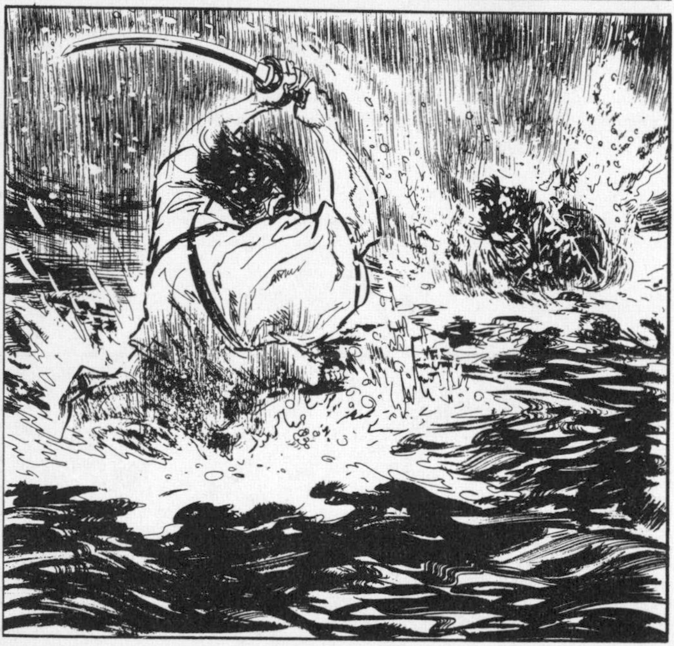

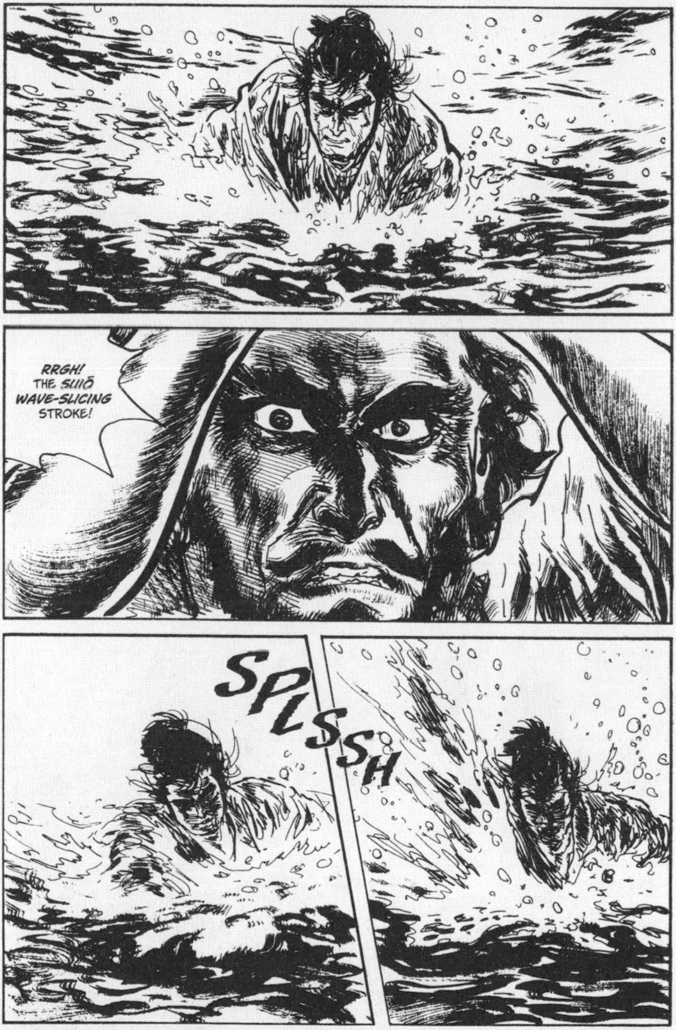
RRGH! THE SUIŌ WAVE-SLICING STROKE!
SPLSSSH

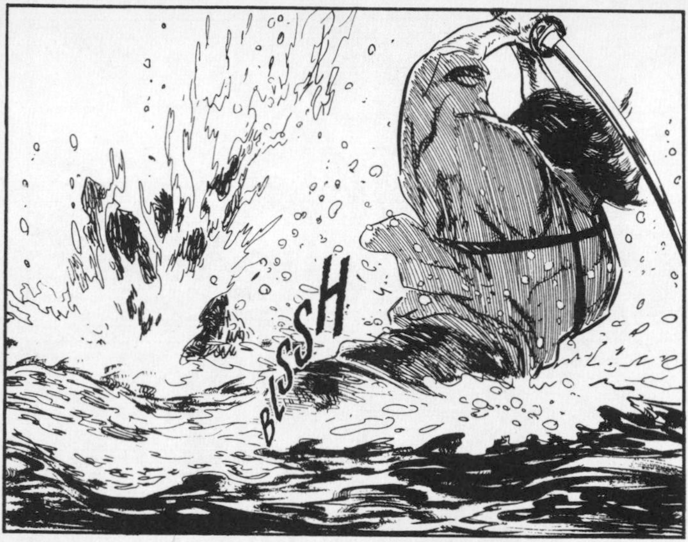
BLSSH
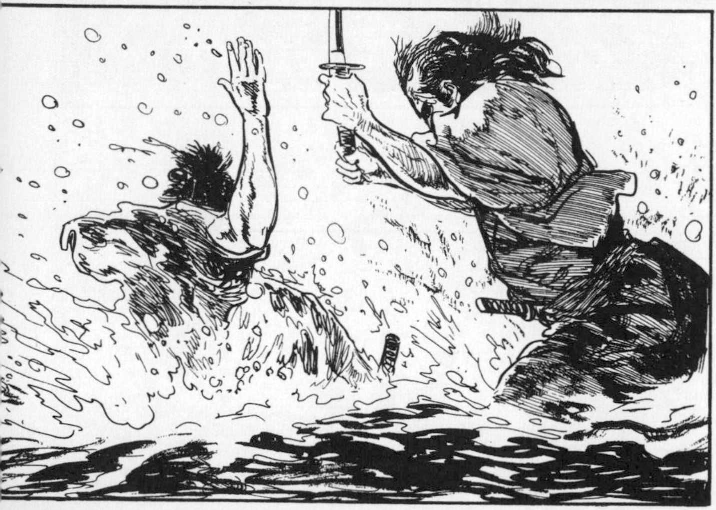

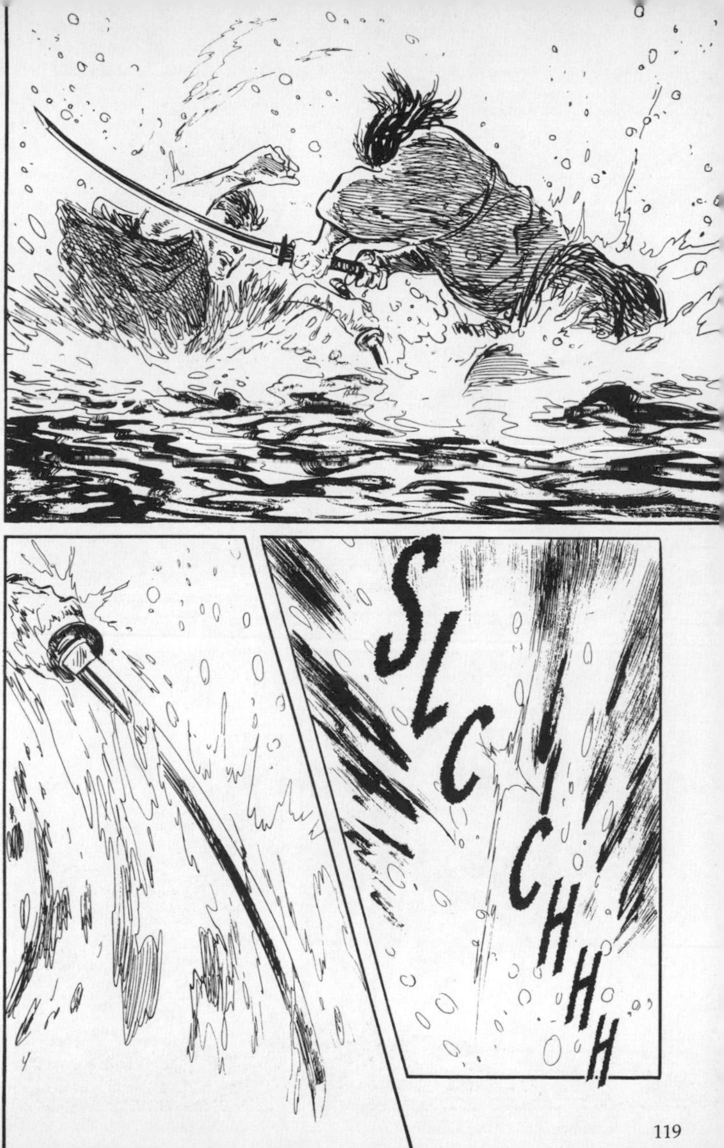
SLCCHHHH

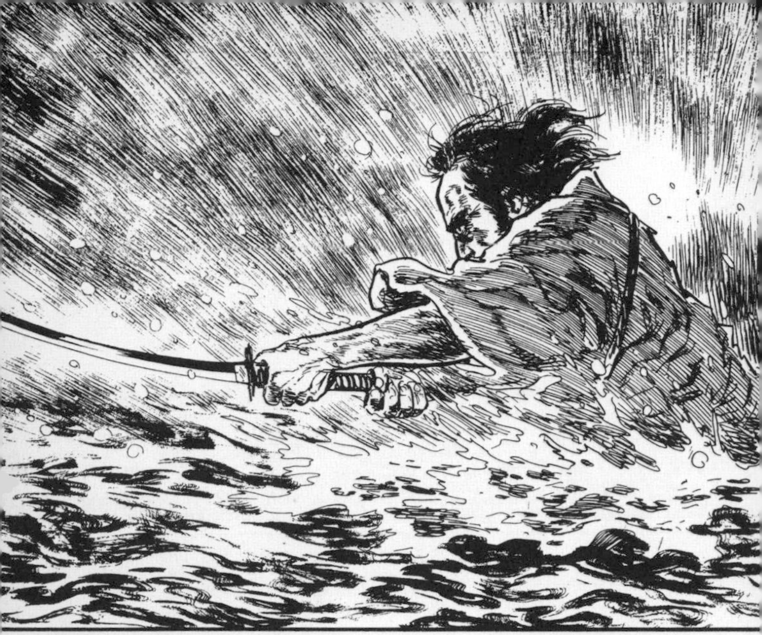
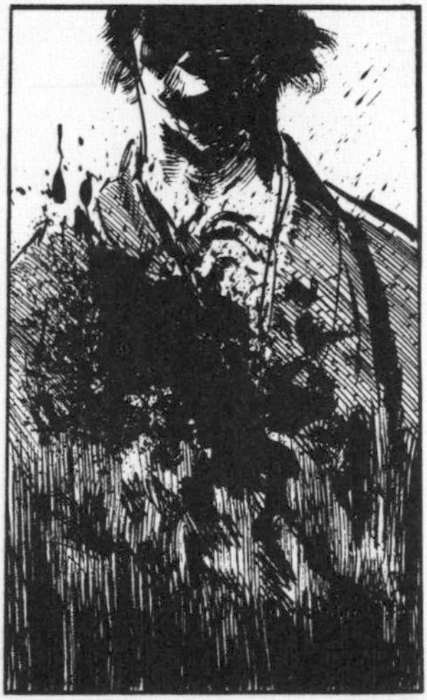
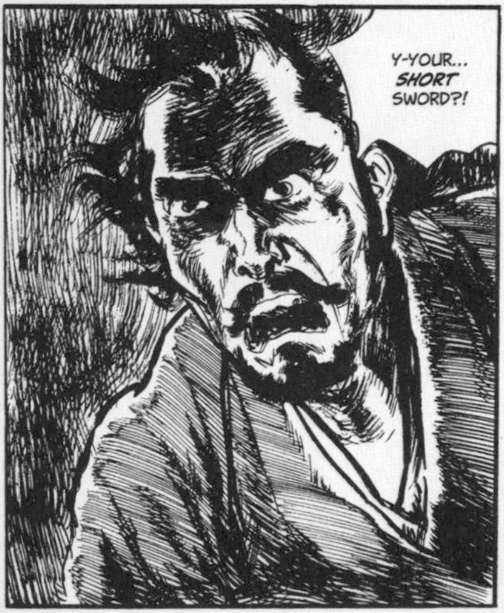
Y-YOUR...
SHORT
SWORD?!

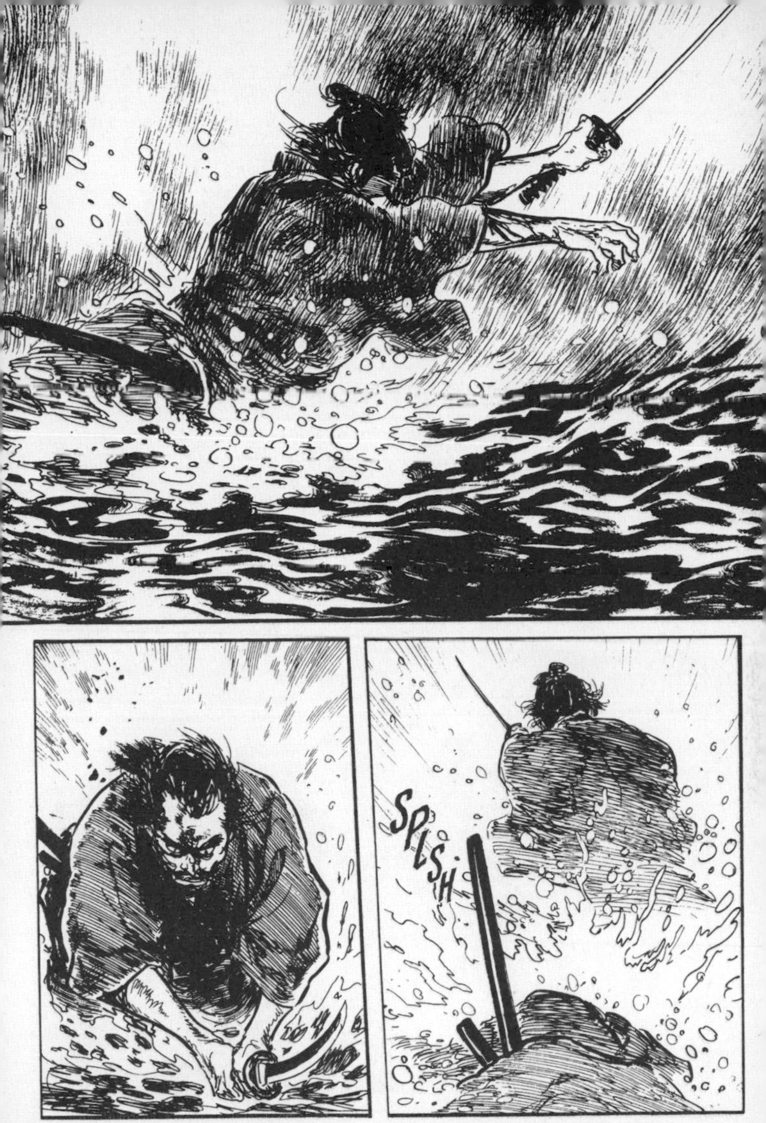
SPLSH

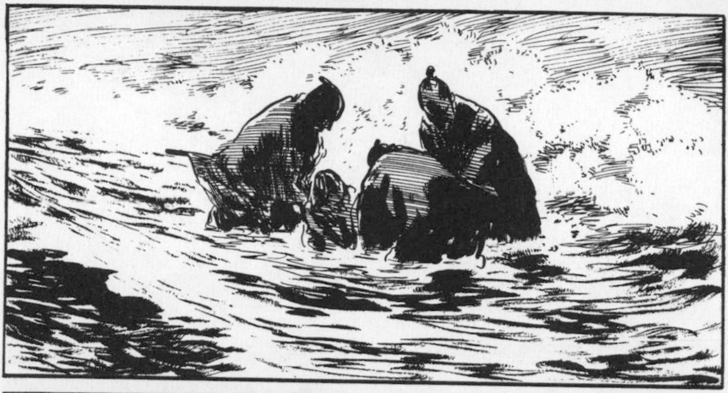
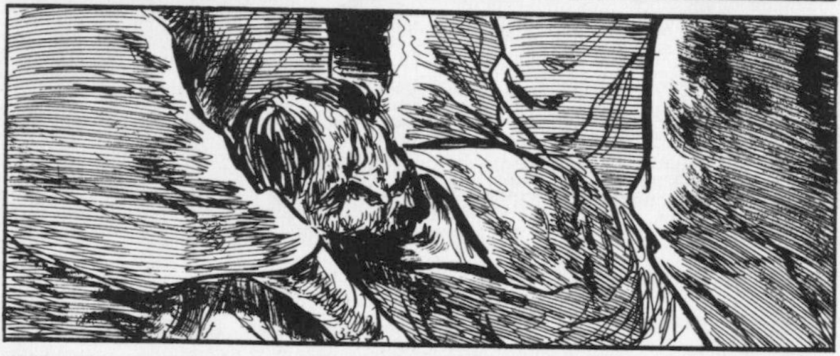
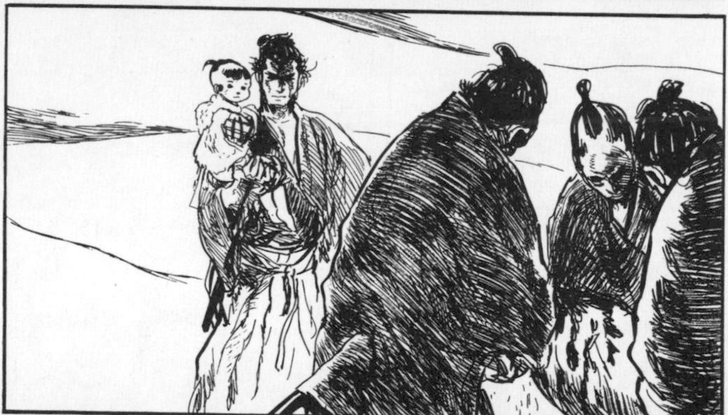

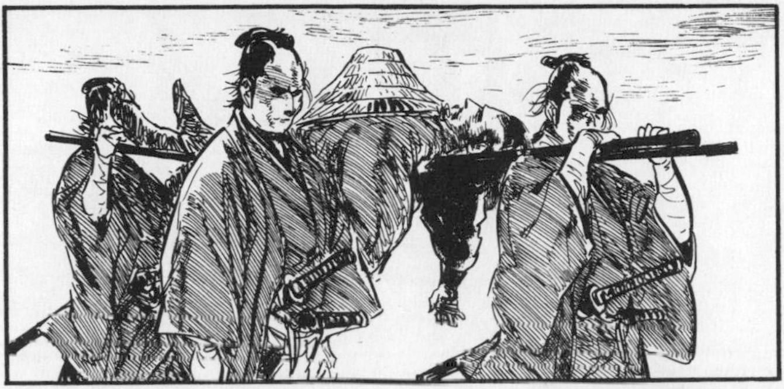

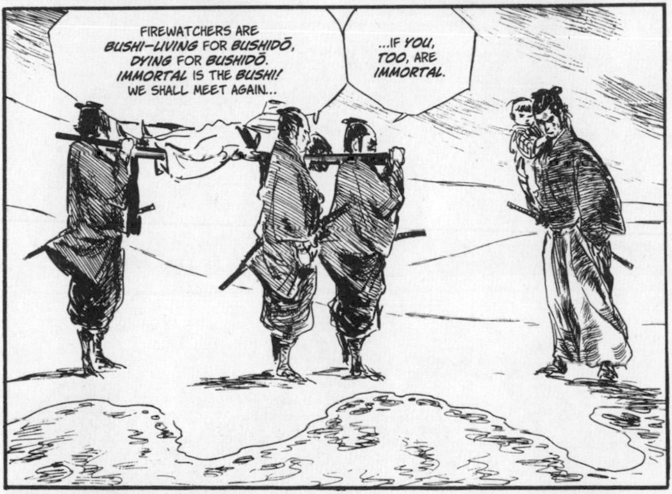
FIREWATCHERS ARE BUSHI—LIVING FOR BUSHIDŌ, DYING FOR BUSHIDŌ. IMMORTAL IS THE BUSHI! WE SHALL MEET AGAIN...
...IF YOU, TOO, ARE IMMORTAL.

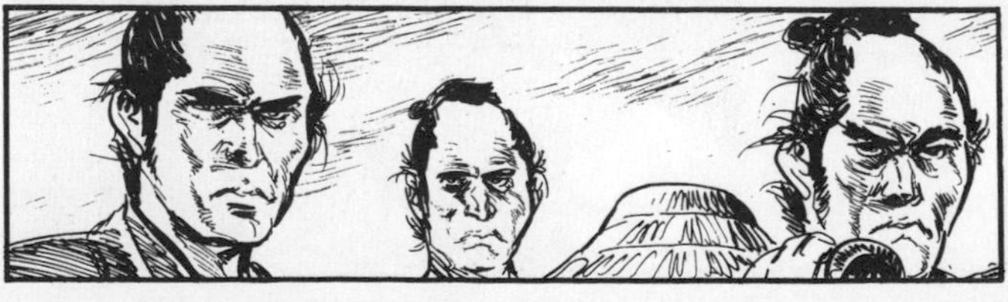

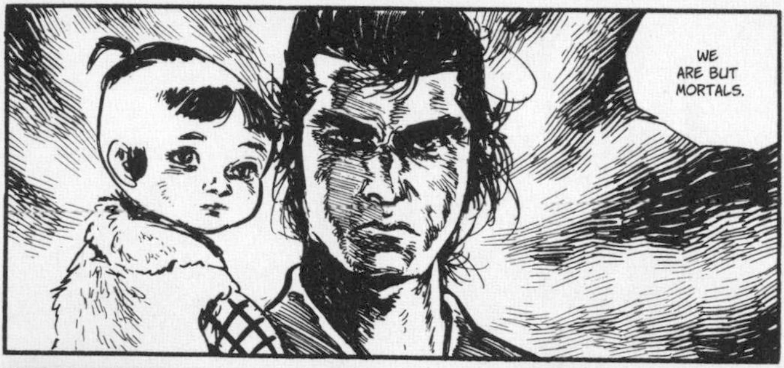
WE ARE BUT MORTALS.
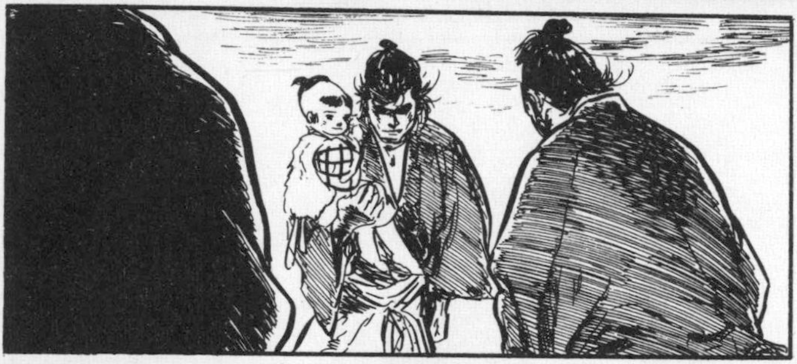
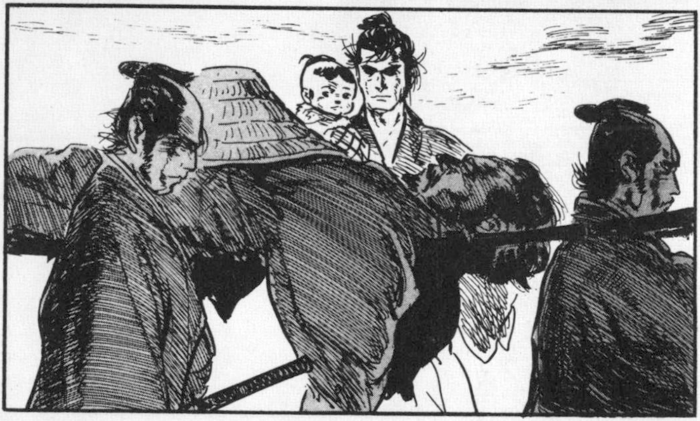

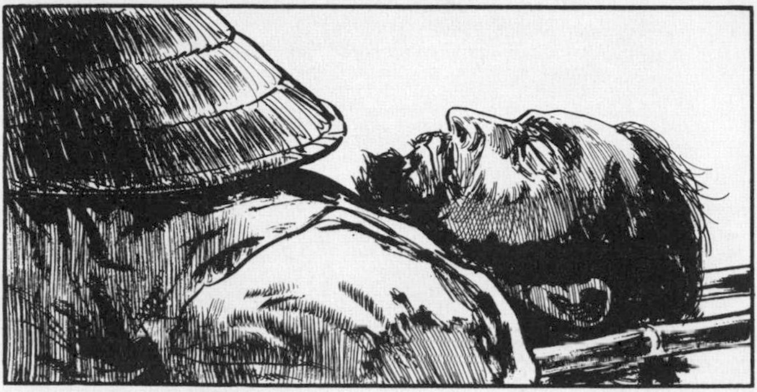
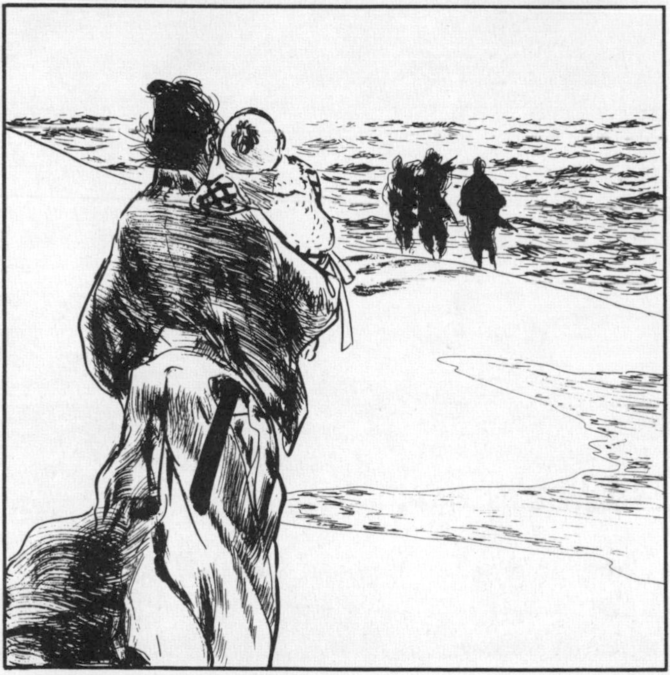

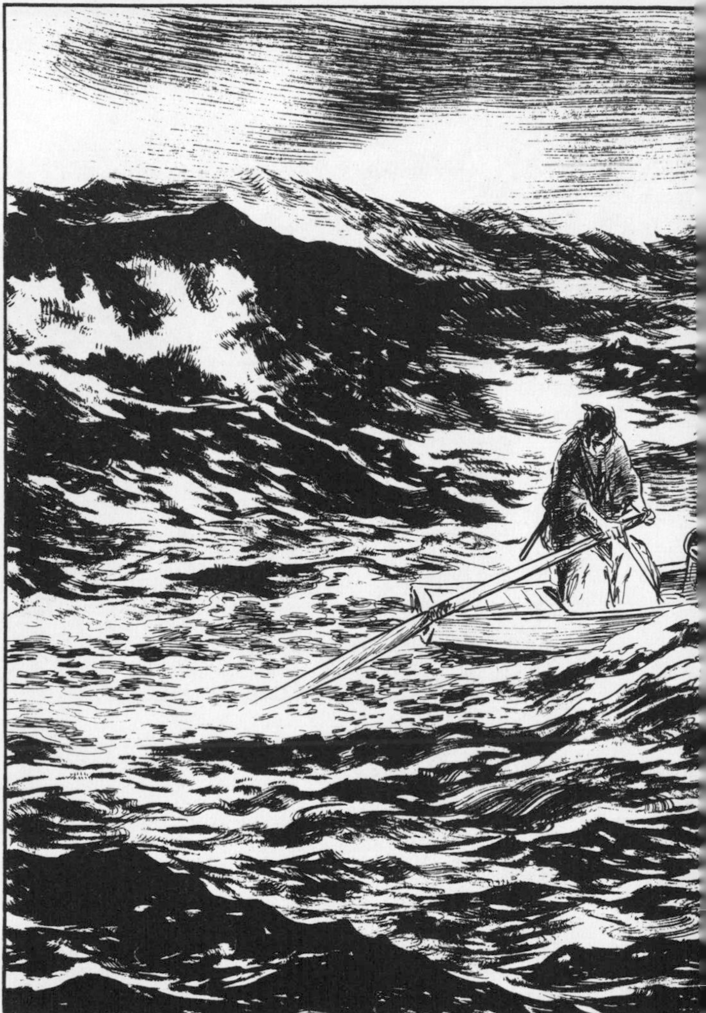

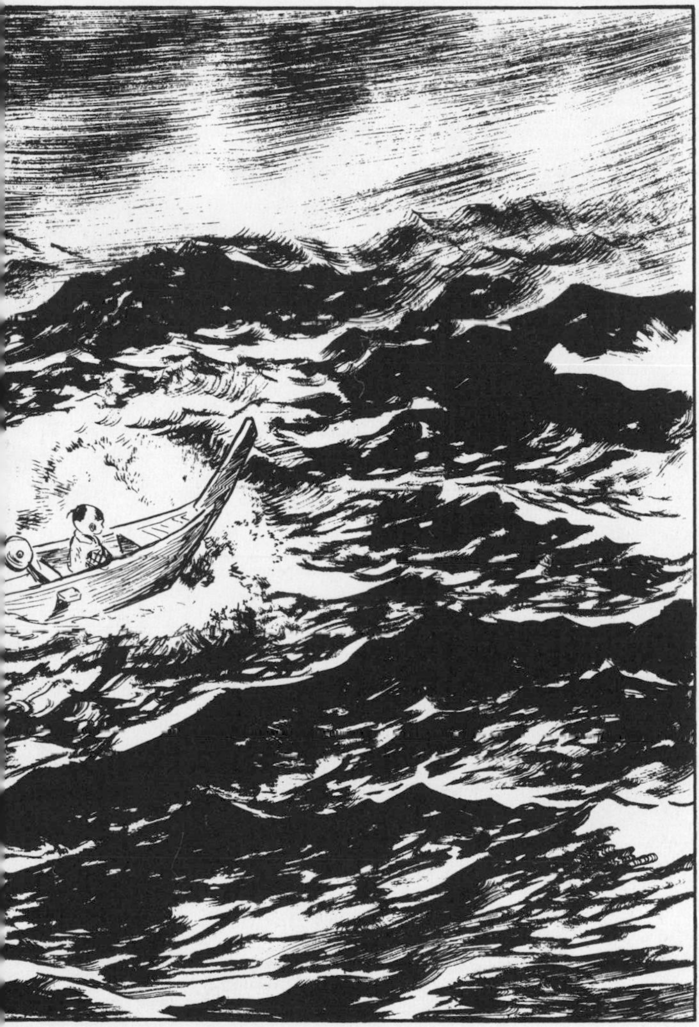

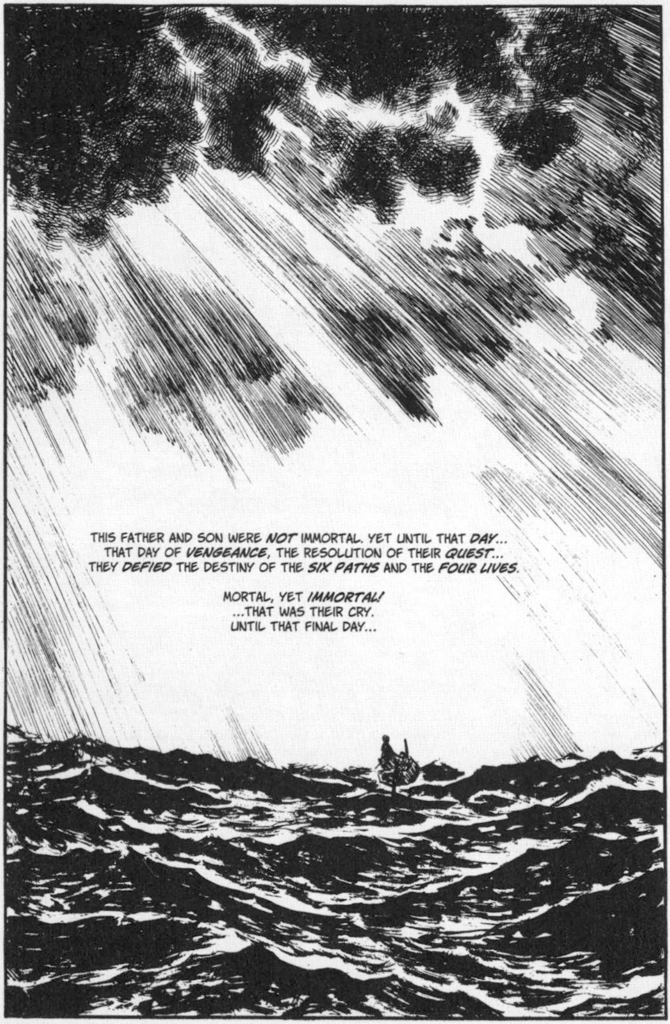
THIS FATHER AND SON WERE NOT IMMORTAL. YET UNTIL THAT DAY...
THAT DAY OF VENGEANCE, THE RESOLUTION OF THEIR QUEST...
THEY DEFIED THE DESTINY OF THE SIX PATHS AND THE FOUR LIVES.
MORTAL, YET IMMORTAL!
...THAT WAS THEIR CRY.
UNTIL THAT FINAL DAY...

the ninetieth

Paper Money

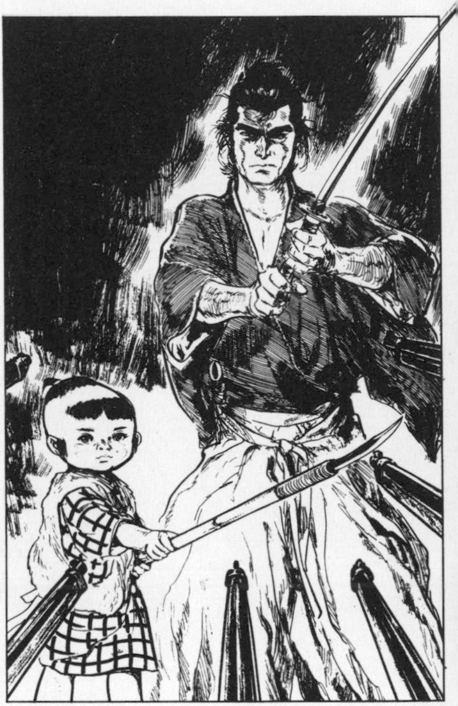

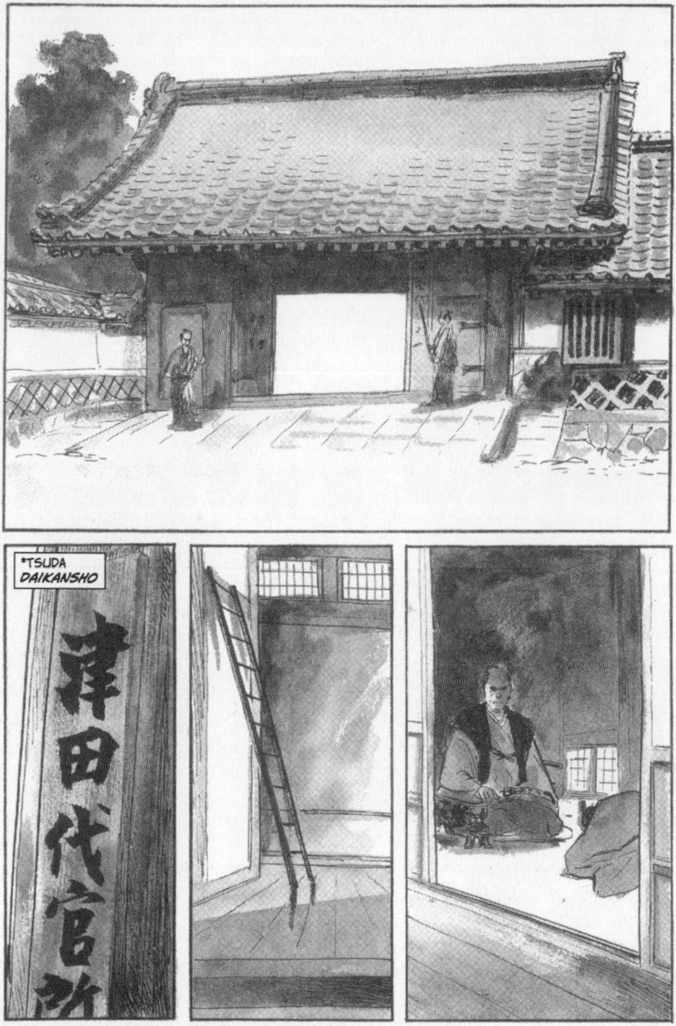
*TSUDA
DAIKANSHO
津田代官所

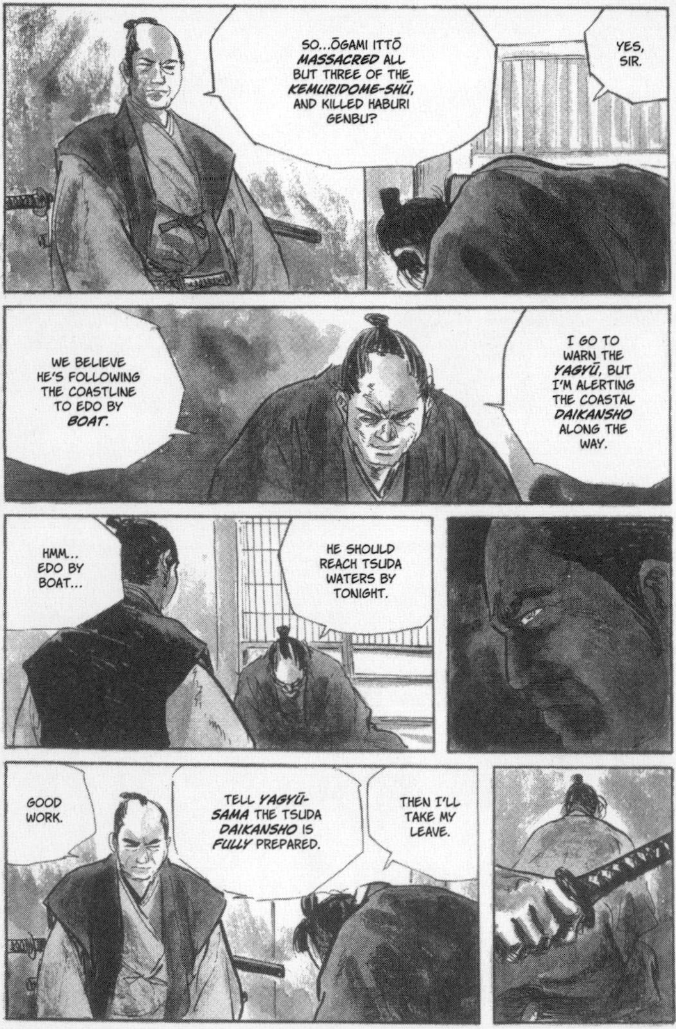
SO...ŌGAMI ITTŌ *MASSACRED* ALL BUT THREE OF THE *KEMURIDOME-SHŪ*, AND KILLED HABURI GENBU?
YES, SIR.
WE BELIEVE HE'S FOLLOWING THE COASTLINE TO EDO BY *BOAT*.
I GO TO WARN THE *YAGYŪ*, BUT I'M ALERTING THE COASTAL *DAIKANSHO* ALONG THE WAY.
HMM.. EDO BY BOAT...
HE SHOULD REACH TSUDA WATERS BY TONIGHT.
GOOD WORK.
TELL *YAGYŪ-SAMA* THE TSUDA *DAIKANSHO* IS *FULLY* PREPARED.
THEN I'LL TAKE MY LEAVE.

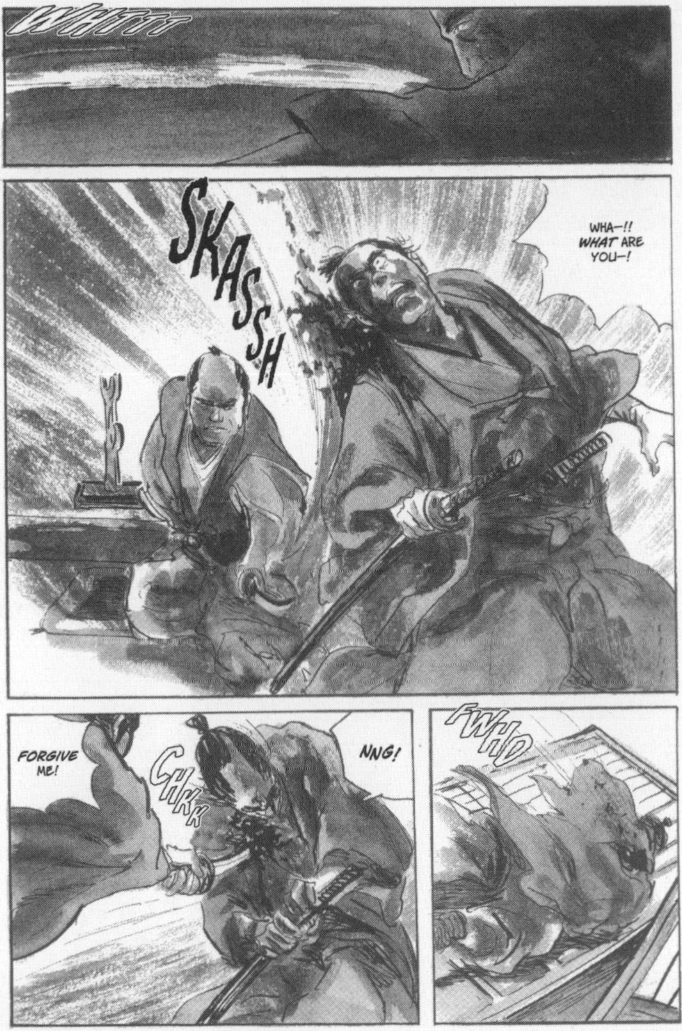
WHITTT
SKASSH
WHA-!! WHAT ARE YOU-!
FORGIVE ME!
CHKK
NNG!
FWHO

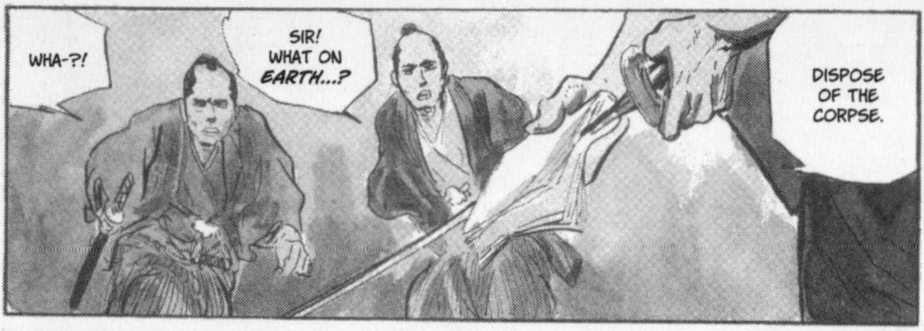
WHA-?!
SIR! WHAT ON *EARTH...?*
DISPOSE OF THE CORPSE.
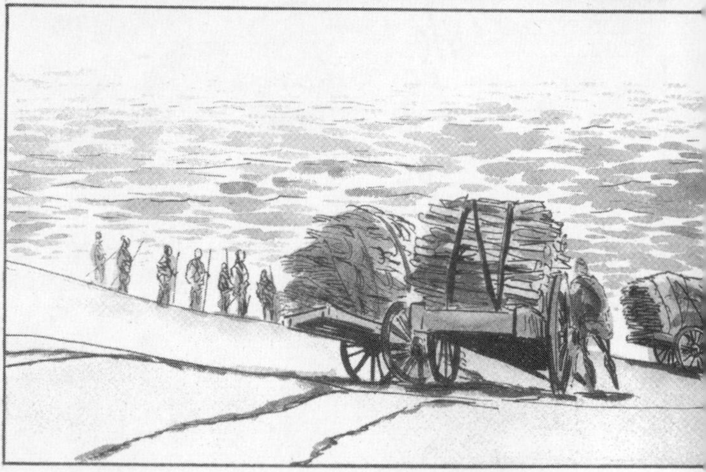
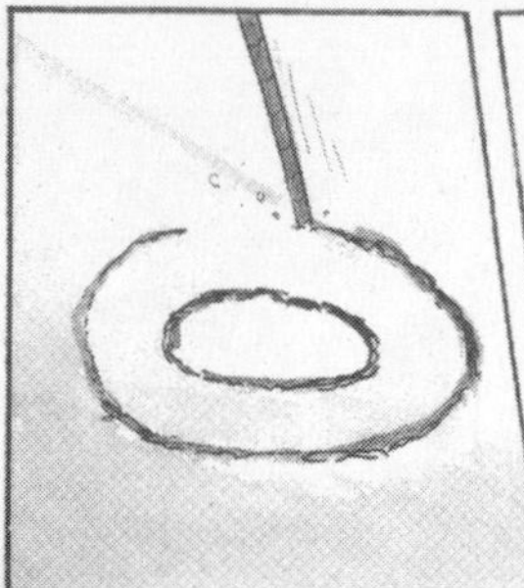
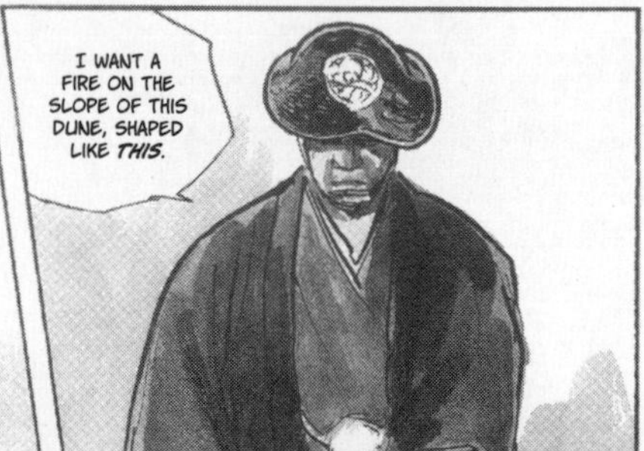
I WANT A FIRE ON THE SLOPE OF THIS DUNE, SHAPED LIKE *THIS*.

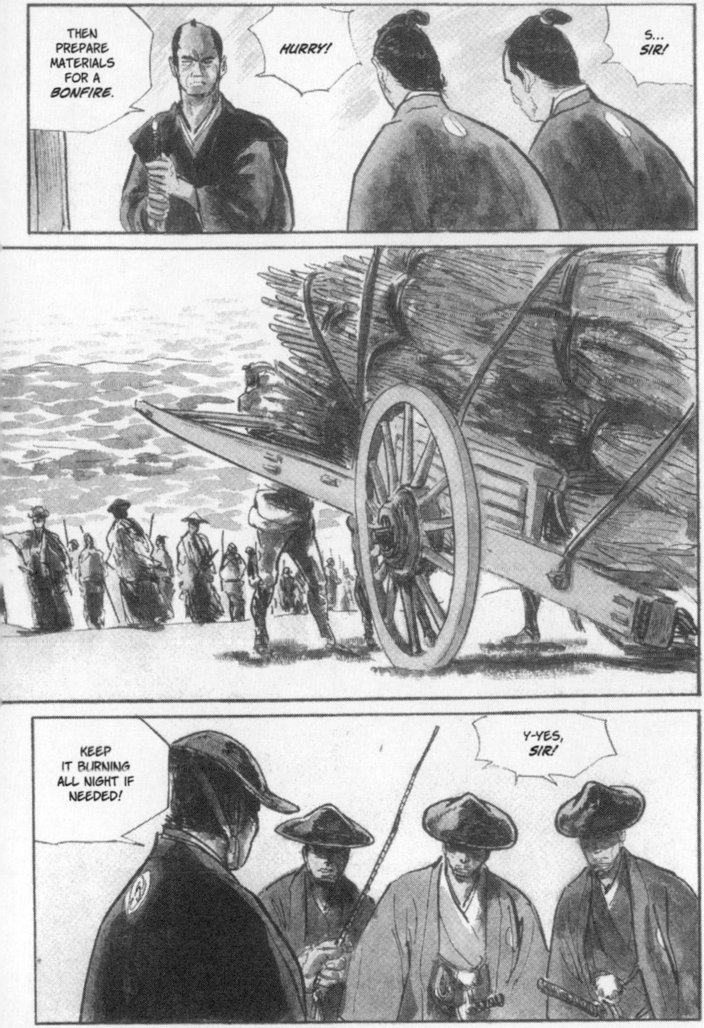
THEN PREPARE MATERIALS FOR A BONFIRE.
HURRY!
S... SIR!
KEEP IT BURNING ALL NIGHT IF NEEDED!
Y-YES, SIR!

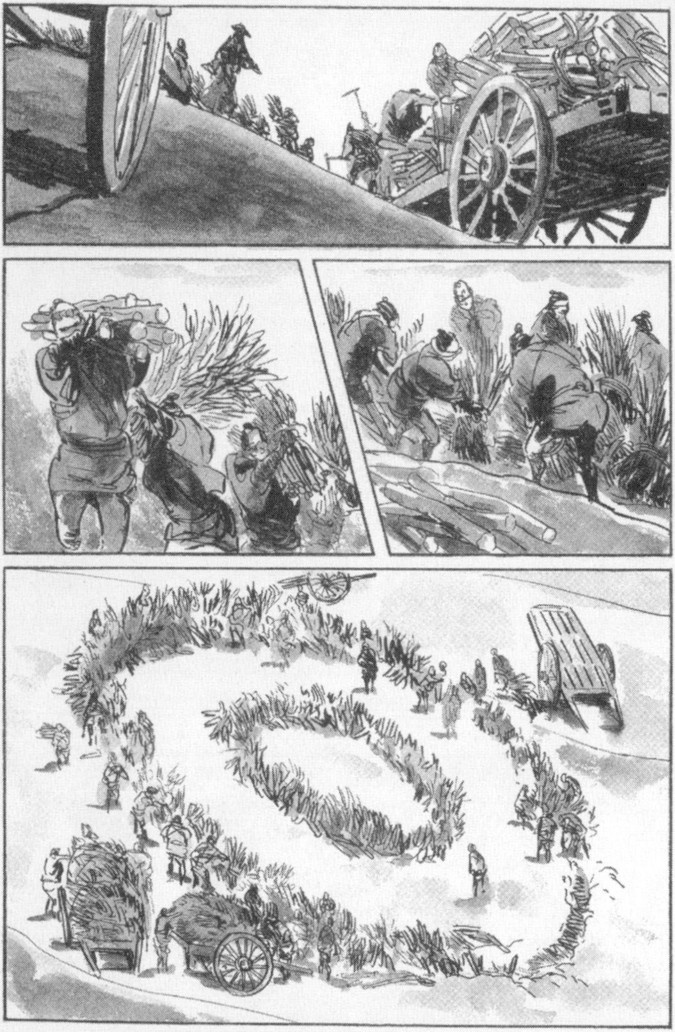

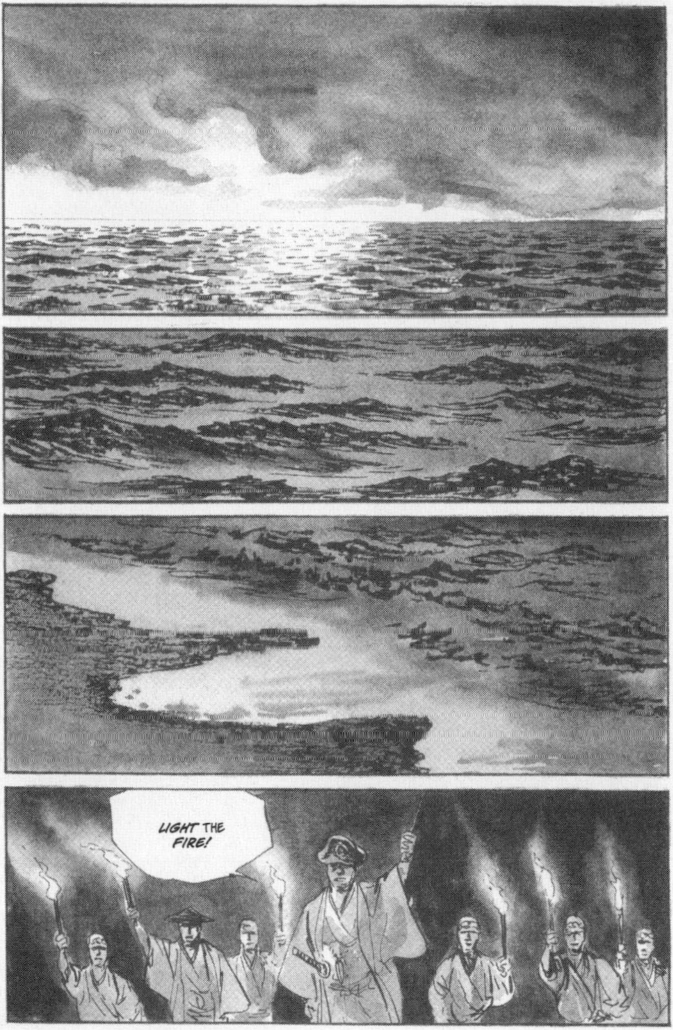
LIGHT THE FIRE!

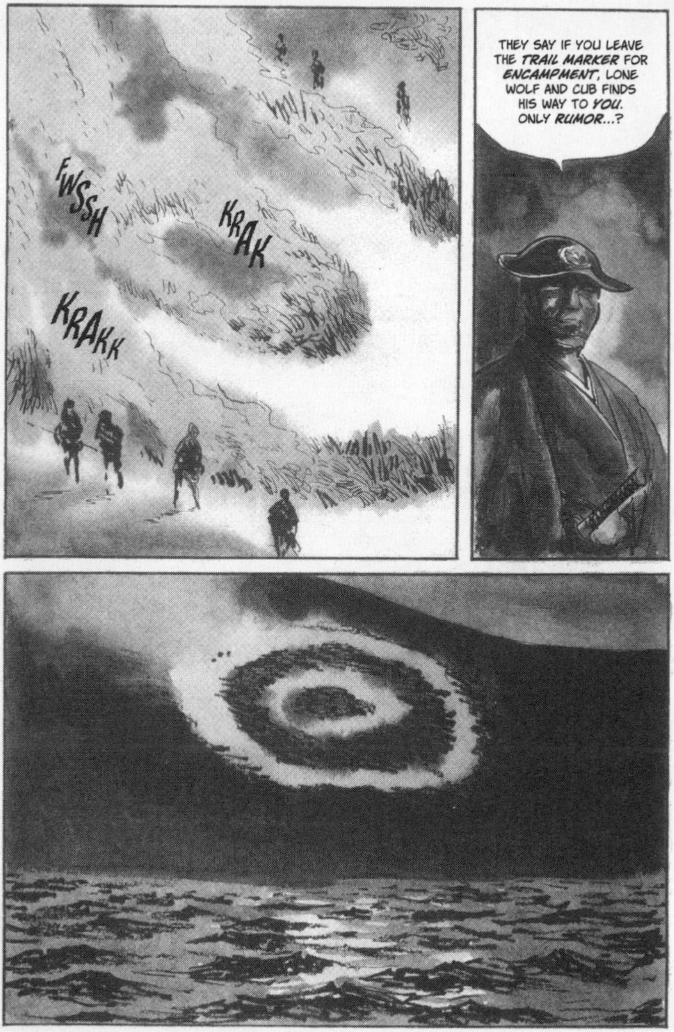
THEY SAY IF YOU LEAVE THE TRAIL MARKER FOR ENCAMPMENT, LONE WOLF AND CUB FINDS HIS WAY TO YOU. ONLY RUMOR...?
KRAK
FWSSH
KRAKK

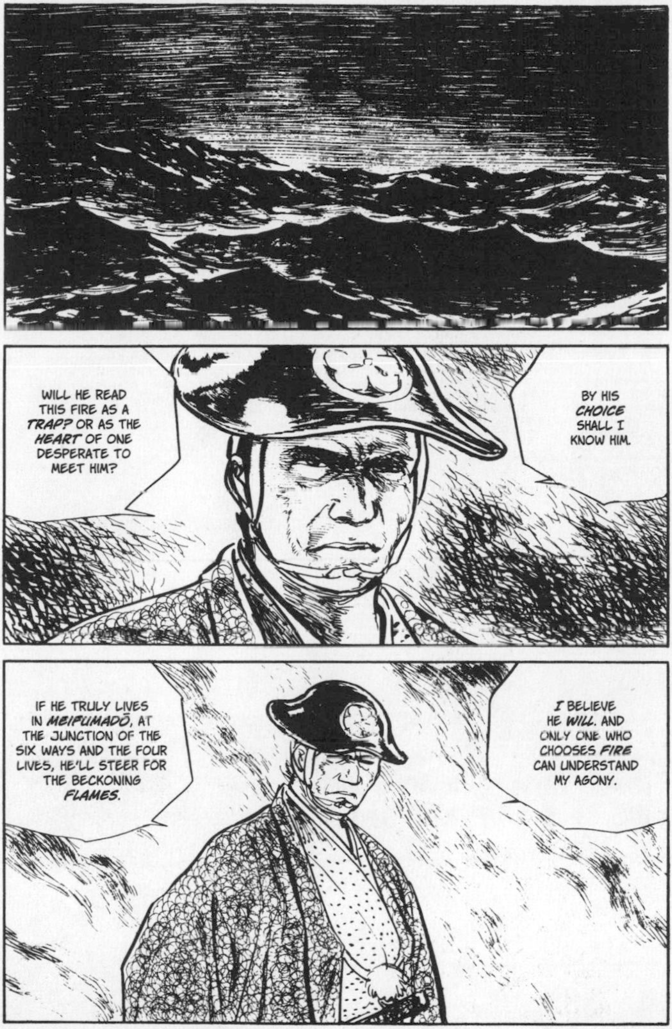
WILL HE READ THIS FIRE AS A *TRAP?* OR AS THE *HEART* OF ONE DESPERATE TO MEET HIM?
BY HIS *CHOICE* SHALL I KNOW HIM.
IF HE TRULY LIVES IN *MEIFUMADŌ*, AT THE JUNCTION OF THE SIX WAYS AND THE FOUR LIVES, HE'LL STEER FOR THE BECKONING *FLAMES*.
I BELIEVE HE *WILL*. AND ONLY ONE WHO CHOOSES *FIRE* CAN UNDERSTAND MY AGONY.

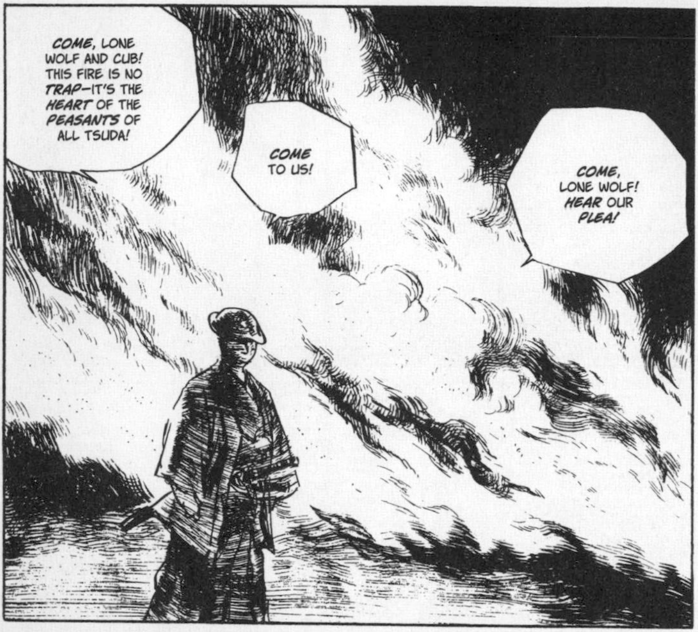
COME, LONE WOLF! HEAR OUR PLEA!
COME TO US!
COME, LONE WOLF AND CUB! THIS FIRE IS NO TRAP—IT'S THE HEART OF THE PEASANTS OF ALL TSUDA!

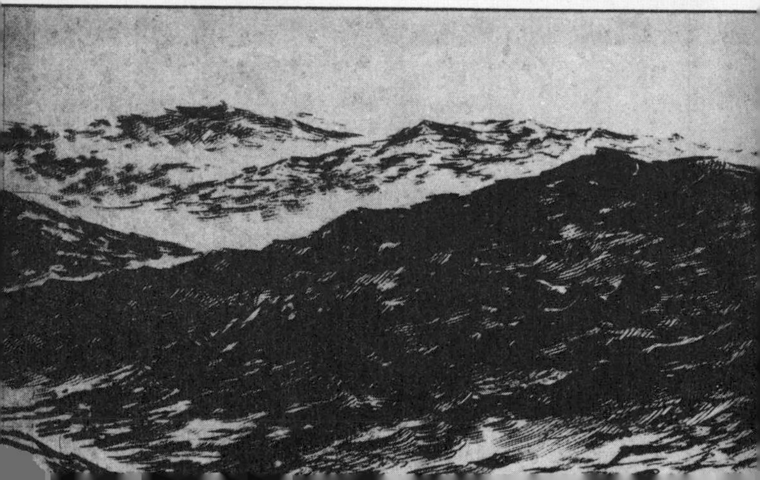

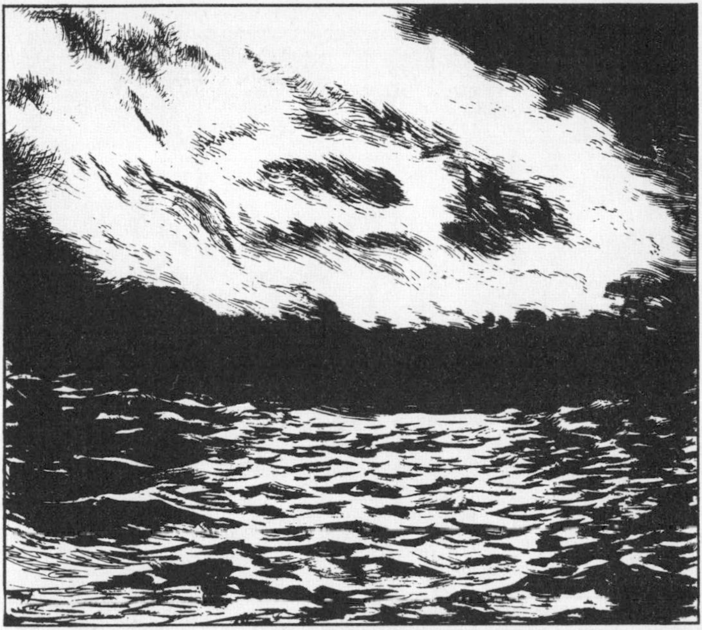
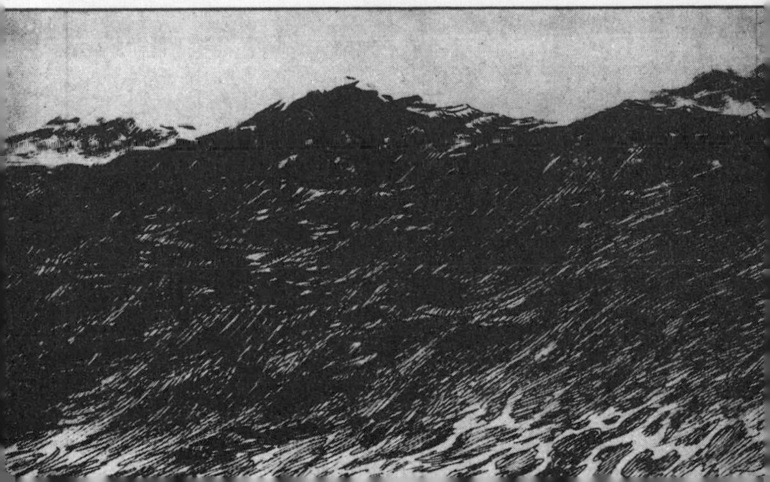

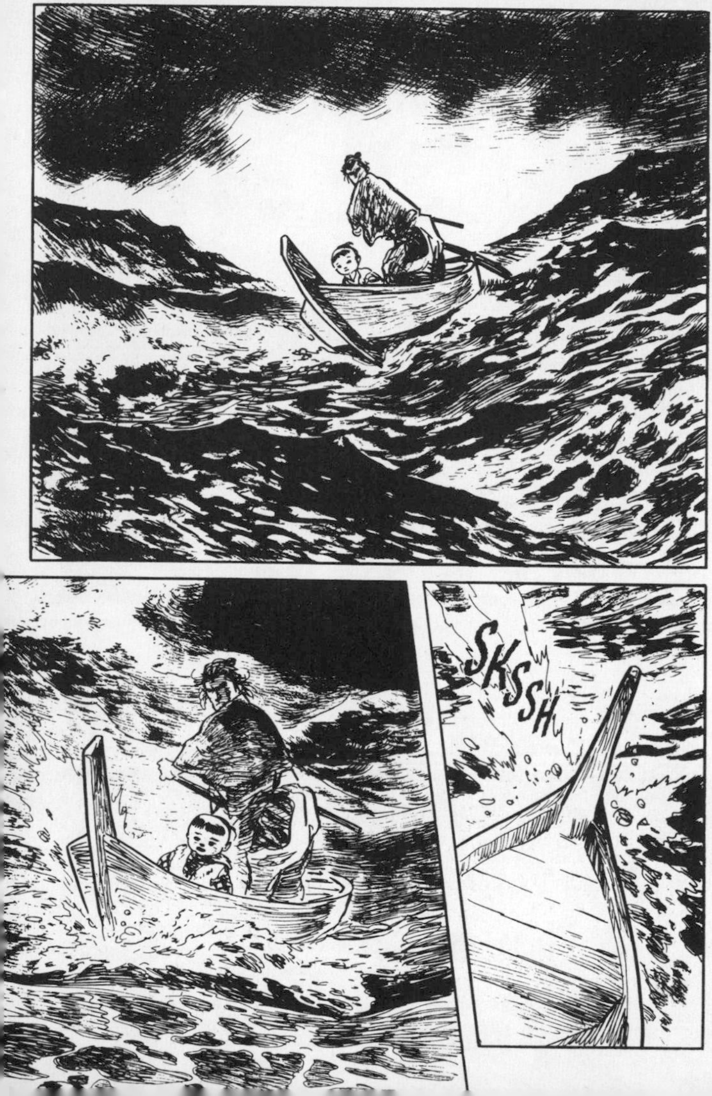
SKSSH

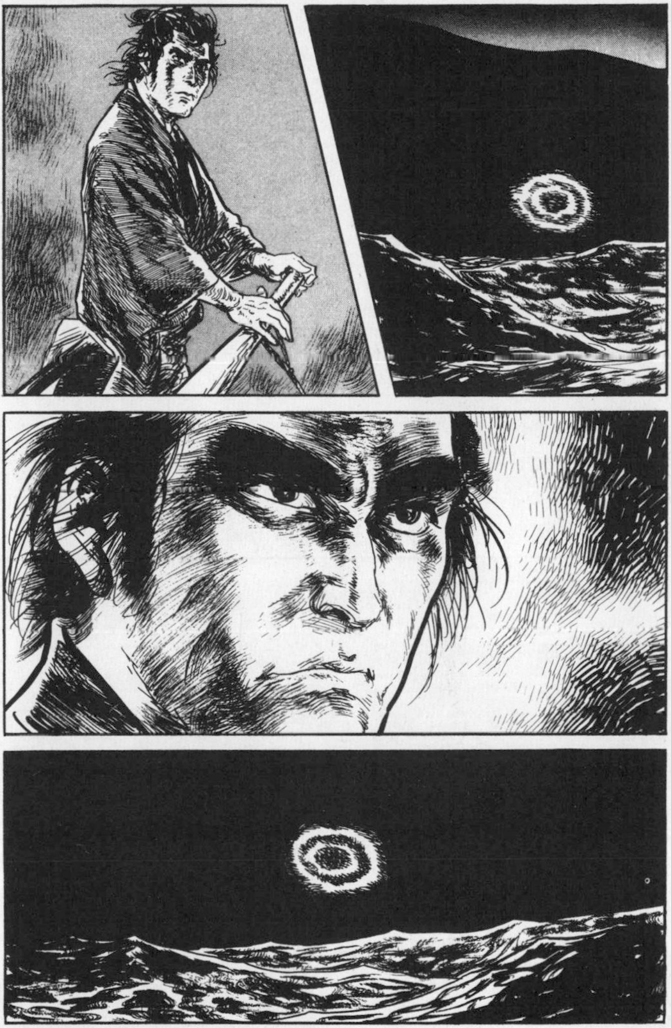

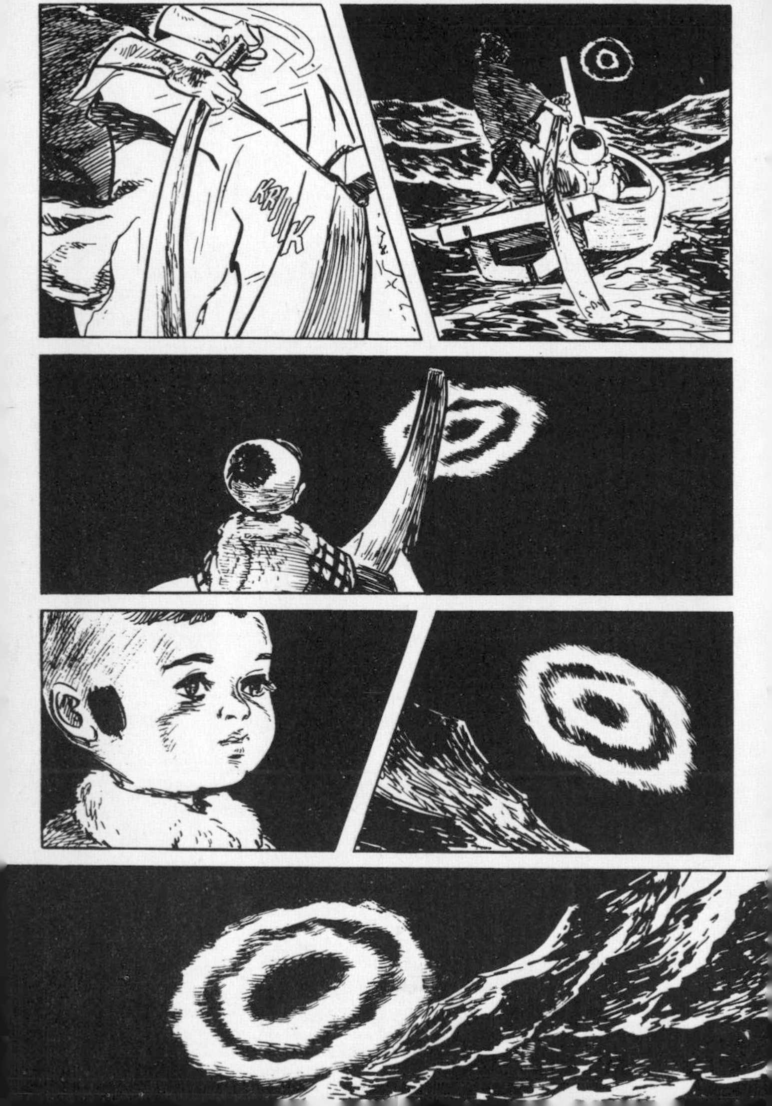
KRIIK

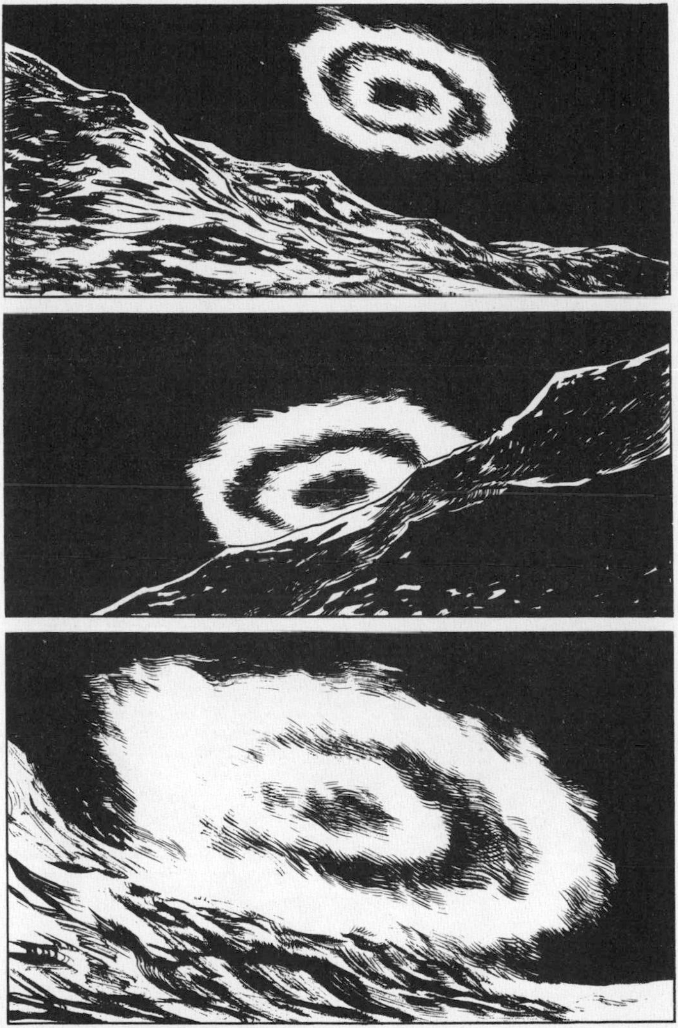

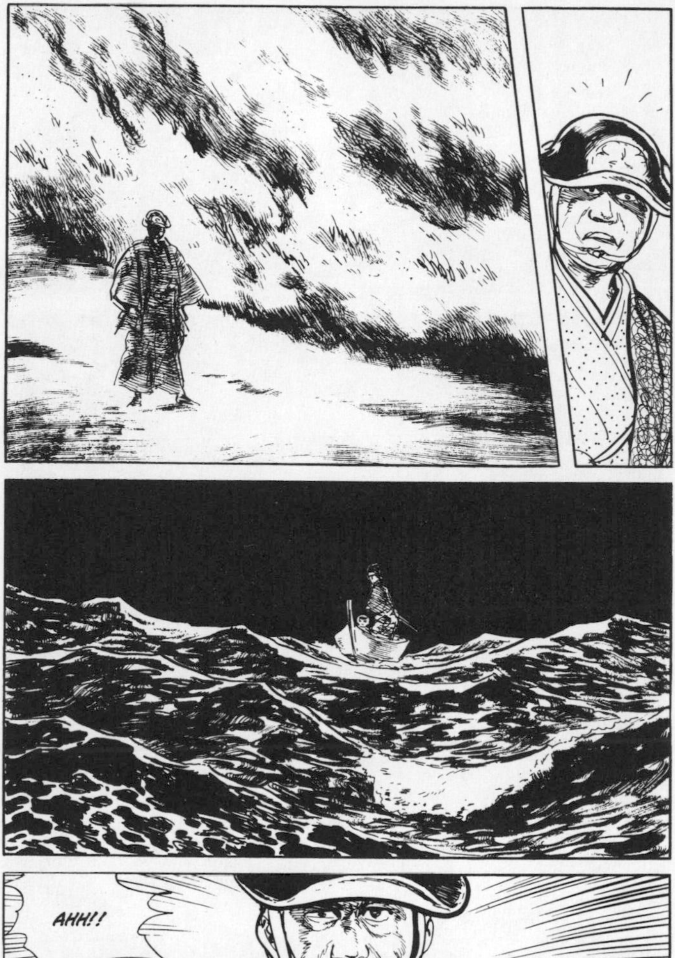
AHH!!

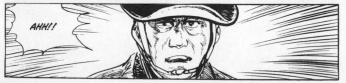

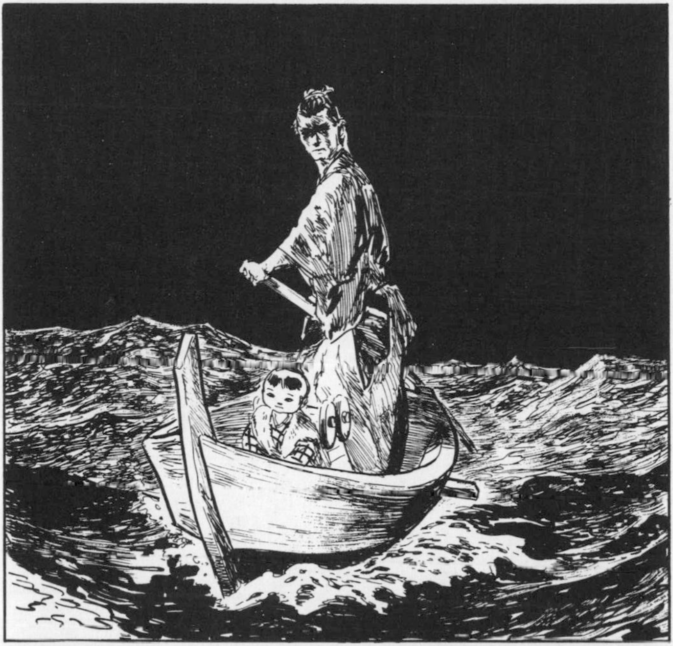

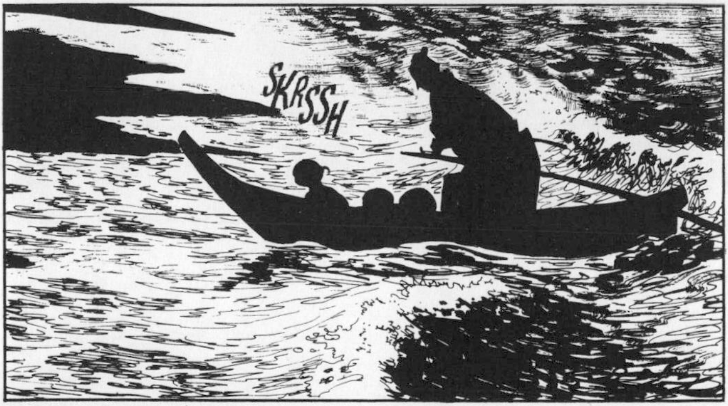
SKRSSH

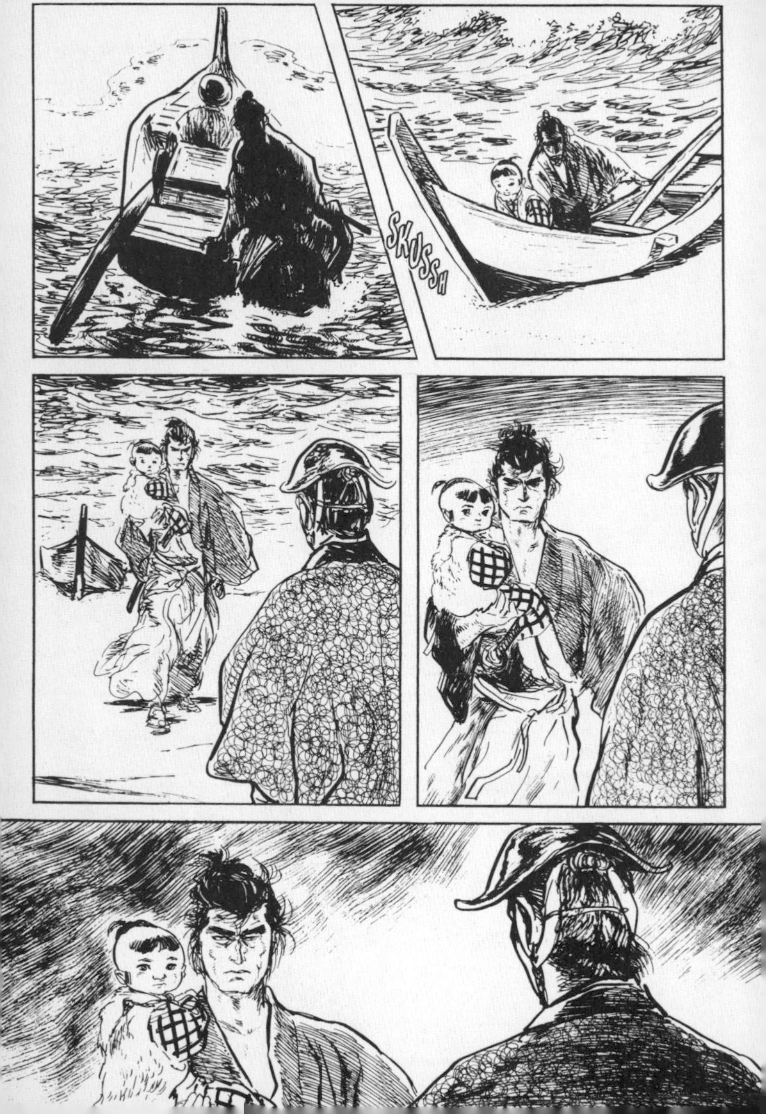
SKUSSH

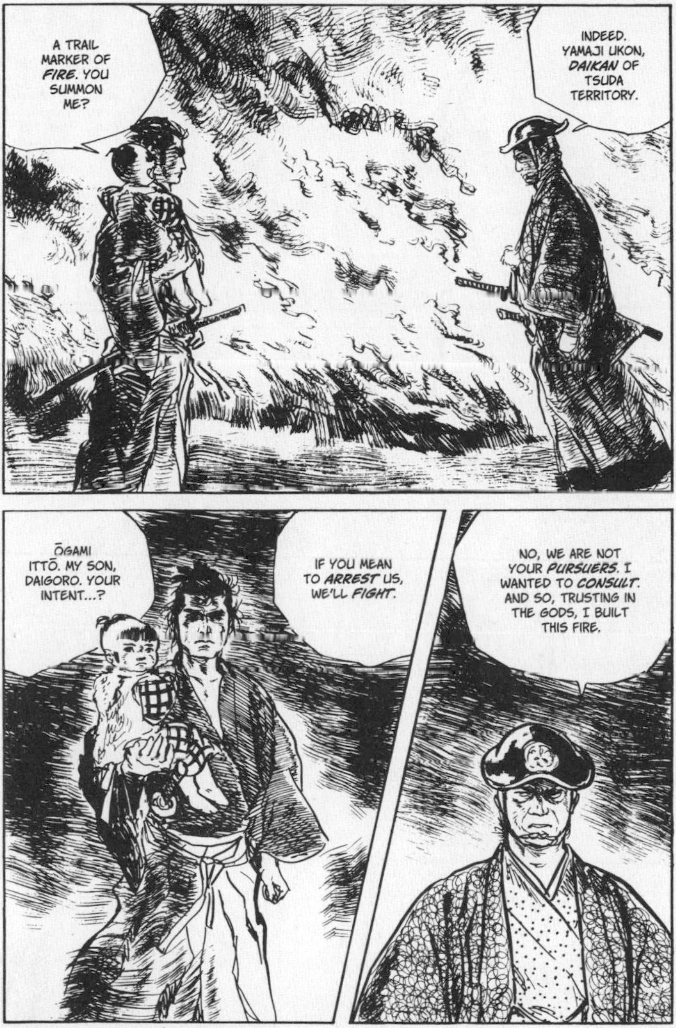
A TRAIL MARKER OF FIRE. YOU SUMMON ME?
INDEED. YAMAJI UKON, DAIKAN OF TSUDA TERRITORY.
ŌGAMI ITTŌ. MY SON, DAIGORO. YOUR INTENT...?
IF YOU MEAN TO ARREST US, WE'LL FIGHT.
NO, WE ARE NOT YOUR PURSUERS. I WANTED TO CONSULT. AND SO, TRUSTING IN THE GODS, I BUILT THIS FIRE.

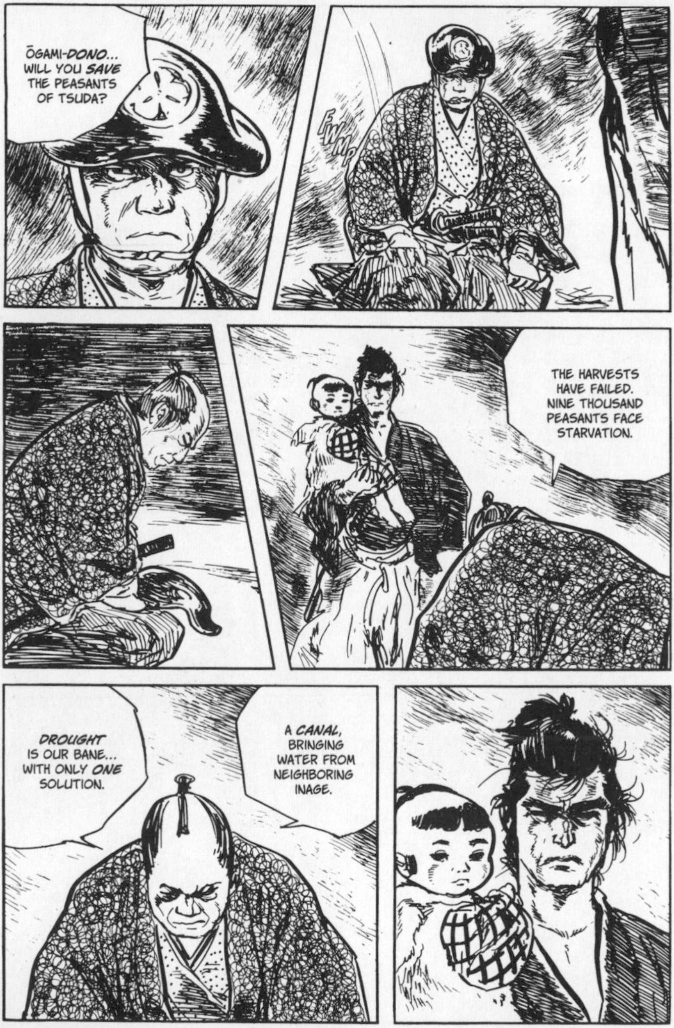
ŌGAMI-*DONO*... WILL YOU *SAVE* THE PEASANTS OF TSUDA?
FWMP
THE HARVESTS HAVE FAILED. NINE THOUSAND PEASANTS FACE STARVATION.
DROUGHT IS OUR BANE... WITH ONLY *ONE* SOLUTION.
A *CANAL*, BRINGING WATER FROM NEIGHBORING INAGE.

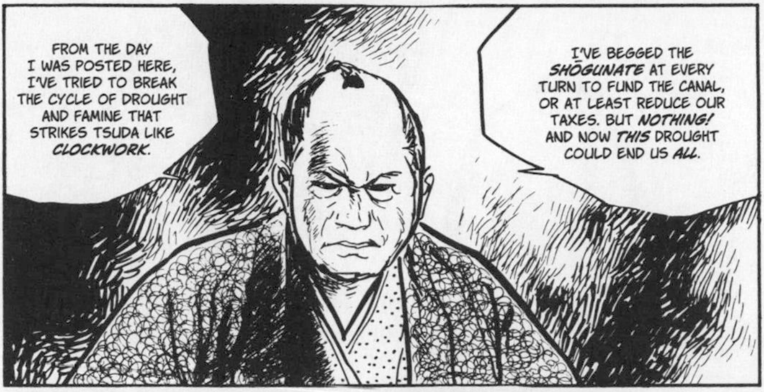
FROM THE DAY I WAS POSTED HERE, I'VE TRIED TO BREAK THE CYCLE OF DROUGHT AND FAMINE THAT STRIKES TSUDA LIKE *CLOCKWORK*.
I'VE BEGGED THE *SHŌGUNATE* AT EVERY TURN TO FUND THE CANAL, OR AT LEAST REDUCE OUR TAXES. BUT *NOTHING!* AND NOW *THIS* DROUGHT COULD END US *ALL*.
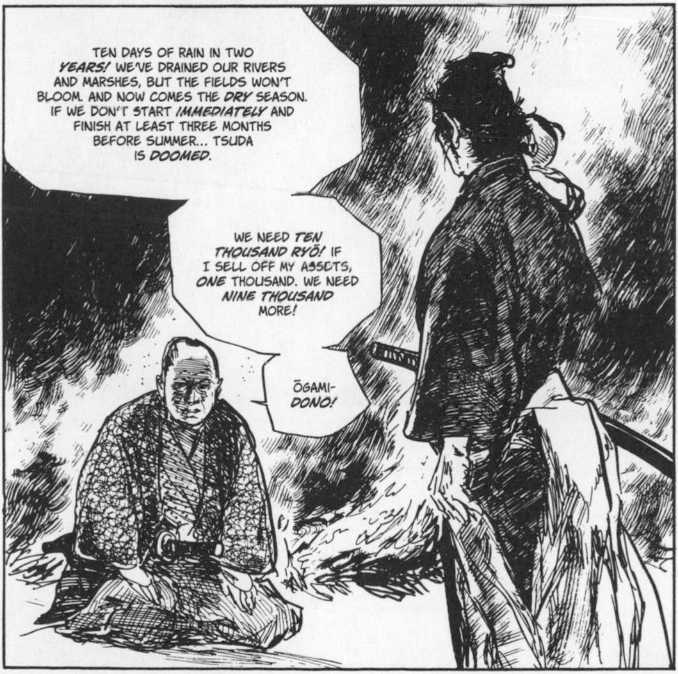
TEN DAYS OF RAIN IN TWO *YEARS!* WE'VE DRAINED OUR RIVERS AND MARSHES, BUT THE FIELDS WON'T BLOOM. AND NOW COMES THE *DRY* SEASON. IF WE DON'T START *IMMEDIATELY* AND FINISH AT LEAST THREE MONTHS BEFORE SUMMER... TSUDA IS *DOOMED*.
WE NEED *TEN THOUSAND RYŌ!* IF I SELL OFF MY ASSETS, *ONE* THOUSAND. WE NEED *NINE THOUSAND* MORE!
ŌGAMI-*DONO!*

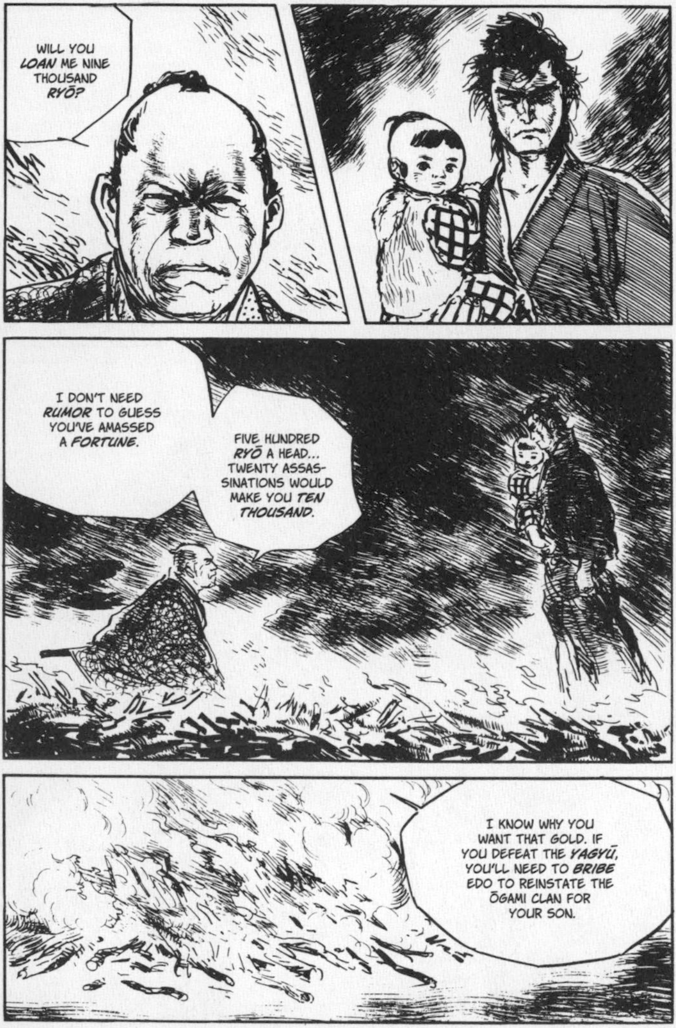
WILL YOU *LOAN* ME NINE THOUSAND *RYŌ?*
I DON'T NEED *RUMOR* TO GUESS YOU'VE AMASSED A *FORTUNE*.
FIVE HUNDRED *RYŌ* A HEAD... TWENTY ASSAS-SINATIONS WOULD MAKE YOU *TEN THOUSAND*.
I KNOW WHY YOU WANT THAT GOLD. IF YOU DEFEAT THE *YAGYŪ*, YOU'LL NEED TO *BRIBE* EDO TO REINSTATE THE ŌGAMI CLAN FOR YOUR SON.

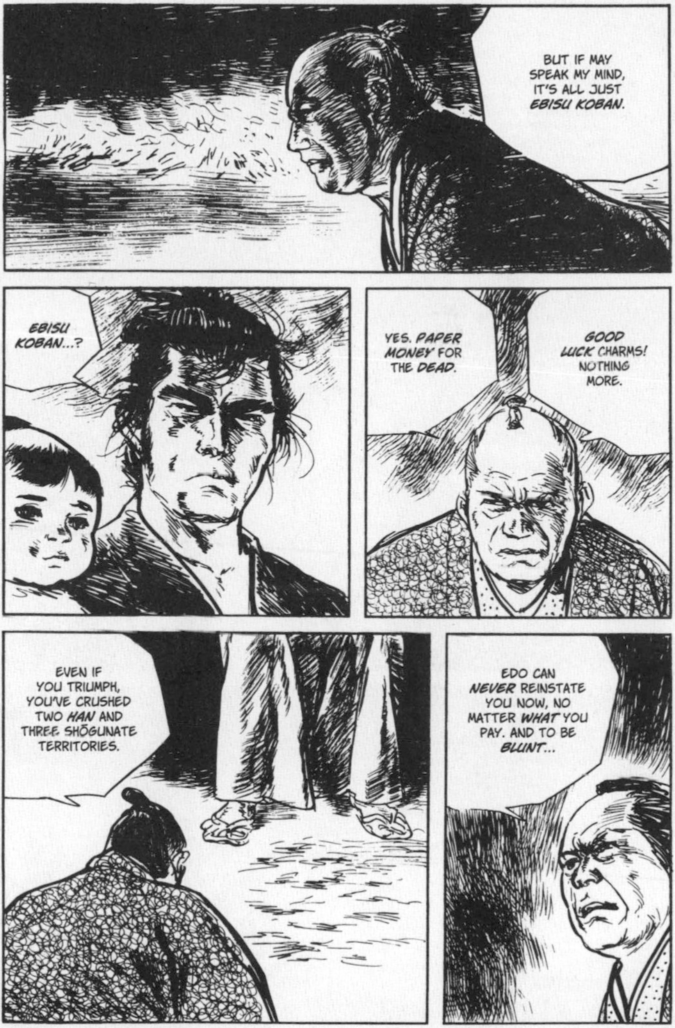
BUT IF MAY SPEAK MY MIND, IT'S ALL JUST *EBISU KOBAN*.
EBISU KOBAN...?
YES. *PAPER MONEY* FOR THE *DEAD*.
GOOD LUCK CHARMS! NOTHING MORE.
EVEN IF YOU TRIUMPH, YOU'VE CRUSHED TWO *HAN* AND THREE SHŌGUNATE TERRITORIES.
EDO CAN *NEVER* REINSTATE YOU NOW, NO MATTER *WHAT* YOU PAY. AND TO BE *BLUNT*...

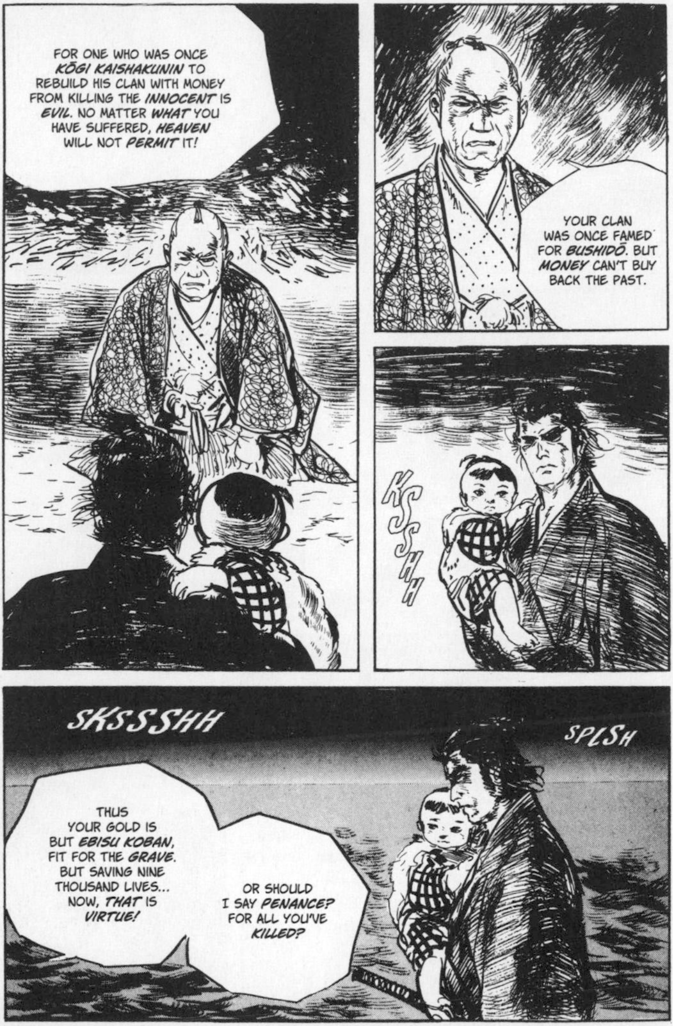
FOR ONE WHO WAS ONCE KŌGI KAISHAKUNIN TO REBUILD HIS CLAN WITH MONEY FROM KILLING THE INNOCENT IS EVIL. NO MATTER WHAT YOU HAVE SUFFERED, HEAVEN WILL NOT PERMIT IT!
YOUR CLAN WAS ONCE FAMED FOR BUSHIDŌ. BUT MONEY CAN'T BUY BACK THE PAST.
KSSSHH
SKSSSHH
SPLSH
THUS YOUR GOLD IS BUT EBISU KOBAN, FIT FOR THE GRAVE. BUT SAVING NINE THOUSAND LIVES... NOW, THAT IS VIRTUE!
OR SHOULD I SAY PENANCE? FOR ALL YOU'VE KILLED?

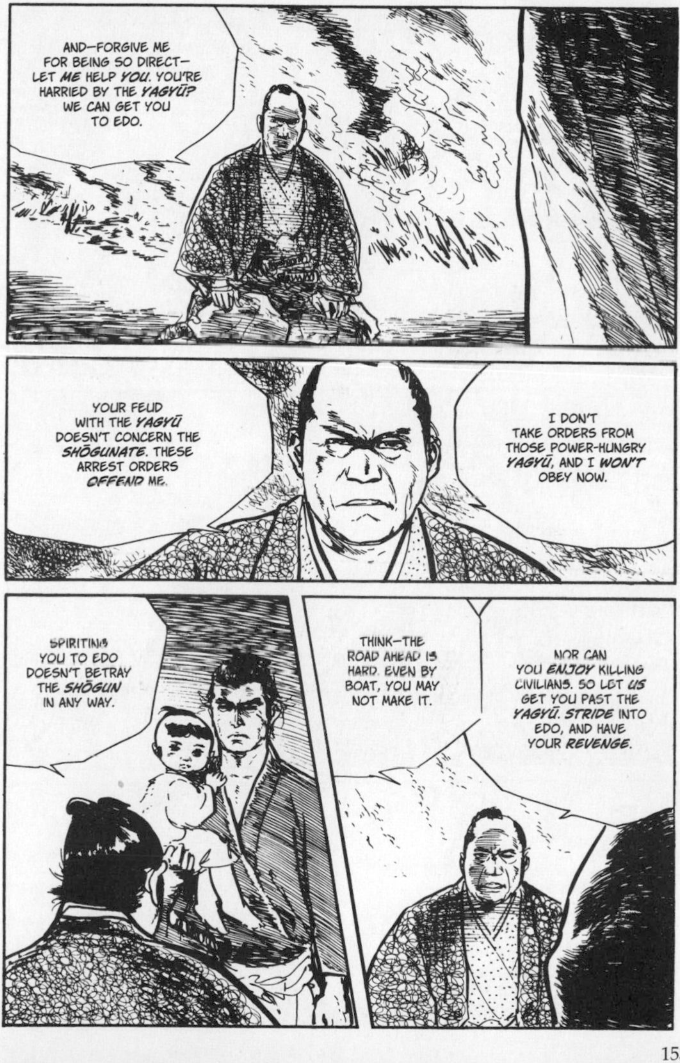

AND—FORGIVE ME FOR BEING SO DIRECT—LET *ME* HELP *YOU*. YOU'RE HARRIED BY THE *YAGYŪ?* WE CAN GET YOU TO EDO.
YOUR FEUD WITH THE *YAGYŪ* DOESN'T CONCERN THE *SHŌGUNATE*. THESE ARREST ORDERS *OFFEND* ME.
I DON'T TAKE ORDERS FROM THOSE POWER-HUNGRY *YAGYŪ*, AND I *WON'T* OBEY NOW.
SPIRITING YOU TO EDO DOESN'T BETRAY THE *SHŌGUN* IN ANY WAY.
THINK—THE ROAD AHEAD IS HARD. EVEN BY BOAT, YOU MAY NOT MAKE IT.
NOR CAN YOU *ENJOY* KILLING CIVILIANS. SO LET *US* GET YOU PAST THE *YAGYŪ*. *STRIDE* INTO EDO, AND HAVE YOUR *REVENGE*.

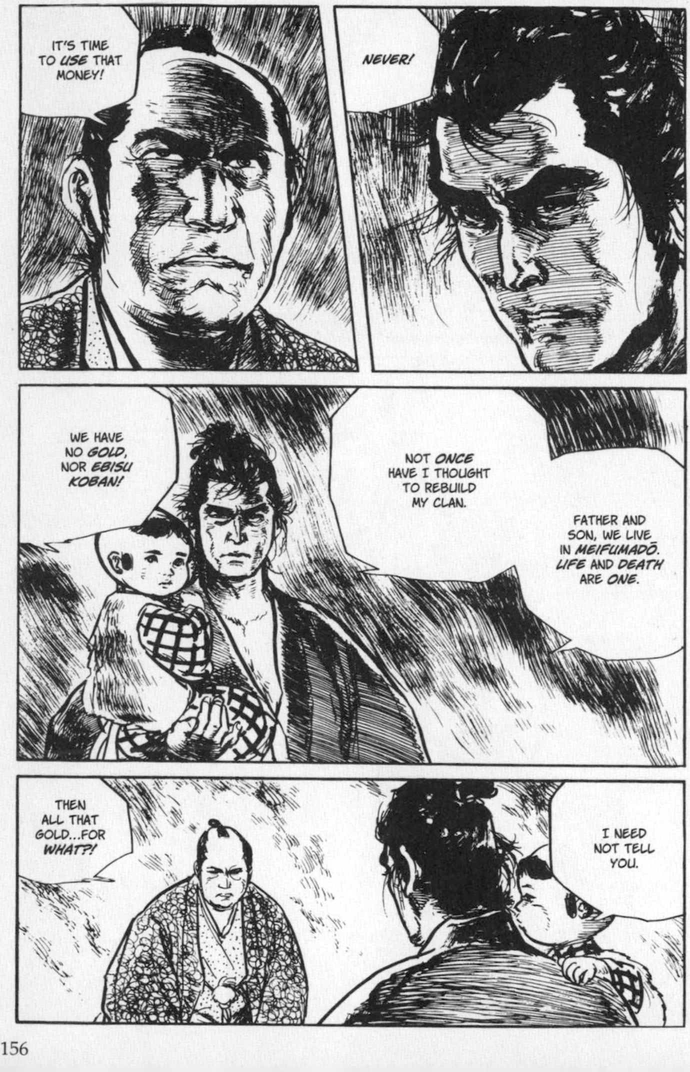
IT'S TIME TO USE THAT MONEY!
NEVER!
WE HAVE NO GOLD, NOR EBISU KOBAN!
NOT ONCE HAVE I THOUGHT TO REBUILD MY CLAN.
FATHER AND SON, WE LIVE IN MEIFUMADŌ. LIFE AND DEATH ARE ONE.
THEN ALL THAT GOLD...FOR WHAT?!
I NEED NOT TELL YOU.

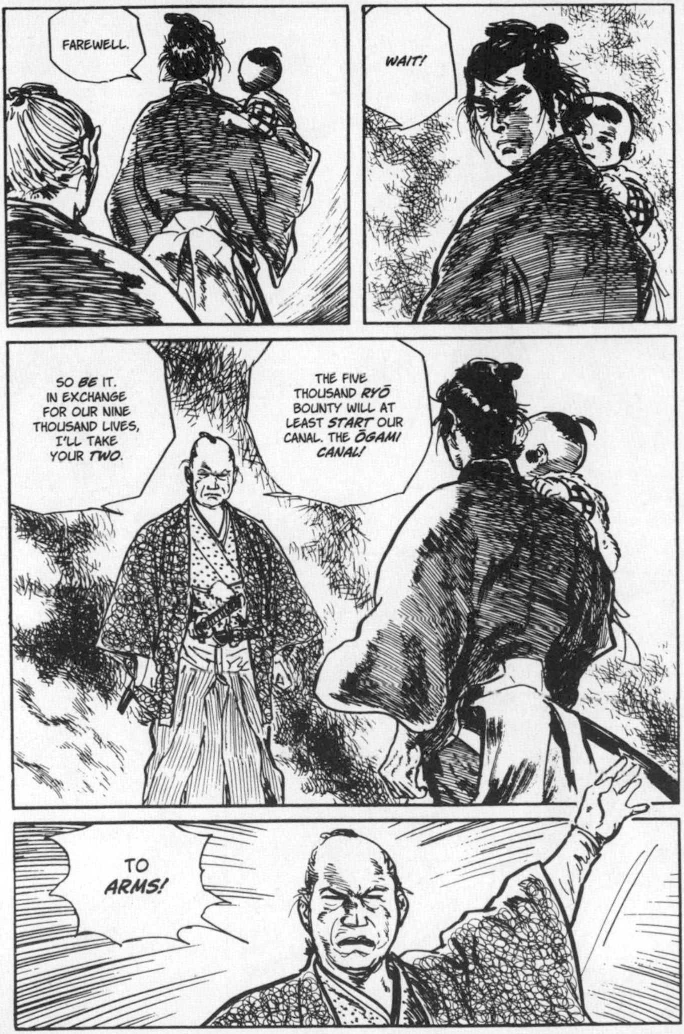
FAREWELL.
WAIT!
SO BE IT. IN EXCHANGE FOR OUR NINE THOUSAND LIVES, I'LL TAKE YOUR TWO.
THE FIVE THOUSAND RYŌ BOUNTY WILL AT LEAST START OUR CANAL. THE ŌGAMI CANAL!
TO ARMS!

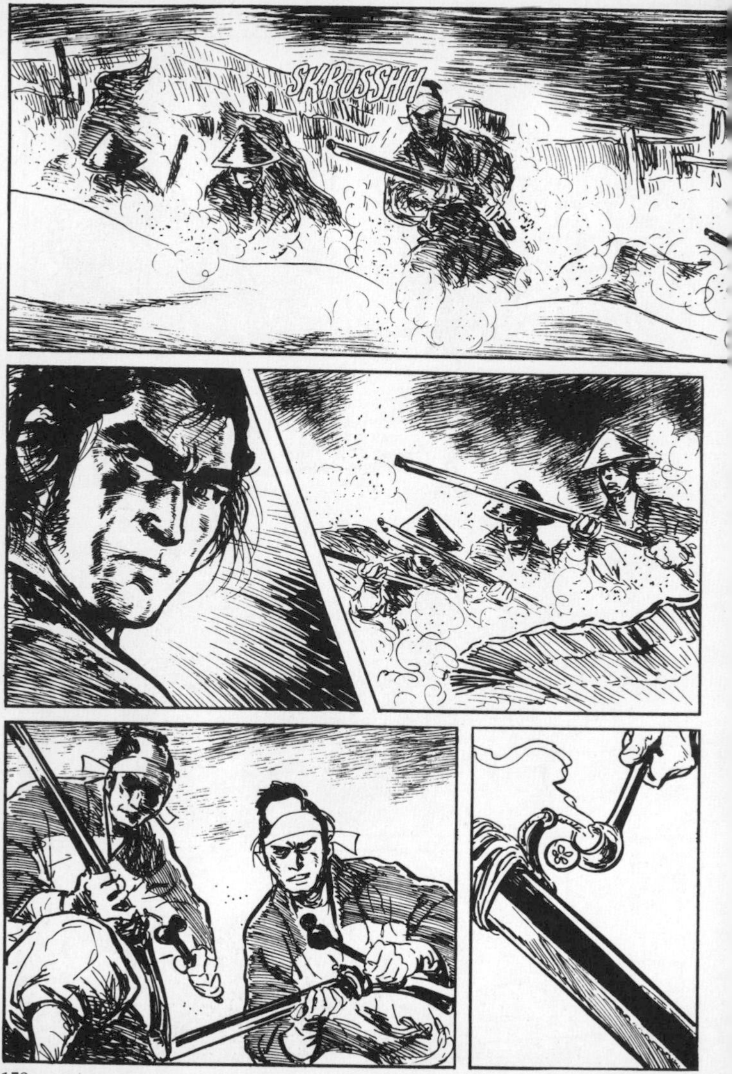
SKRUSSHH

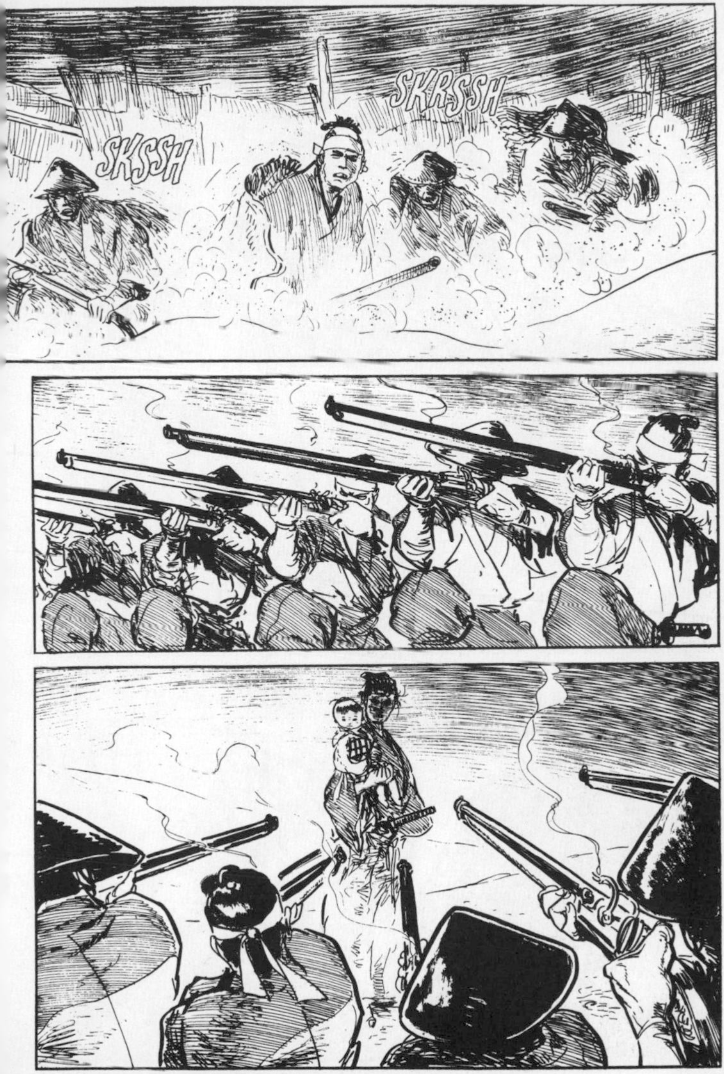
SKRSSH
SKSSH

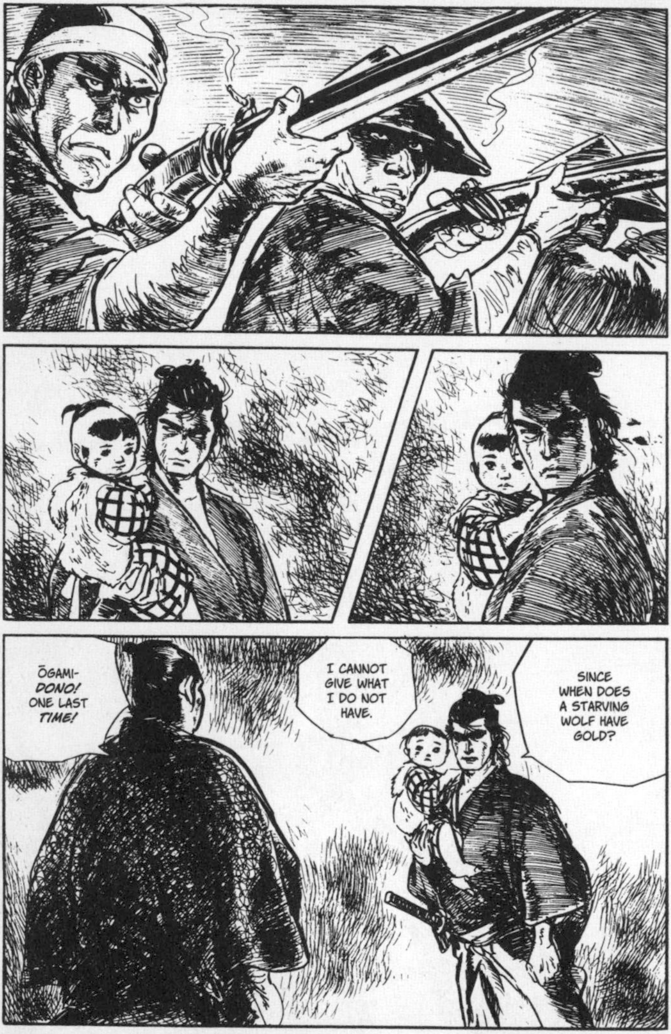
ŌGAMI-DONO! ONE LAST TIME!
I CANNOT GIVE WHAT I DO NOT HAVE.
SINCE WHEN DOES A STARVING WOLF HAVE GOLD?

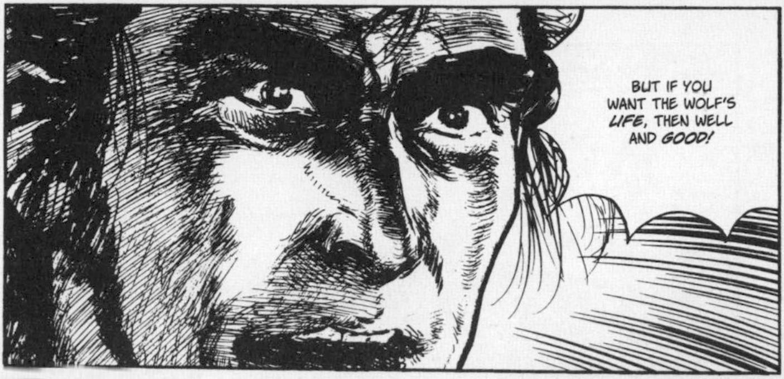
BUT IF YOU WANT THE WOLF'S *LIFE*, THEN WELL AND *GOOD!*
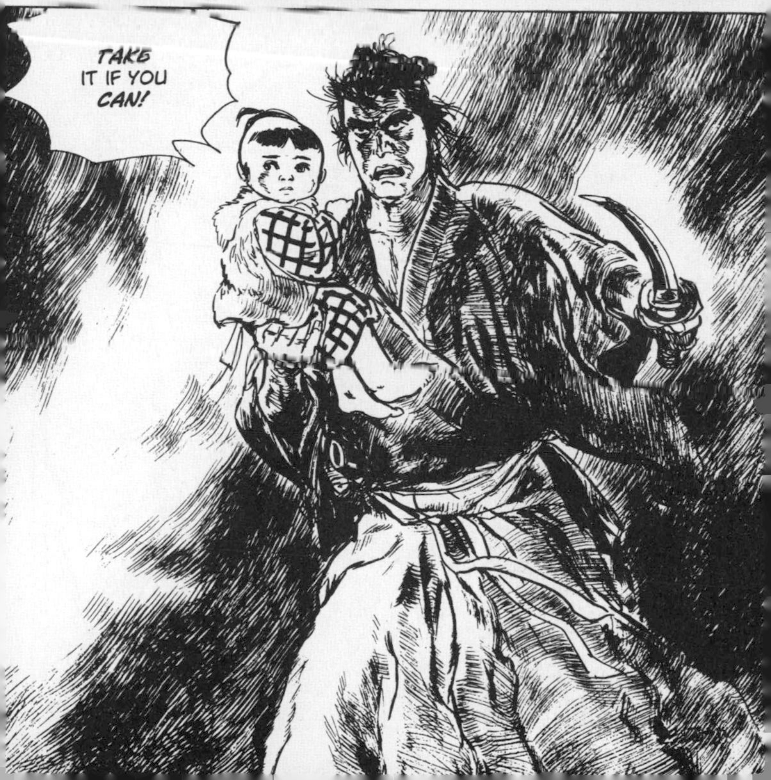
TAKE IT IF YOU *CAN!*

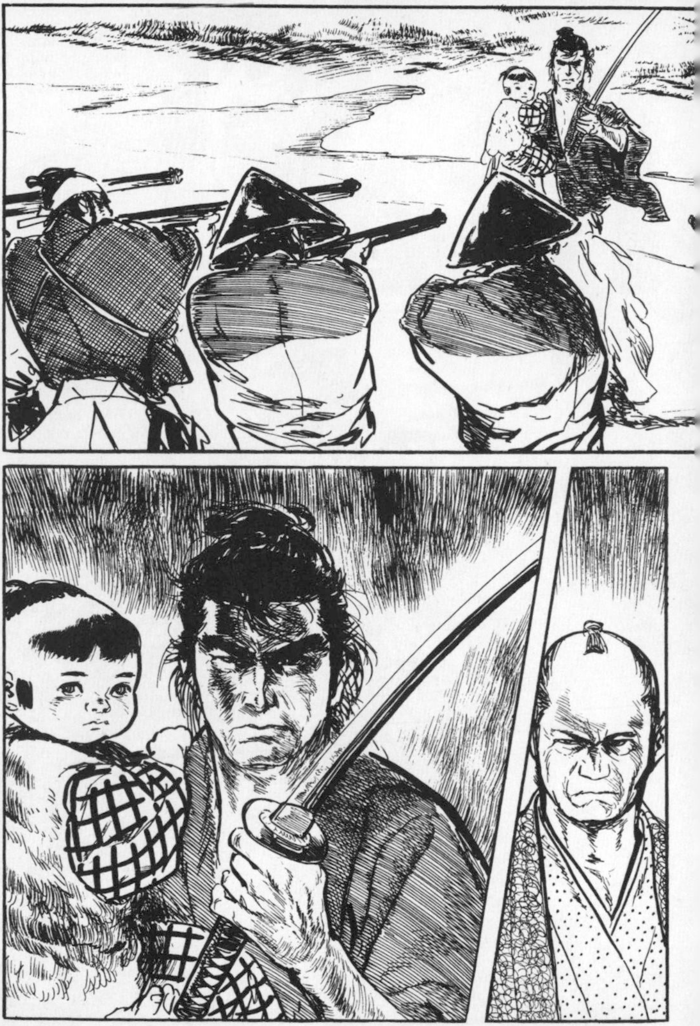

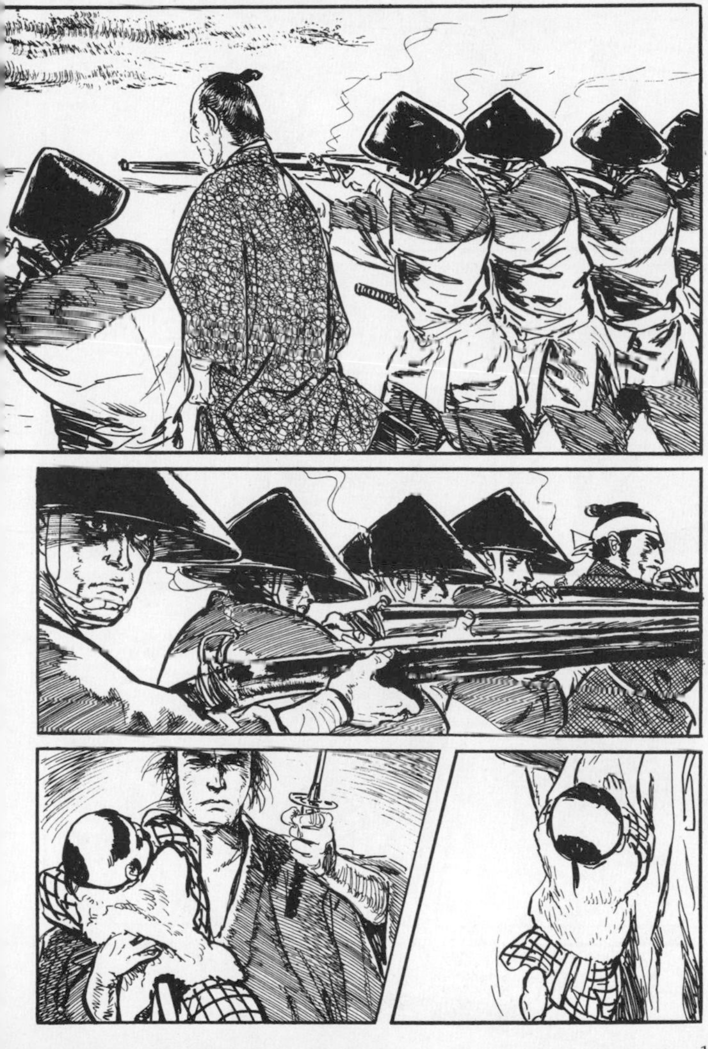

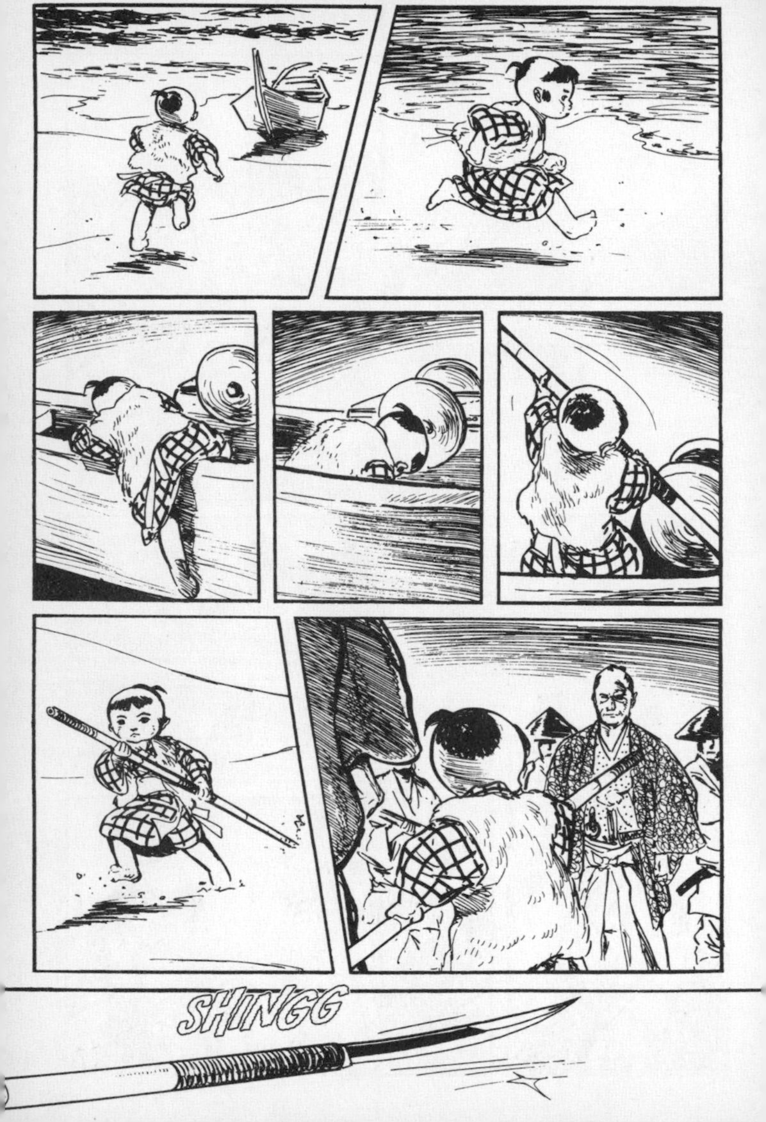
SHINGG

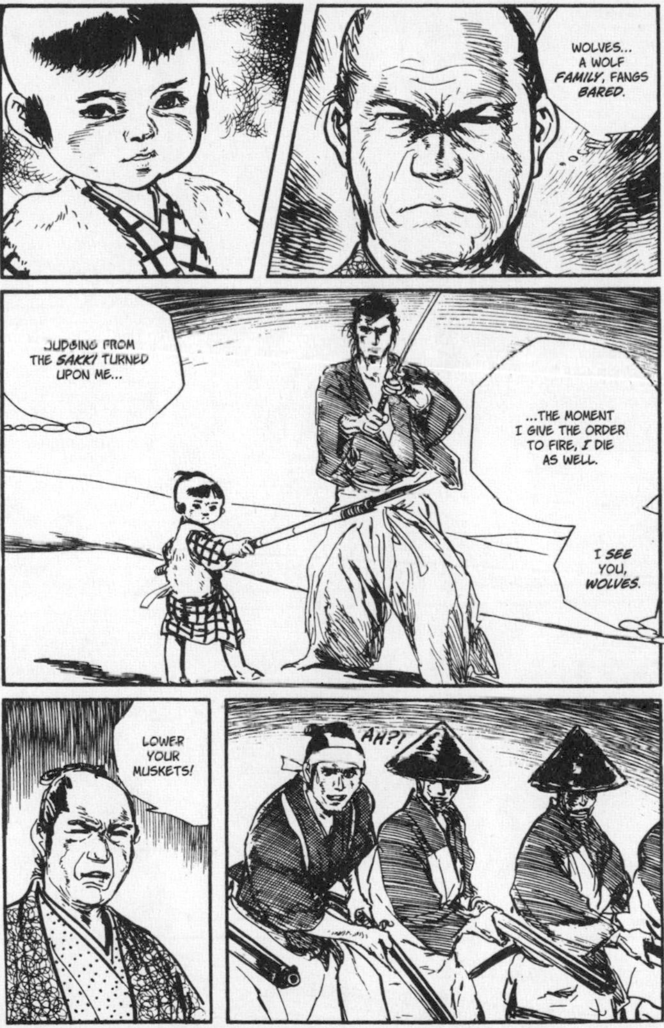
WOLVES... A WOLF *FAMILY*, FANGS *BARED*.
JUDGING FROM THE *SAKKI* TURNED UPON ME...
...THE MOMENT I GIVE THE ORDER TO FIRE, *I* DIE AS WELL.
I *SEE* YOU, *WOLVES*.
AH?!
LOWER YOUR MUSKETS!

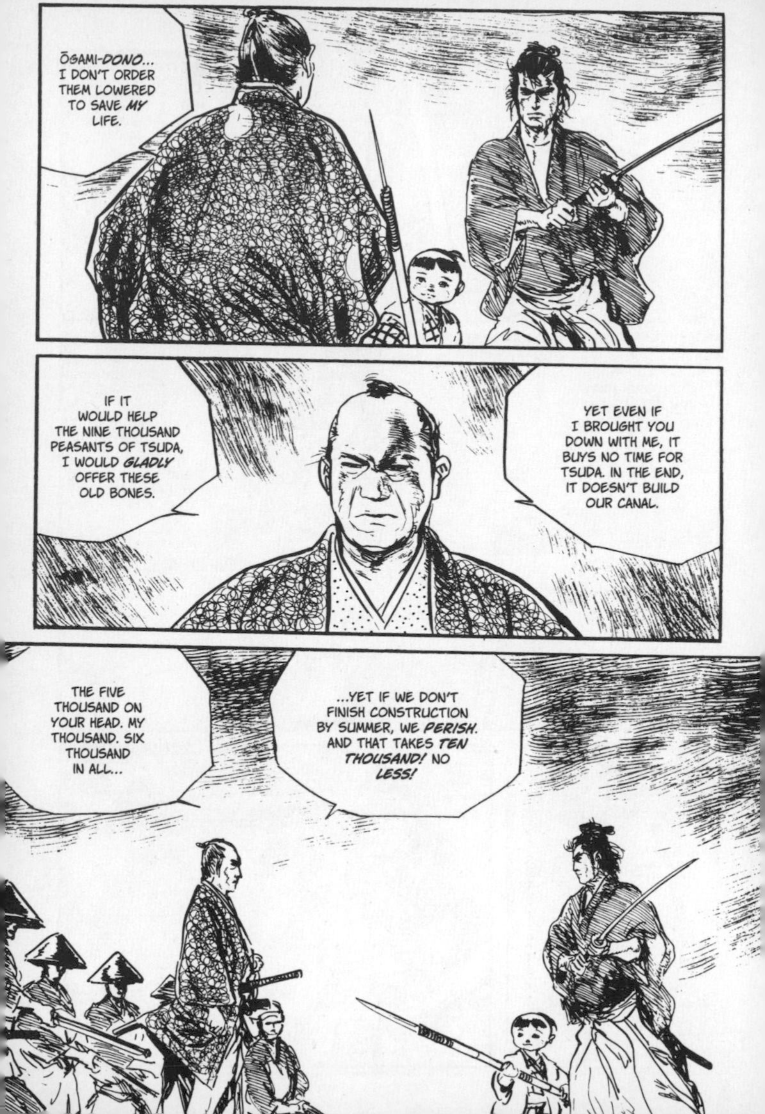
ŌGAMI-*DONO*... I DON'T ORDER THEM LOWERED TO SAVE *MY* LIFE.
IF IT WOULD HELP THE NINE THOUSAND PEASANTS OF TSUDA, I WOULD *GLADLY* OFFER THESE OLD BONES.
YET EVEN IF I BROUGHT YOU DOWN WITH ME, IT BUYS NO TIME FOR TSUDA. IN THE END, IT DOESN'T BUILD OUR CANAL.
THE FIVE THOUSAND ON YOUR HEAD. MY THOUSAND. SIX THOUSAND IN ALL...
...YET IF WE DON'T FINISH CONSTRUCTION BY SUMMER, WE *PERISH*. AND THAT TAKES *TEN THOUSAND!* NO *LESS!*

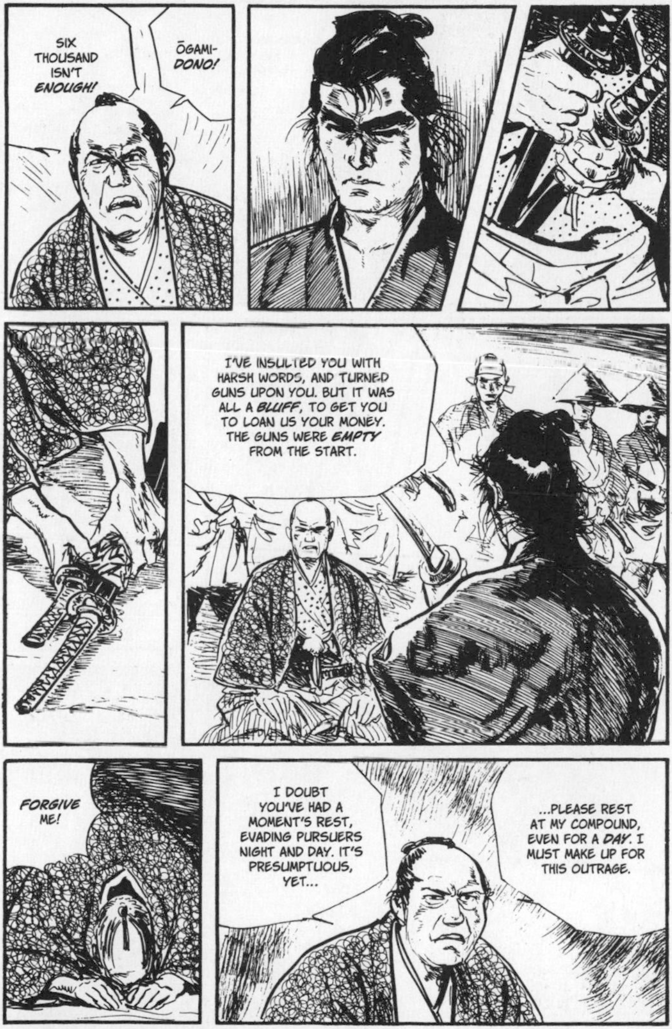

SIX THOUSAND ISN'T *ENOUGH!*
ŌGAMI-*DONO!*
I'VE INSULTED YOU WITH HARSH WORDS, AND TURNED GUNS UPON YOU. BUT IT WAS ALL A *BLUFF*, TO GET YOU TO LOAN US YOUR MONEY. THE GUNS WERE *EMPTY* FROM THE START.
FORGIVE ME!
I DOUBT YOU'VE HAD A MOMENT'S REST, EVADING PURSUERS NIGHT AND DAY. IT'S PRESUMPTUOUS, YET...
...PLEASE REST AT MY COMPOUND, EVEN FOR A *DAY*. I MUST MAKE UP FOR THIS OUTRAGE.

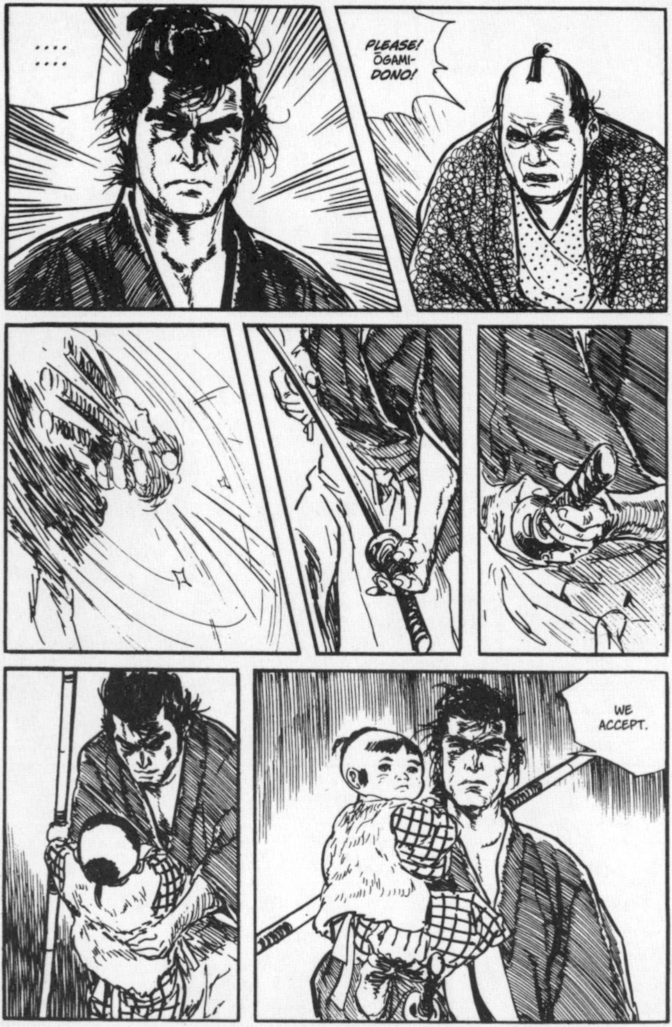
PLEASE! ŌGAMI-DONO!
....
....
WE ACCEPT.

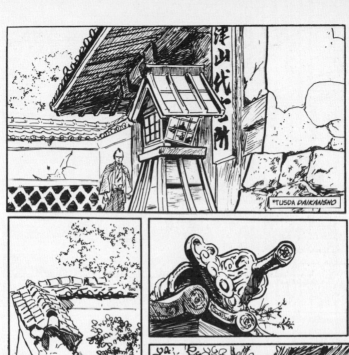

*TUSDA DAIKANSHO

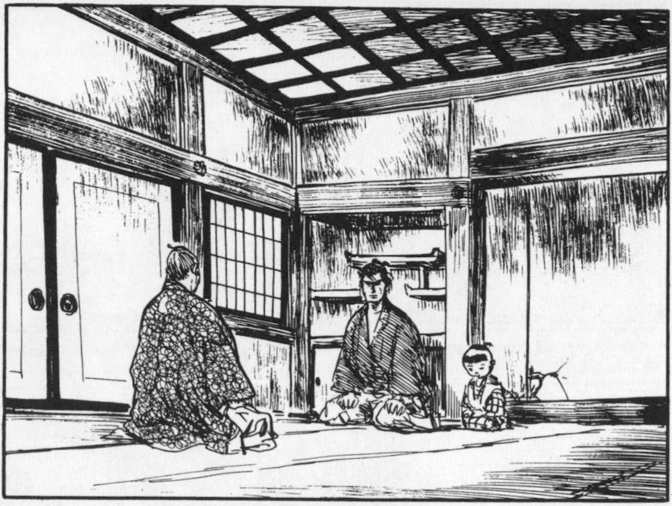

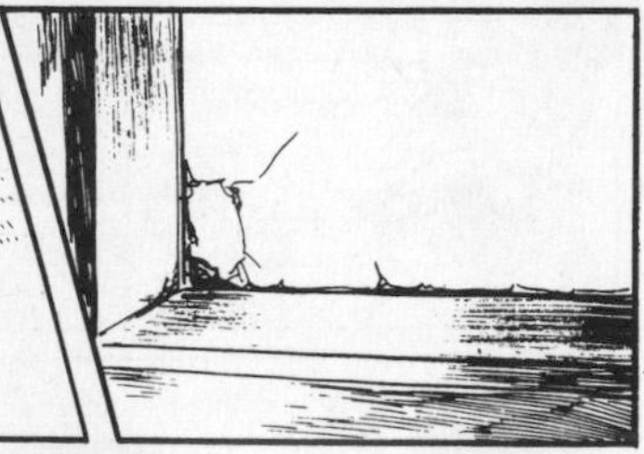

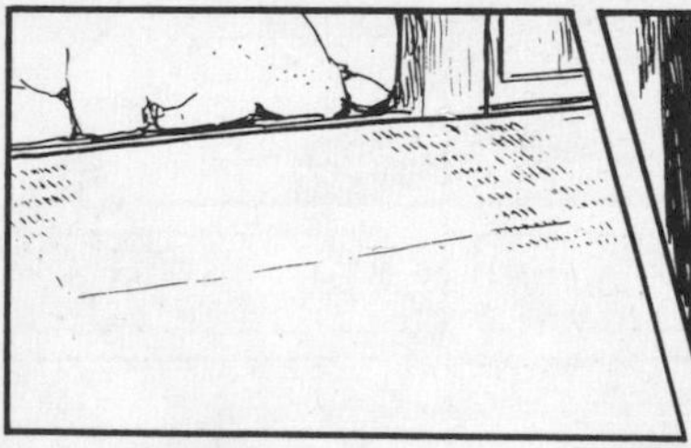

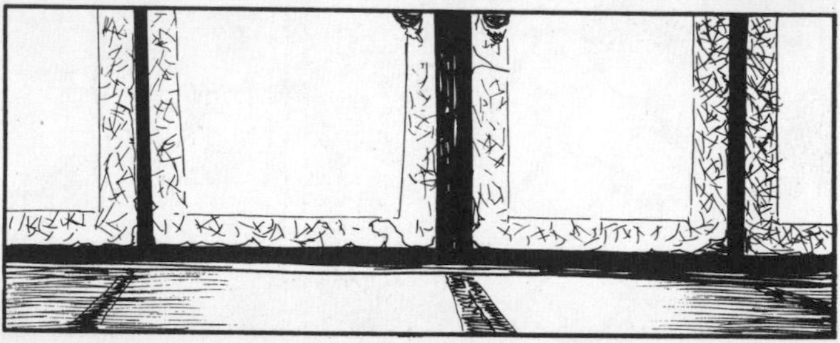

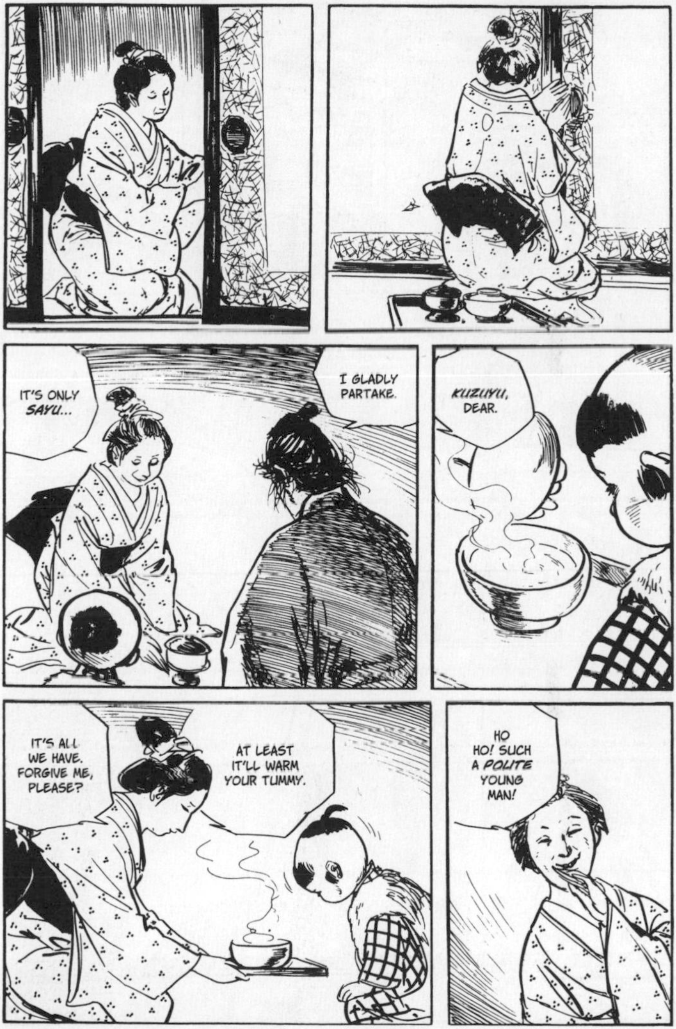
IT'S ONLY SAYU...
I GLADLY PARTAKE.
KUZUYU, DEAR.
IT'S ALL WE HAVE. FORGIVE ME, PLEASE?
AT LEAST IT'LL WARM YOUR TUMMY.
HO HO! SUCH A POLITE YOUNG MAN!

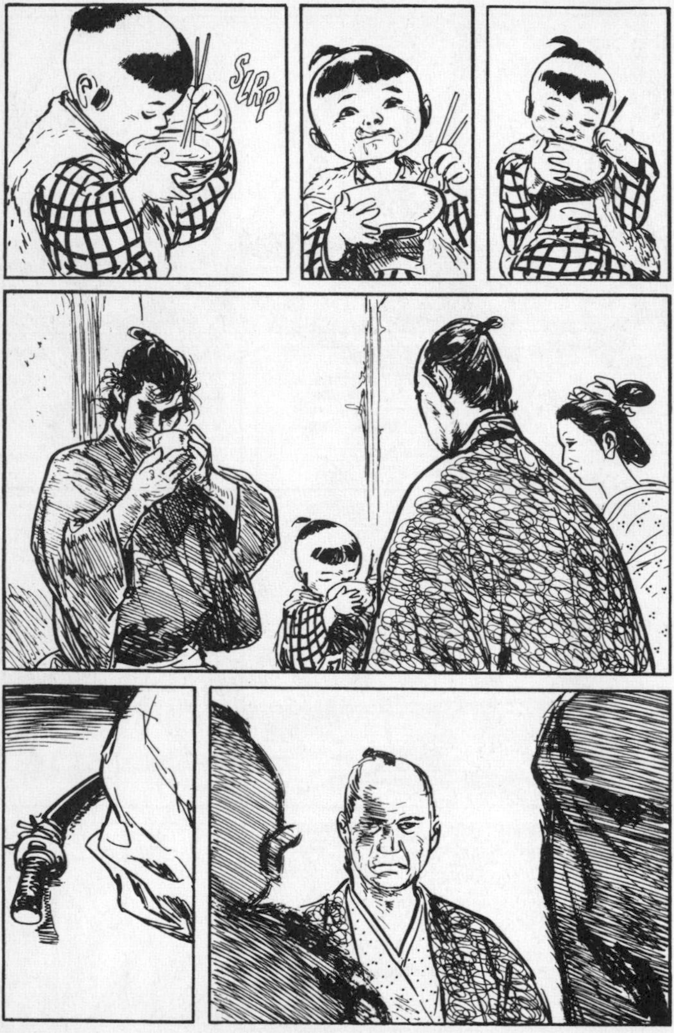
SLRP

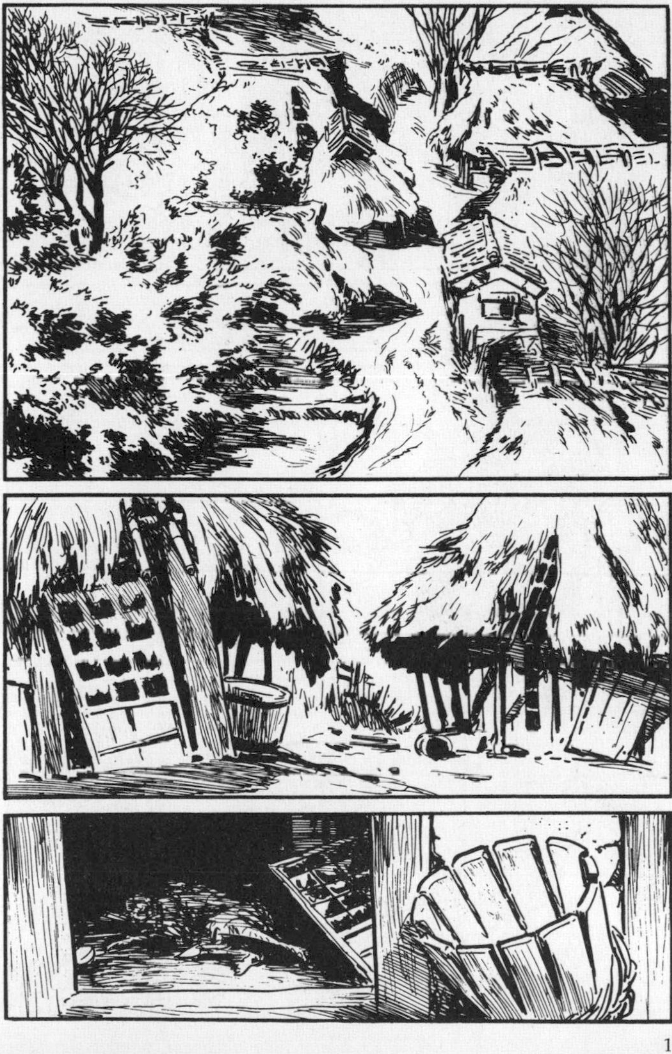

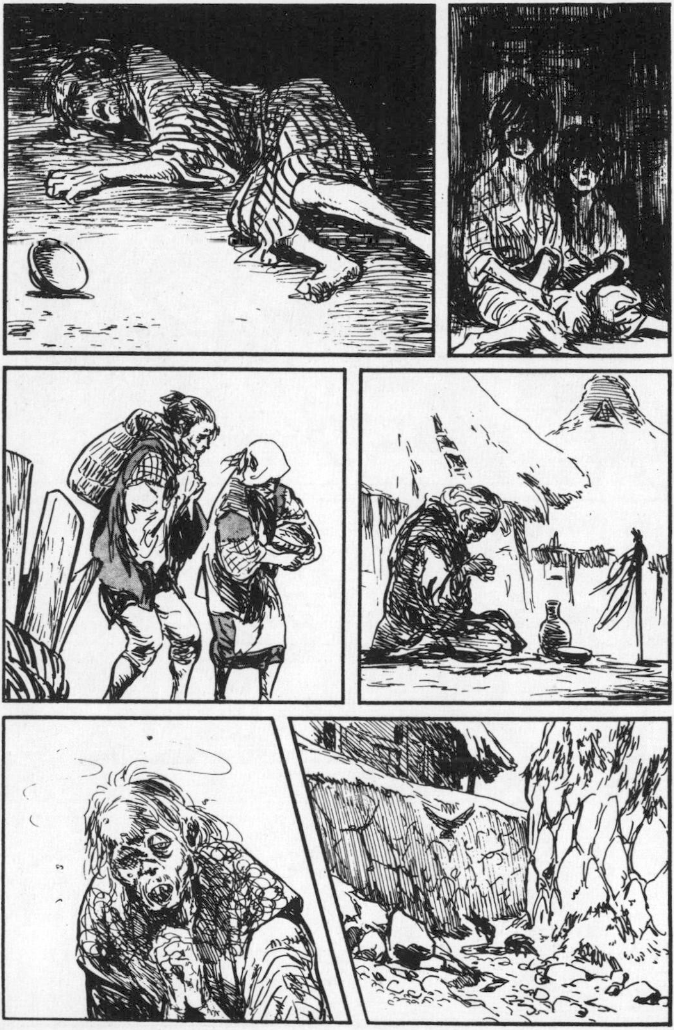

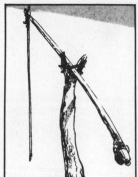

175

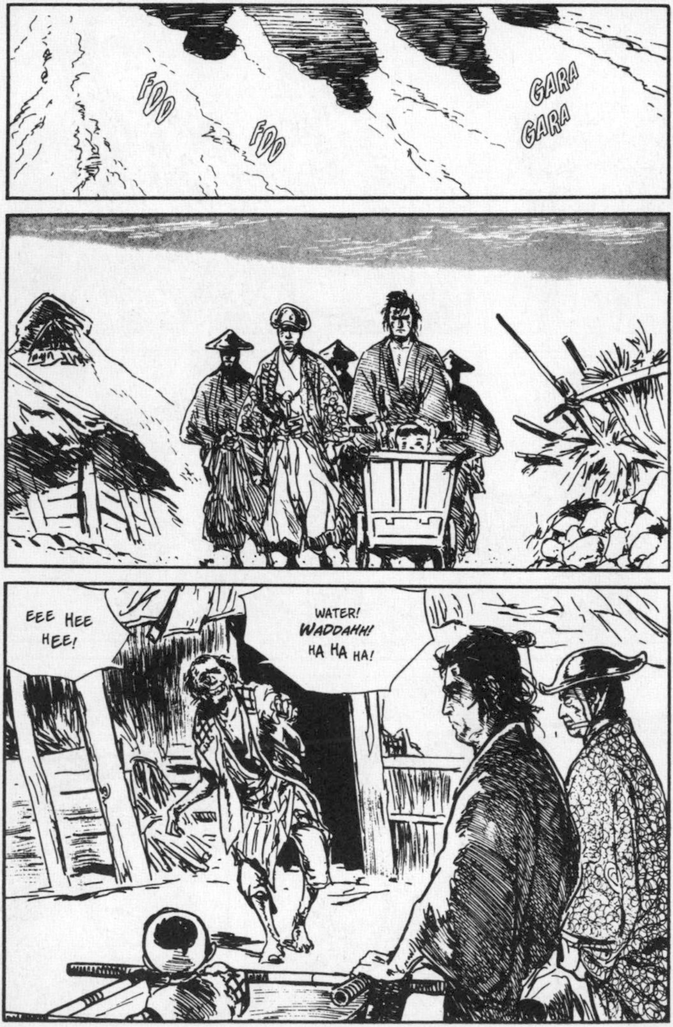
GARA GARA
FDO
FDO
WATER! WADDAHH! HA HA HA!
EEE HEE HEE!

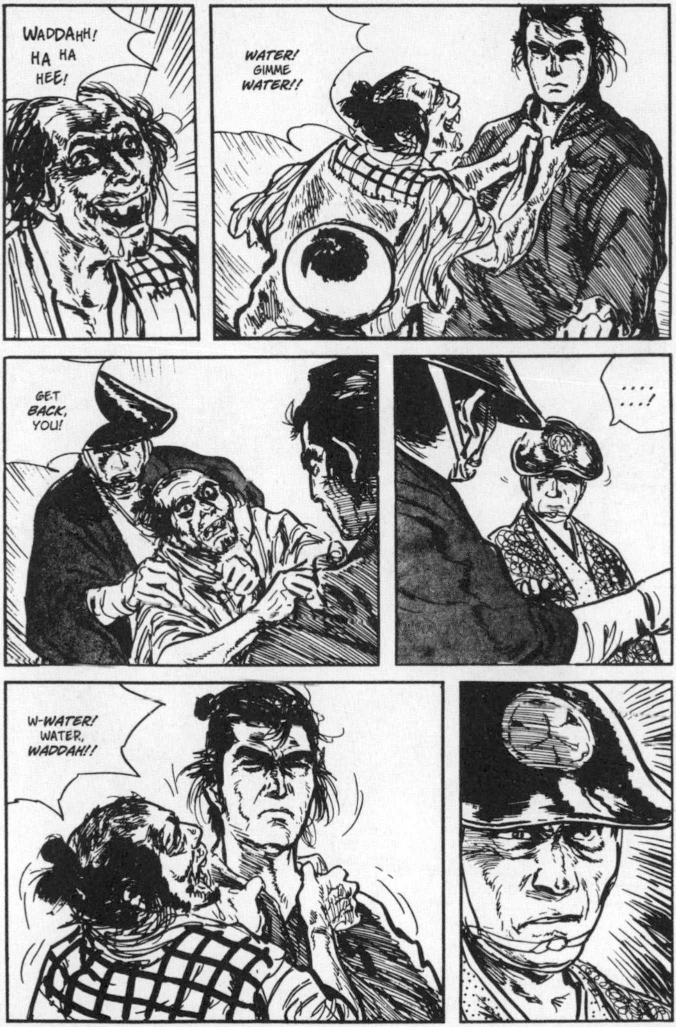
WADDAHH! HA HA HEE!
WATER! GIMME WATER!!
GET BACK, YOU!
....!
W-WATER! WATER, WADDAH!!

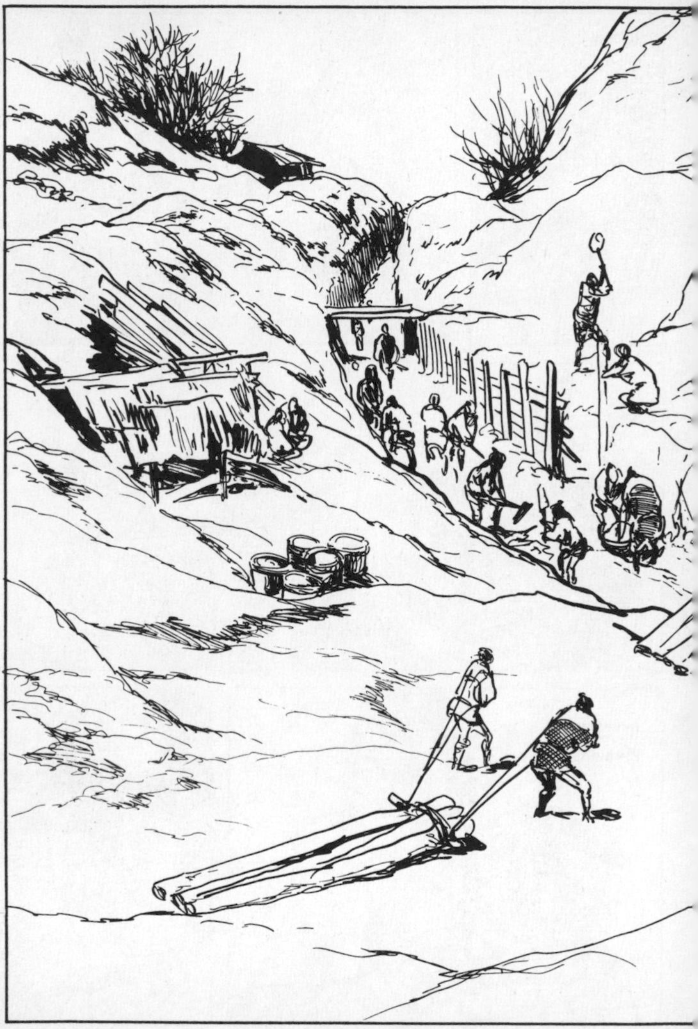

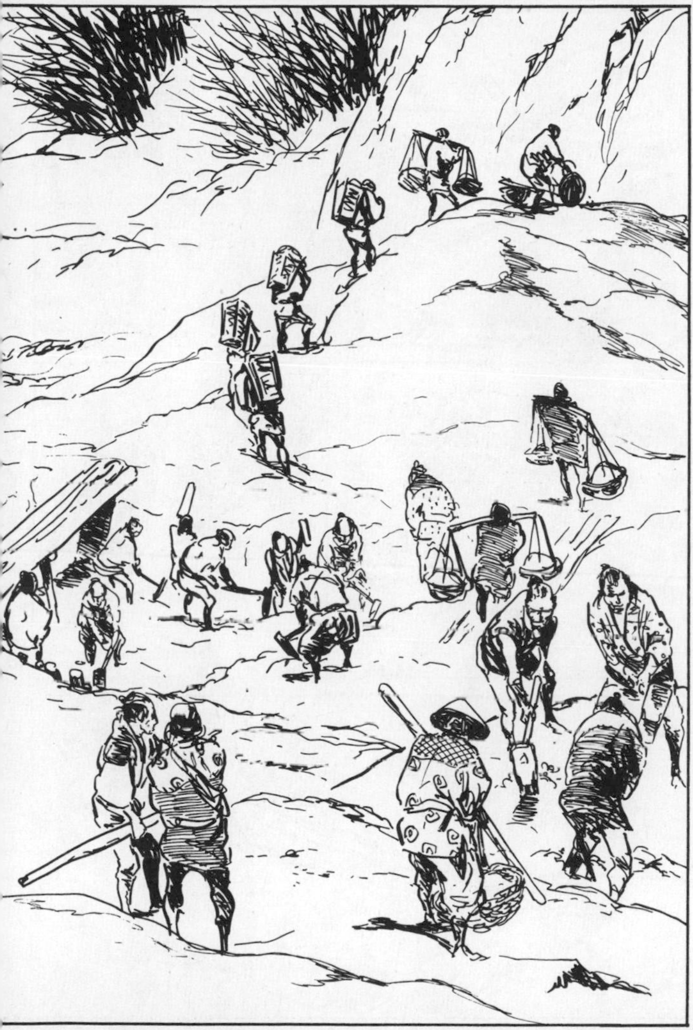

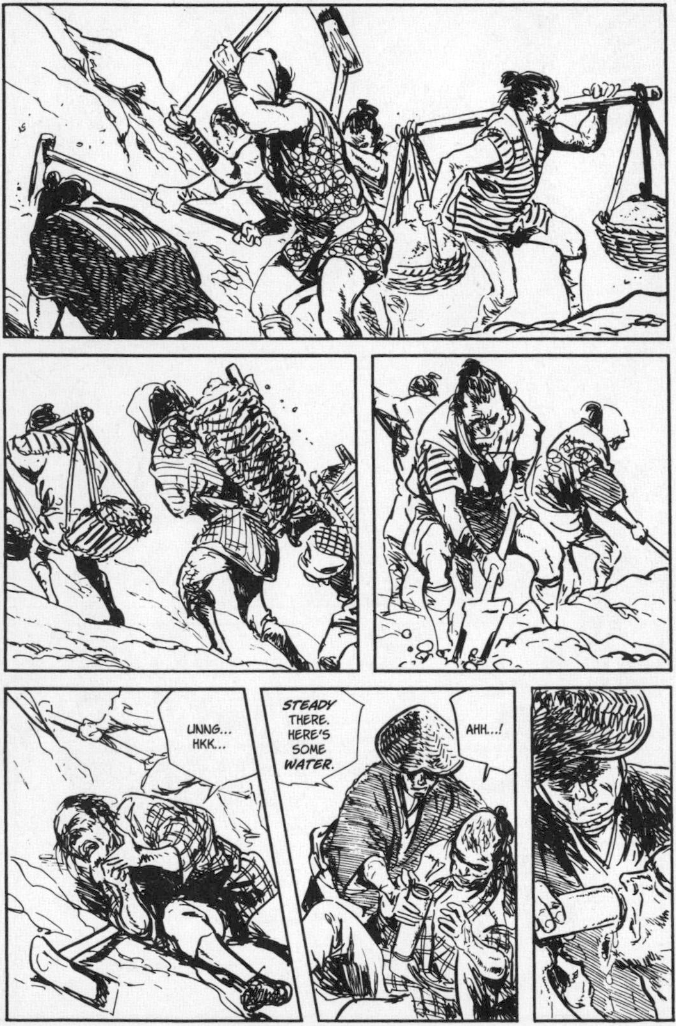
UNNG... HKK...
STEADY THERE. HERE'S SOME WATER.
AHH...!

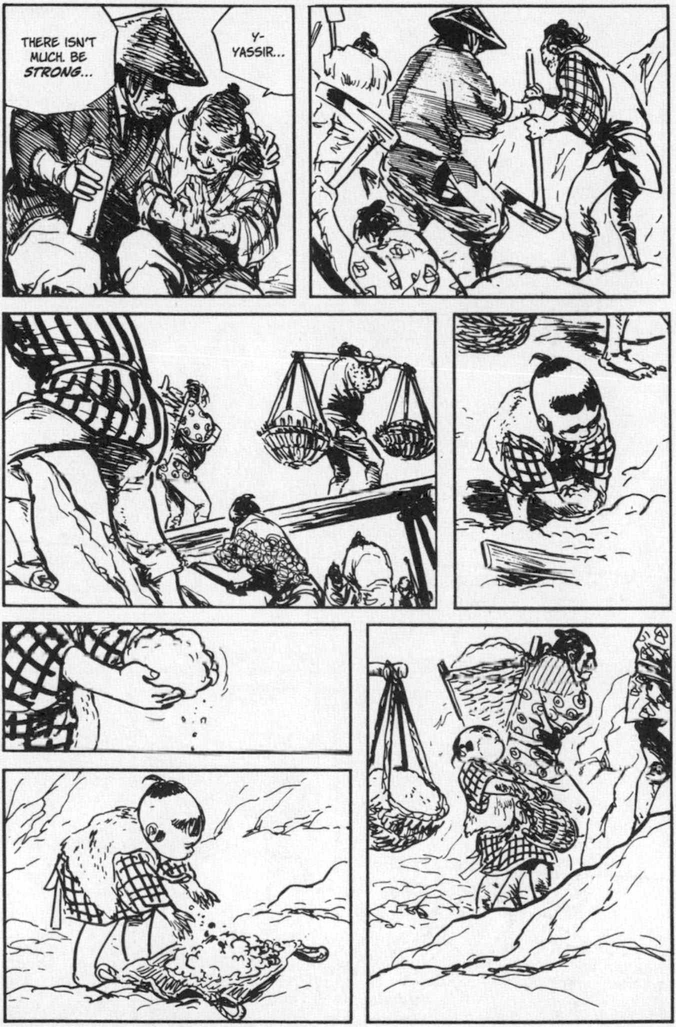
Y-
YASSIR...
THERE ISN'T
MUCH. BE
STRONG...

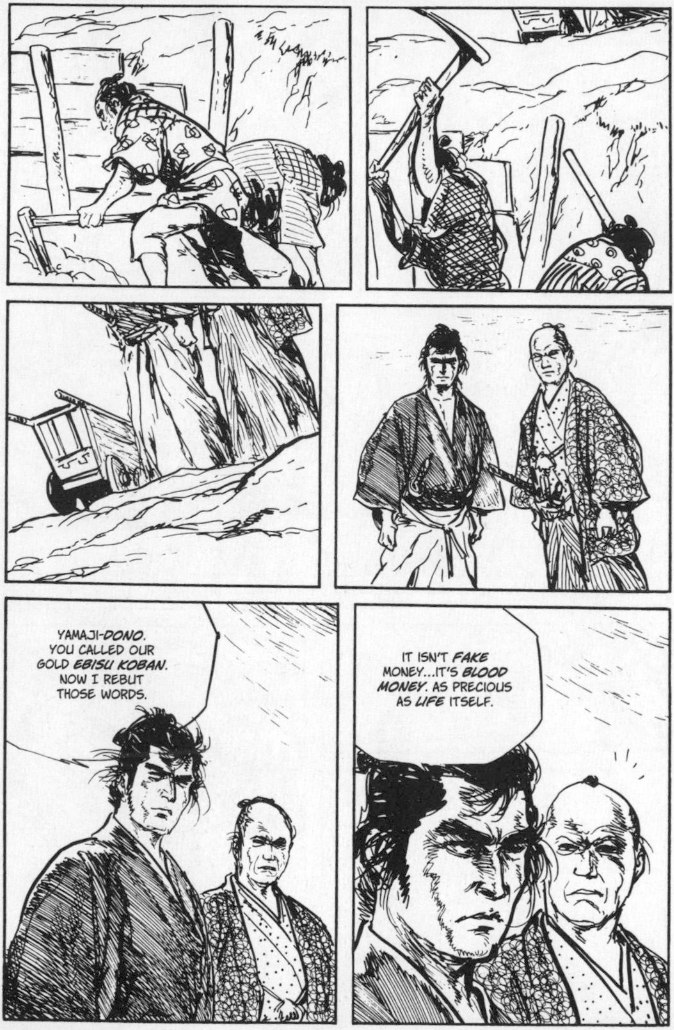
YAMAJI-DONO. YOU CALLED OUR GOLD EBISU KOBAN. NOW I REBUT THOSE WORDS.
IT ISN'T FAKE MONEY...IT'S BLOOD MONEY. AS PRECIOUS AS LIFE ITSELF.

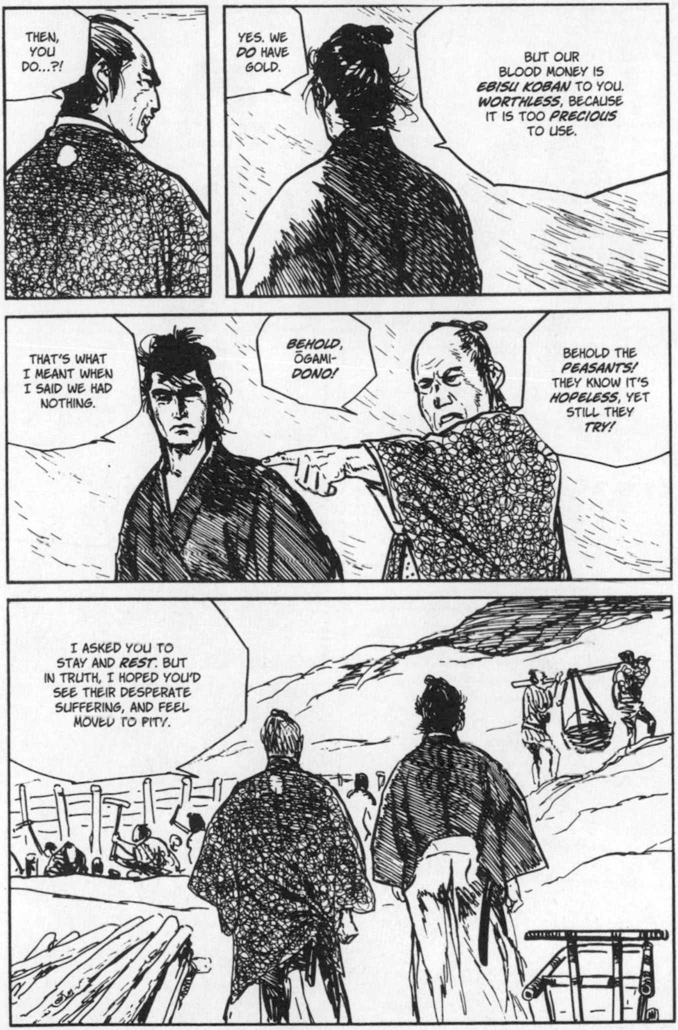
THEN, YOU DO...?!
YES. WE DO HAVE GOLD.
BUT OUR BLOOD MONEY IS EBISU KOBAN TO YOU. WORTHLESS, BECAUSE IT IS TOO PRECIOUS TO USE.
THAT'S WHAT I MEANT WHEN I SAID WE HAD NOTHING.
BEHOLD, ŌGAMI-DONO!
BEHOLD THE PEASANTS! THEY KNOW IT'S HOPELESS, YET STILL THEY TRY!
I ASKED YOU TO STAY AND REST. BUT IN TRUTH, I HOPED YOU'D SEE THEIR DESPERATE SUFFERING, AND FEEL MOVED TO PITY.

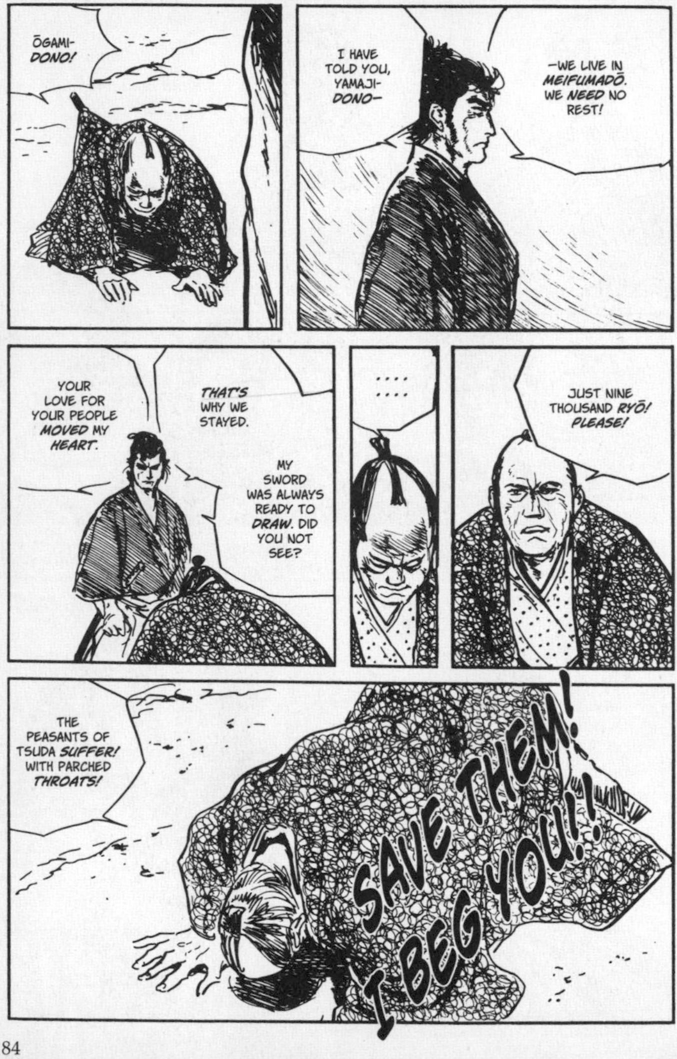
ŌGAMI-DONO!
I HAVE TOLD YOU, YAMAJI-DONO—
—WE LIVE IN MEIFUMADŌ. WE NEED NO REST!
YOUR LOVE FOR YOUR PEOPLE MOVED MY HEART.
THAT'S WHY WE STAYED.
MY SWORD WAS ALWAYS READY TO DRAW. DID YOU NOT SEE?
....
....
JUST NINE THOUSAND RYŌ! PLEASE!
THE PEASANTS OF TSUDA SUFFER! WITH PARCHED THROATS!
SAVE THEM! I BEG YOU!!

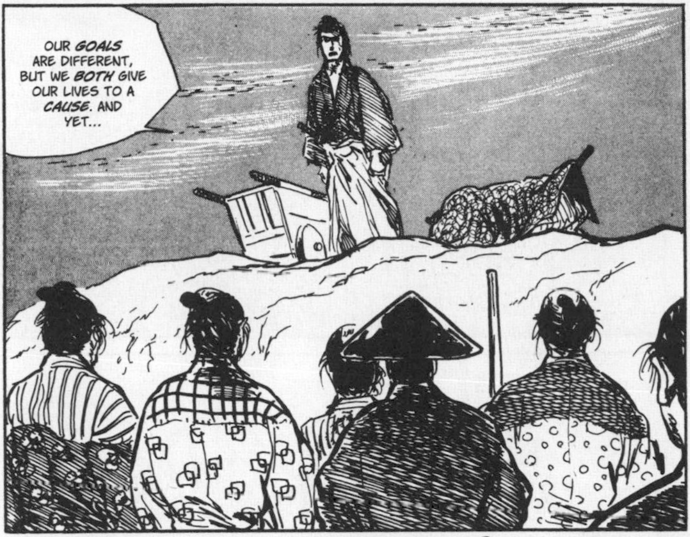
OUR GOALS ARE DIFFERENT, BUT WE BOTH GIVE OUR LIVES TO A CAUSE. AND YET...

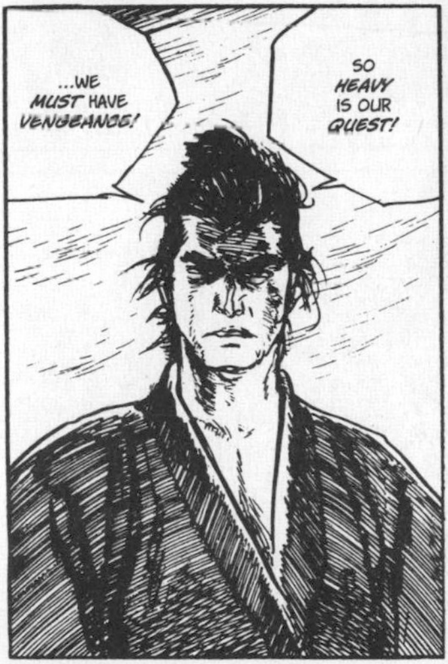
...WE MUST HAVE VENGEANCE!
SO HEAVY IS OUR QUEST!

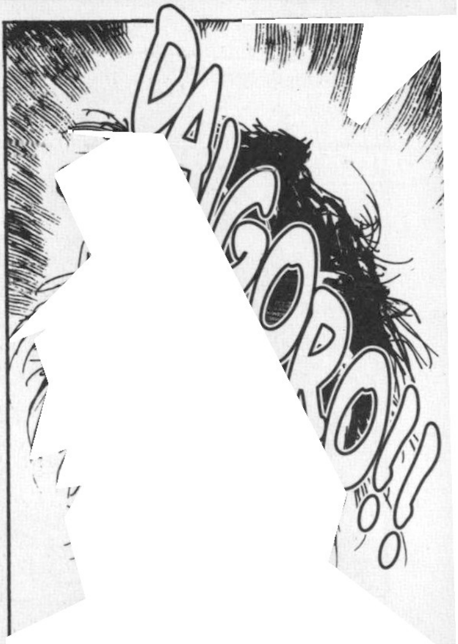
DAIGORO!!

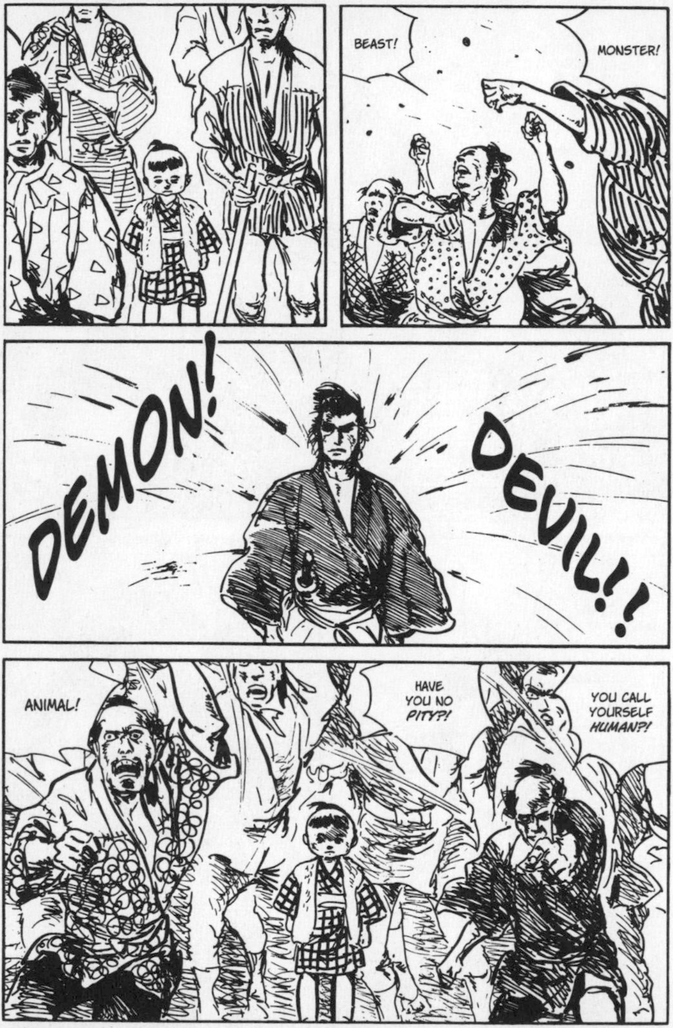
BEAST!
MONSTER!
DEMON!
DEVIL!!!
ANIMAL!
HAVE YOU NO *PITY?!*
YOU CALL YOURSELF *HUMAN?!*

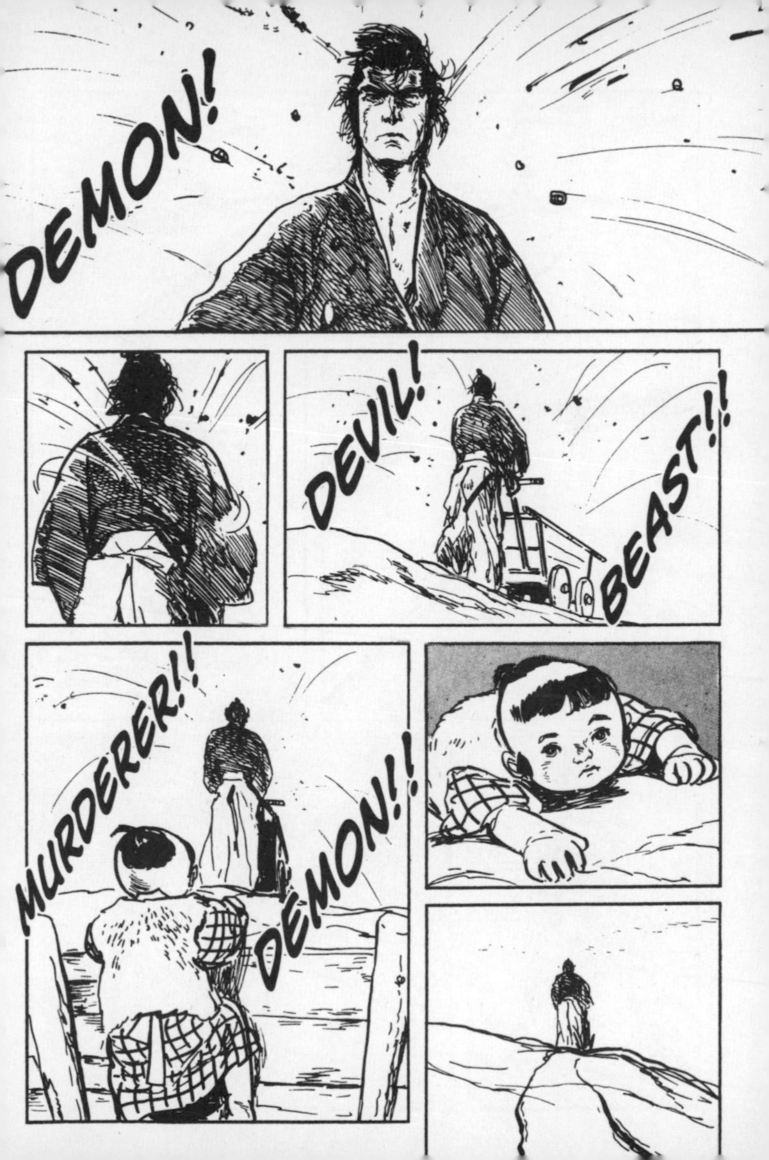
DEMON!
DEVIL!
BEAST!!
DEMON!!
MURDERER!!

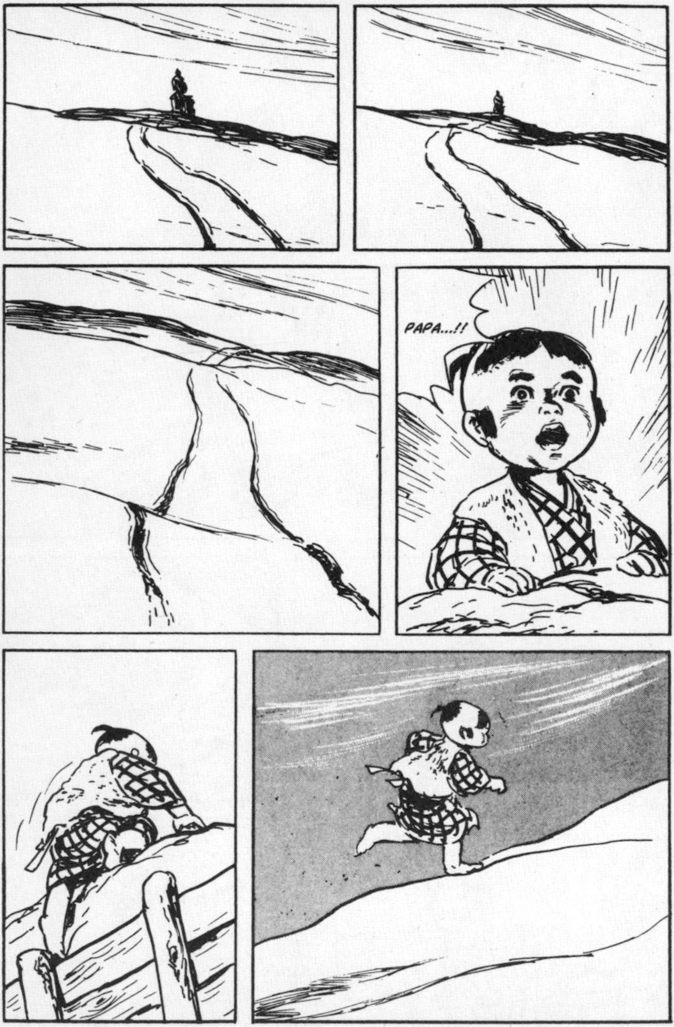
PAPA...!!

the ninety-first

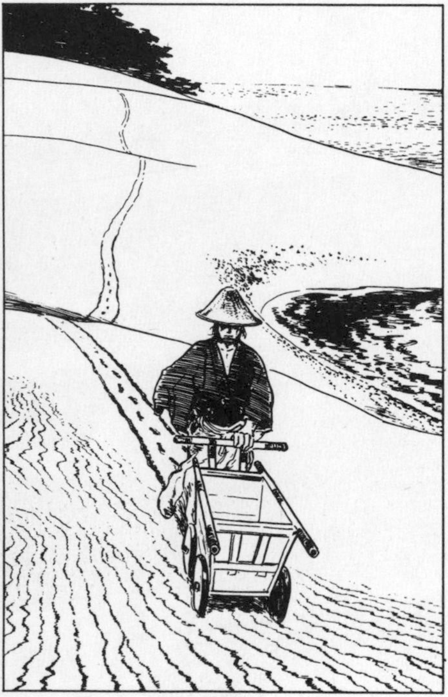

Lifeline

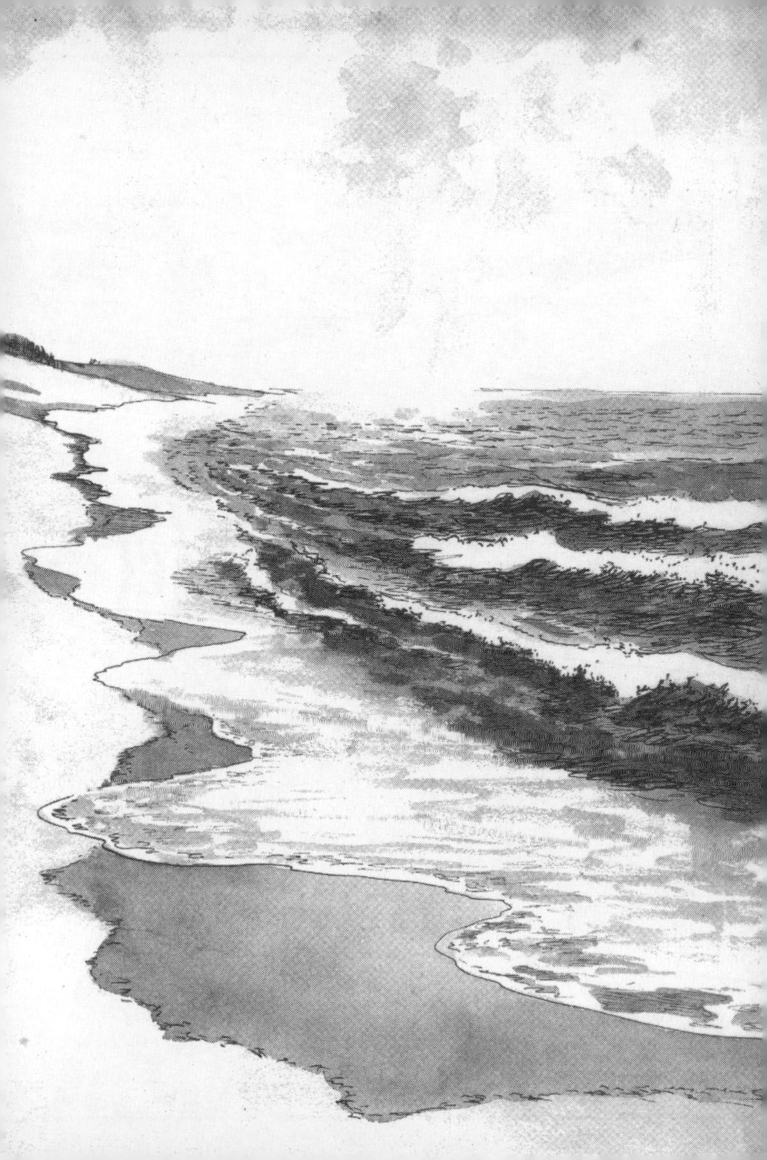

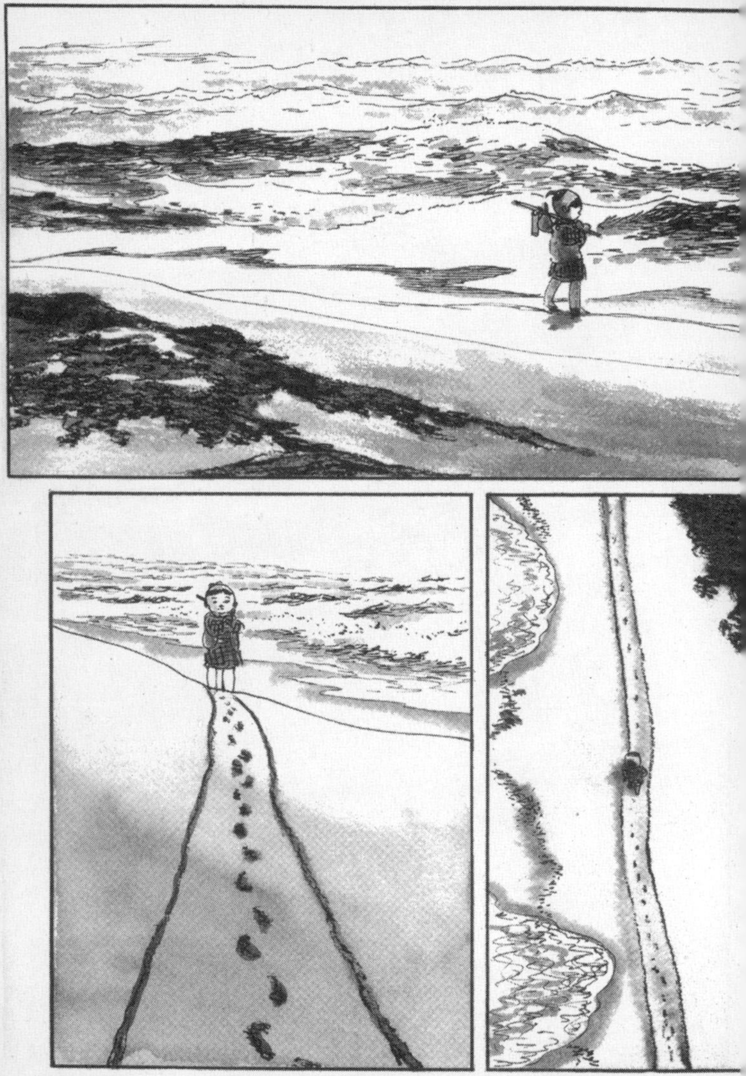

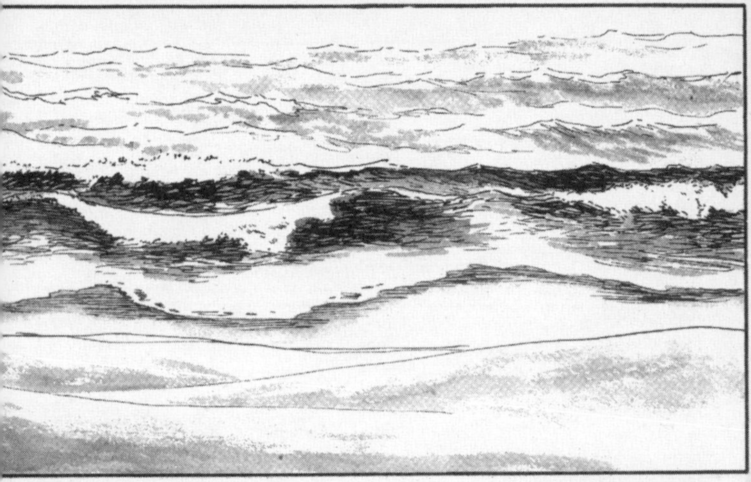

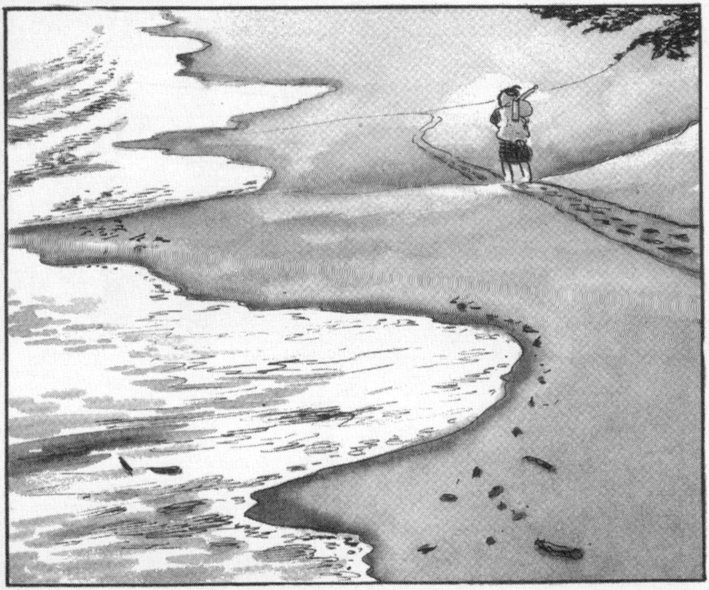

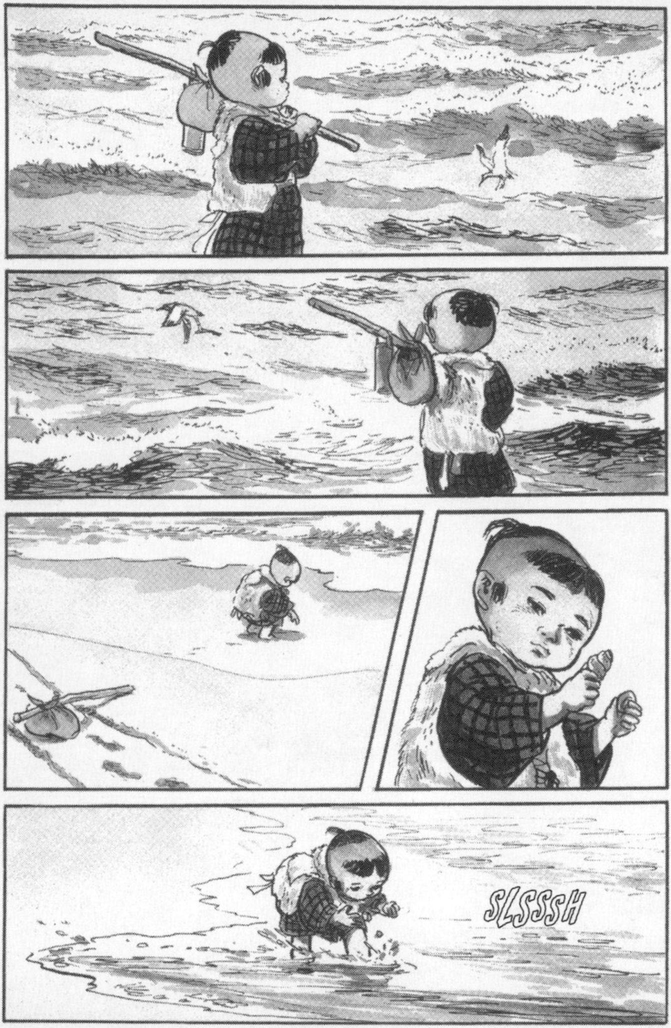
SLSSSH

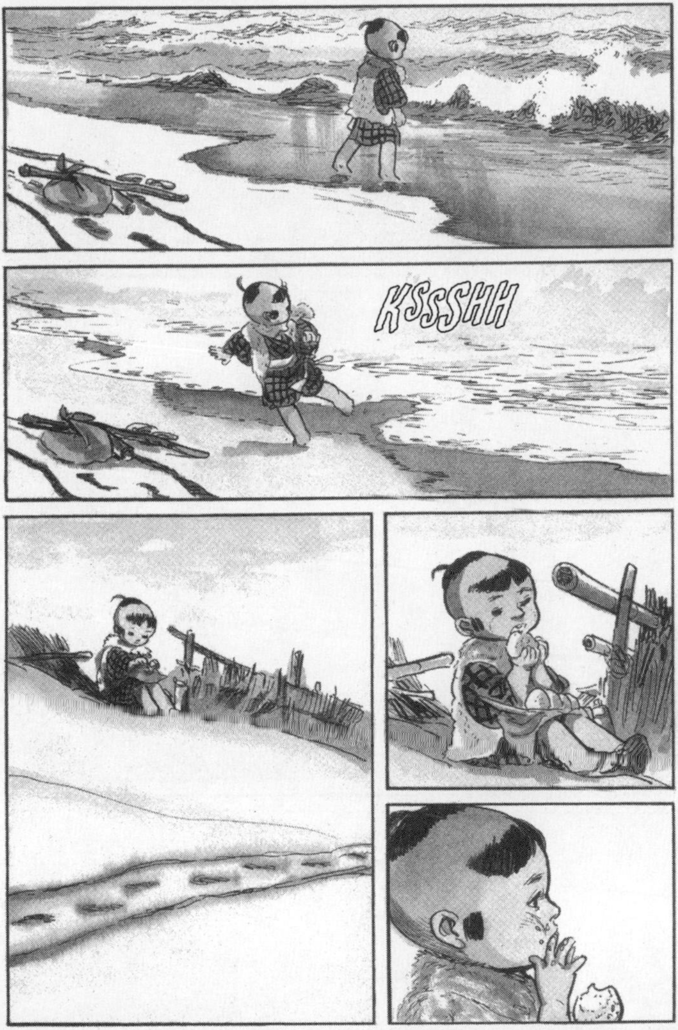
KSSSHH

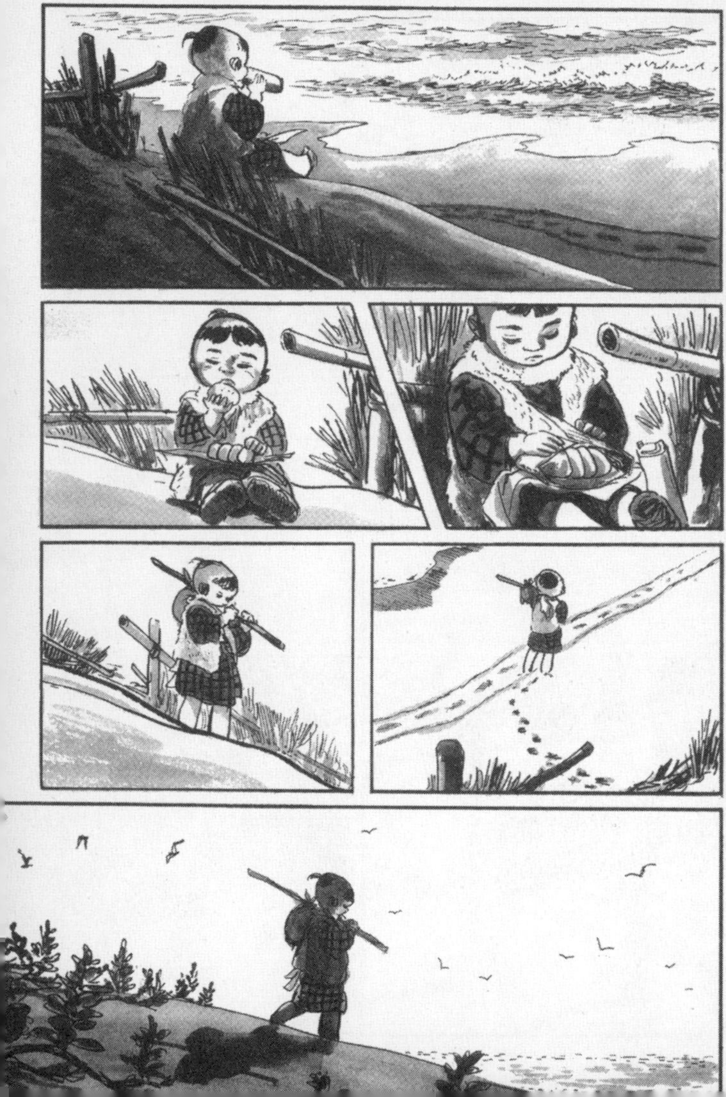

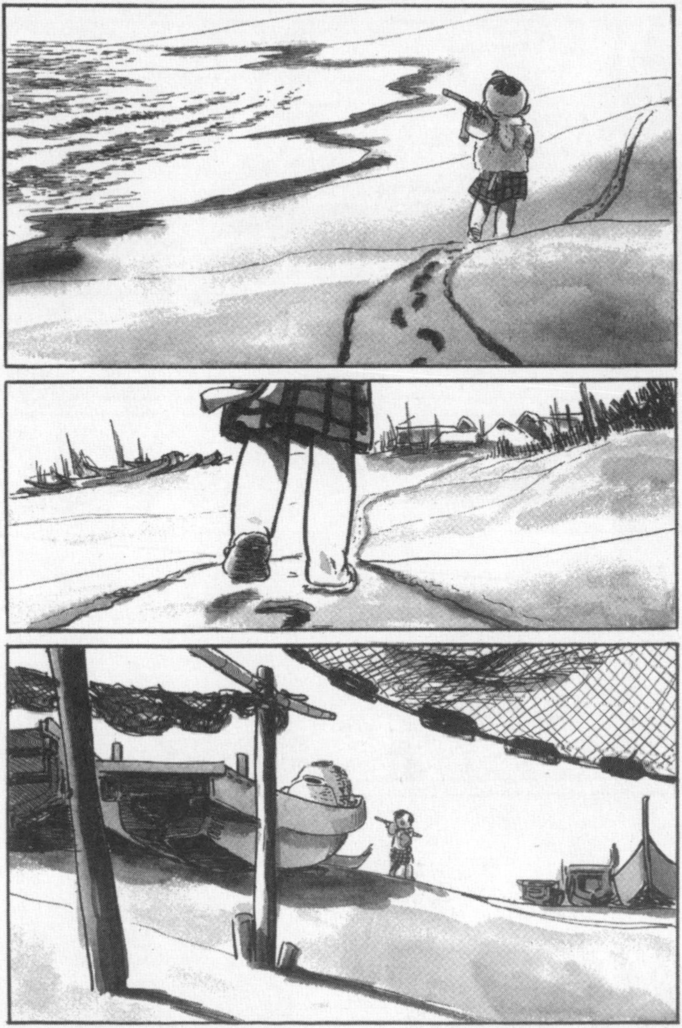

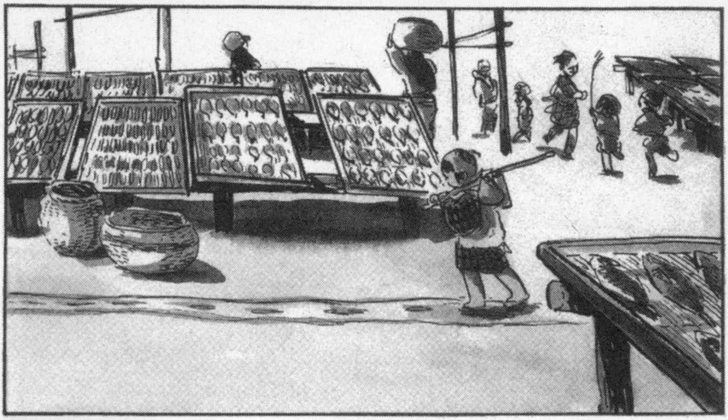

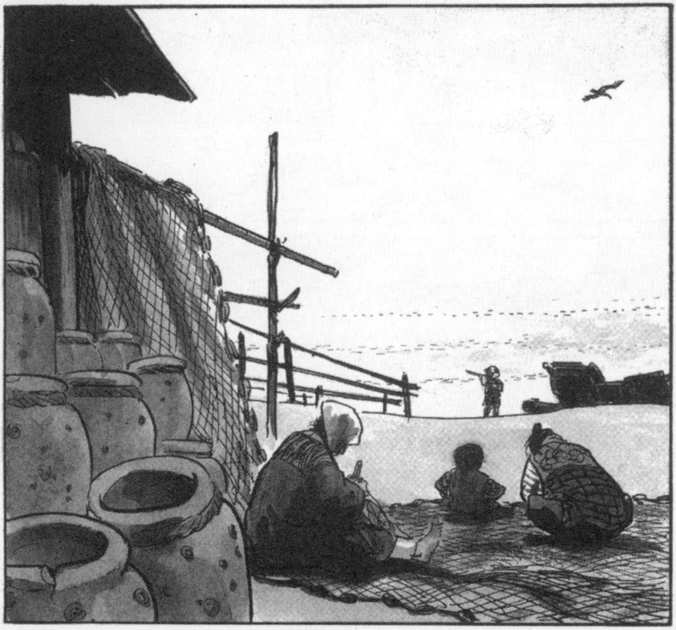

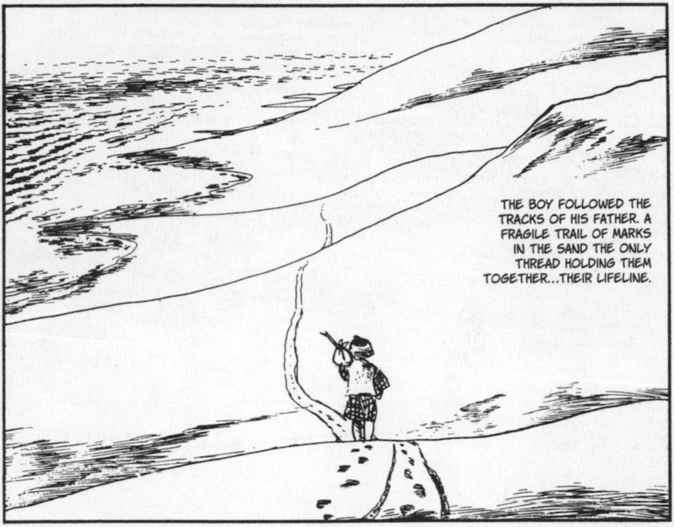
THE BOY FOLLOWED THE TRACKS OF HIS FATHER. A FRAGILE TRAIL OF MARKS IN THE SAND THE ONLY THREAD HOLDING THEM TOGETHER...THEIR LIFELINE.

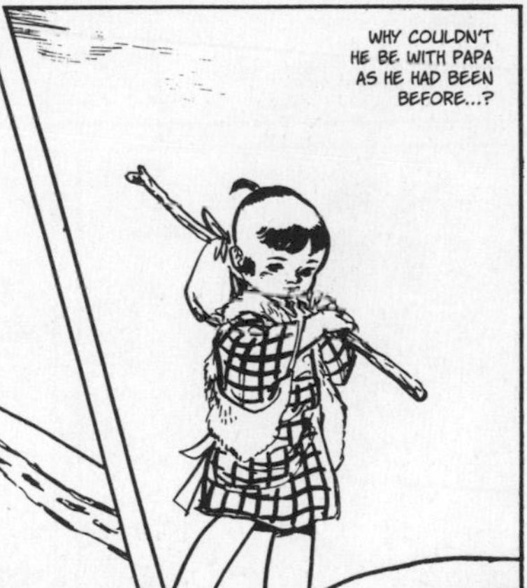
WHY COULDN'T HE BE WITH PAPA AS HE HAD BEEN BEFORE...?

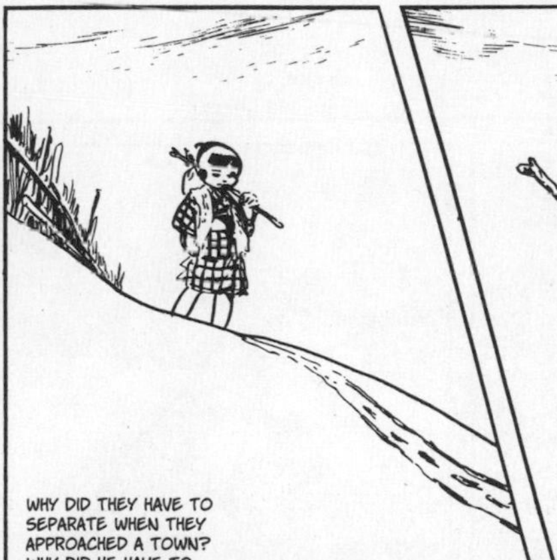
WHY DID THEY HAVE TO SEPARATE WHEN THEY APPROACHED A TOWN? WHY DID HE HAVE TO FOLLOW HIS FATHER'S FOOTSTEPS FROM SO FAR AWAY...?

THEY WERE PURSUED.
TO AVOID SHEDDING
INNOCENT BLOOD, IT
WAS BEST TO AVOID
HOSTILE EYES. SO
REASONABLE...BUT DID
THE BOY UNDERSTAND?

HE ONLY
FOLLOWED
HIS FATHER'S
FOOTPRINTS.

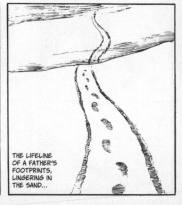

THE LIFELINE
OF A FATHER'S
FOOTPRINTS,
LINGERING IN
THE SAND...

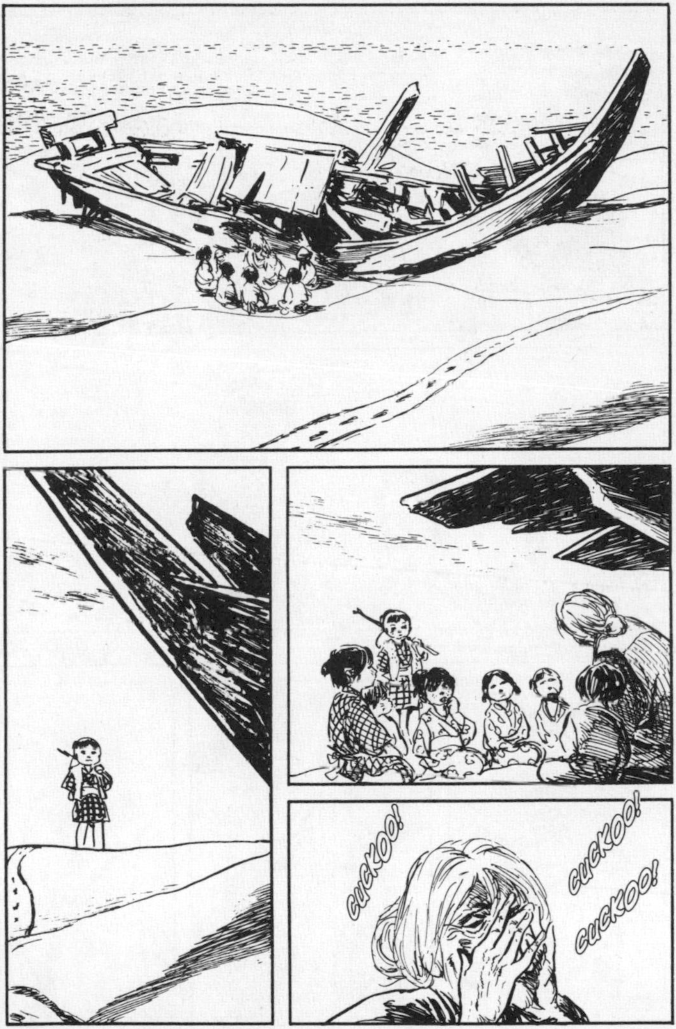
CUCKOO!
CUCKOO!
CUCKOO!

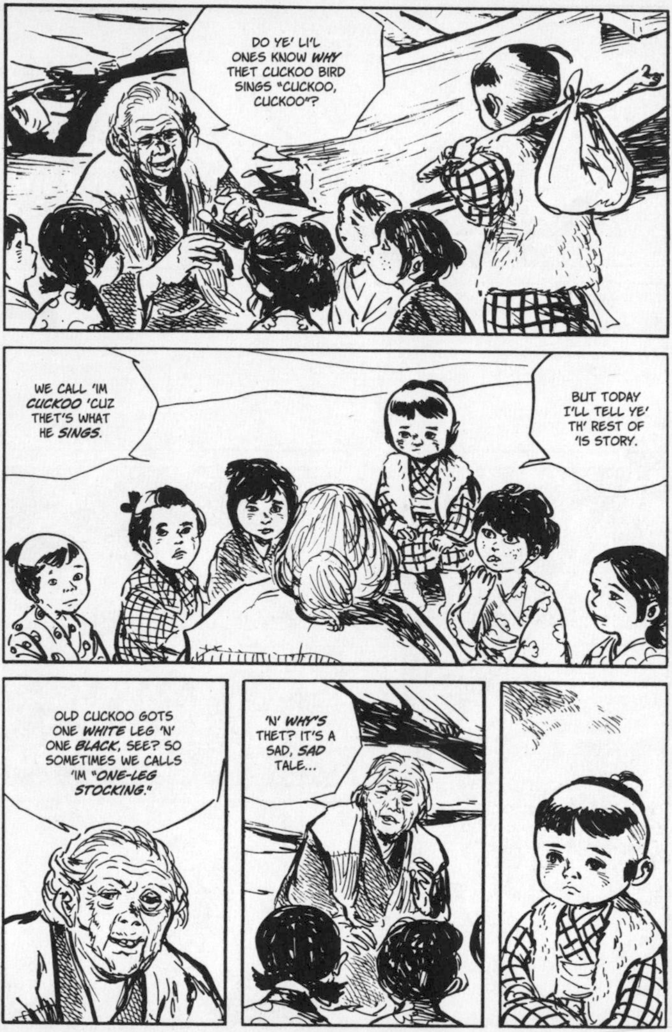
DO YE' LI'L ONES KNOW *WHY* THET CUCKOO BIRD SINGS "CUCKOO, CUCKOO"?
WE CALL 'IM *CUCKOO* 'CUZ THET'S WHAT HE *SINGS*.
BUT TODAY I'LL TELL YE' TH' REST OF 'IS STORY.
OLD CUCKOO GOTS ONE *WHITE* LEG 'N' ONE *BLACK*, SEE? SO SOMETIMES WE CALLS 'IM *"ONE-LEG STOCKING."*
'N' *WHY'S* THET? IT'S A SAD, *SAD* TALE...

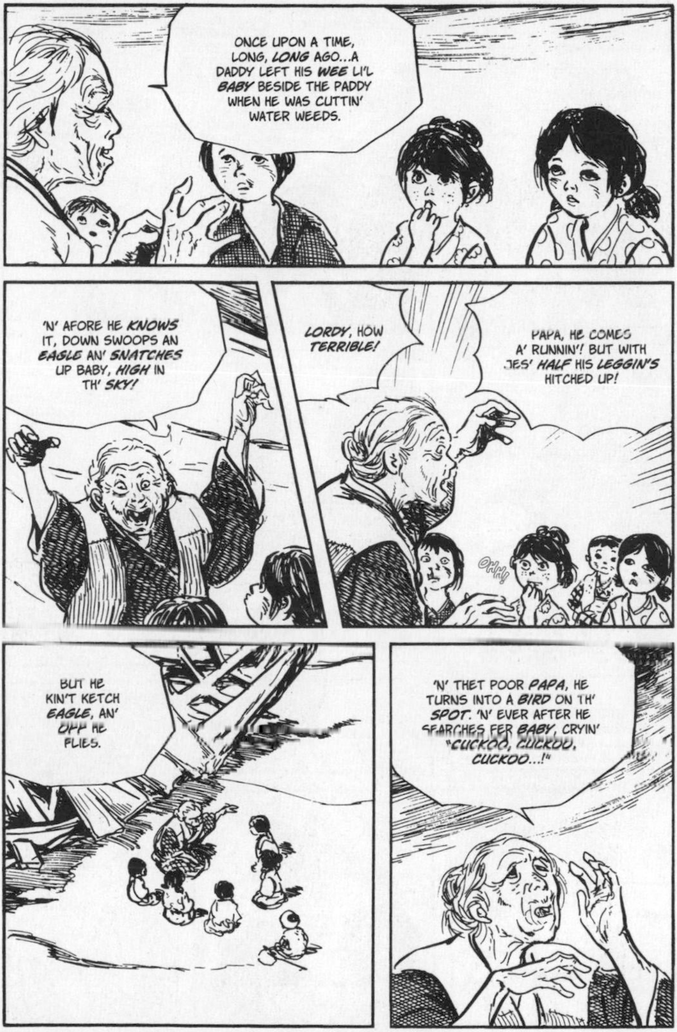
ONCE UPON A TIME, LONG, LONG AGO...A DADDY LEFT HIS WEE LI'L BABY BESIDE THE PADDY WHEN HE WAS CUTTIN' WATER WEEDS.
'N' AFORE HE KNOWS IT, DOWN SWOOPS AN EAGLE AN' SNATCHES UP BABY, HIGH IN TH' SKY!
LORDY, HOW TERRIBLE!
PAPA, HE COMES A' RUNNIN'! BUT WITH JES' HALF HIS LEGGIN'S HITCHED UP!
OHH!
BUT HE KIN'T KETCH EAGLE, AN' OFF HE FLIES.
'N' THET POOR PAPA, HE TURNS INTO A BIRD ON TH' SPOT. 'N' EVER AFTER HE SEARCHES FER BABY, CRYIN' "CUCKOO, CUCKOO, CUCKOO...!"

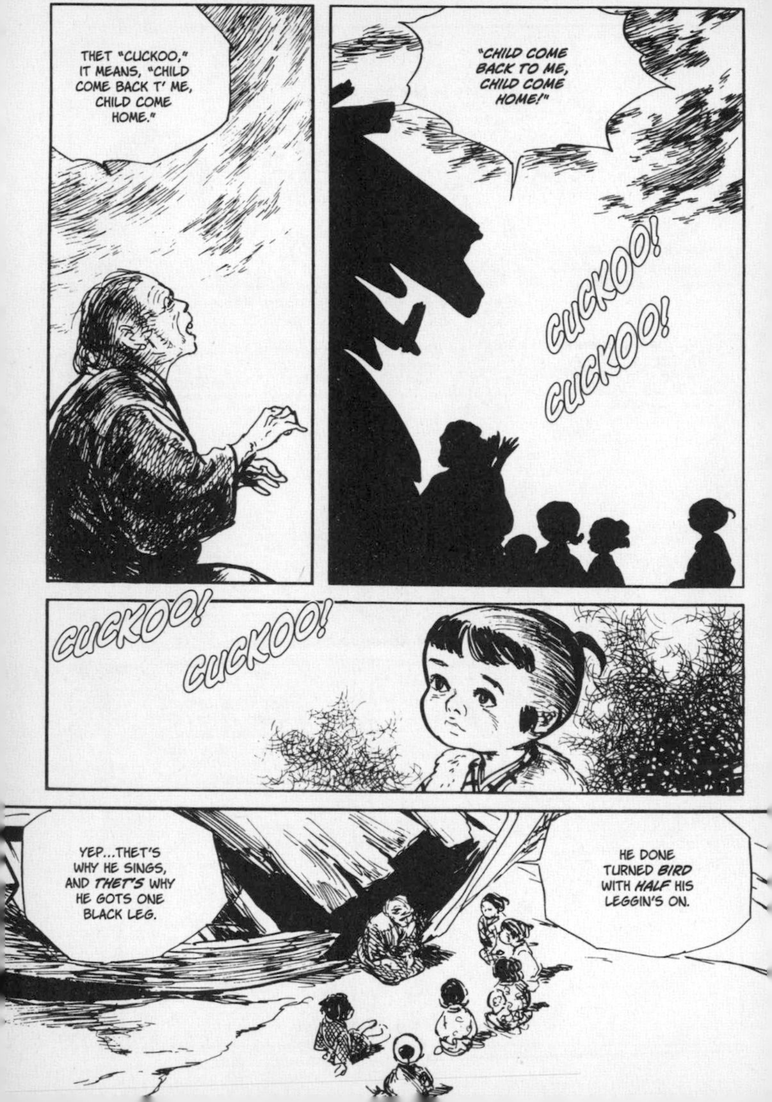
THET "CUCKOO," IT MEANS, "CHILD COME BACK T' ME, CHILD COME HOME."
"CHILD COME BACK TO ME, CHILD COME HOME!"
CUCKOO! CUCKOO!
CUCKOO! CUCKOO!
YEP...THET'S WHY HE SINGS, AND *THET'S* WHY HE GOTS ONE BLACK LEG.
HE DONE TURNED *BIRD* WITH *HALF* HIS LEGGIN'S ON.

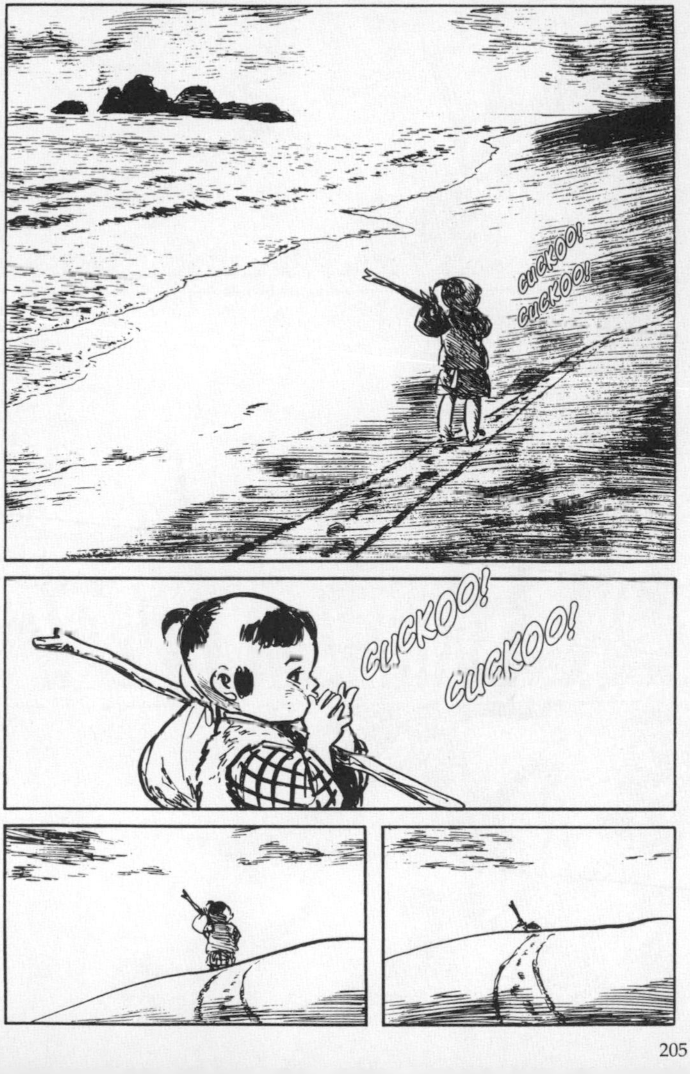
CUCKOO!
CUCKOO!
CUCKOO!
CUCKOO!

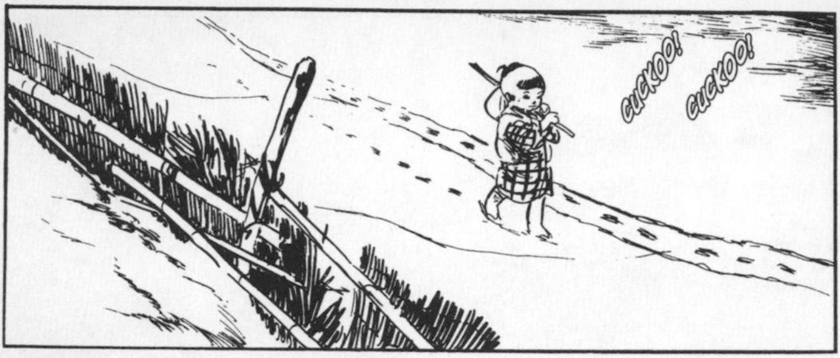
CUCKOO!
CUCKOO!

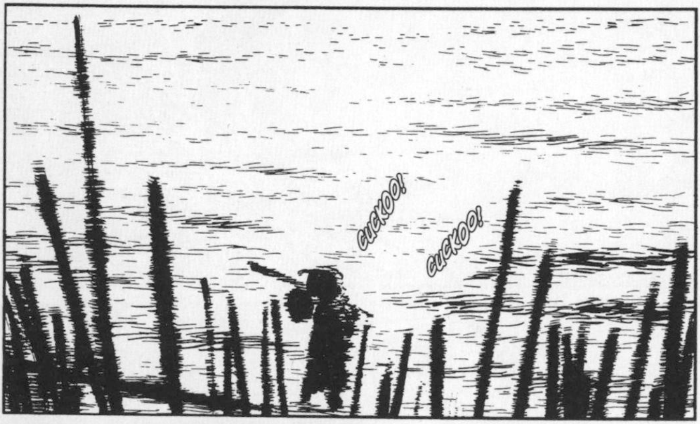
CUCKOO!
CUCKOO!

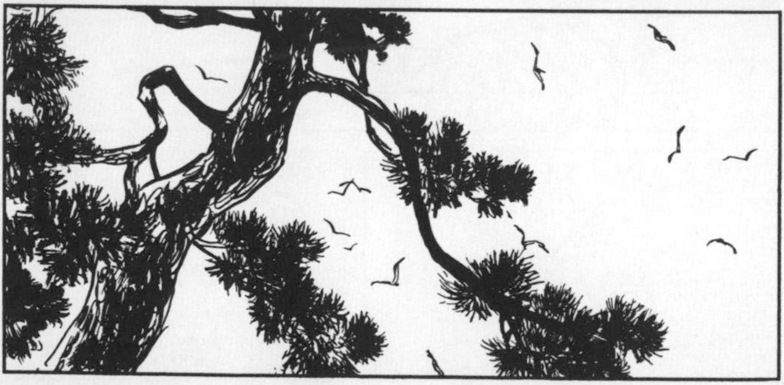

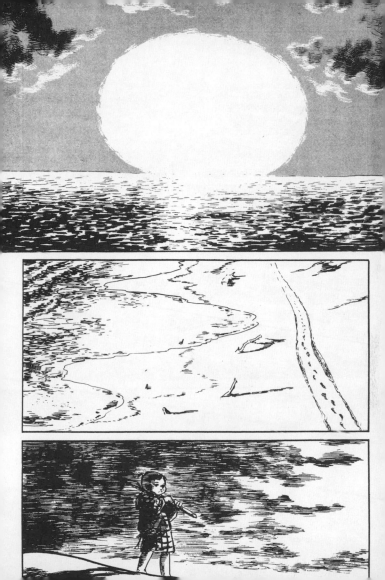

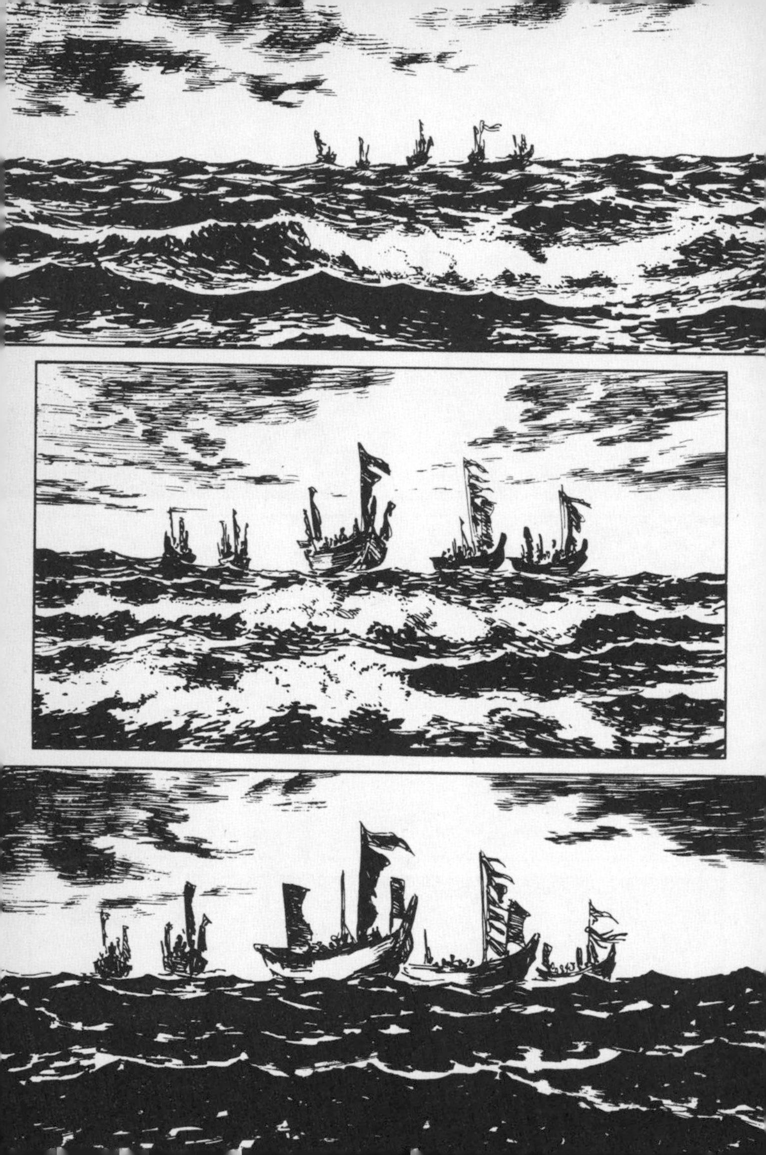

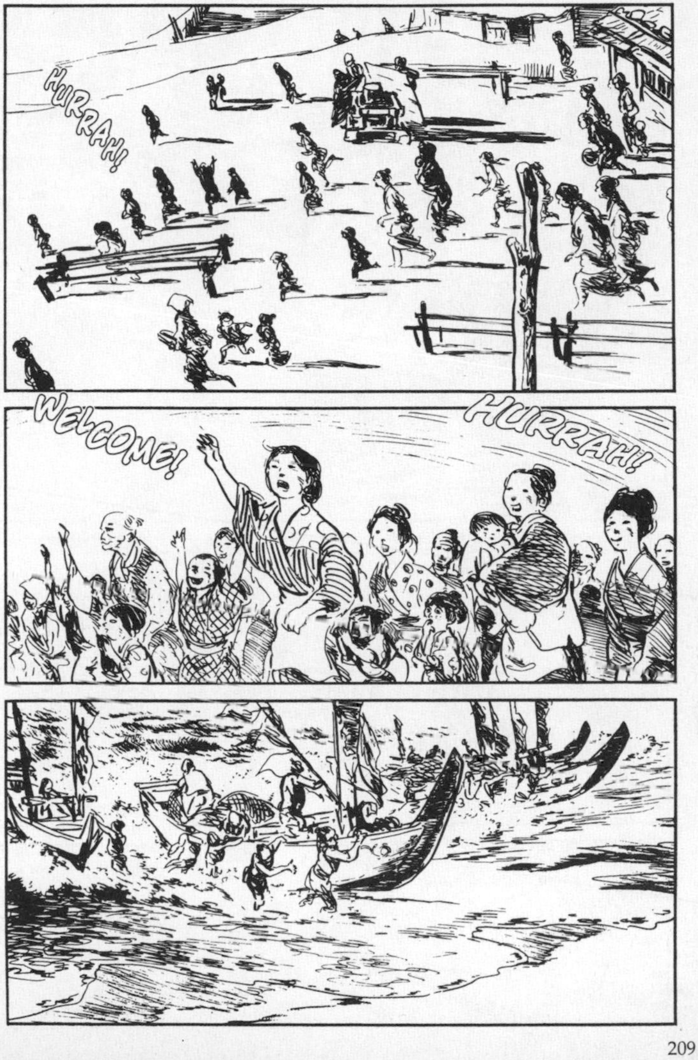
HURRAH!
HURRAH!
WELCOME!

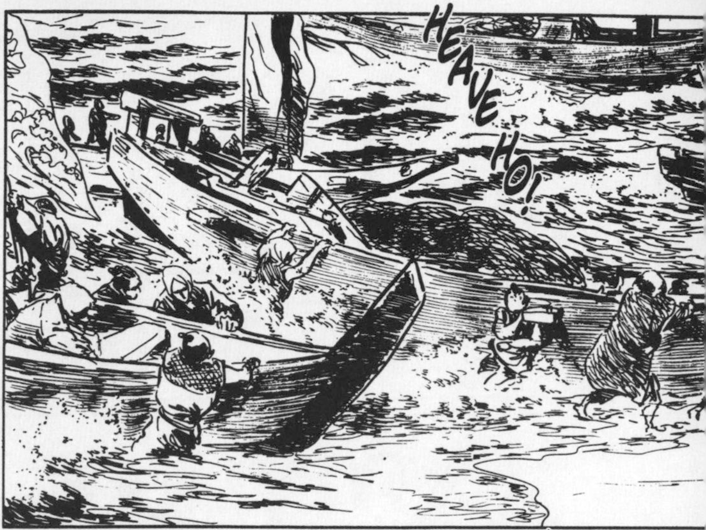
HEAVE HO!

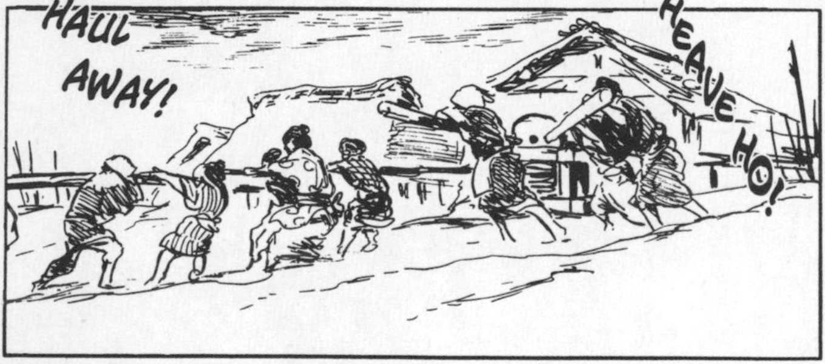
HEAVE HO!
HAUL AWAY!

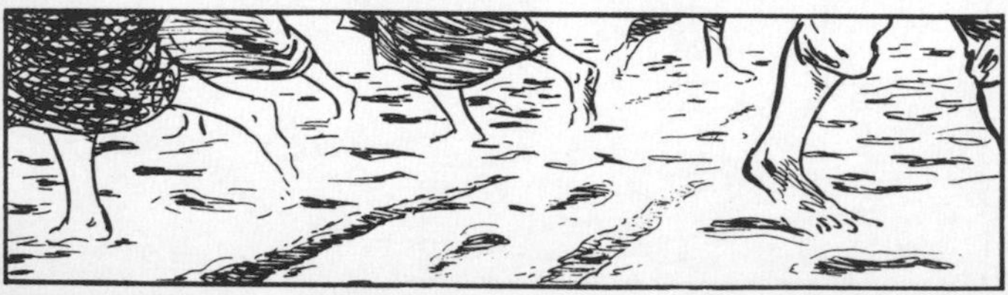

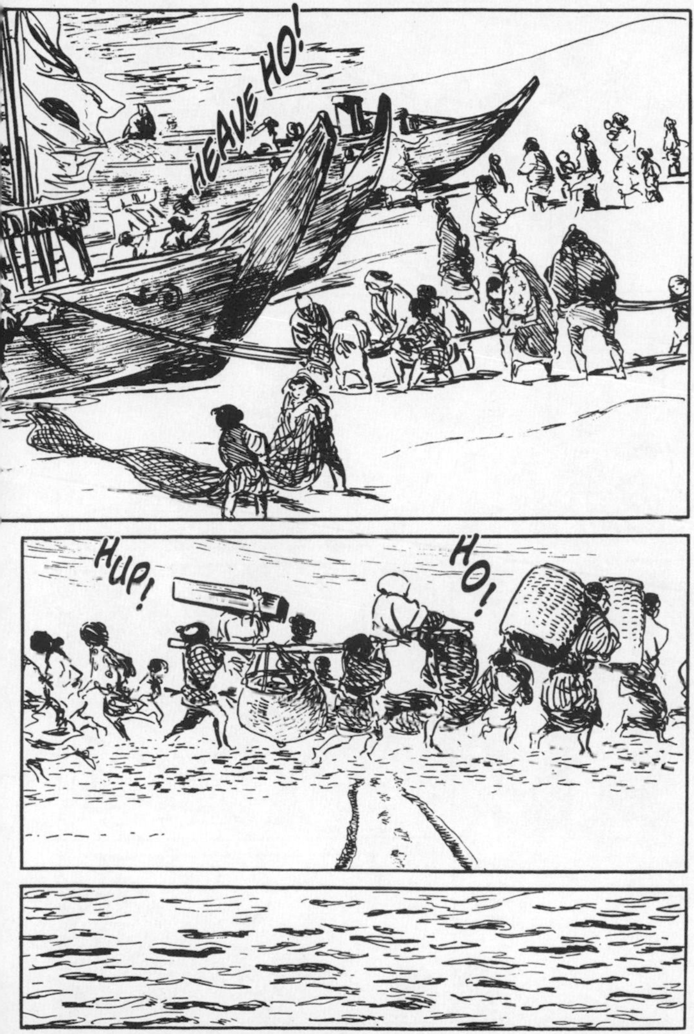
HEAVE HO!
HO!
HUP!

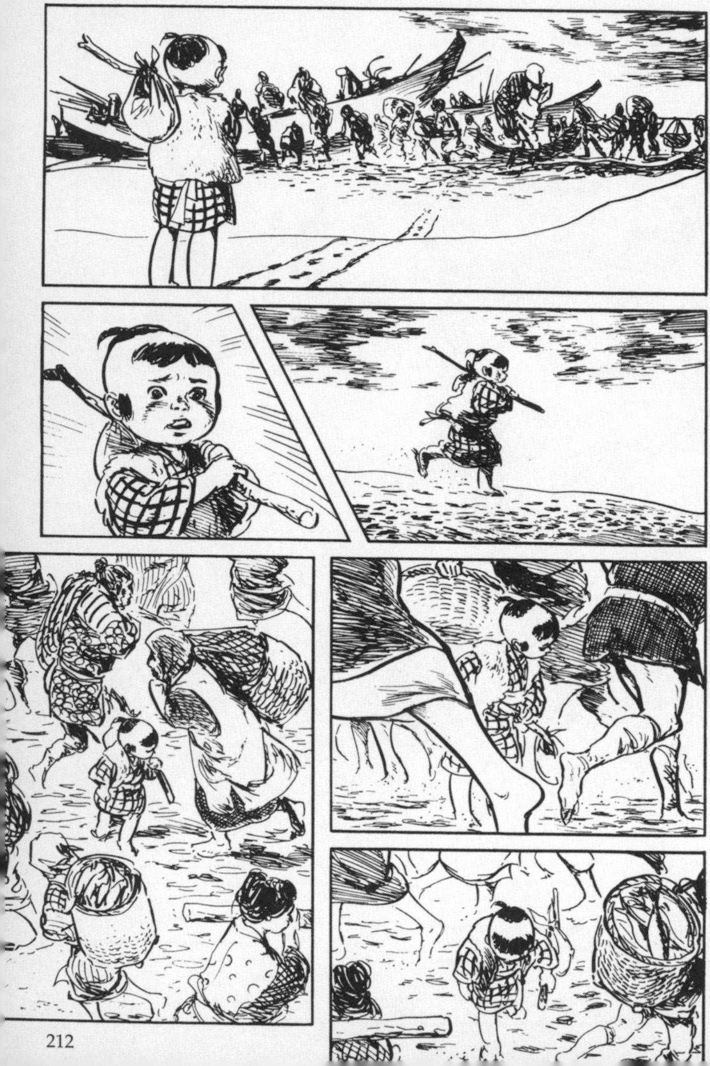

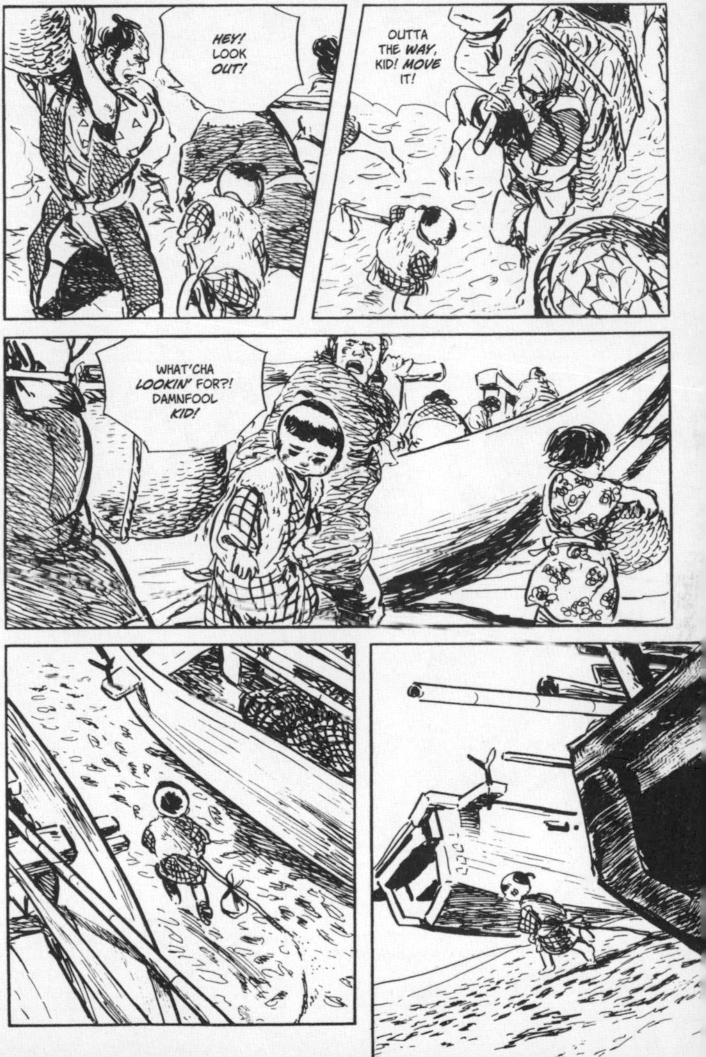
HEY! LOOK OUT!
OUTTA THE WAY, KID! MOVE IT!
WHAT'CHA LOOKIN' FOR?! DAMNFOOL KID!

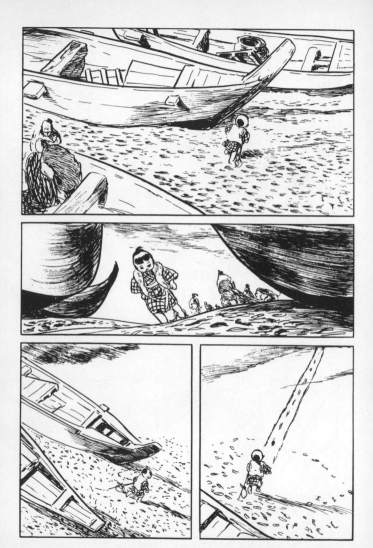

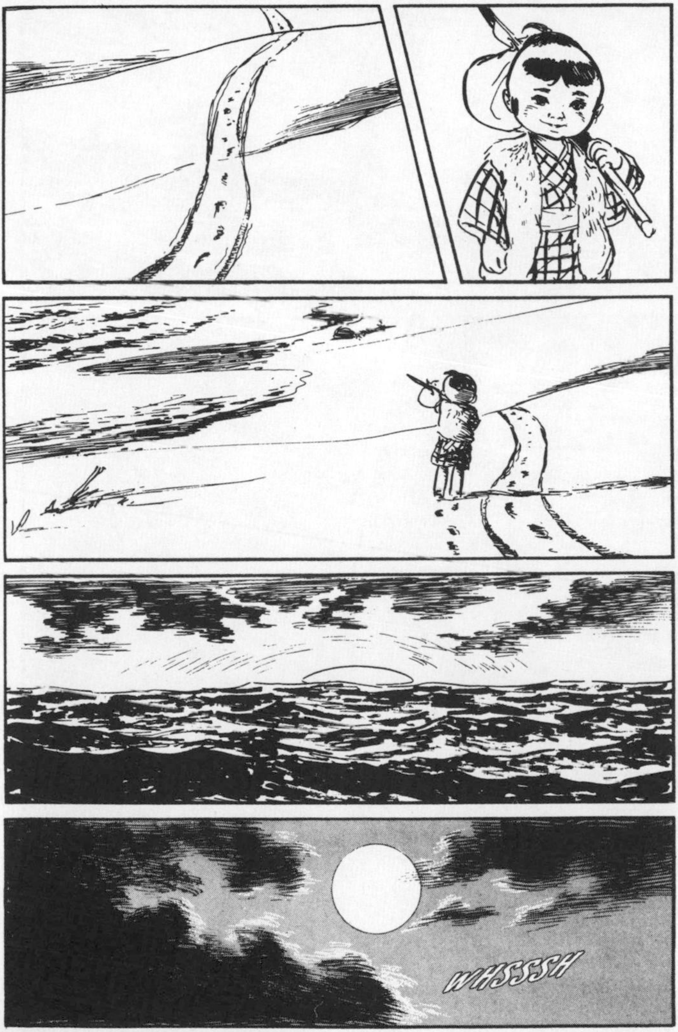
WHSSSH

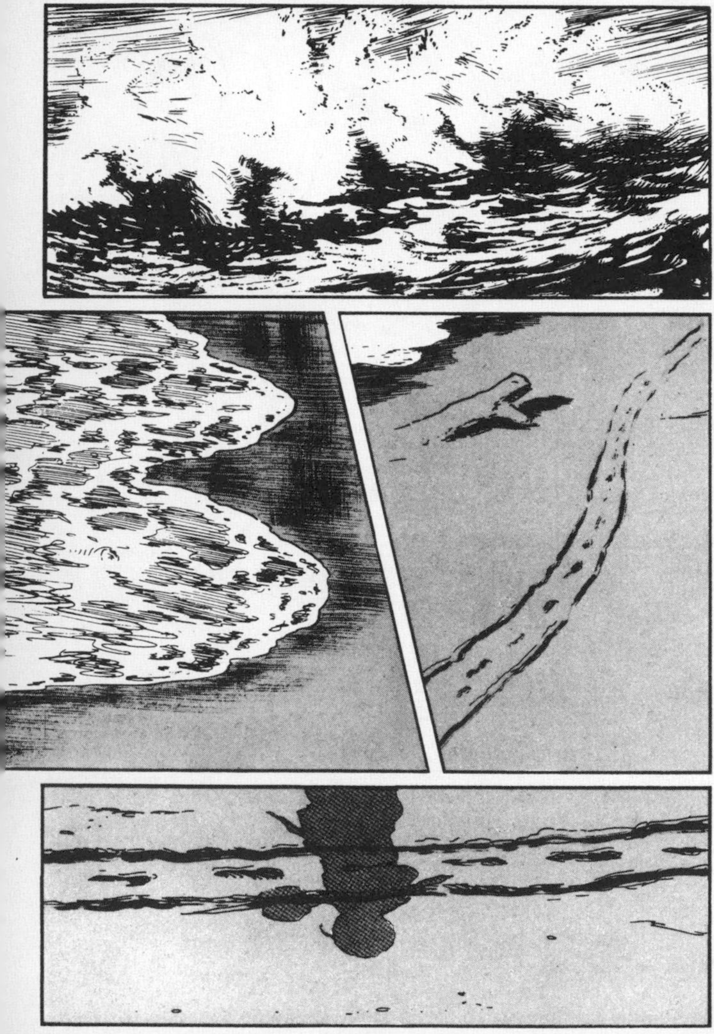

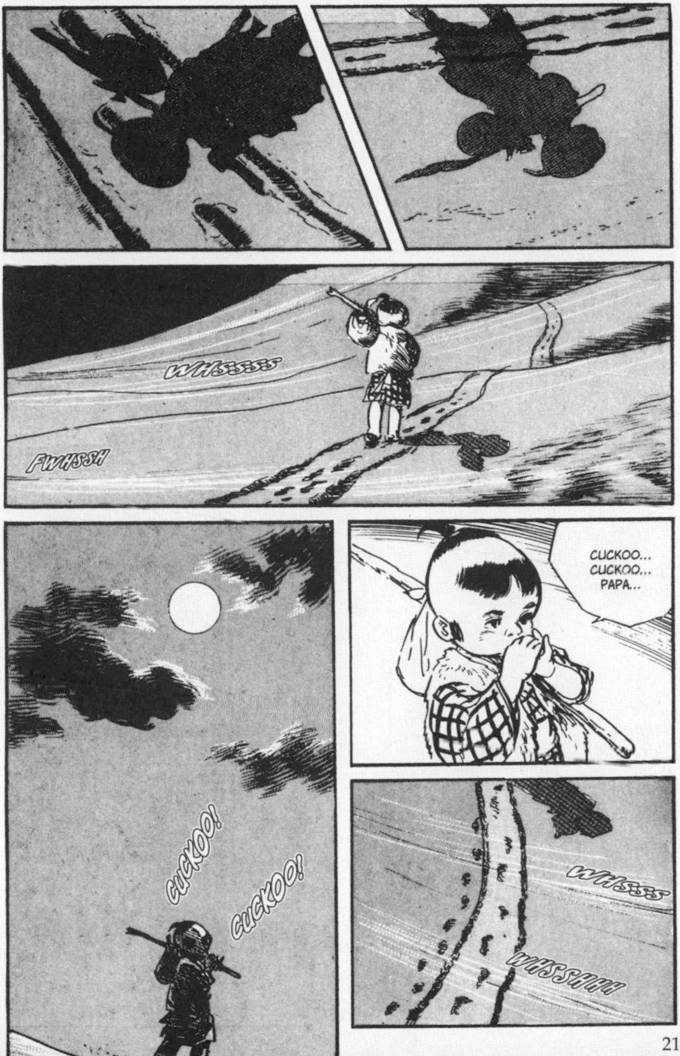
WHSSSS
FWHSSH
CUCKOO... CUCKOO... PAPA...
WHSSSS
WHSSHHH
CUCKOO!
CUCKOO!

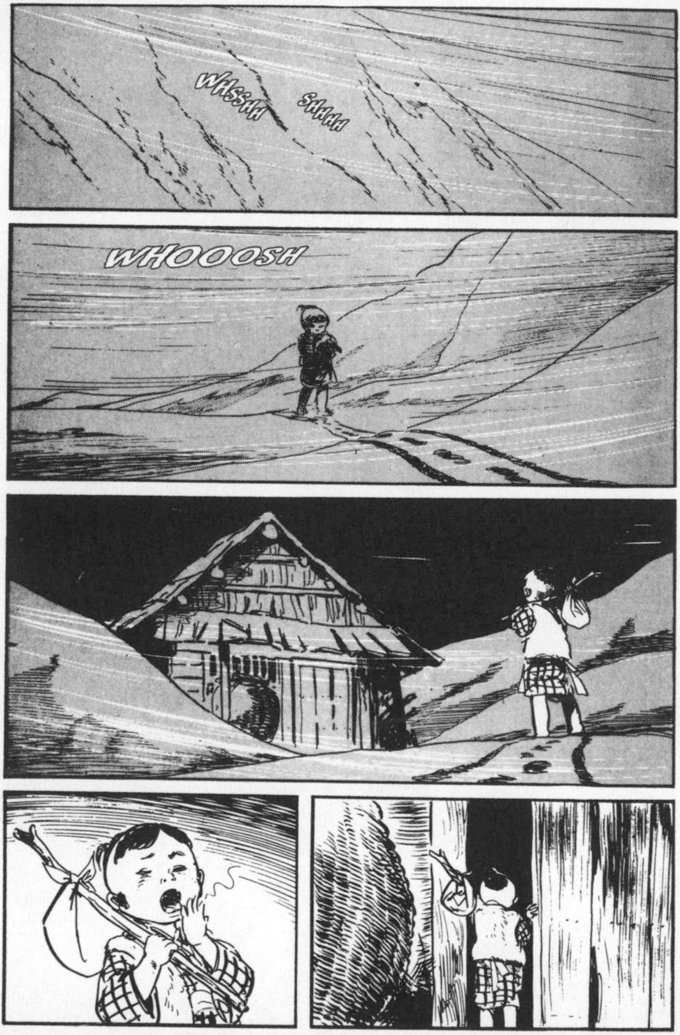
WHSSHH
SHHHH
WHOOOSH

WHSSSSSH

FWSSSSH

FWHSSSHH

TAK
KTAK
KAK

KTAK BAM

KTAK

WHSSSSH

WHOOOSH

WHSSSSSH

219

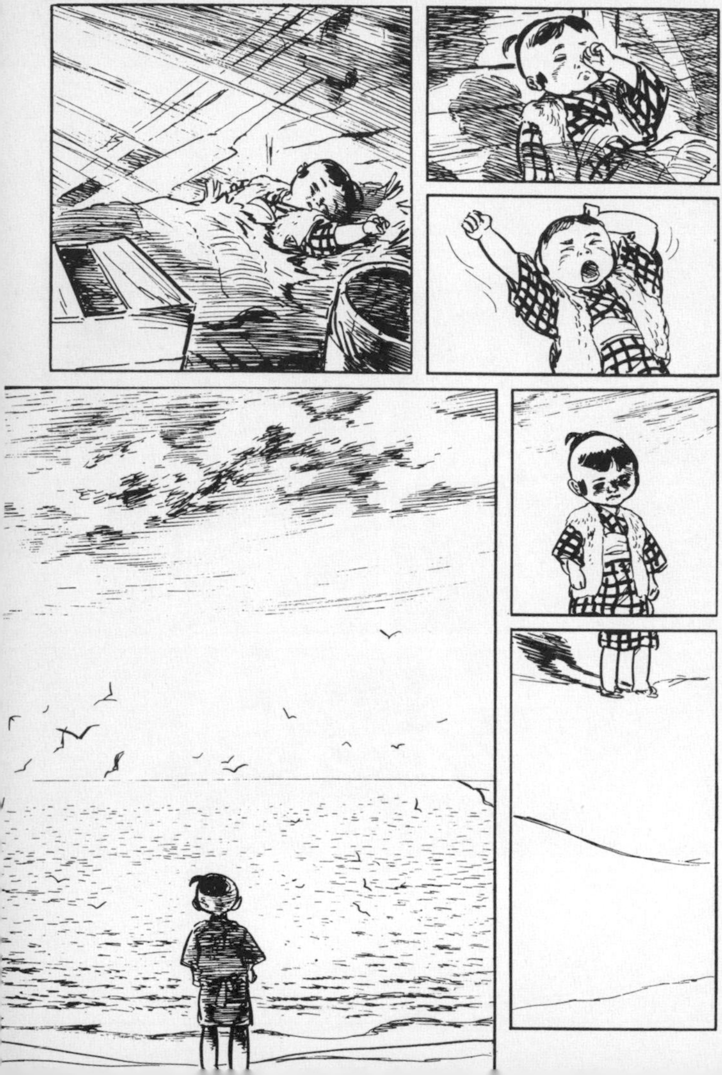

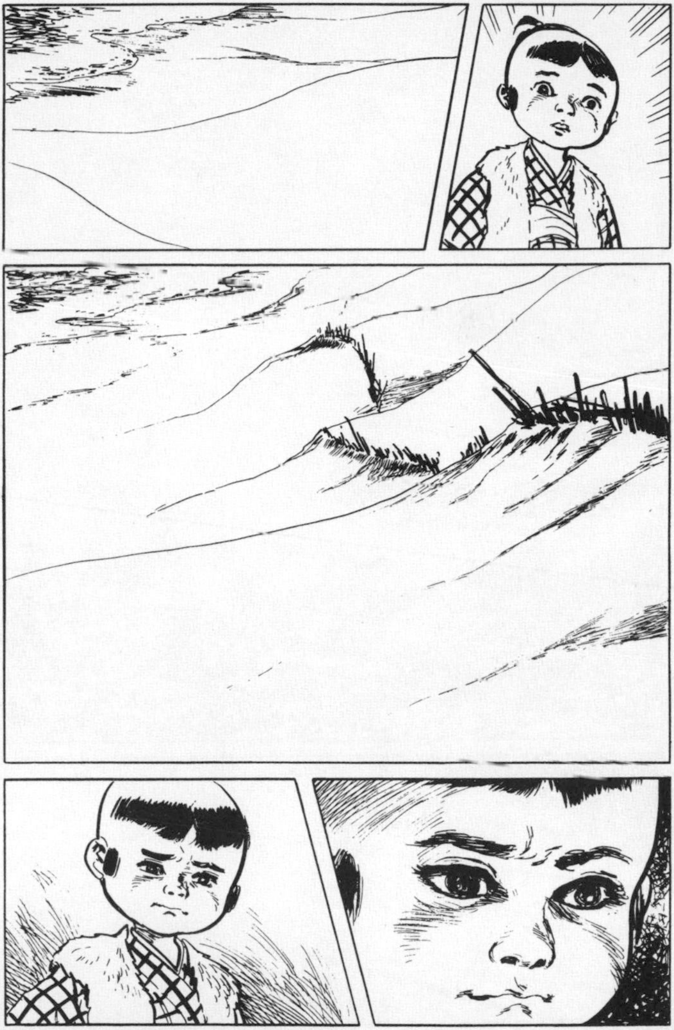

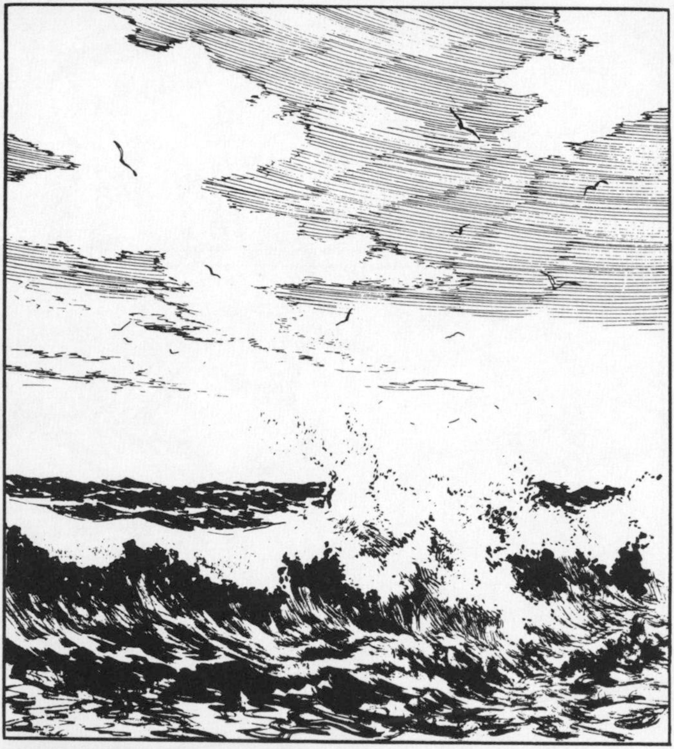
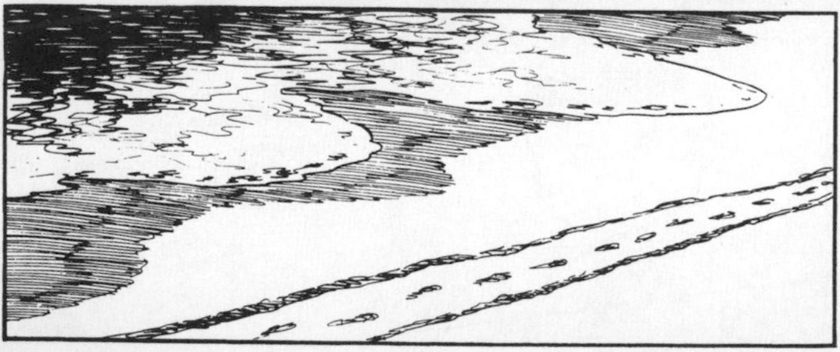

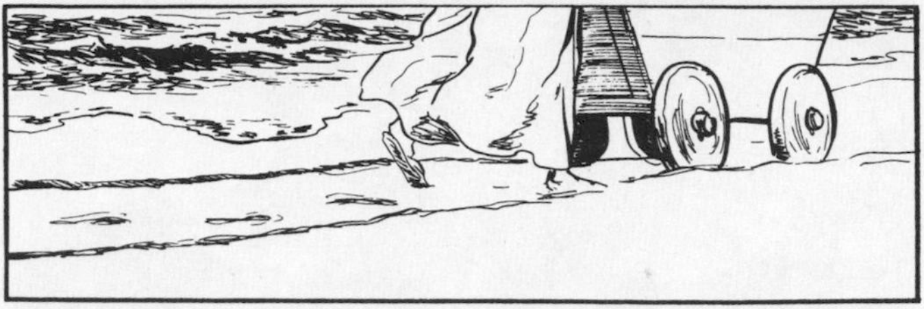
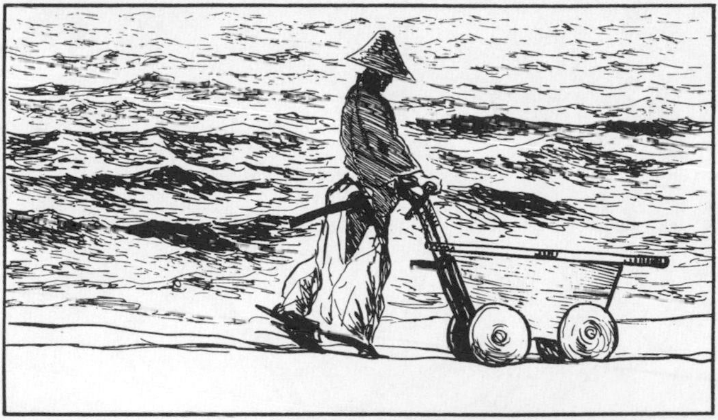
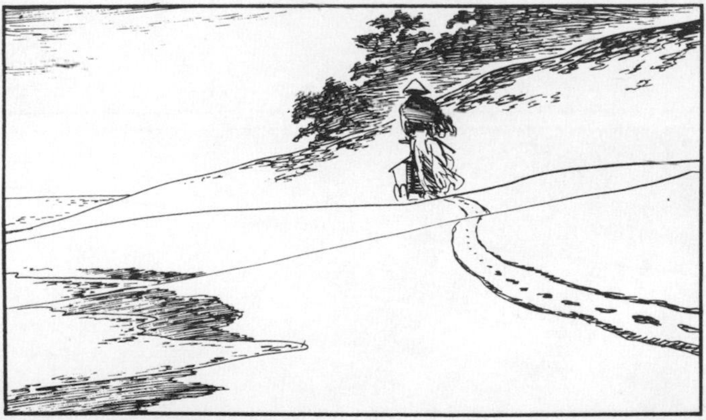

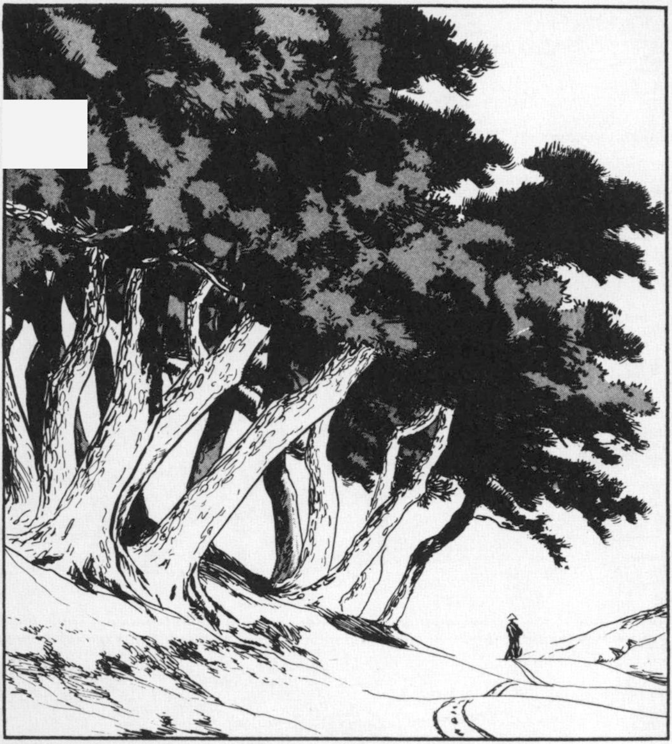

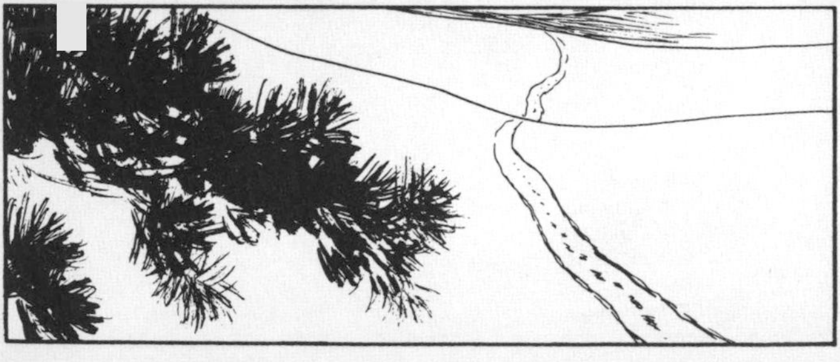

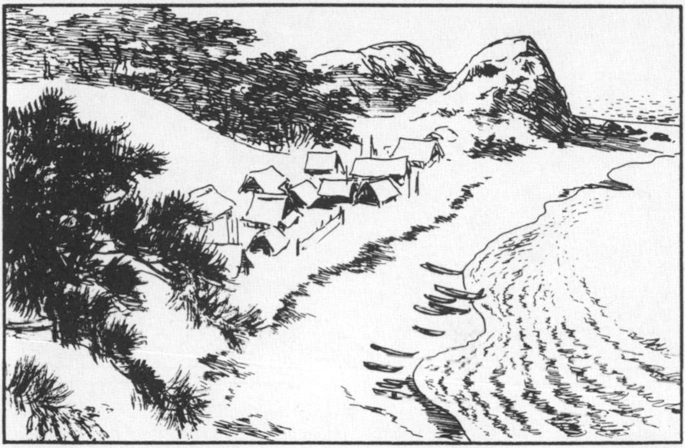
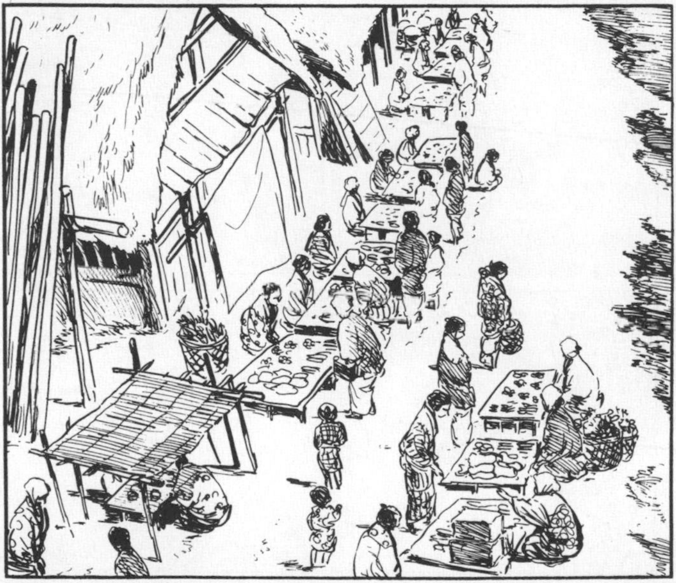

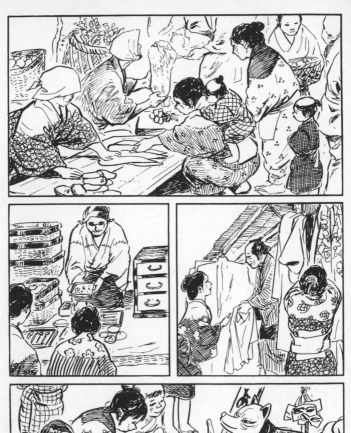

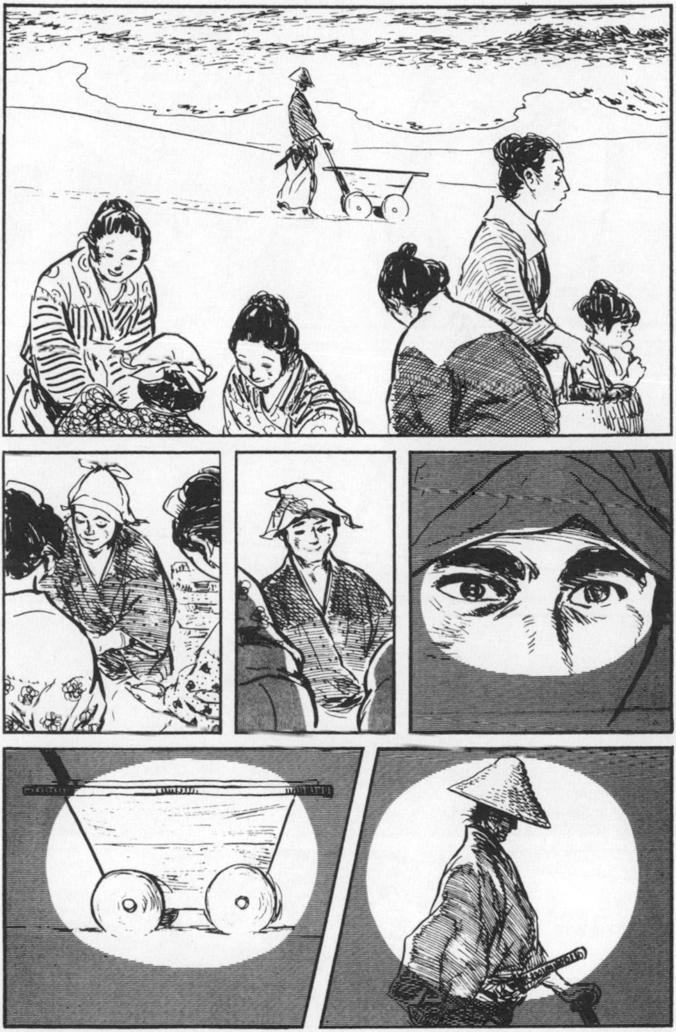

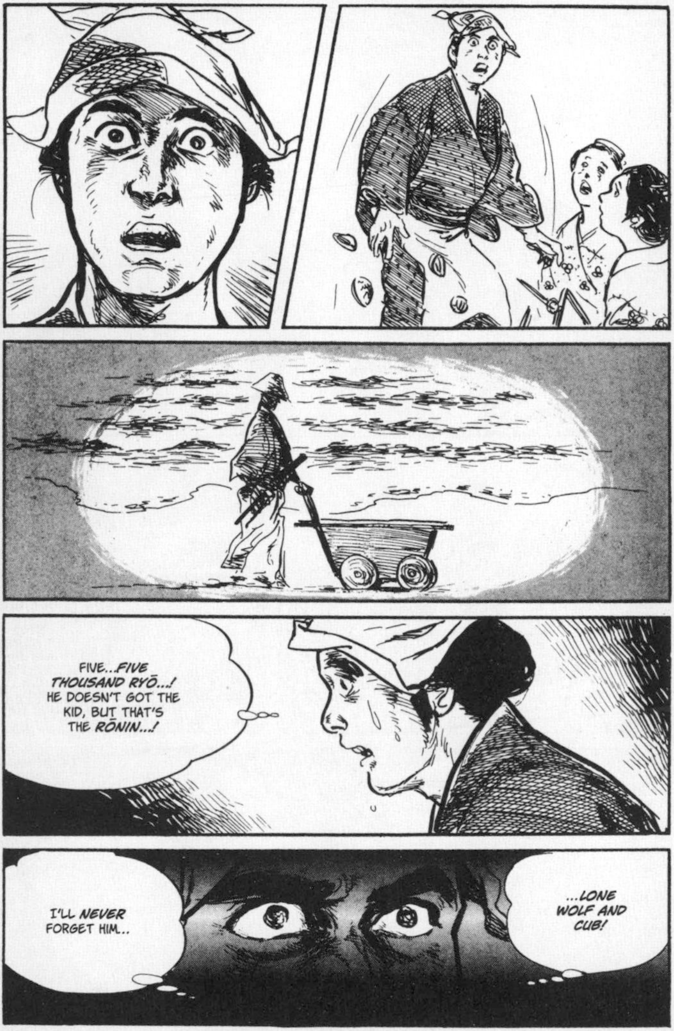
FIVE...*FIVE THOUSAND RYŌ*...!
HE DOESN'T GOT THE KID, BUT THAT'S THE *RŌNIN*...!
...*LONE WOLF AND CUB!*
I'LL *NEVER* FORGET HIM...

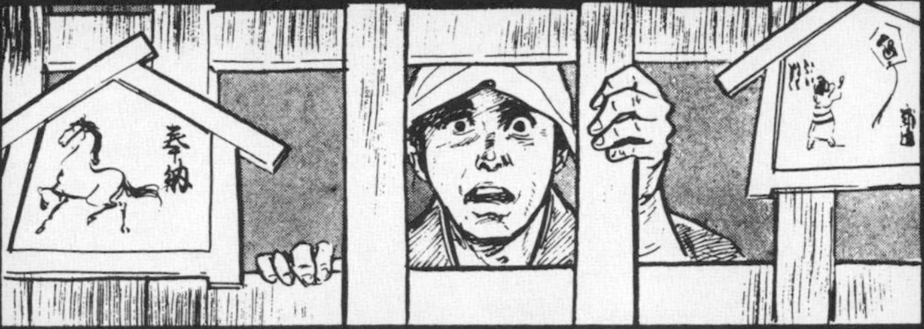
奉納

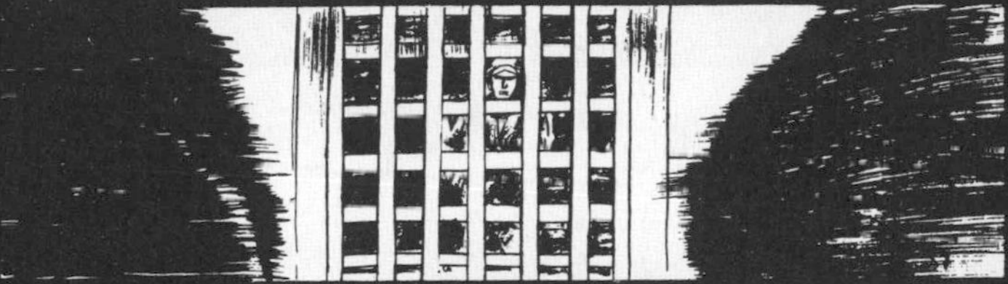

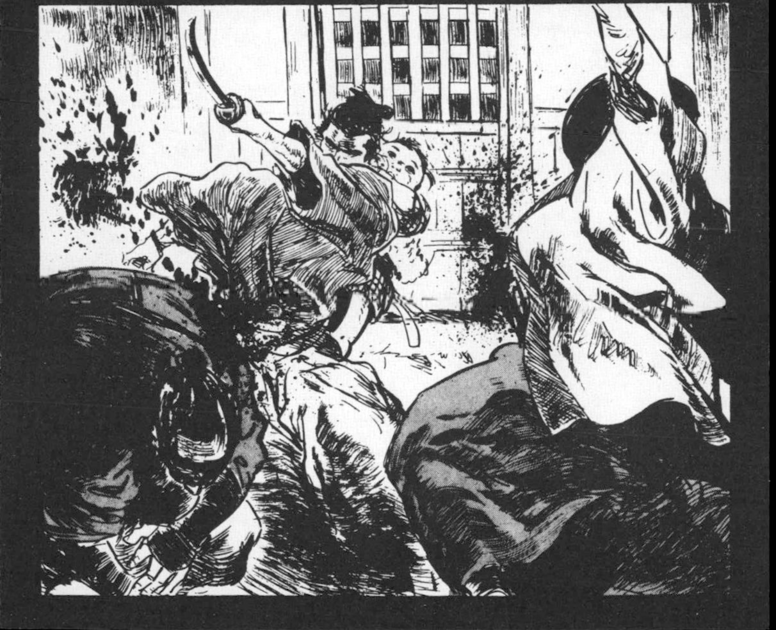

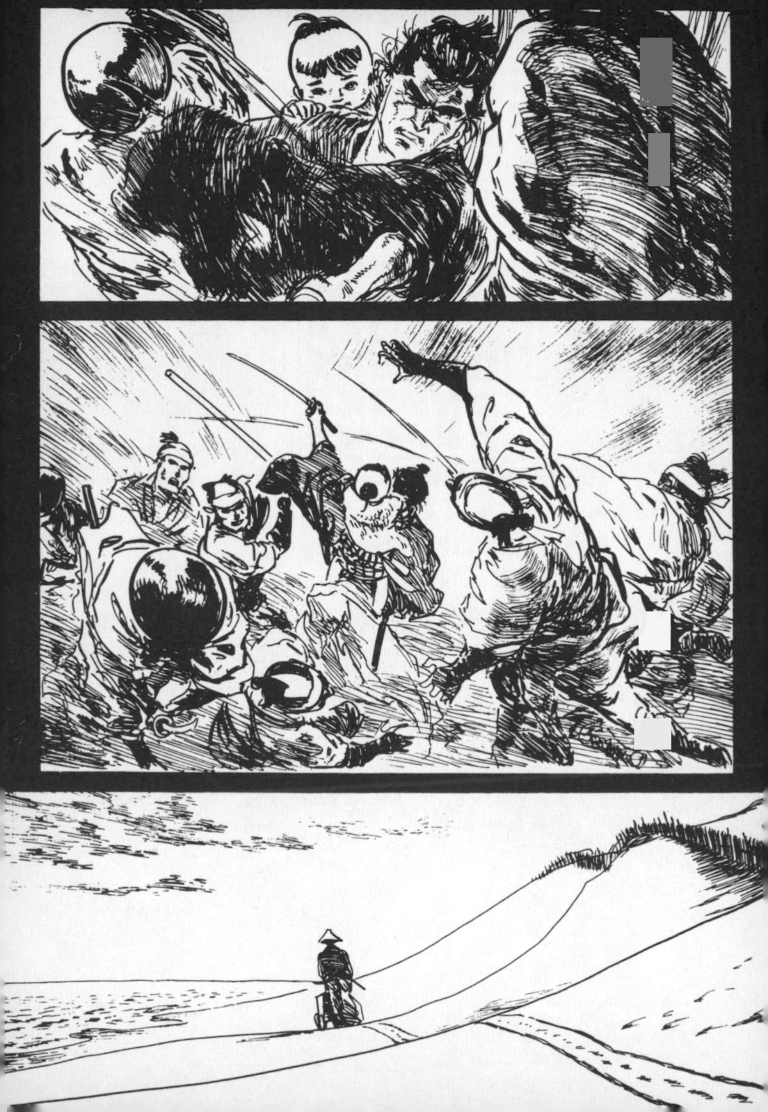

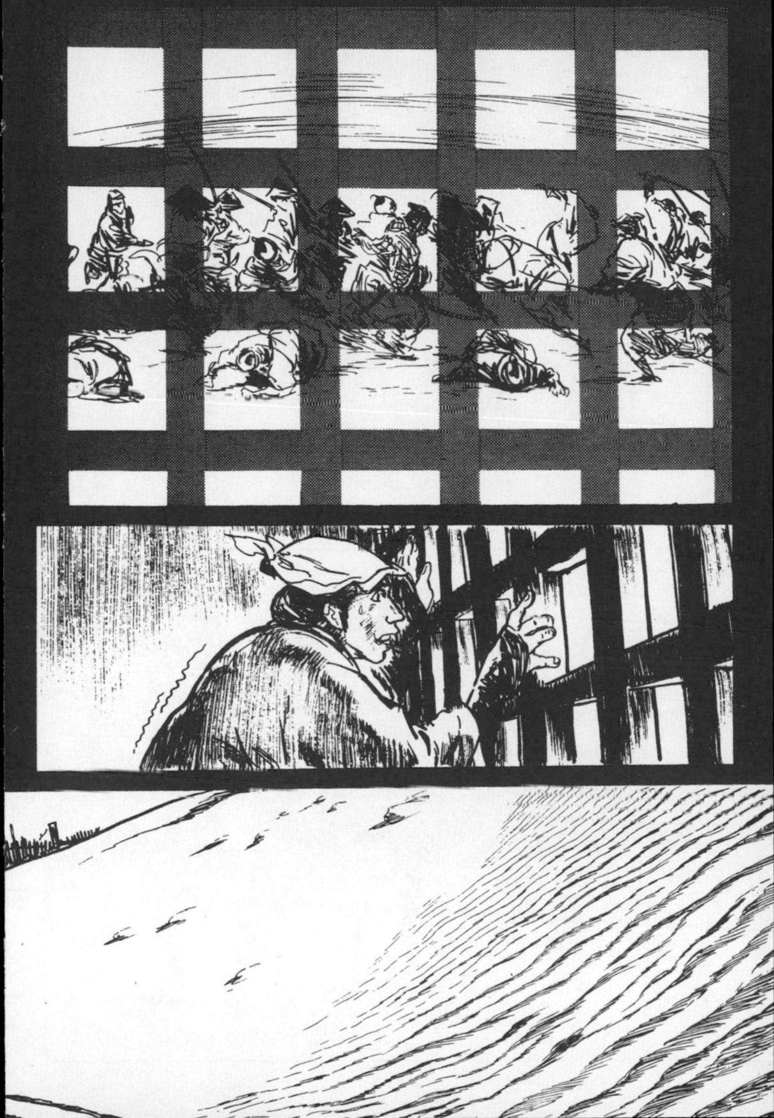

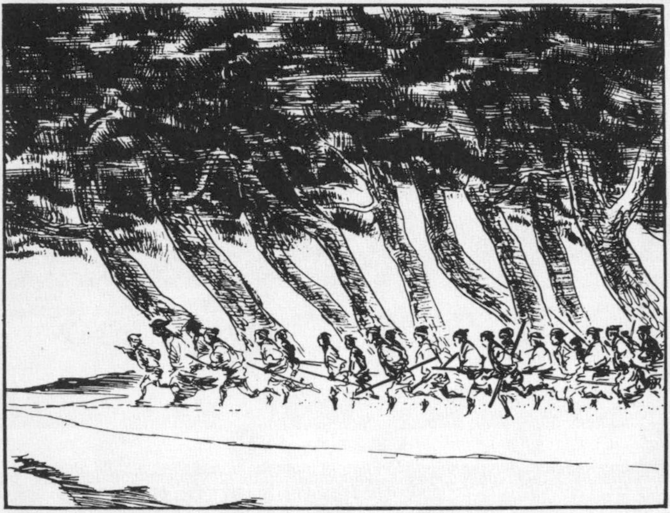
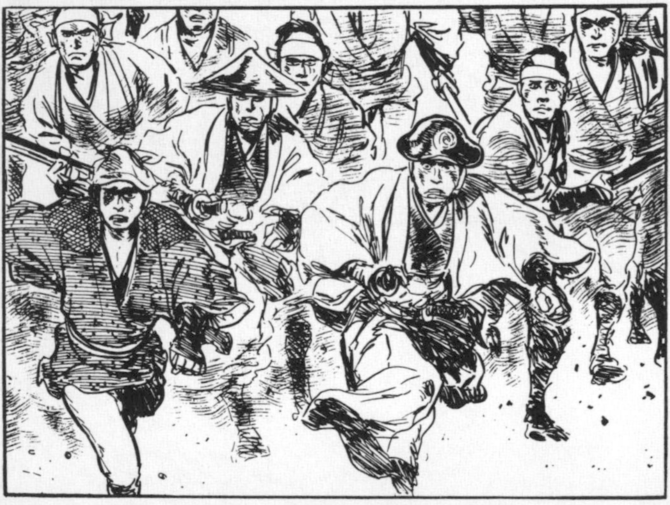

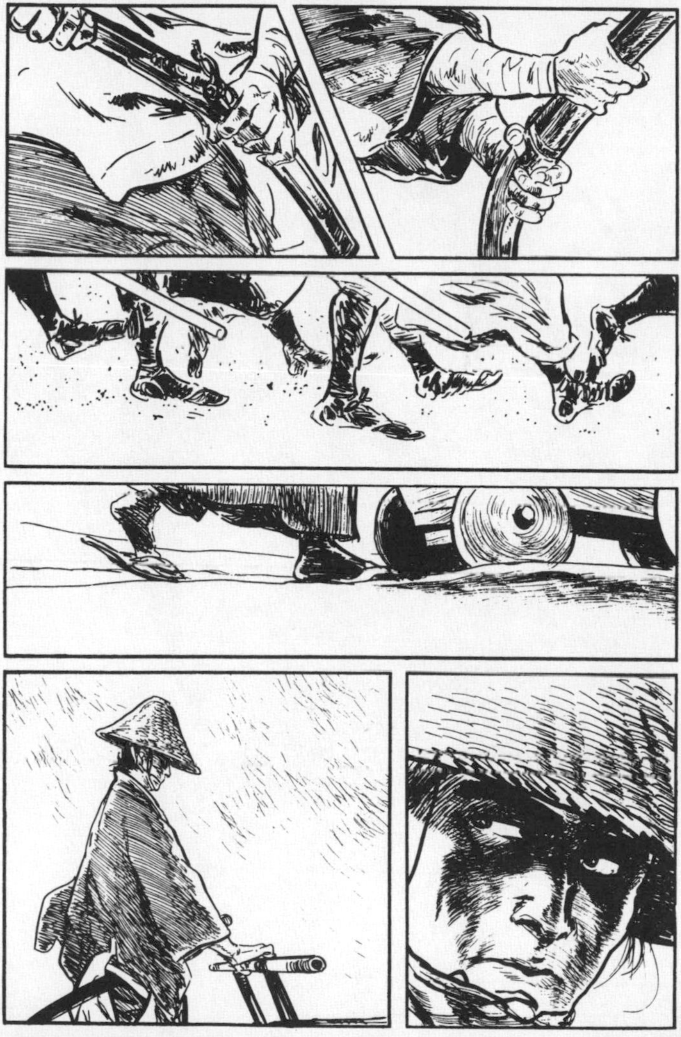

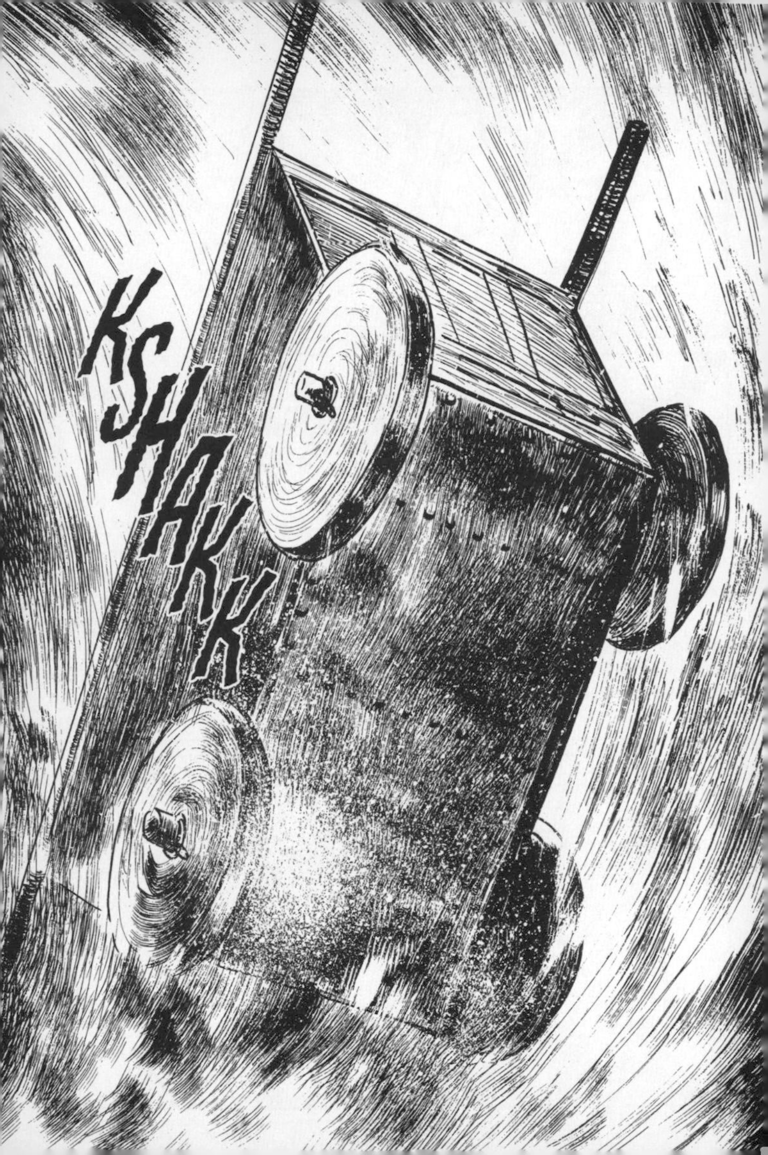
KSHAKK

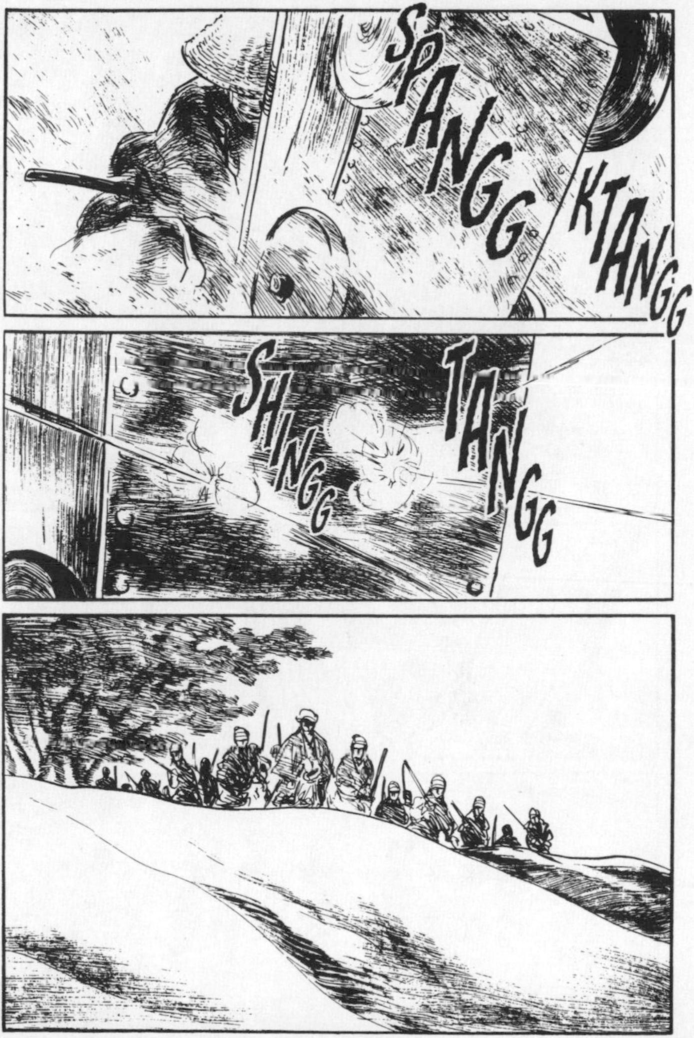
KTANGG
SPANGG
TANGG
SHINGG

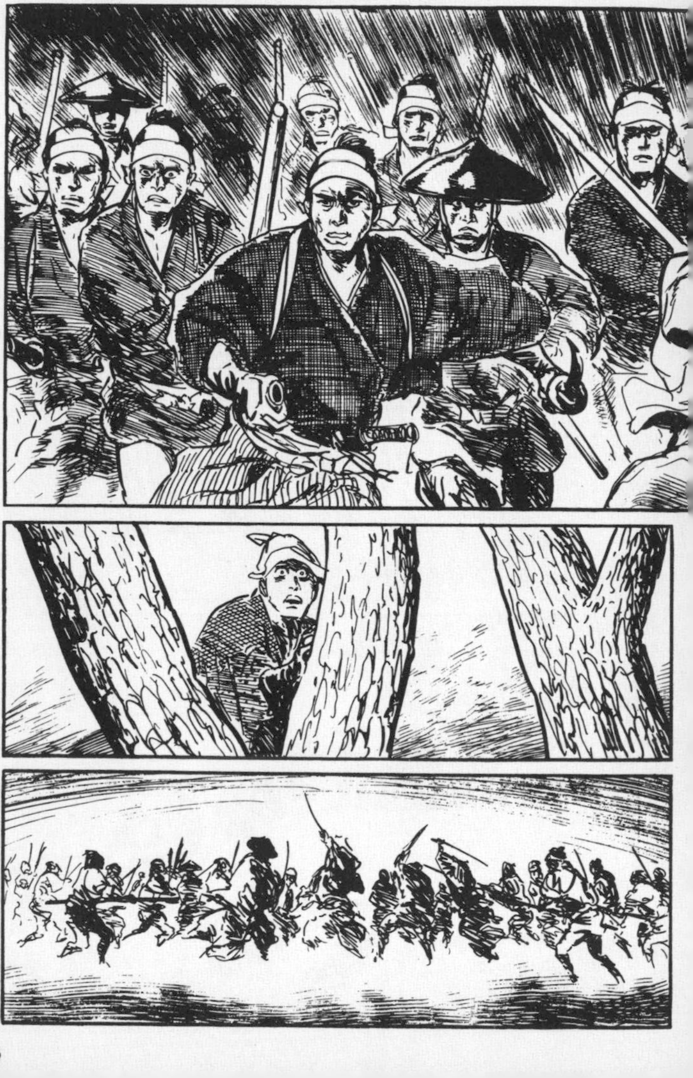

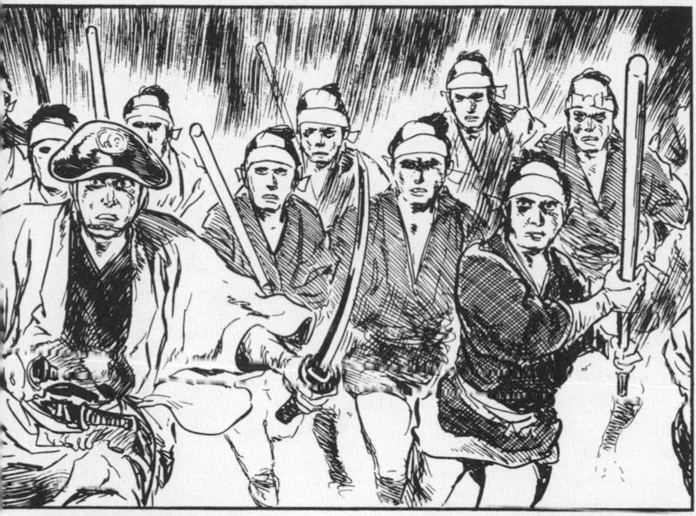
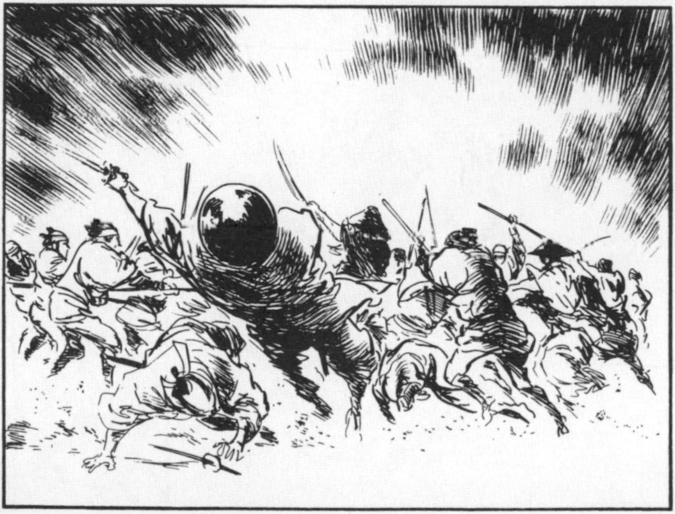

L...
LORD!

ƎULP!Ǝ

ALIUGGH!!

239

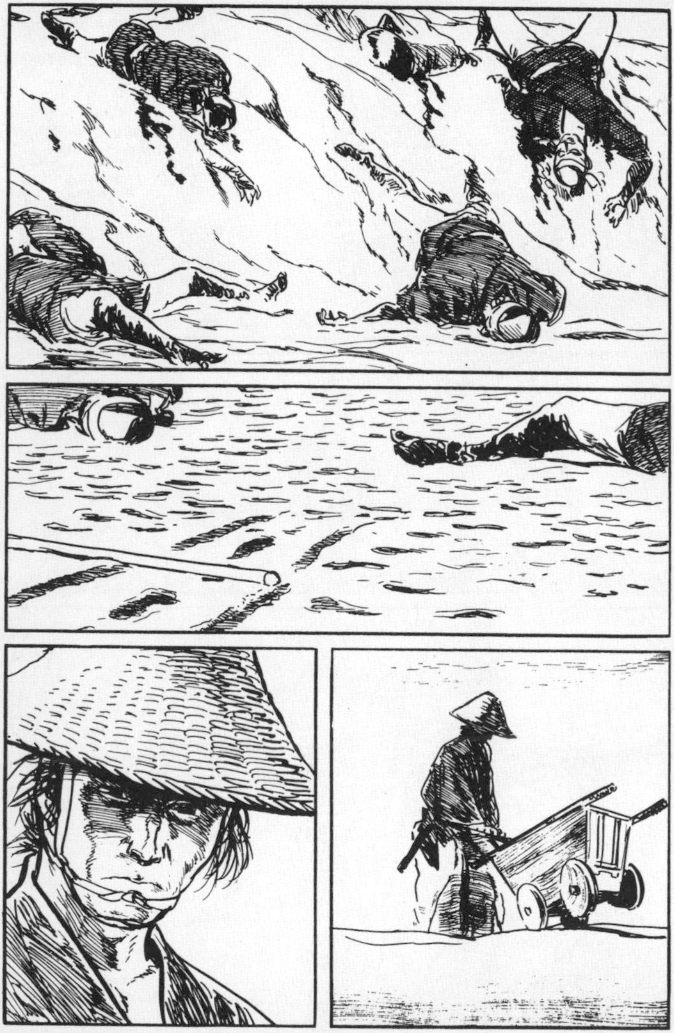

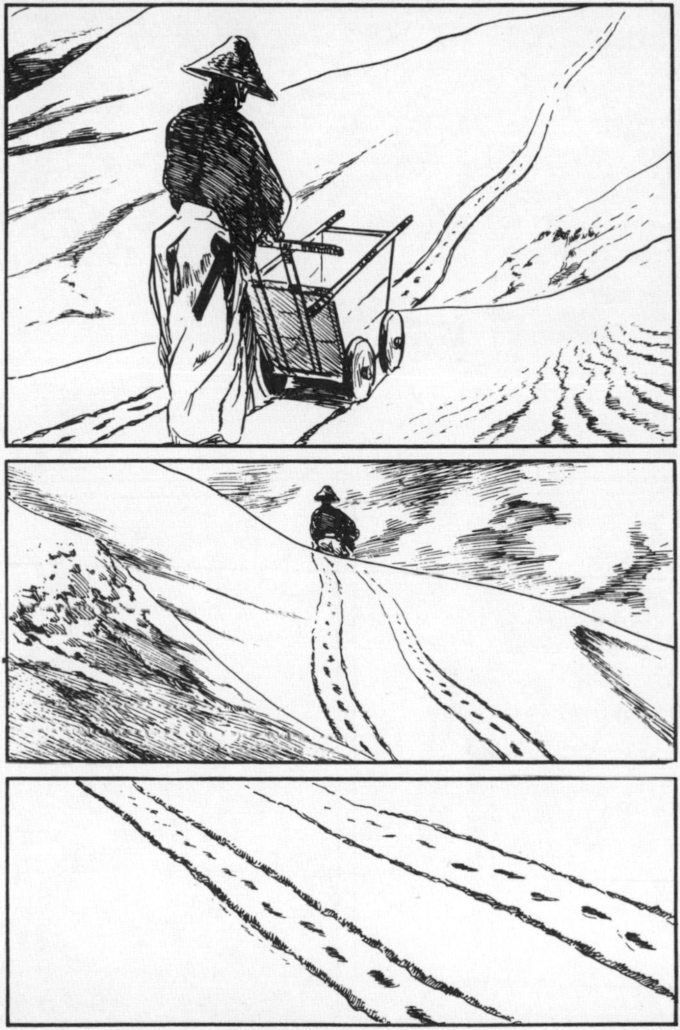

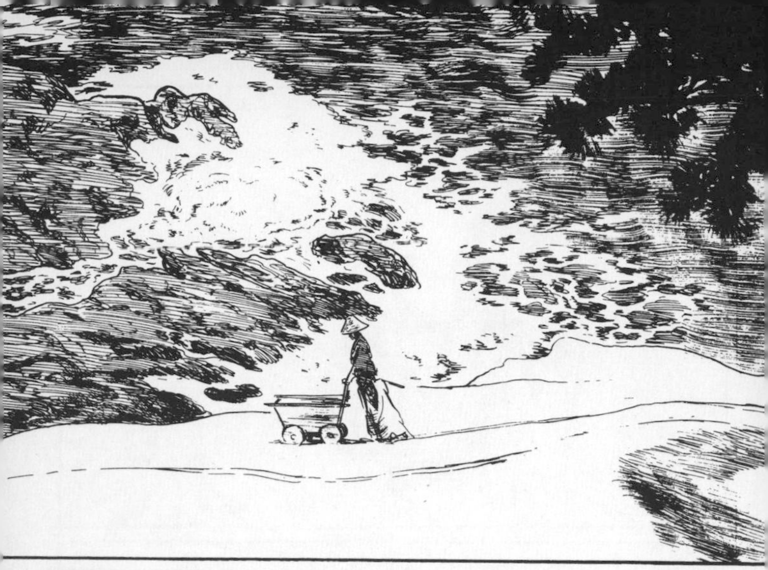
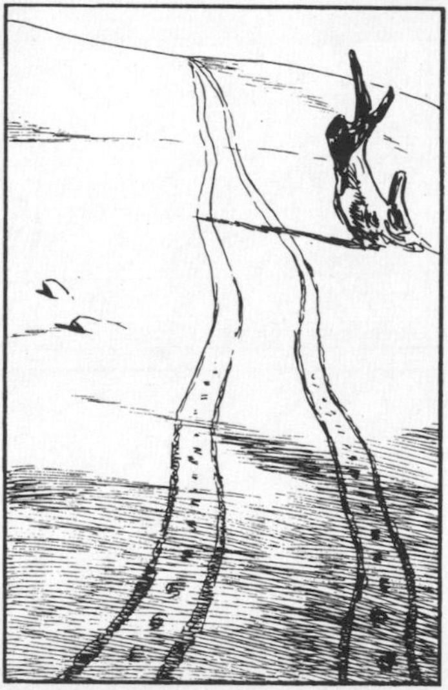
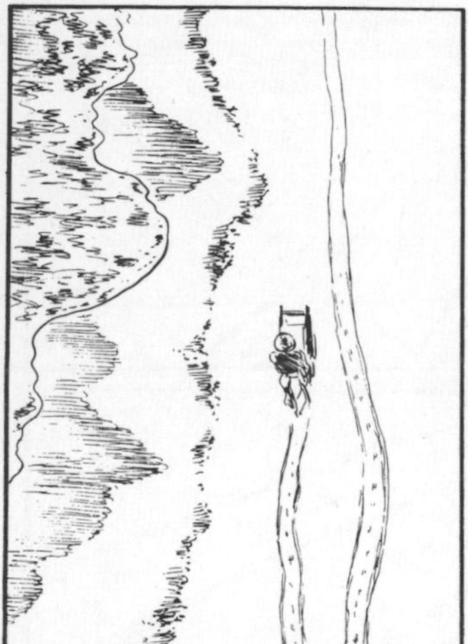

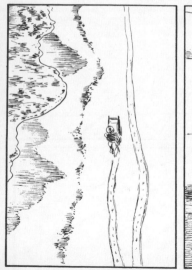

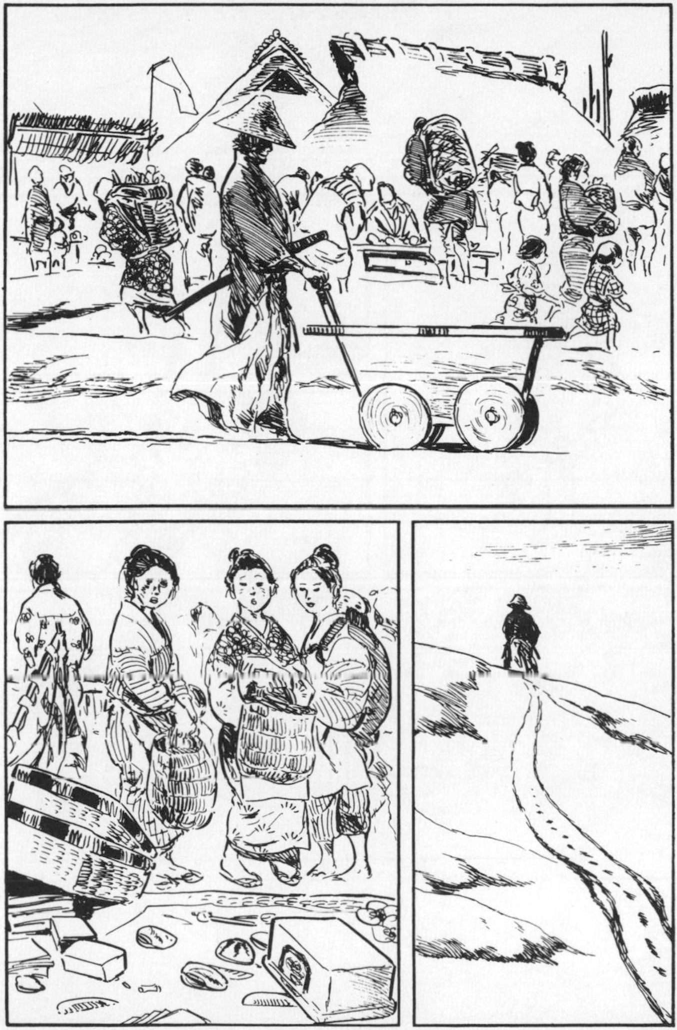

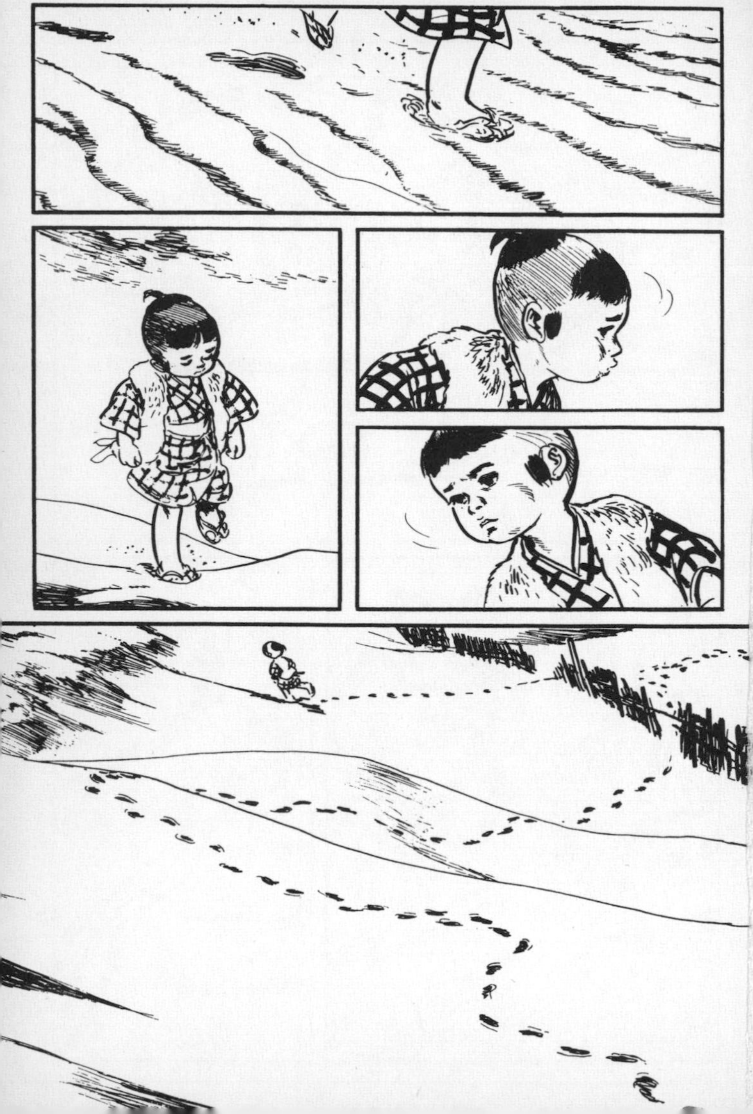

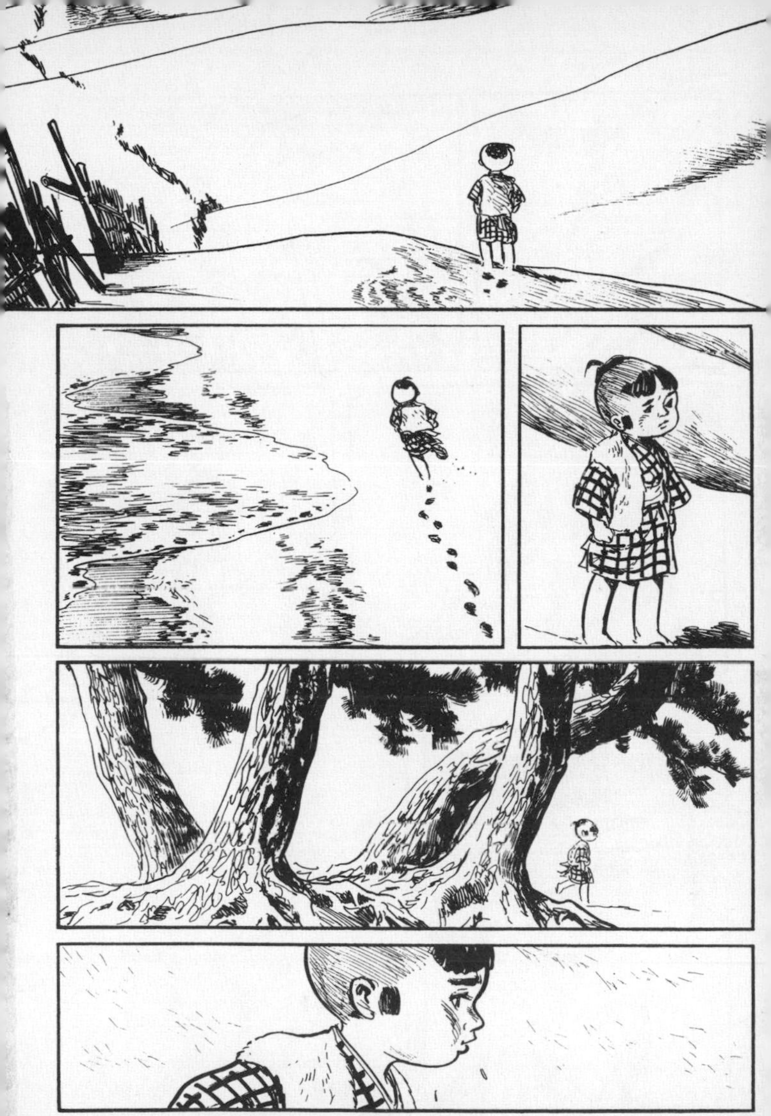

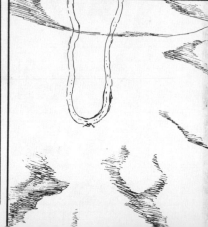

246

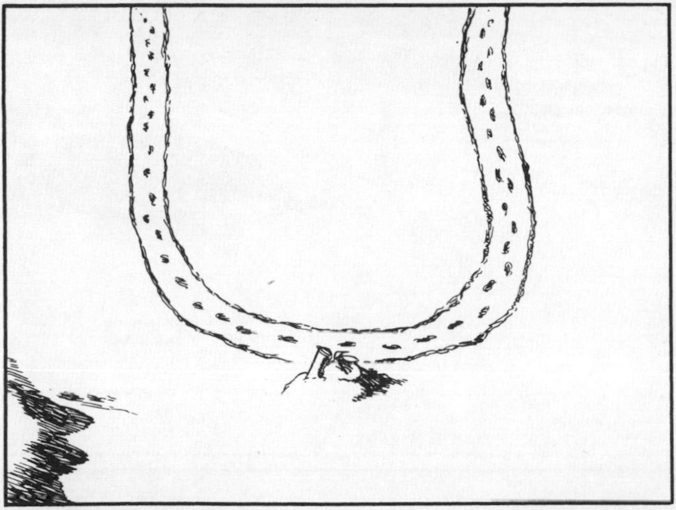
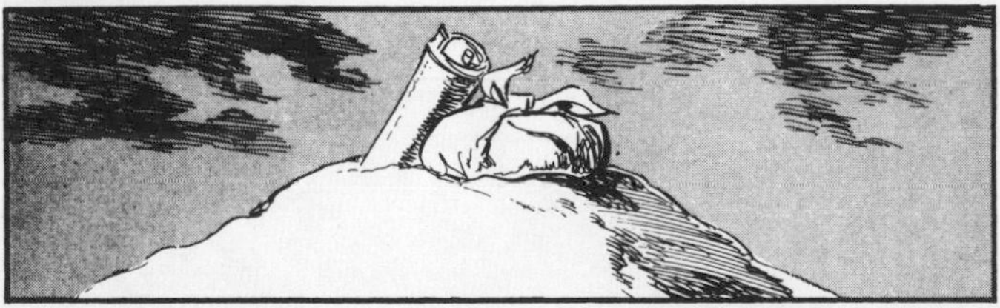
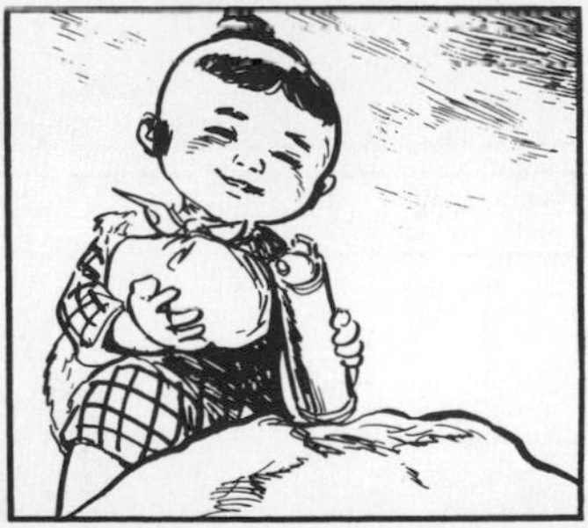
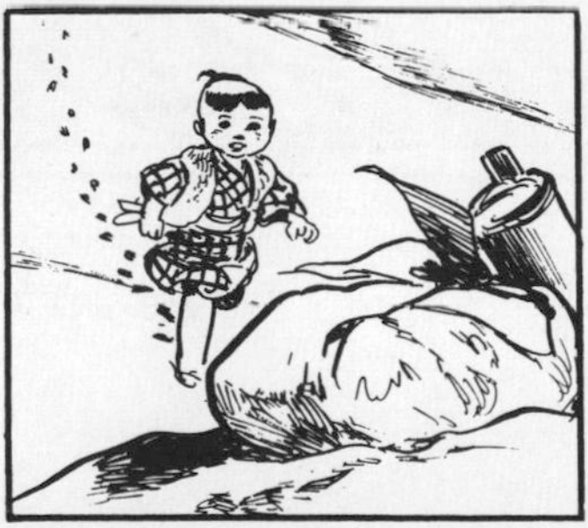

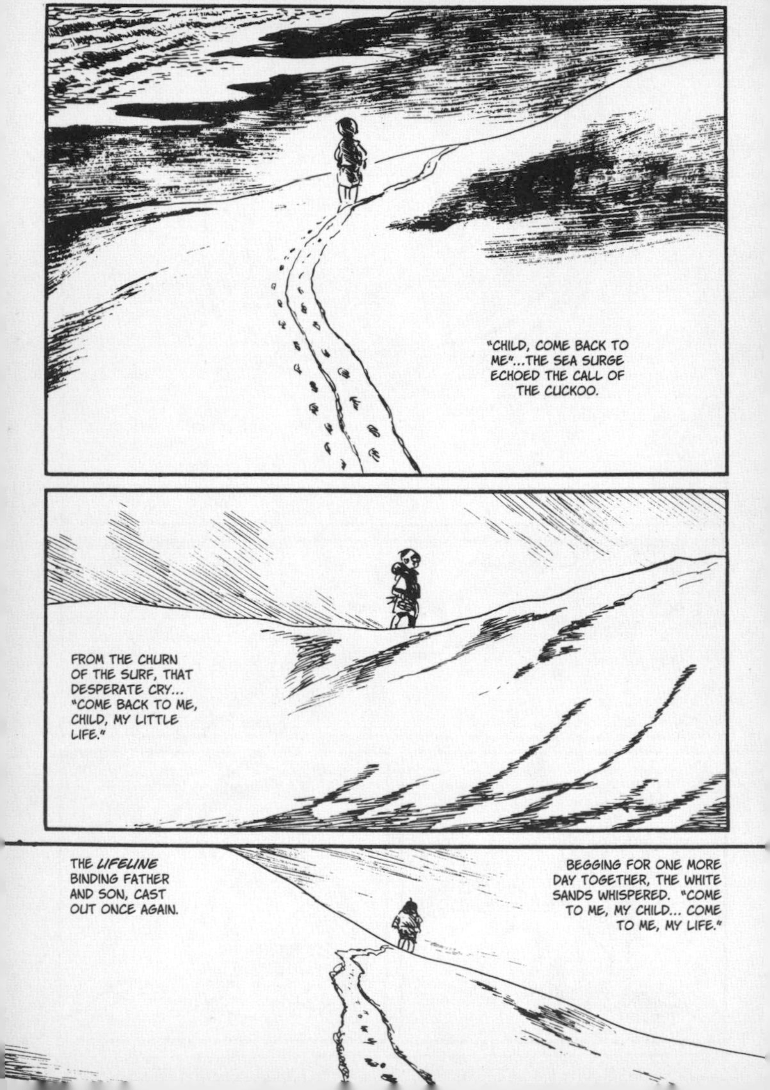
"CHILD, COME BACK TO ME"...THE SEA SURGE ECHOED THE CALL OF THE CUCKOO.
FROM THE CHURN OF THE SURF, THAT DESPERATE CRY... "COME BACK TO ME, CHILD, MY LITTLE LIFE."
BEGGING FOR ONE MORE DAY TOGETHER, THE WHITE SANDS WHISPERED. "COME TO ME, MY CHILD... COME TO ME, MY LIFE."
THE *LIFELINE* BINDING FATHER AND SON, CAST OUT ONCE AGAIN.

the ninety-second

Twilight of the Kurokuwa

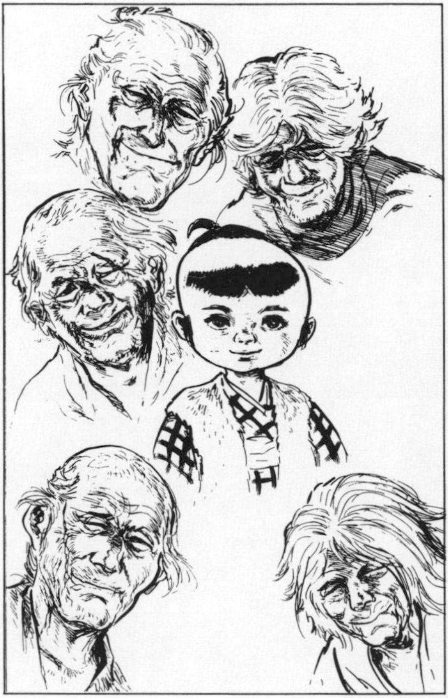

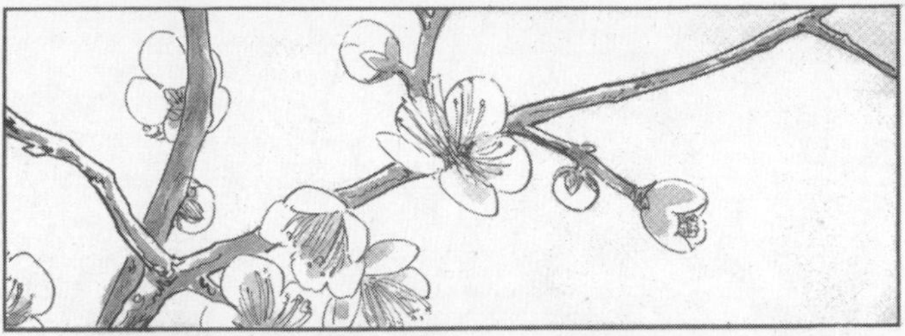

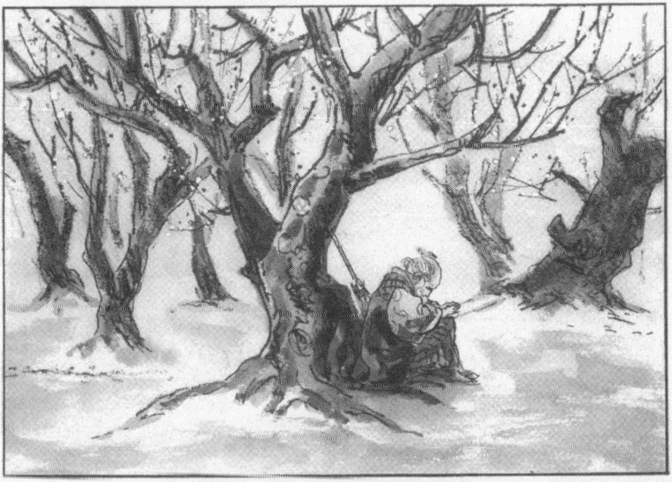

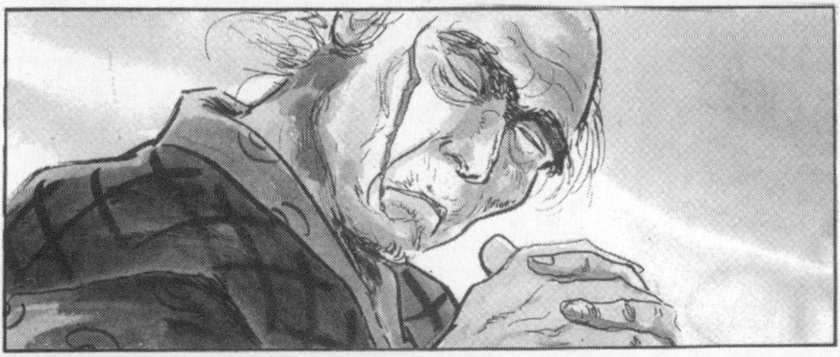

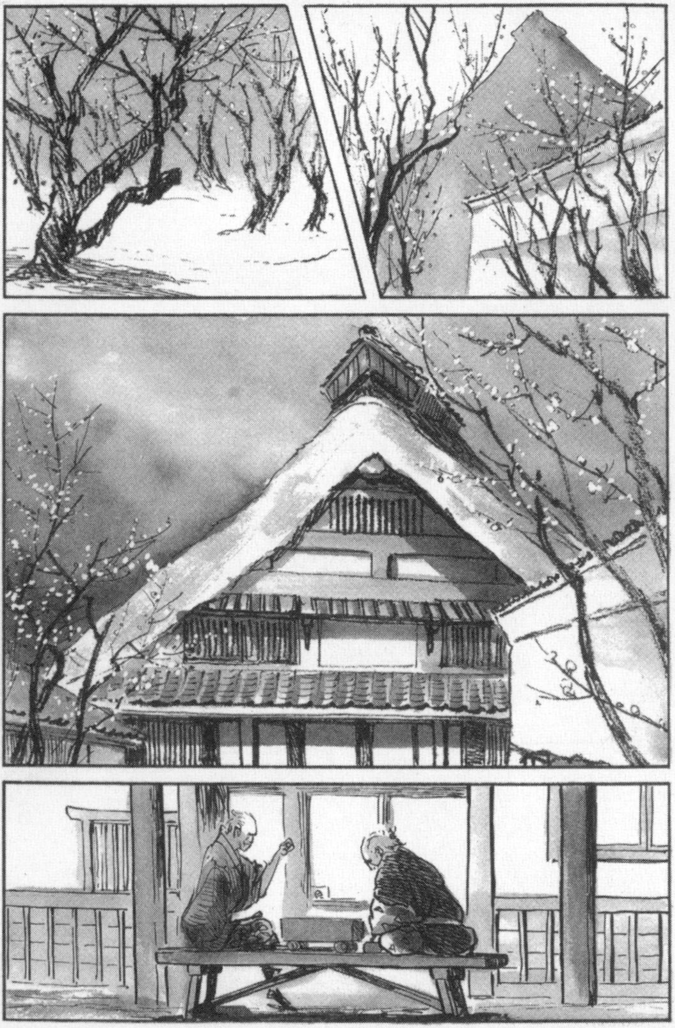

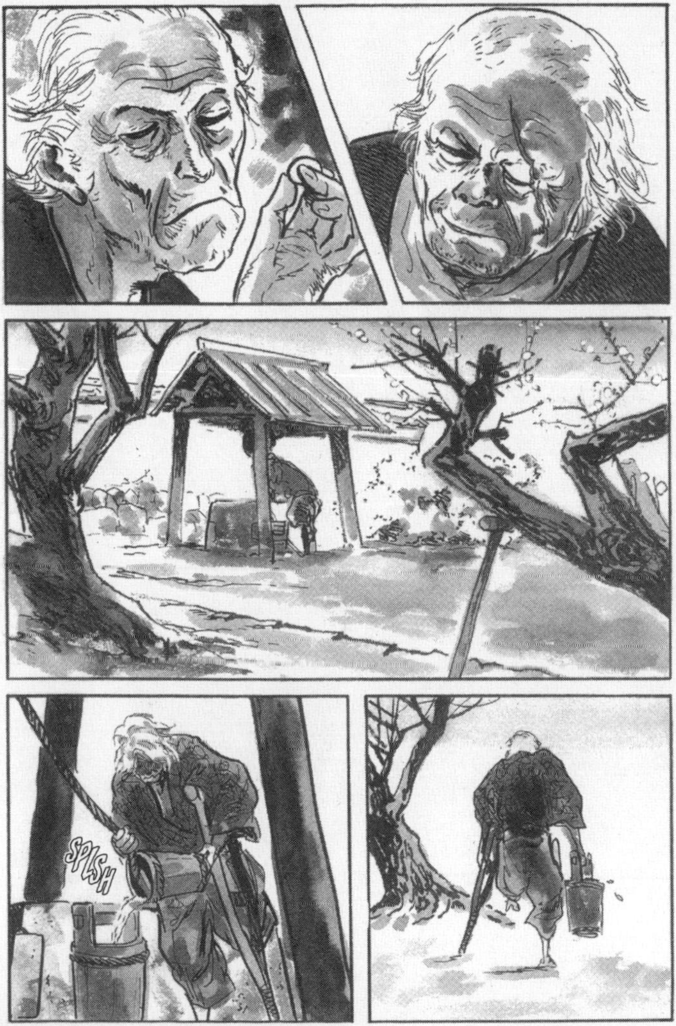
SPLSH

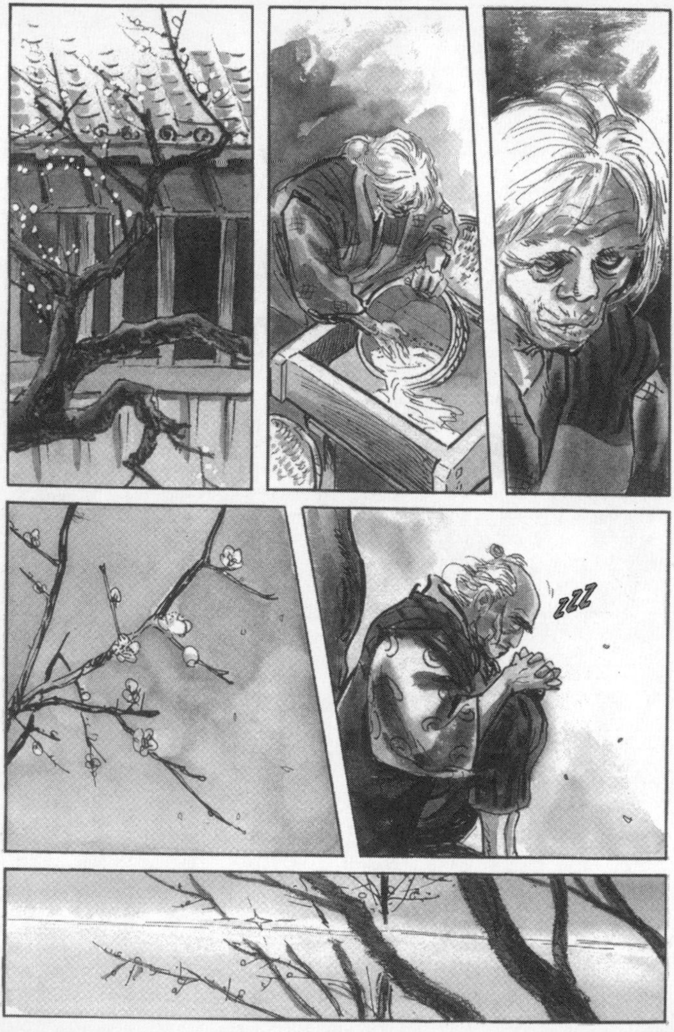
ZZZ

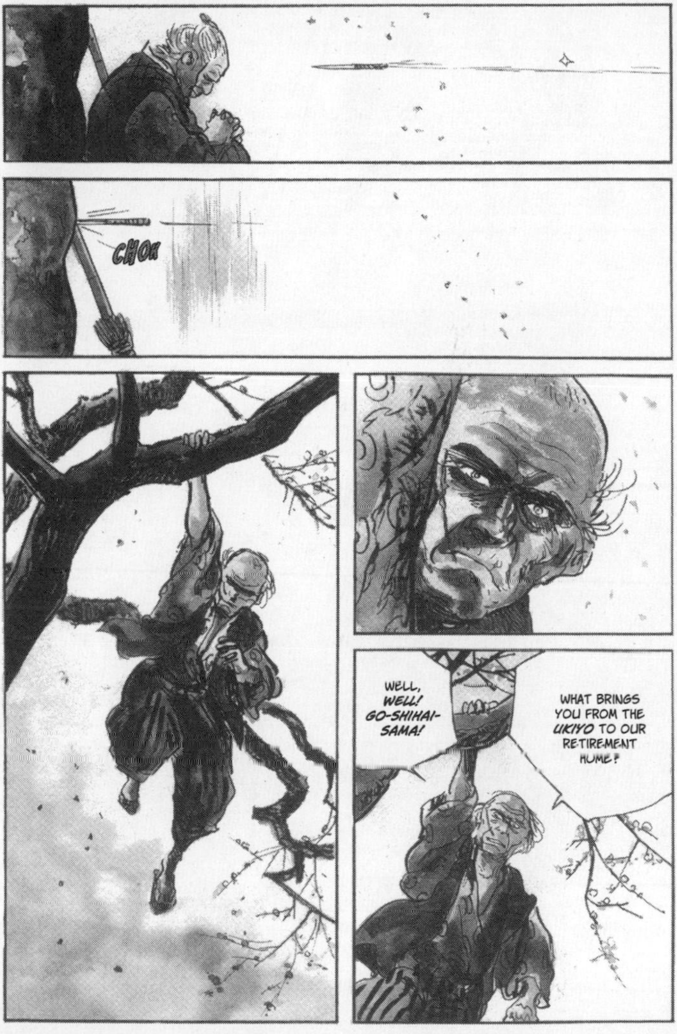
CHOK
WELL, WELL! GO-SHIHAI-SAMA!
WHAT BRINGS YOU FROM THE UKIYO TO OUR RETIREMENT HOME?

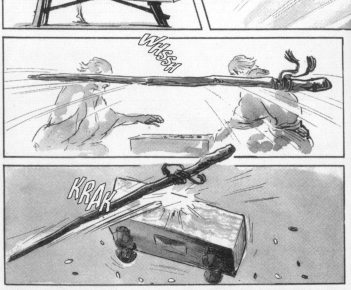

WHSSH

KRAK

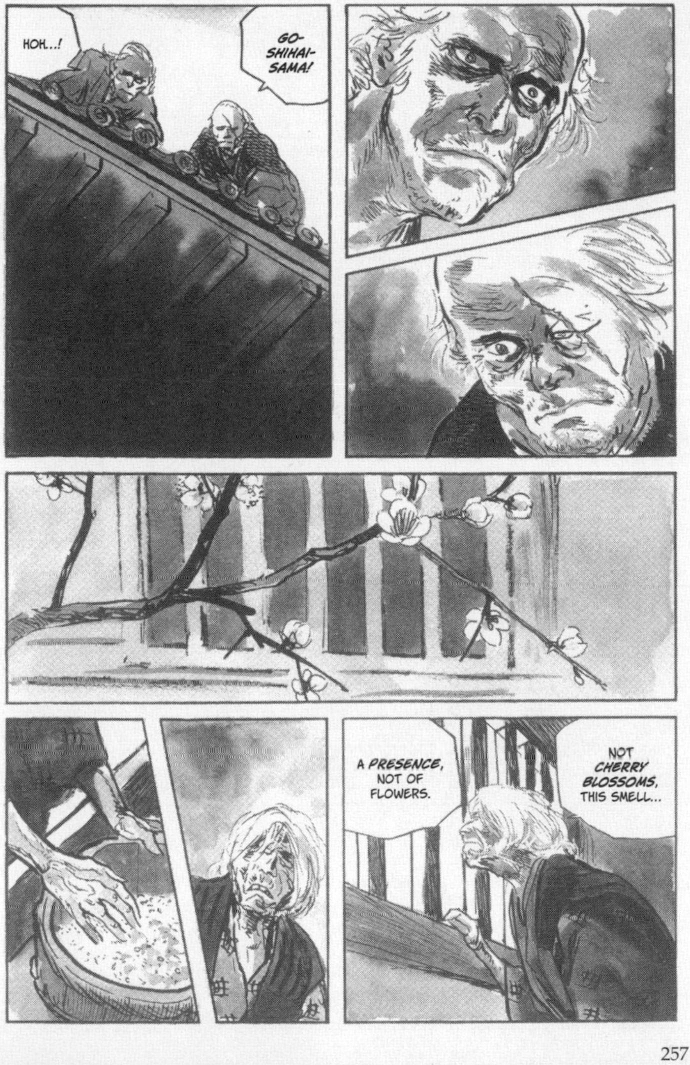
GO-SHIHAI-SAMA!
HOH...!
NOT CHERRY BLOSSOMS, THIS SMELL...
A PRESENCE, NOT OF FLOWERS.

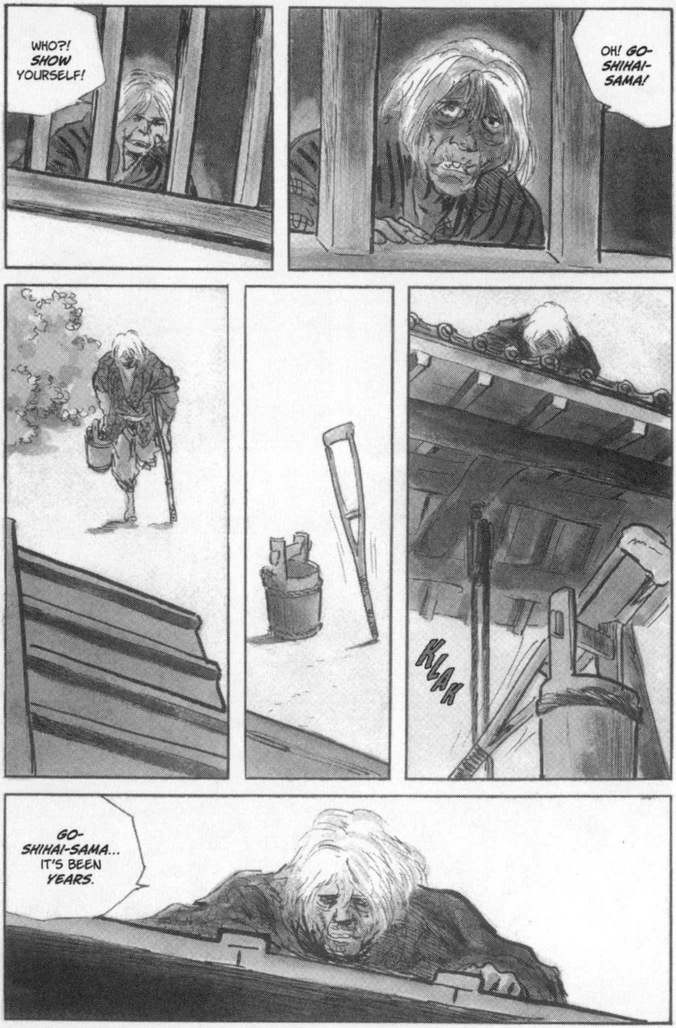
WHO?! SHOW YOURSELF!
OH! GO-SHIHAI-SAMA!
KLAK
GO-SHIHAI-SAMA... IT'S BEEN YEARS.

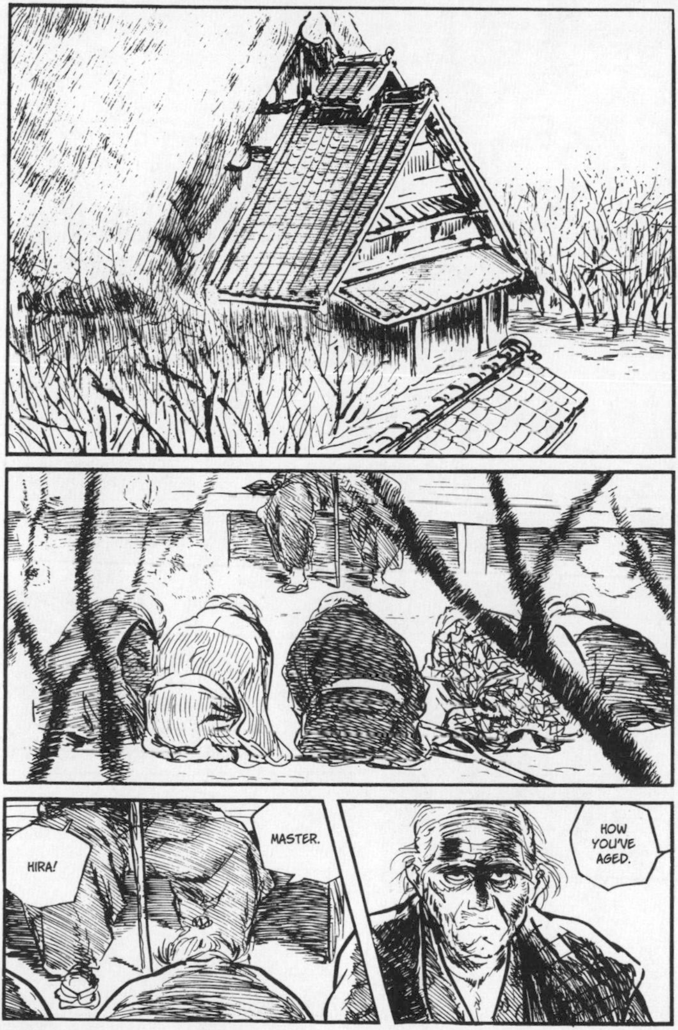
HIRA!
MASTER.
HOW YOU'VE AGED.

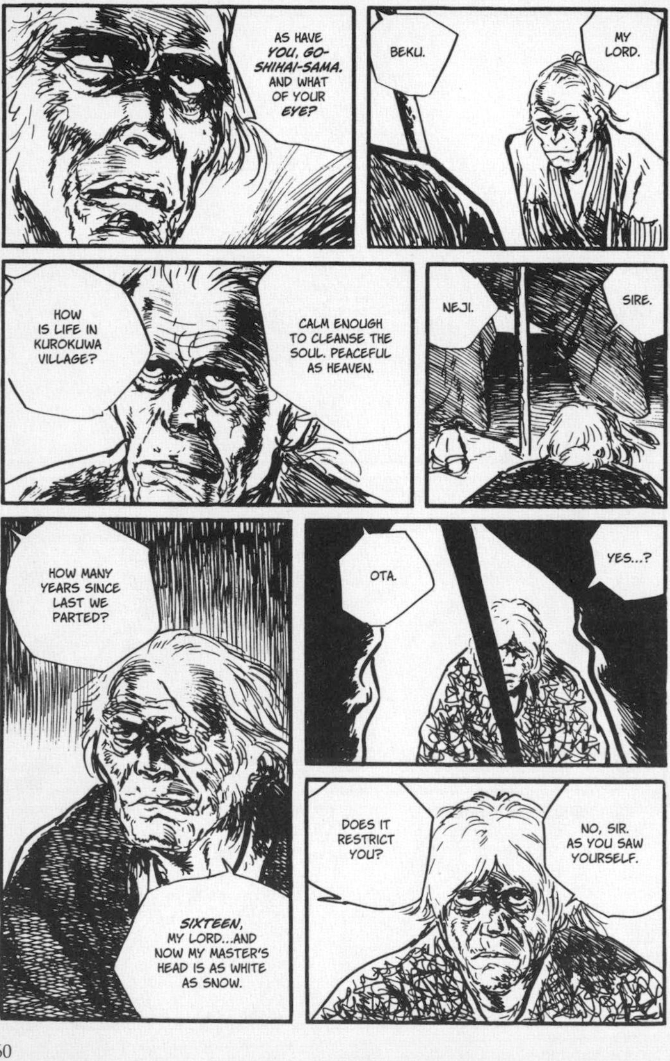
AS HAVE *YOU, GO-SHIHAI-SAMA.* AND WHAT OF YOUR *EYE?*
BEKU.
MY LORD.
HOW IS LIFE IN KUROKUWA VILLAGE?
CALM ENOUGH TO CLEANSE THE SOUL. PEACEFUL AS HEAVEN.
NEJI.
SIRE.
HOW MANY YEARS SINCE LAST WE PARTED?
SIXTEEN, MY LORD...AND NOW MY MASTER'S HEAD IS AS WHITE AS SNOW.
OTA.
YES...?
DOES IT RESTRICT YOU?
NO, SIR. AS YOU SAW YOURSELF.

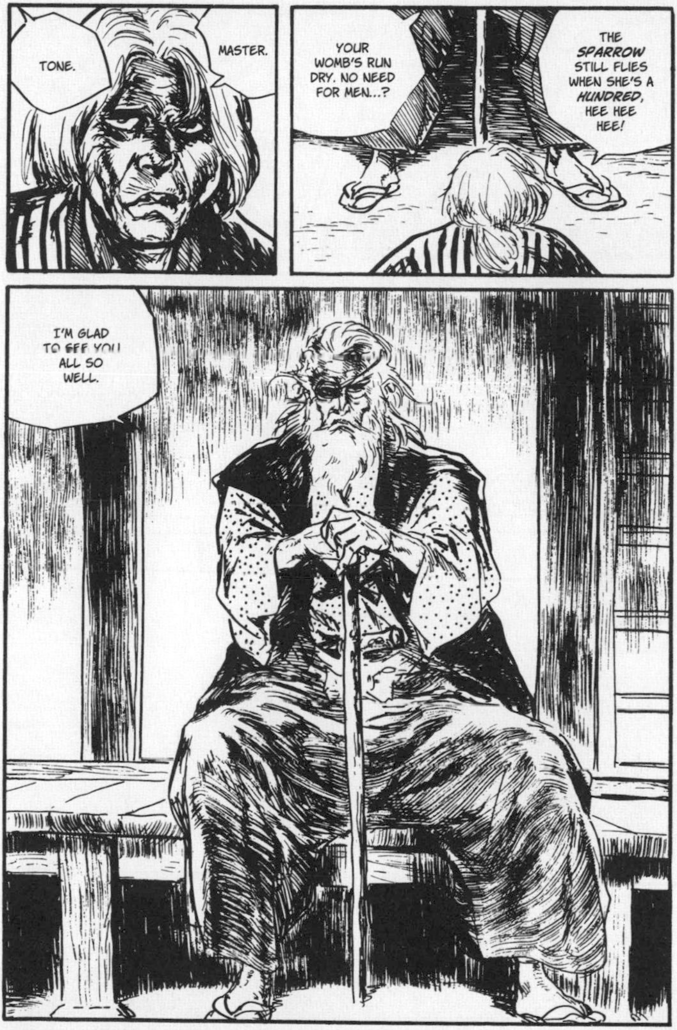
THE *SPARROW* STILL FLIES WHEN SHE'S A *HUNDRED*, HEE HEE HEE!
YOUR WOMB'S RUN DRY. NO NEED FOR MEN...?
MASTER.
TONE.
I'M GLAD TO SEE YOU ALL SO WELL.

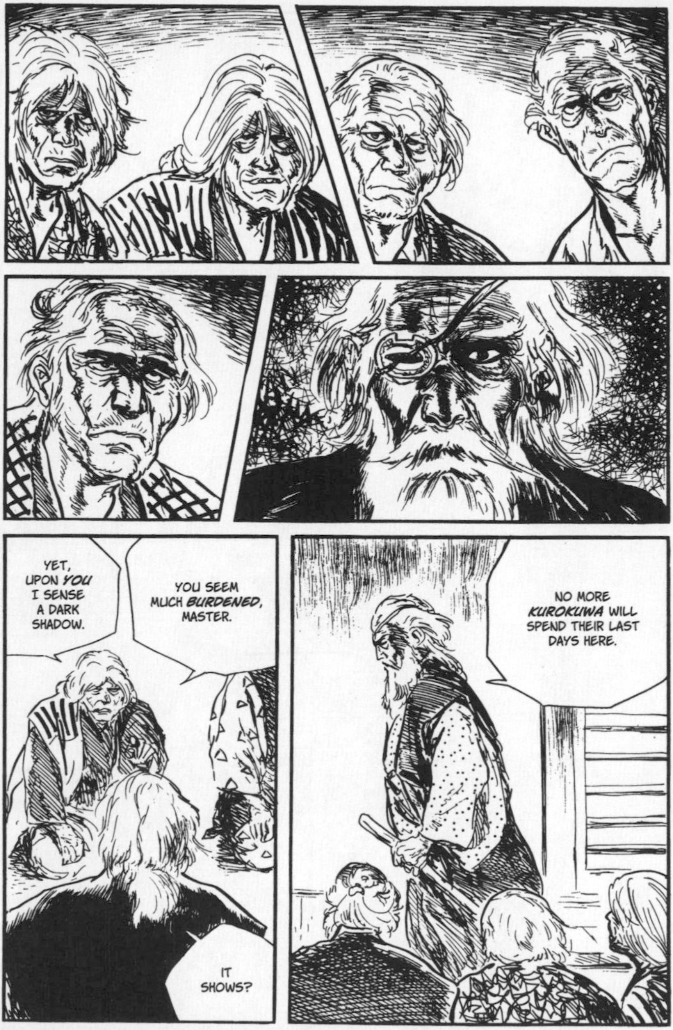
NO MORE *KUROKUWA* WILL SPEND THEIR LAST DAYS HERE.
YOU SEEM MUCH *BURDENED*, MASTER.
YET, UPON *YOU* I SENSE A DARK SHADOW.
IT SHOWS?

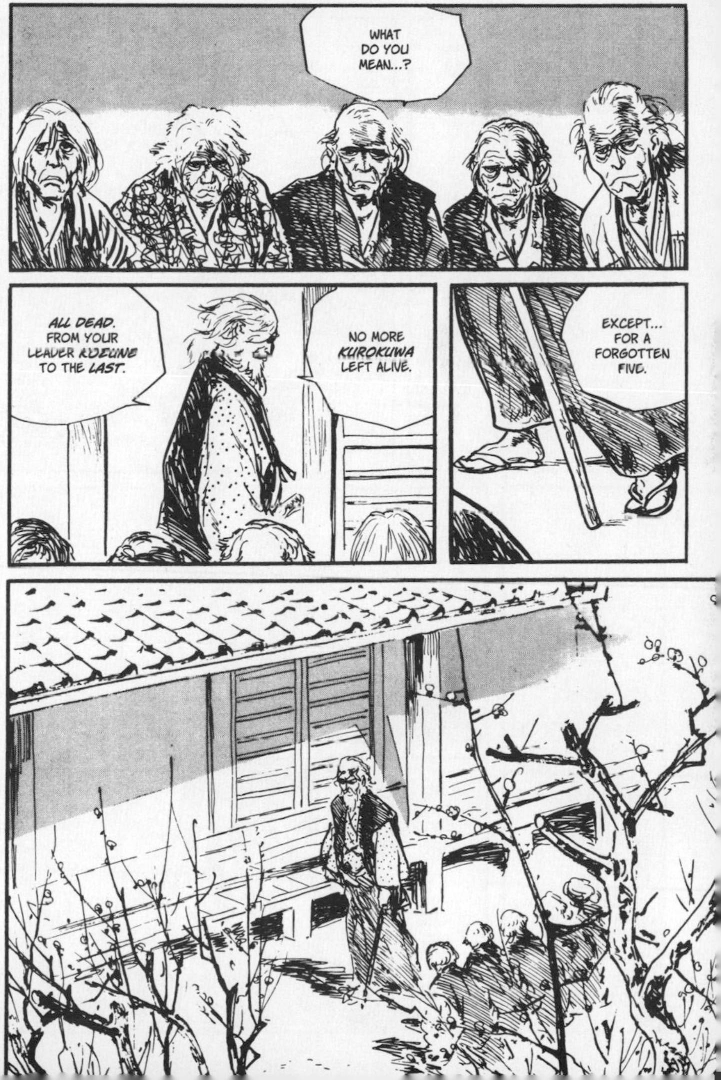
WHAT DO YOU MEAN...?
ALL DEAD. FROM YOUR LEADER KOZUNE TO THE LAST.
NO MORE KUROKUWA LEFT ALIVE.
EXCEPT... FOR A FORGOTTEN FIVE.

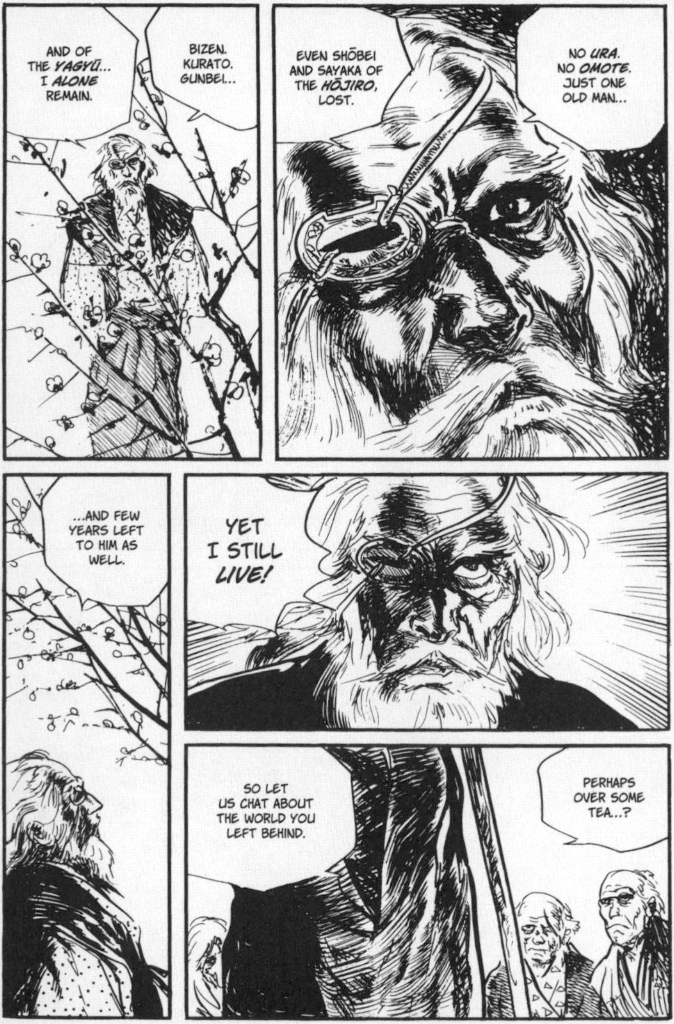
AND OF THE *YAGYŪ*... I *ALONE* REMAIN.
BIZEN. KURATO. GUNBEI...
EVEN SHŌBEI AND SAYAKA OF THE *HŌJIRO*, LOST.
NO *URA*. NO *OMOTE*. JUST ONE OLD MAN...
...AND FEW YEARS LEFT TO HIM AS WELL.
YET I STILL *LIVE!*
SO LET US CHAT ABOUT THE WORLD YOU LEFT BEHIND.
PERHAPS OVER SOME TEA...?

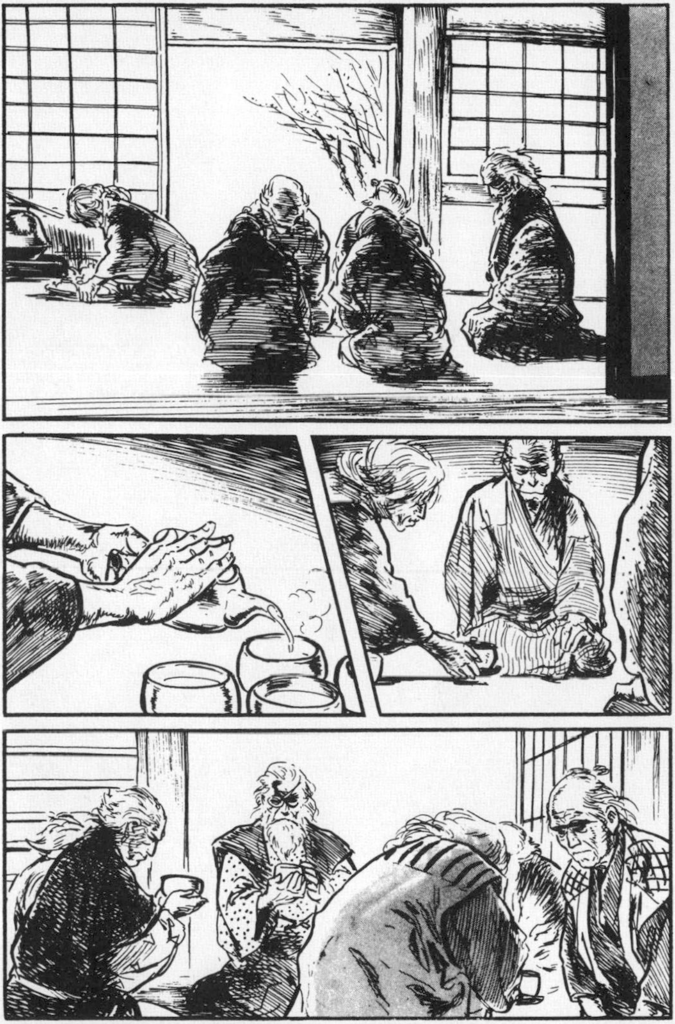

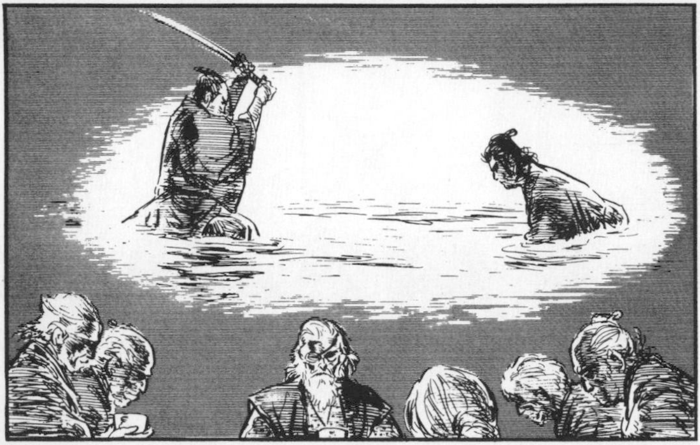
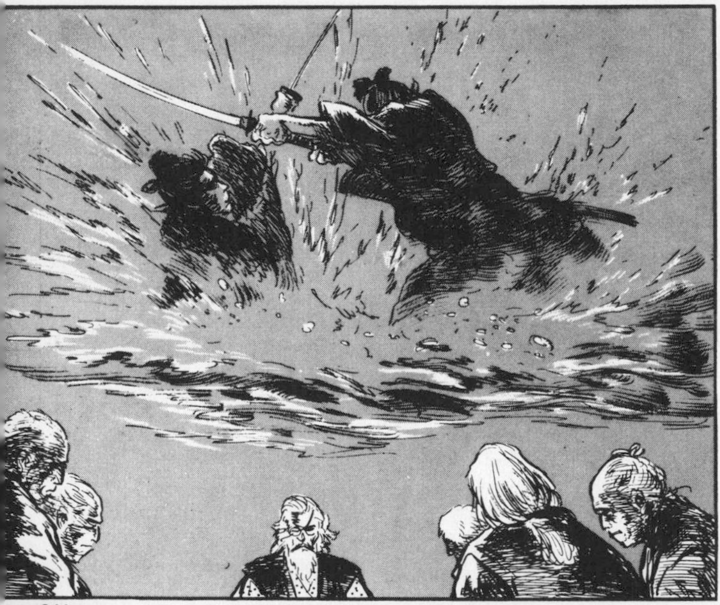

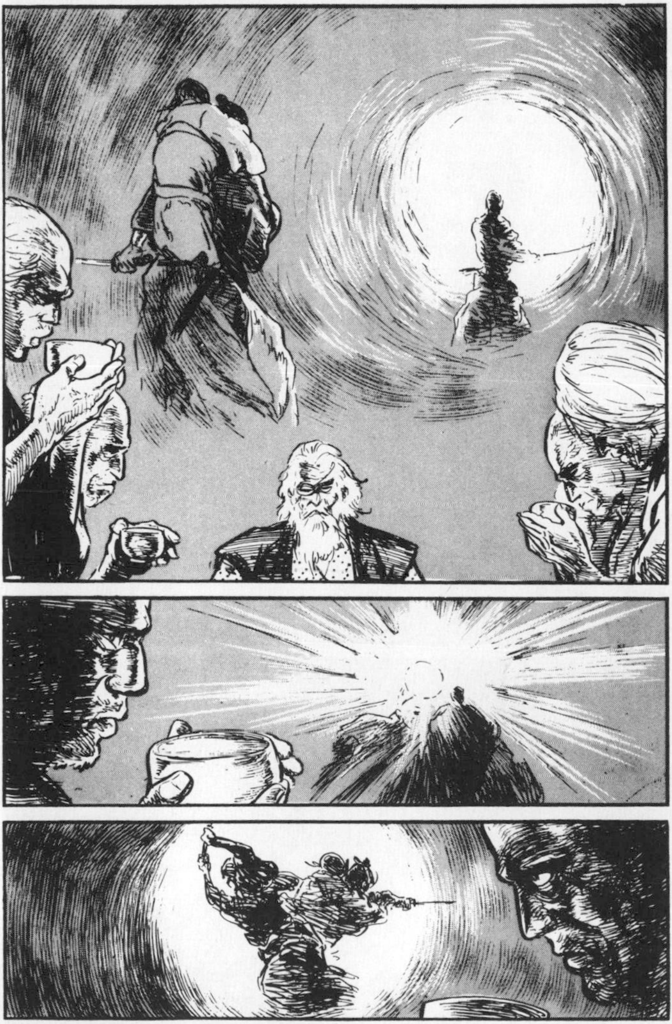

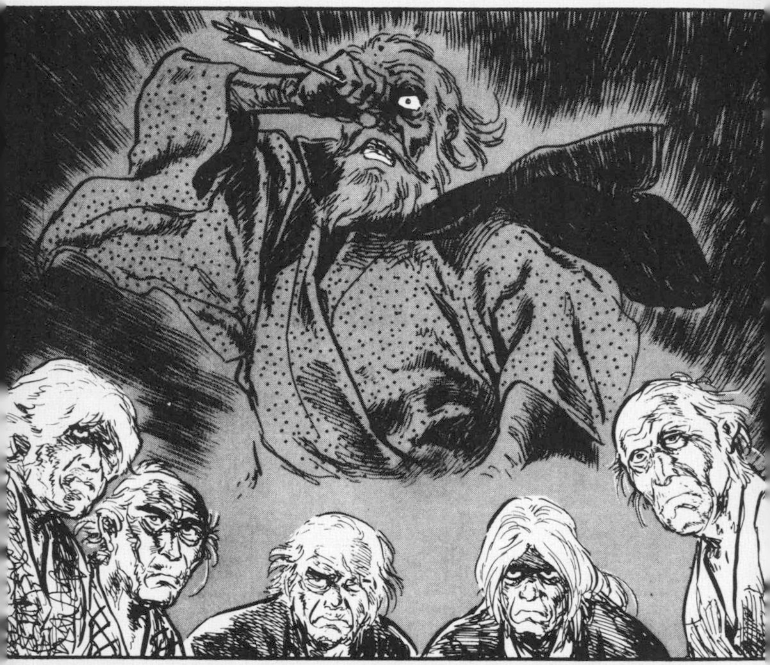

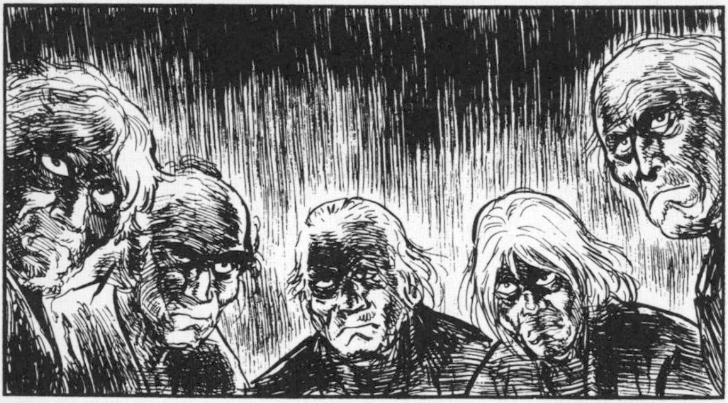

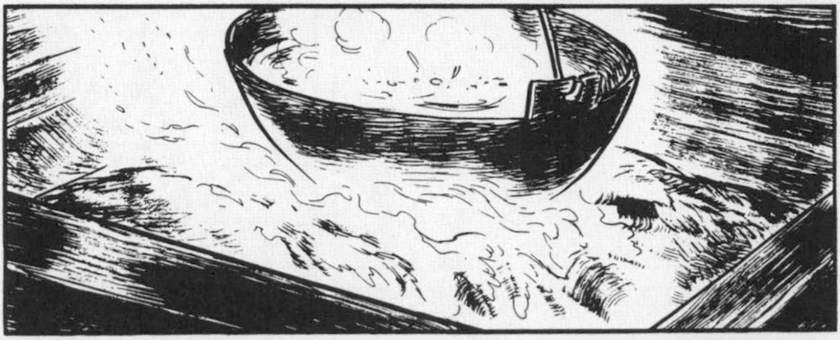
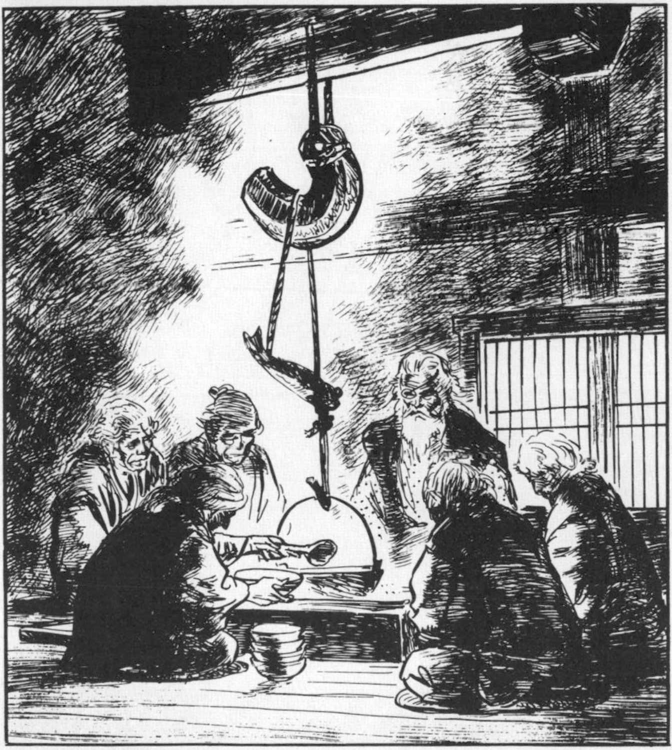

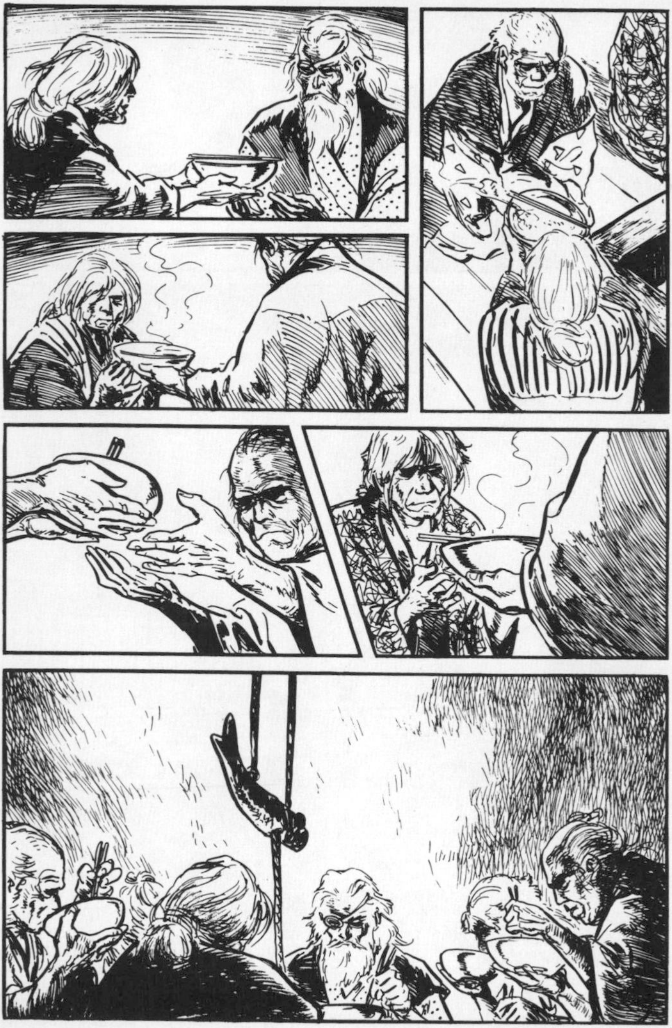

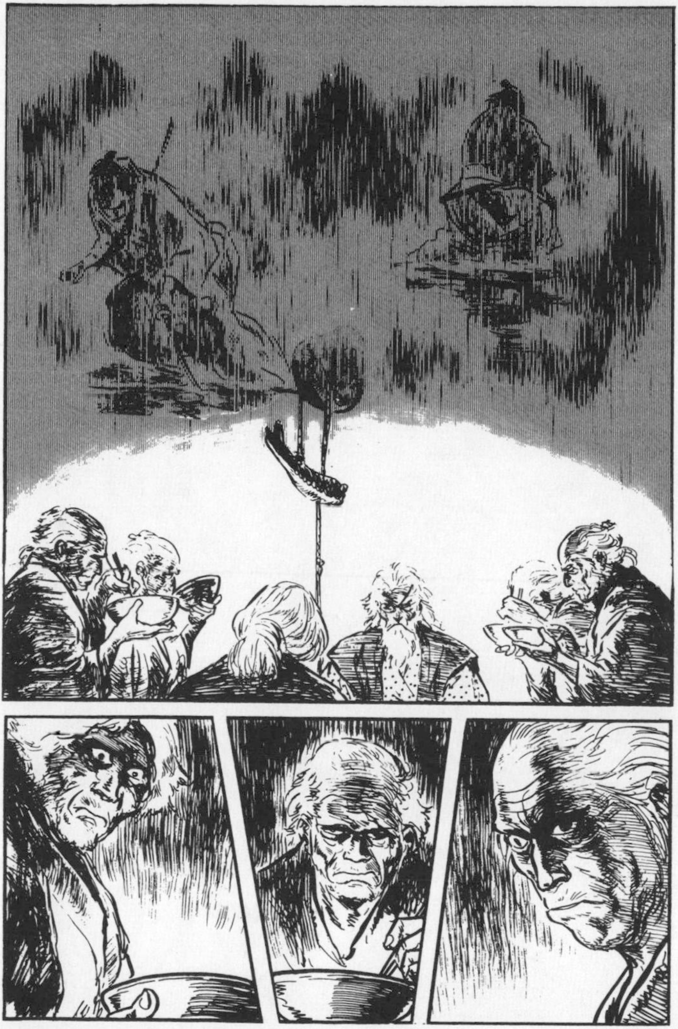

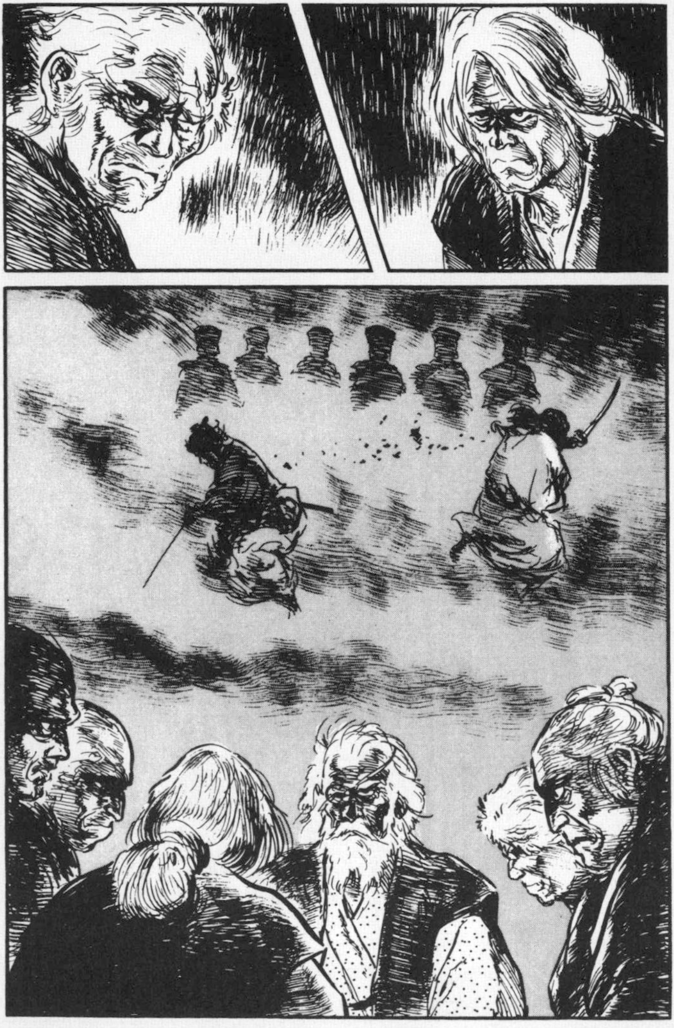

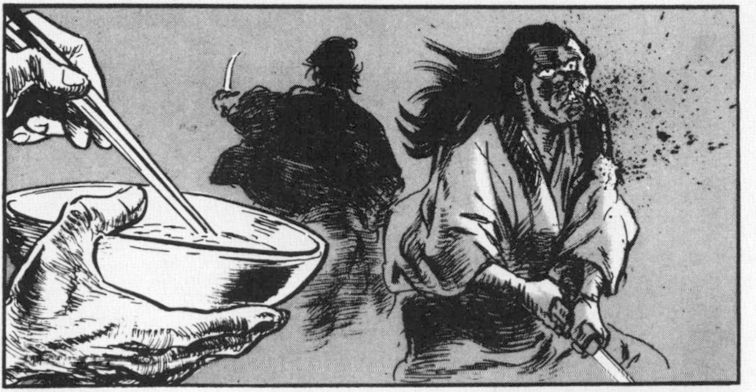
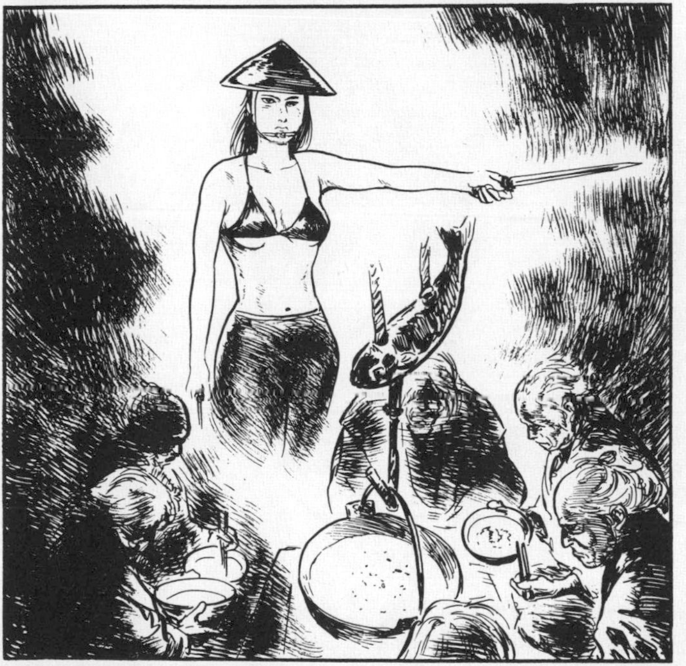

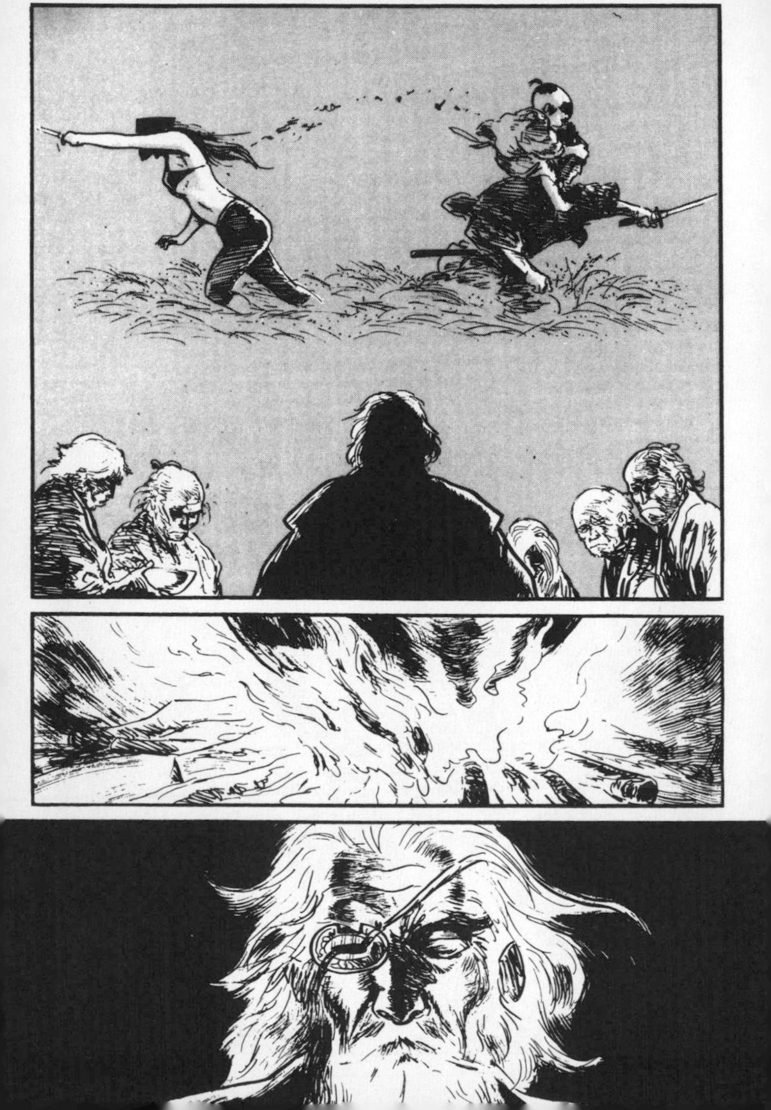

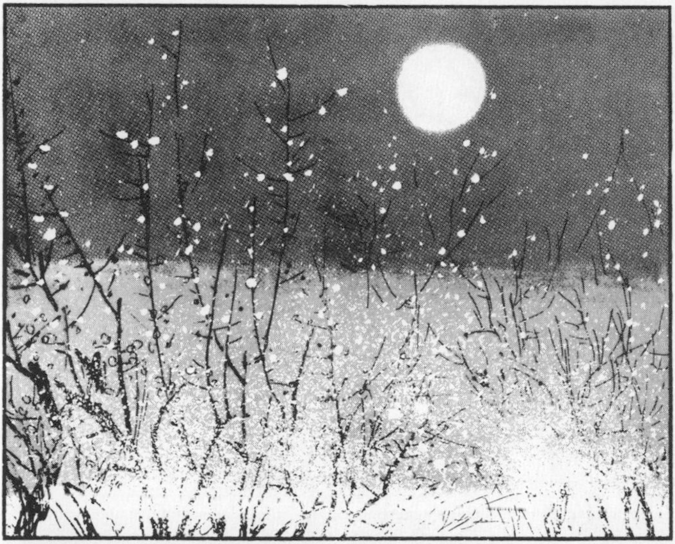
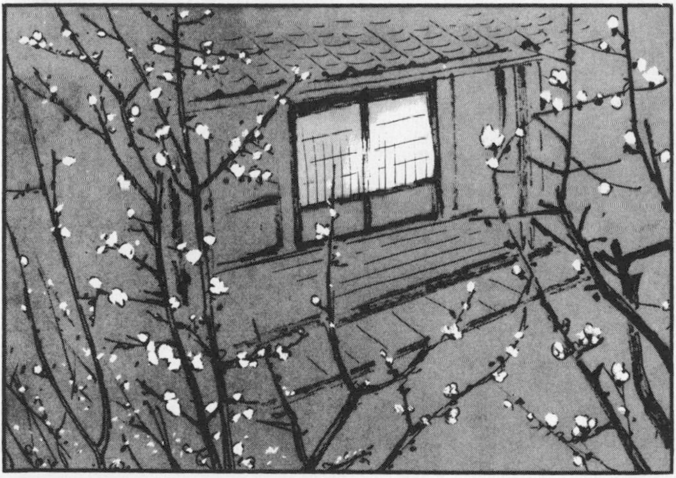

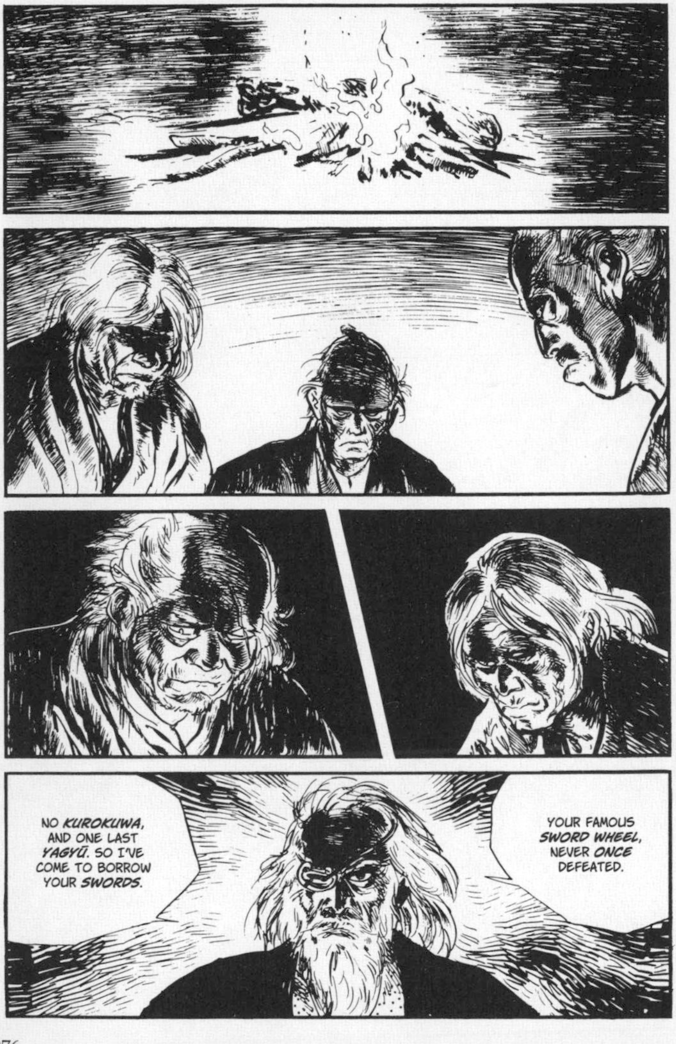
YOUR FAMOUS *SWORD WHEEL*, NEVER *ONCE* DEFEATED.
NO *KUROKUWA*, AND ONE LAST *YAGYŪ*. SO I'VE COME TO BORROW YOUR *SWORDS*.

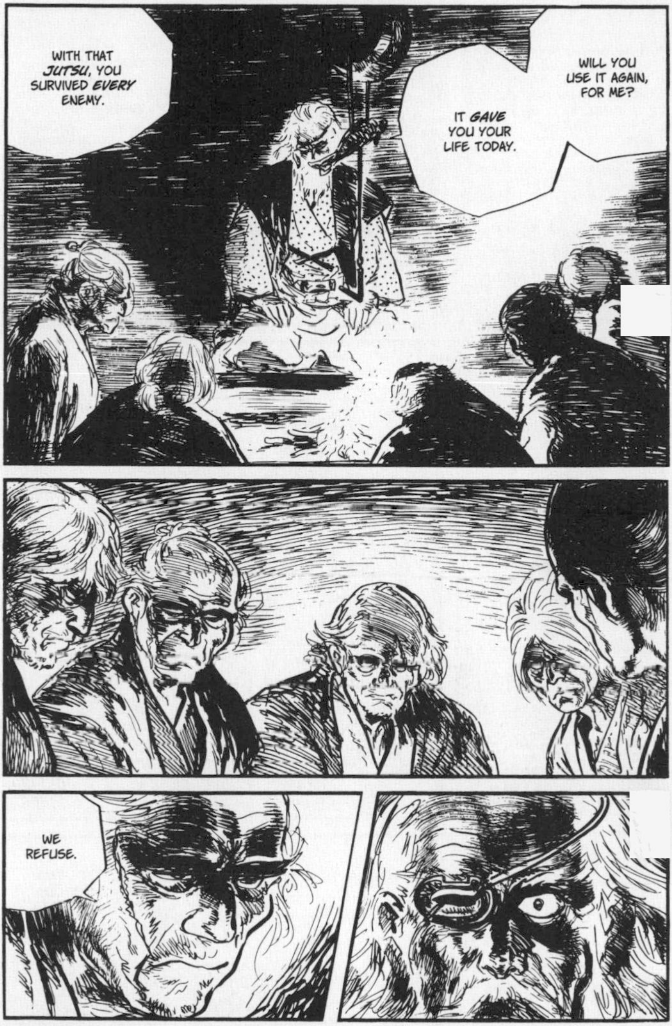
WITH THAT *JUTSU*, YOU SURVIVED *EVERY* ENEMY.
IT *GAVE* YOU YOUR LIFE TODAY.
WILL YOU USE IT AGAIN, FOR ME?
WE REFUSE.

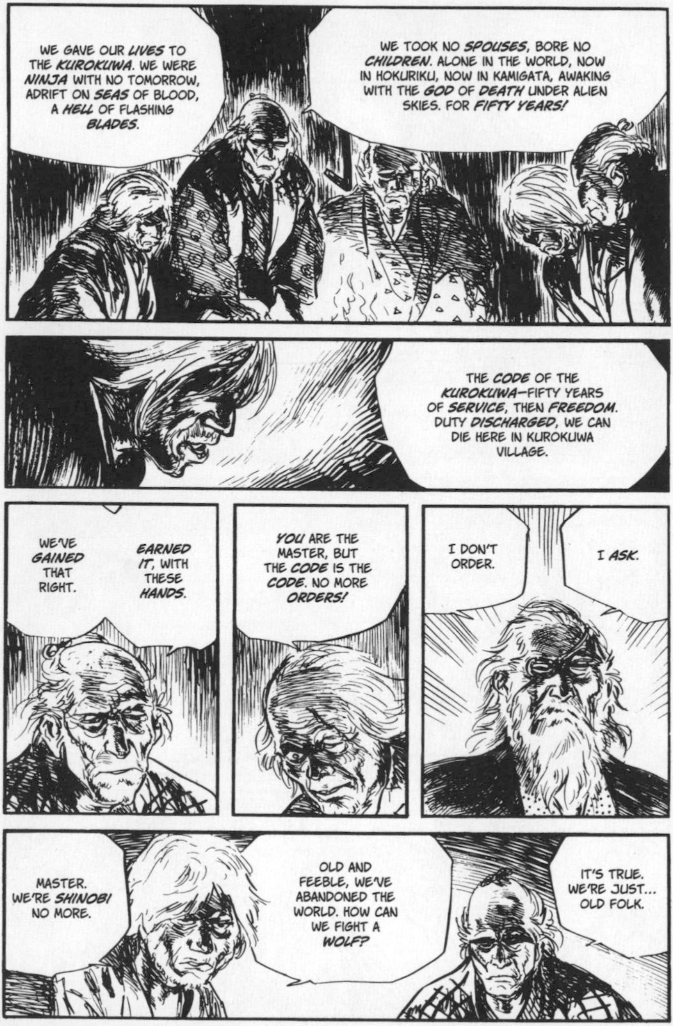
WE GAVE OUR LIVES TO THE KUROKUWA. WE WERE NINJA WITH NO TOMORROW, ADRIFT ON SEAS OF BLOOD, A HELL OF FLASHING BLADES.
WE TOOK NO SPOUSES, BORE NO CHILDREN. ALONE IN THE WORLD, NOW IN HOKURIKU, NOW IN KAMIGATA, AWAKING WITH THE GOD OF DEATH UNDER ALIEN SKIES. FOR FIFTY YEARS!
THE CODE OF THE KUROKUWA—FIFTY YEARS OF SERVICE, THEN FREEDOM. DUTY DISCHARGED, WE CAN DIE HERE IN KUROKUWA VILLAGE.
WE'VE GAINED THAT RIGHT.
EARNED IT, WITH THESE HANDS.
YOU ARE THE MASTER, BUT THE CODE IS THE CODE. NO MORE ORDERS!
I DON'T ORDER.
I ASK.
MASTER. WE'RE SHINOBI NO MORE.
OLD AND FEEBLE, WE'VE ABANDONED THE WORLD. HOW CAN WE FIGHT A WOLF?
IT'S TRUE. WE'RE JUST... OLD FOLK.

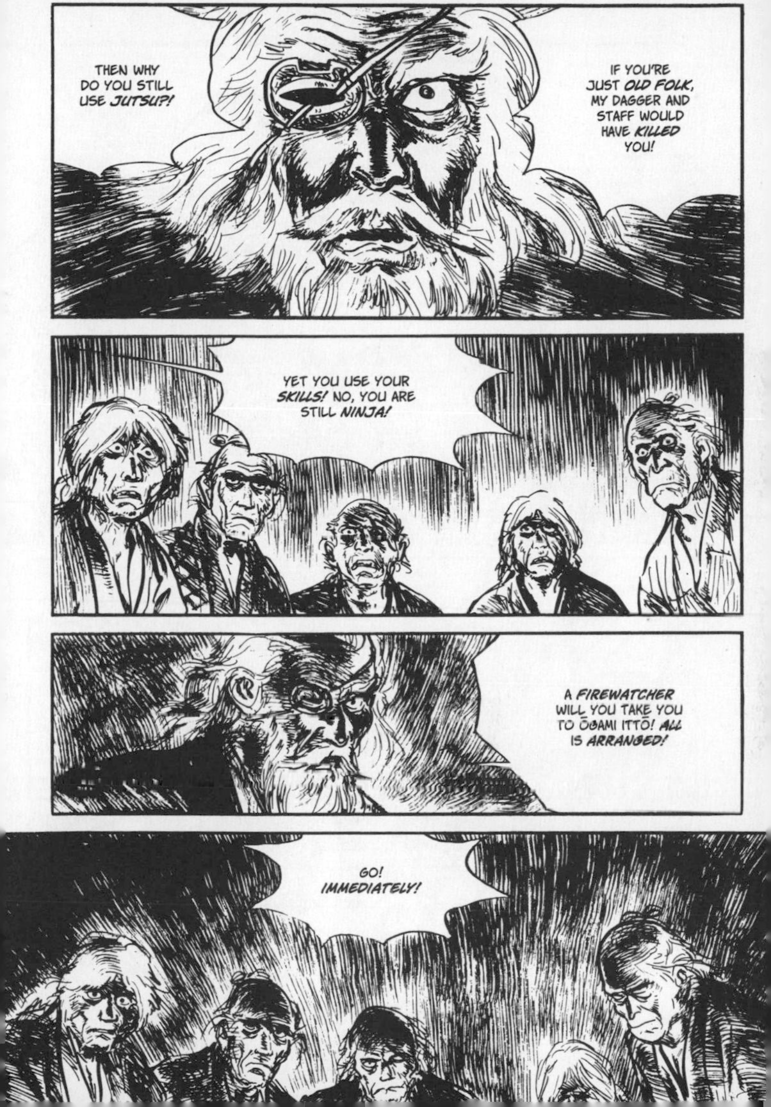
IF YOU'RE JUST OLD FOLK, MY DAGGER AND STAFF WOULD HAVE KILLED YOU!
THEN WHY DO YOU STILL USE JUTSU?!
YET YOU USE YOUR SKILLS! NO, YOU ARE STILL NINJA!
A FIREWATCHER WILL YOU TAKE YOU TO ŌGAMI ITTŌ! ALL IS ARRANGED!
GO! IMMEDIATELY!

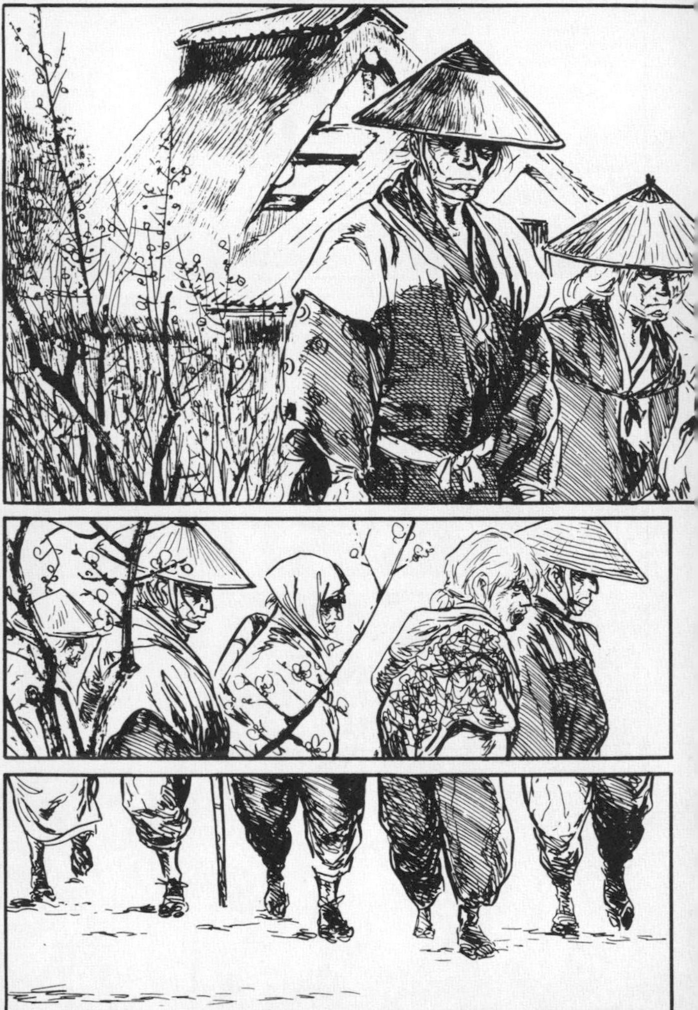

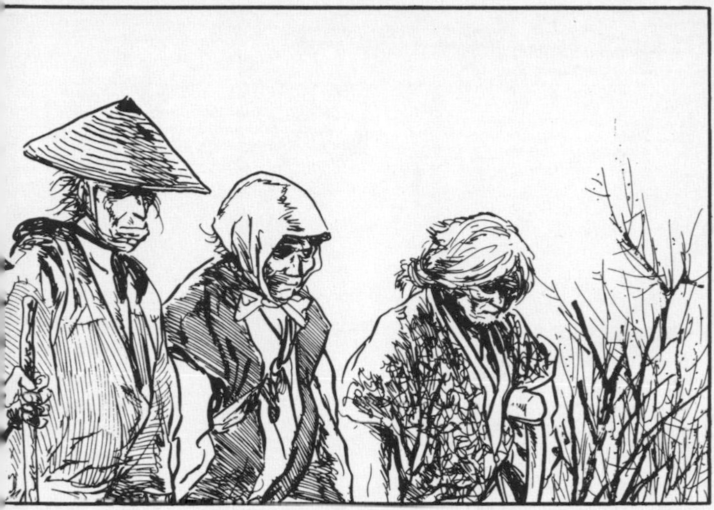
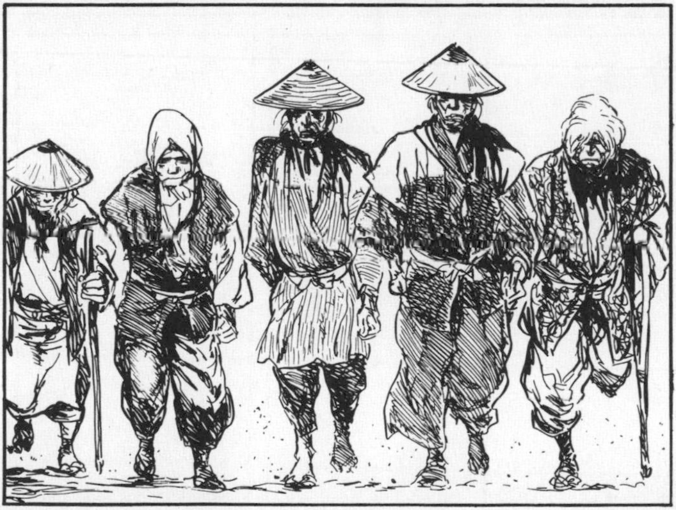

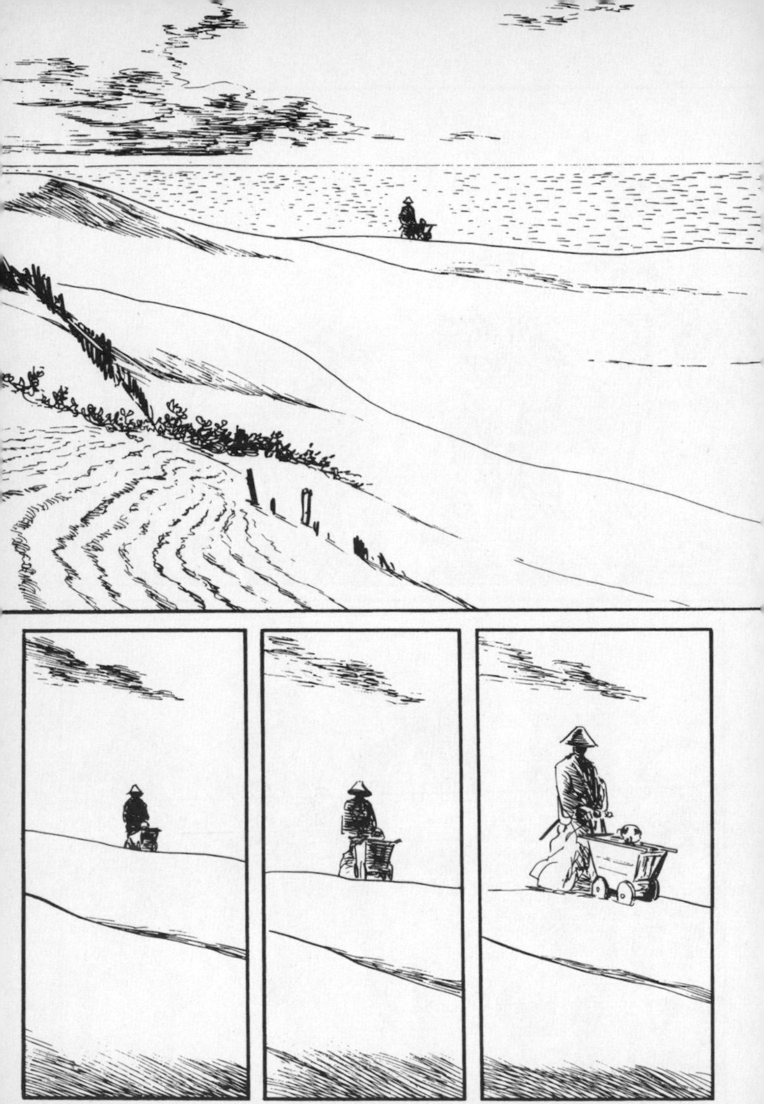

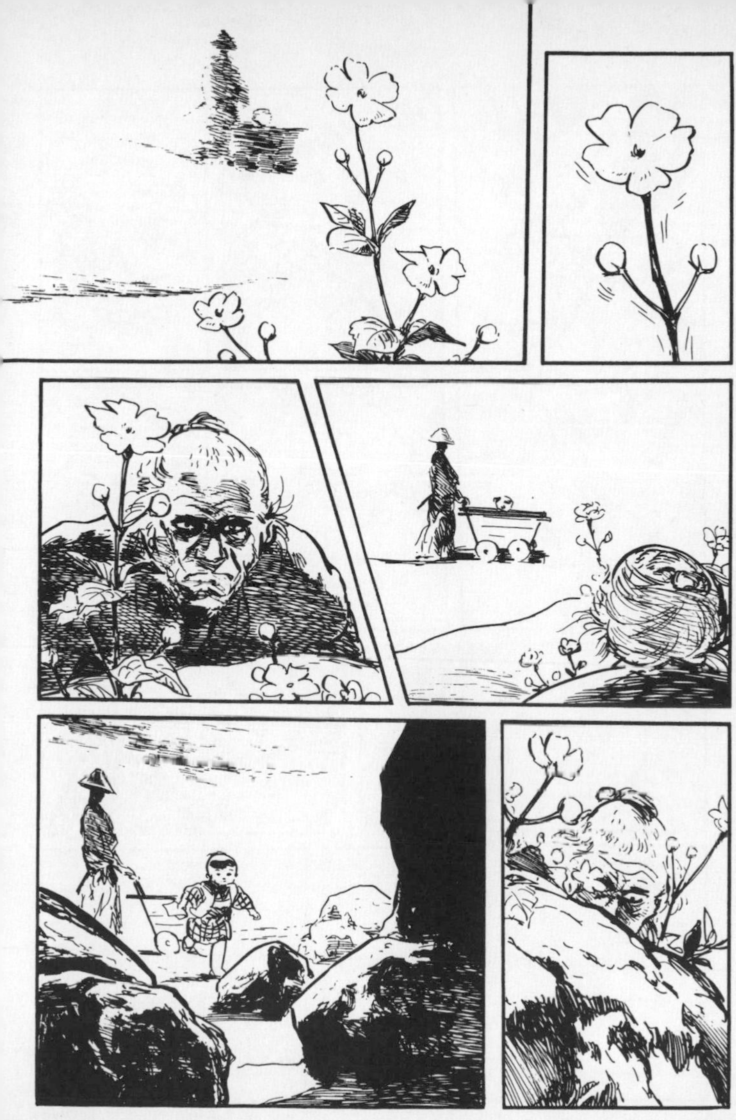

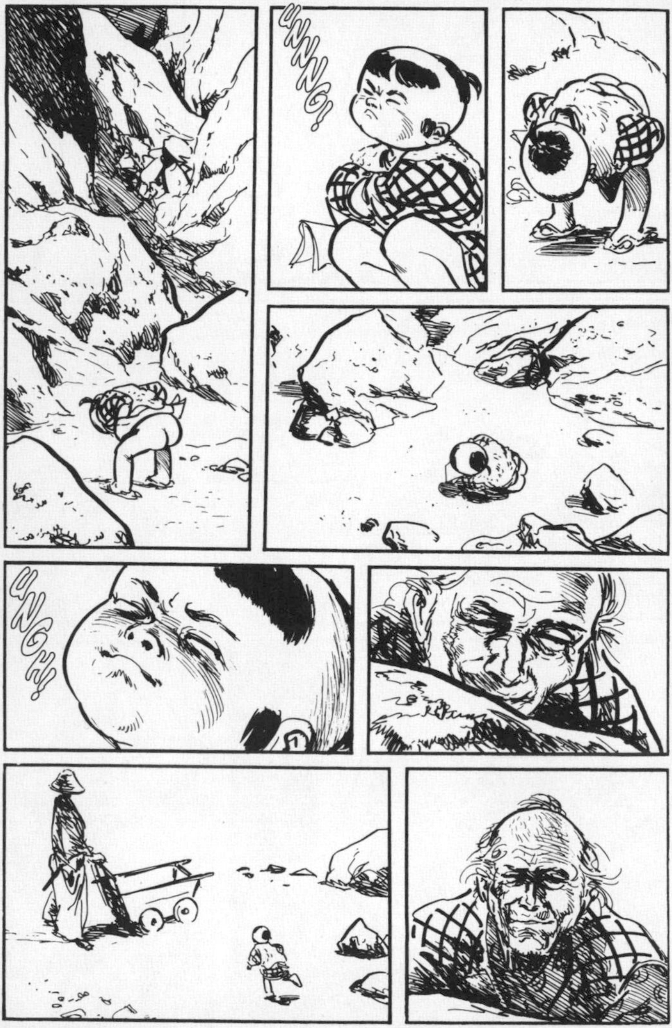
UNNNG!
UNGH!

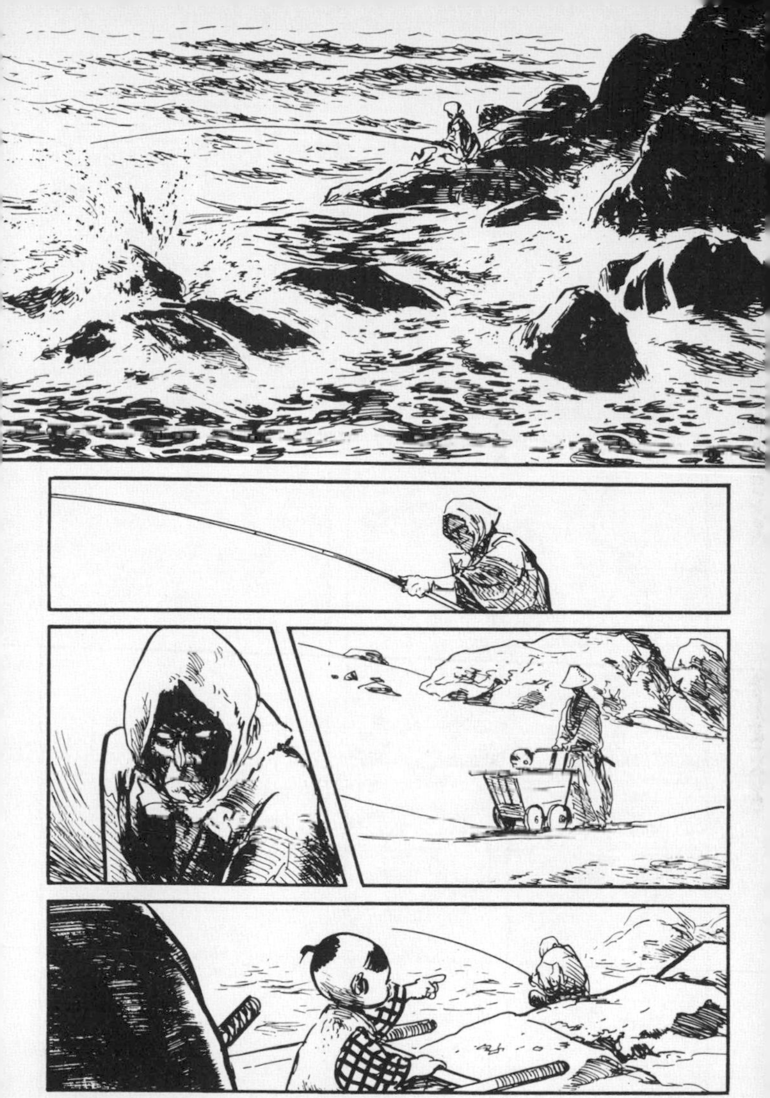

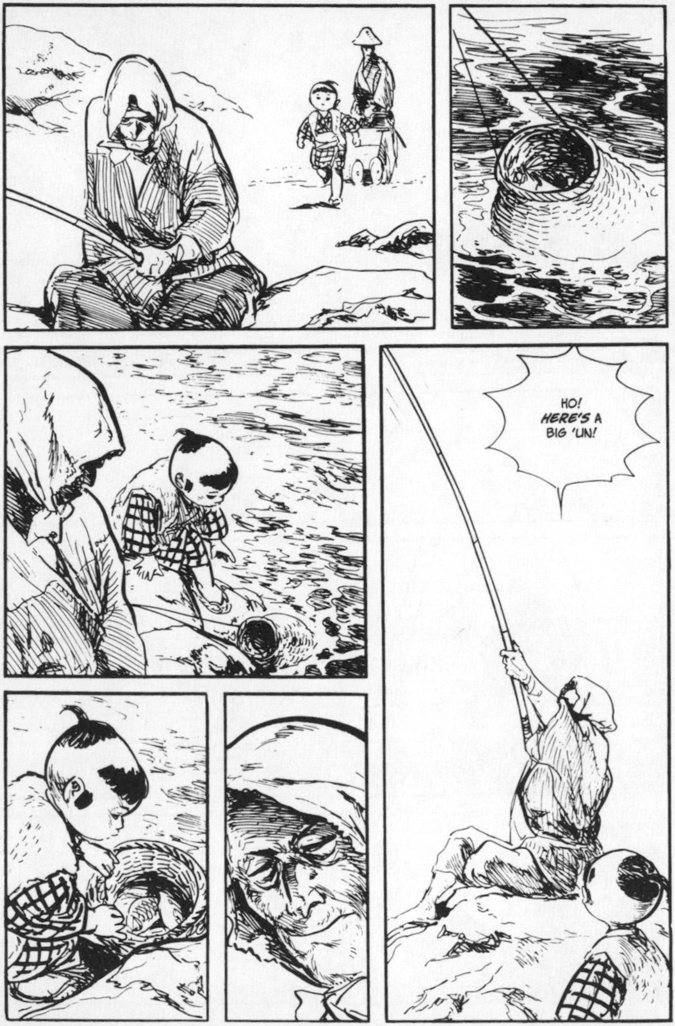
HO! ***HERE'S*** A BIG 'UN!

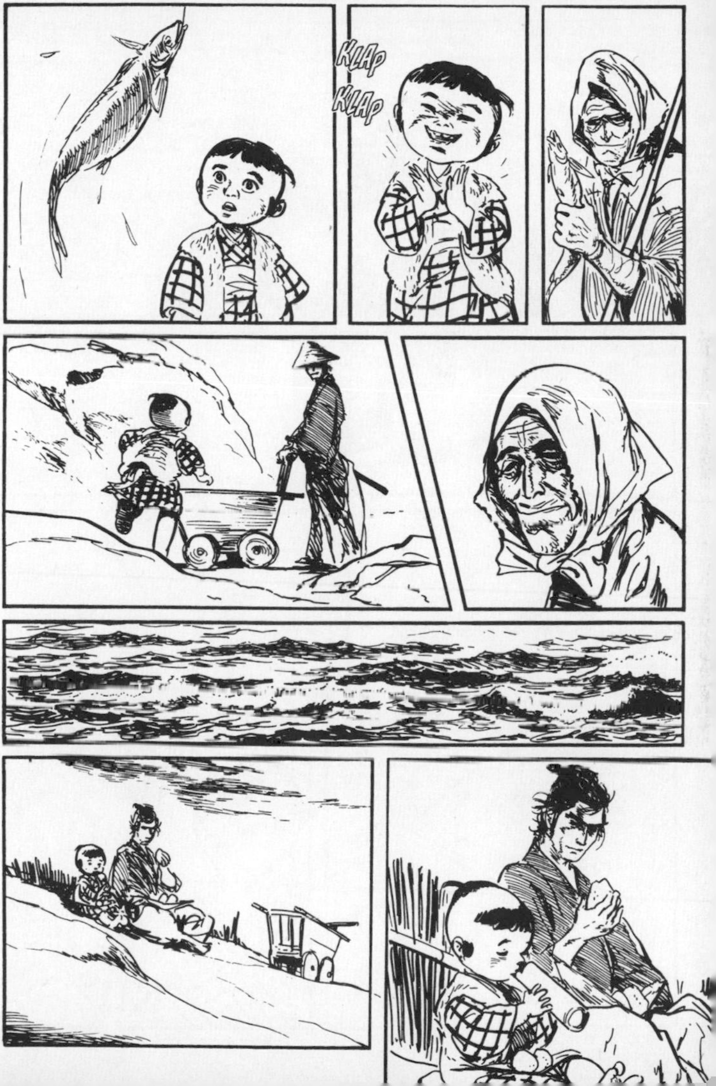
KLAP
KLAP

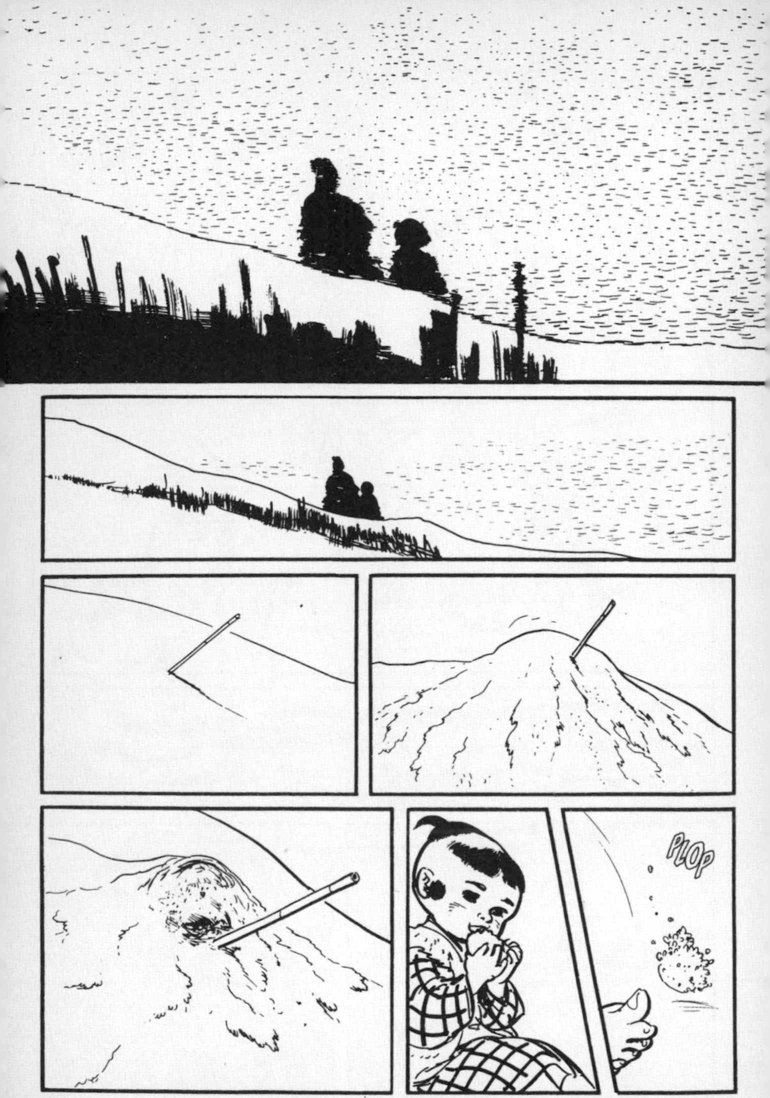
PLOP

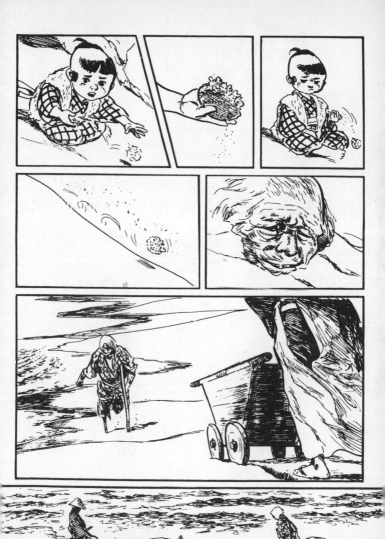

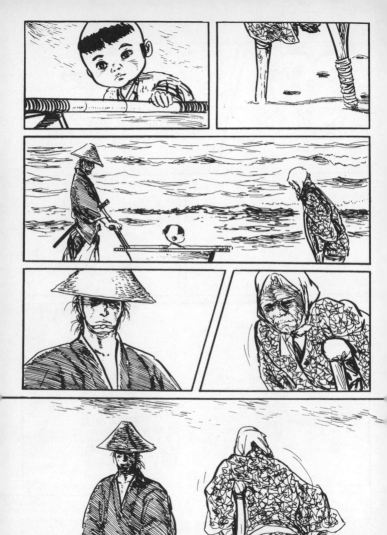

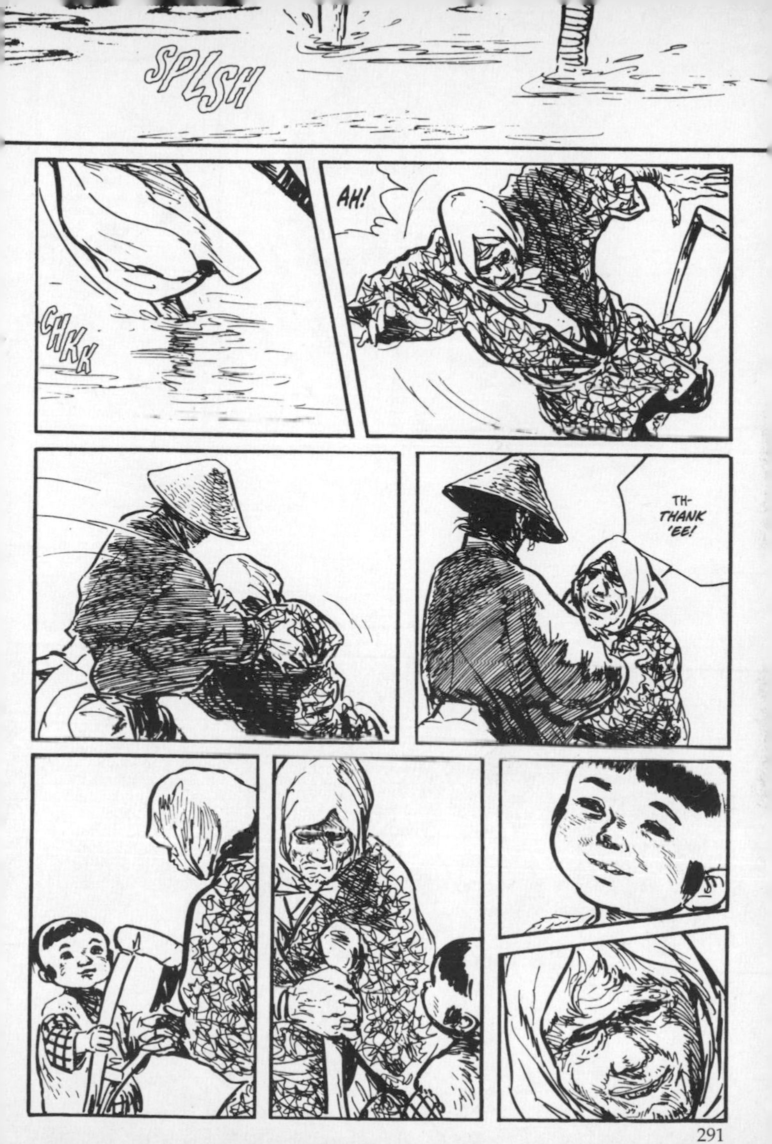
SPLSH
AH!
CHKK
TH- THANK 'EE!

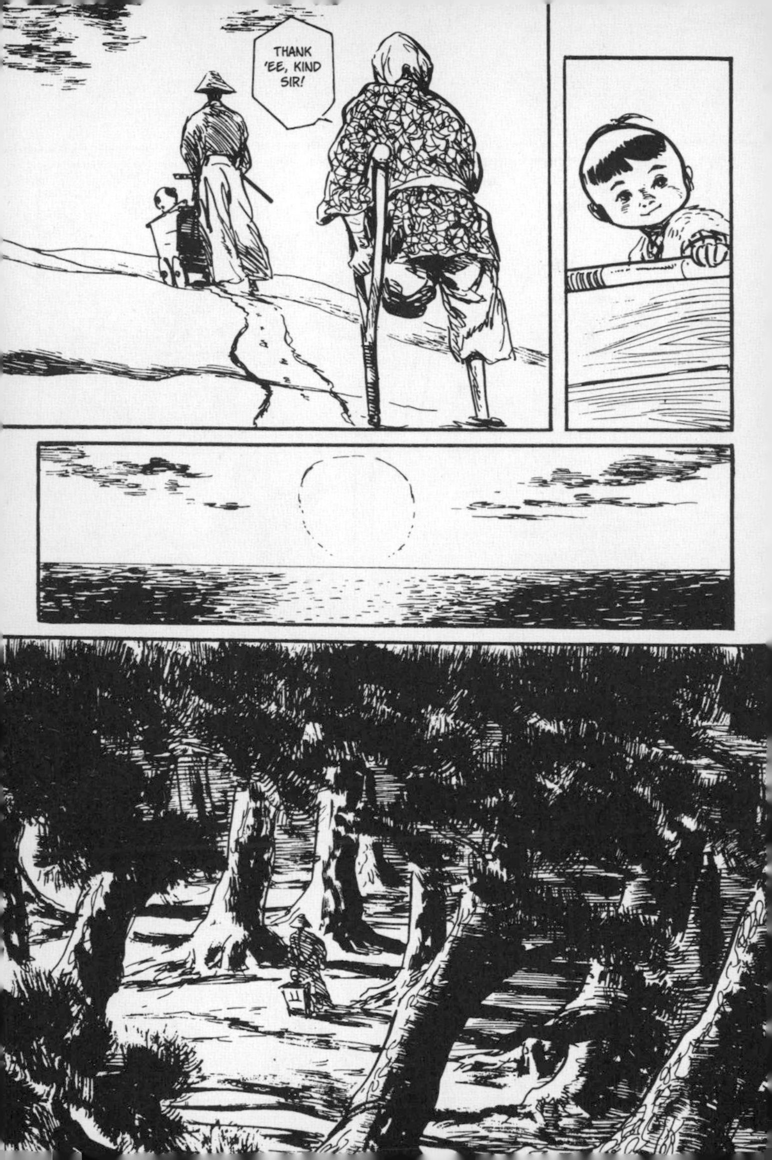
THANK 'EE, KIND SIR!

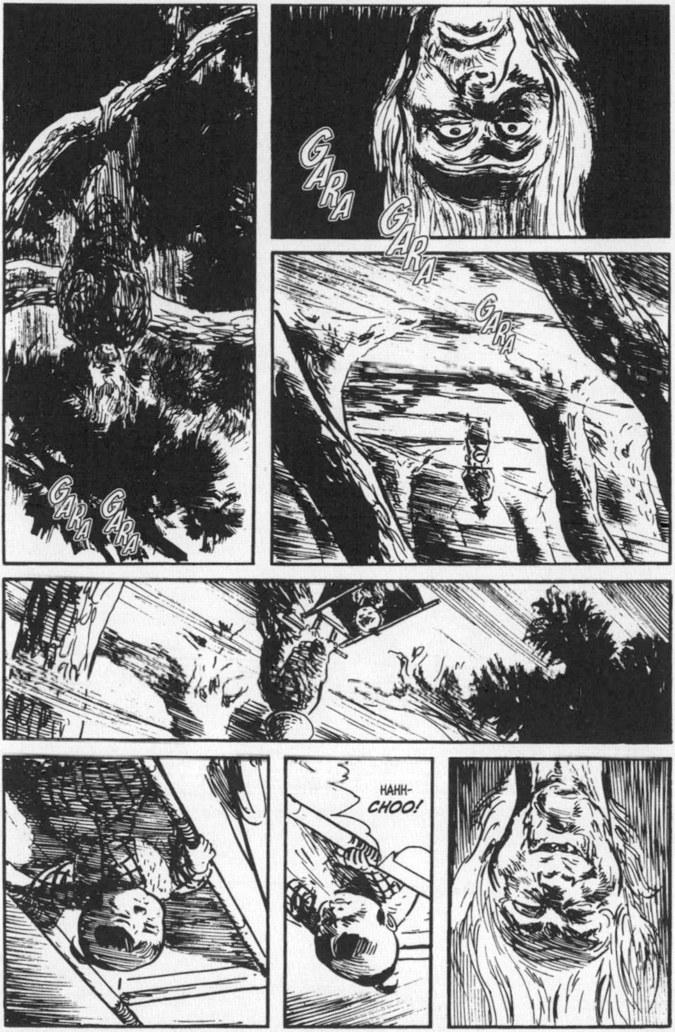
GARA
GARA
GARA
GARA GARA
HAHH-CHOO!

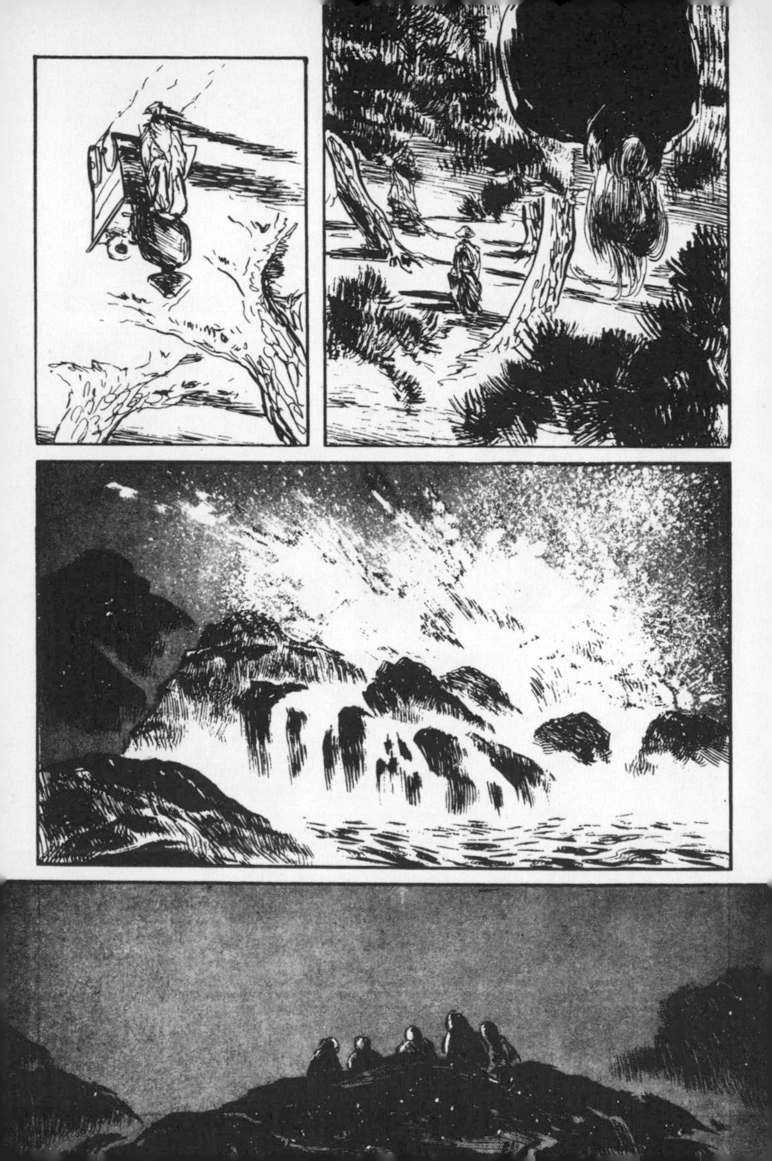

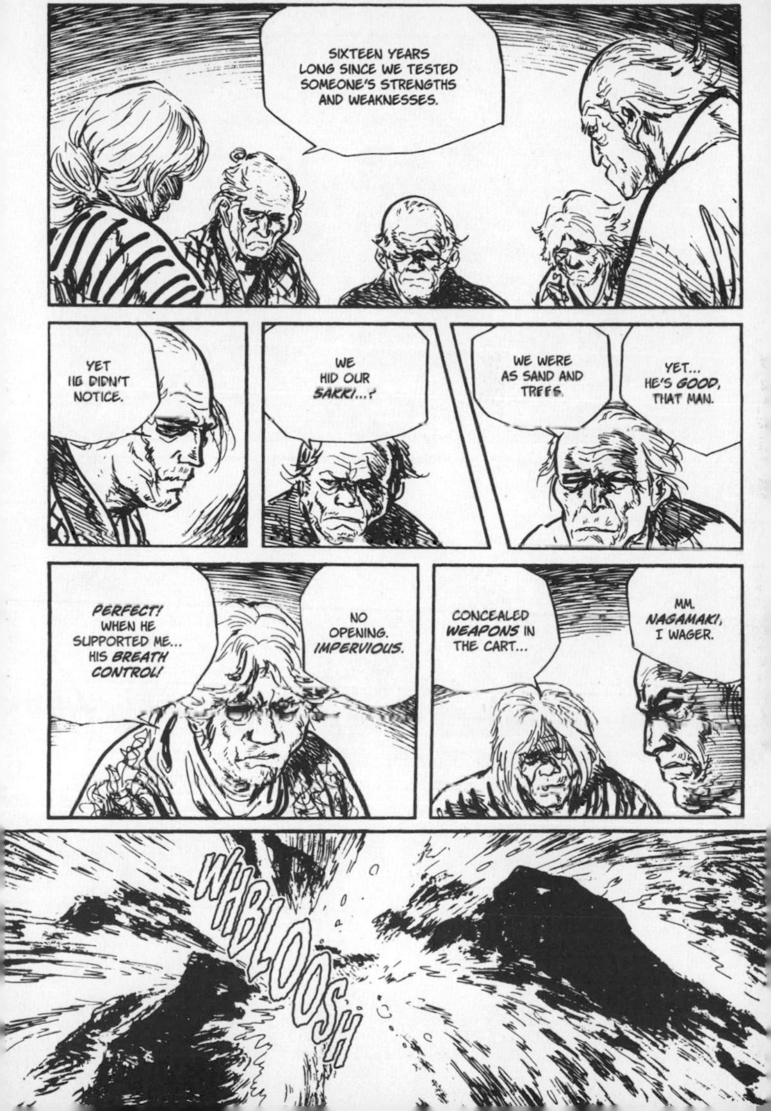
SIXTEEN YEARS LONG SINCE WE TESTED SOMEONE'S STRENGTHS AND WEAKNESSES.
YET HE DIDN'T NOTICE.
WE HID OUR *SAKKI*...?
WE WERE AS SAND AND TREES.
YET... HE'S *GOOD,* THAT MAN.
PERFECT! WHEN HE SUPPORTED ME... HIS *BREATH CONTROL!*
NO OPENING. *IMPERVIOUS.*
CONCEALED *WEAPONS* IN THE CART...
MM. *NAGAMAKI,* I WAGER.
WHBLOOSH

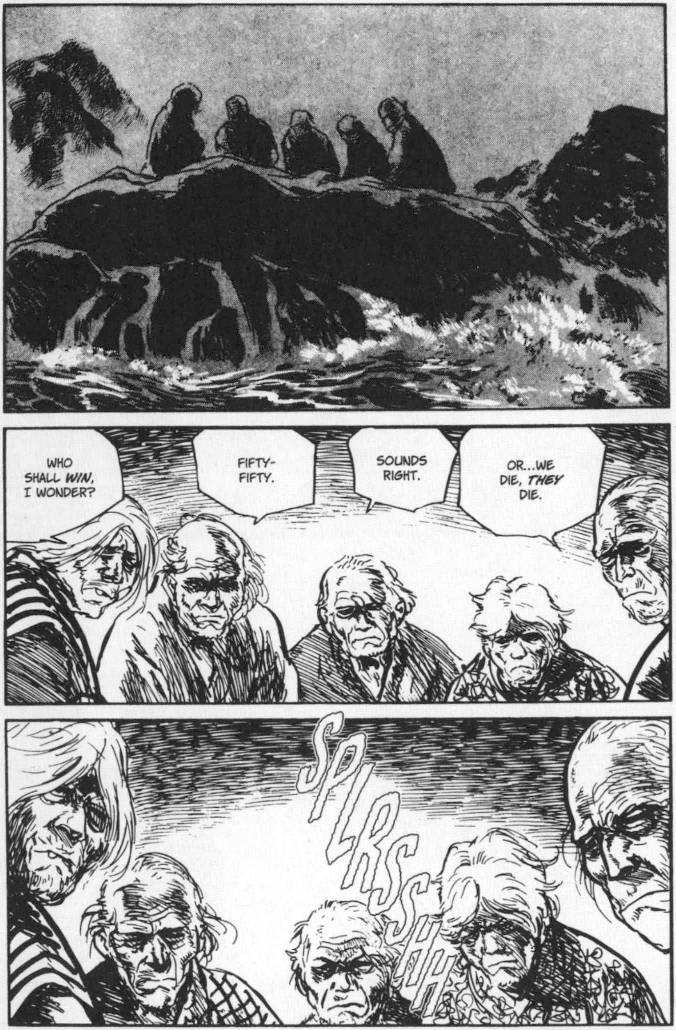
WHO SHALL *WIN*, I WONDER?
FIFTY-FIFTY.
SOUNDS RIGHT.
OR...WE DIE, *THEY* DIE.
SPLRSSHH

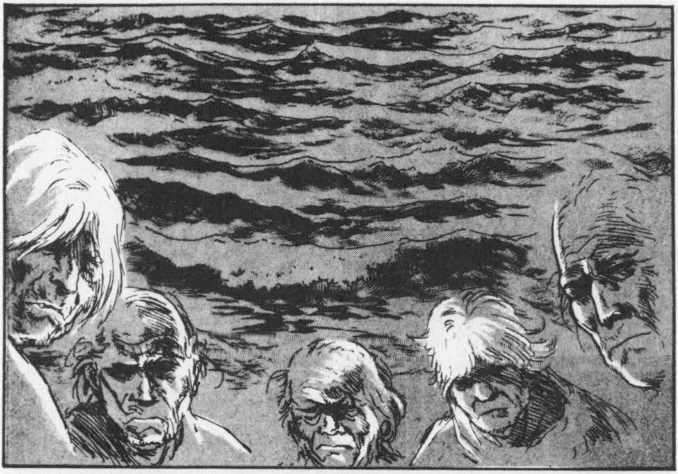
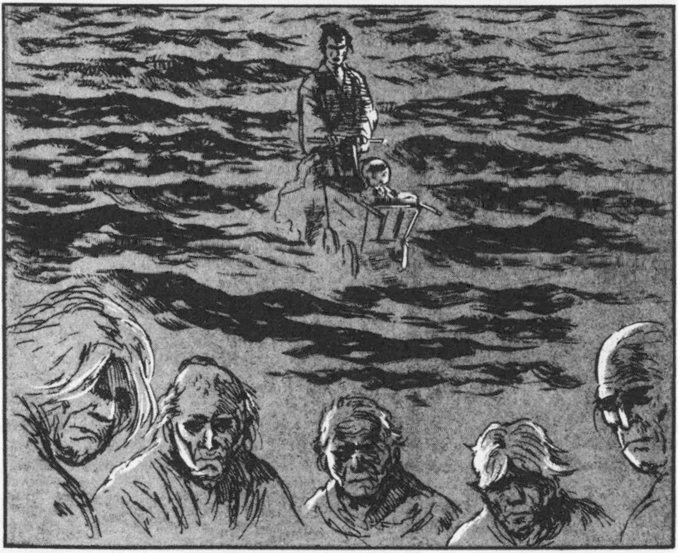

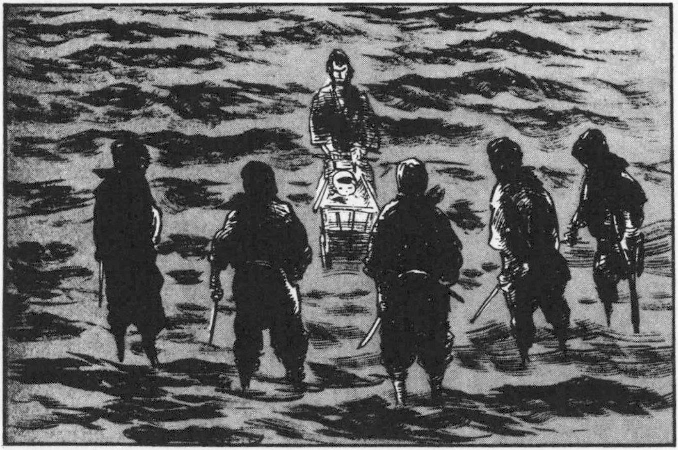
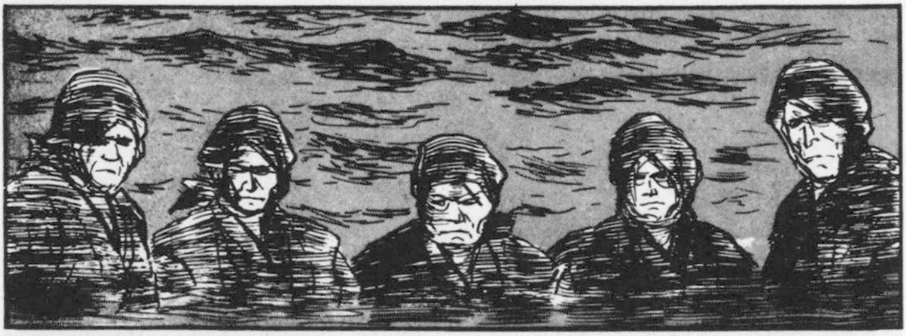
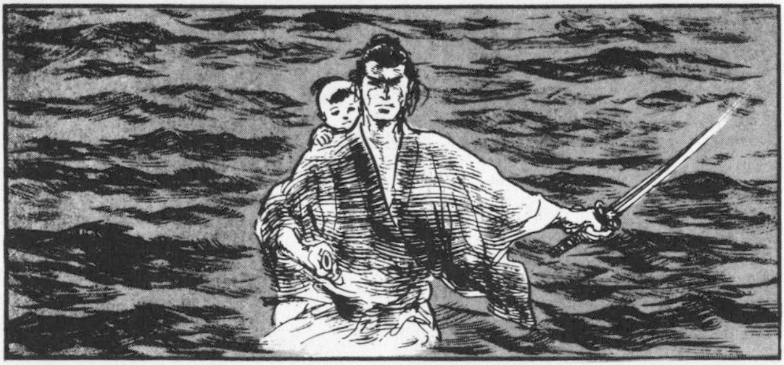

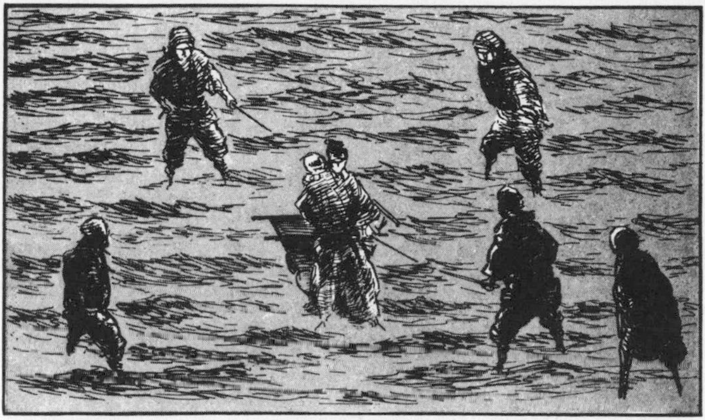

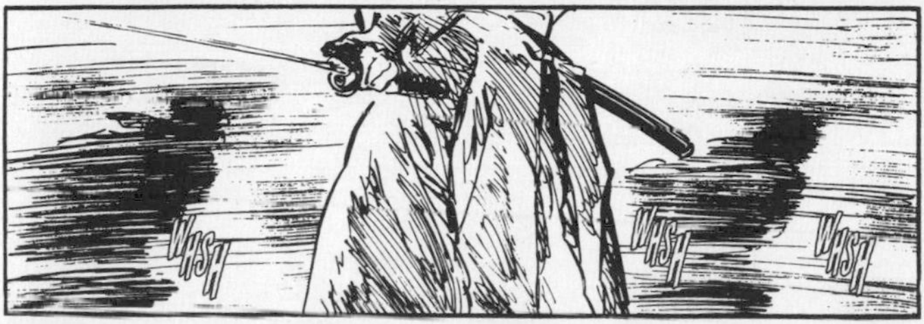
WHSH
WHSH
WHSH

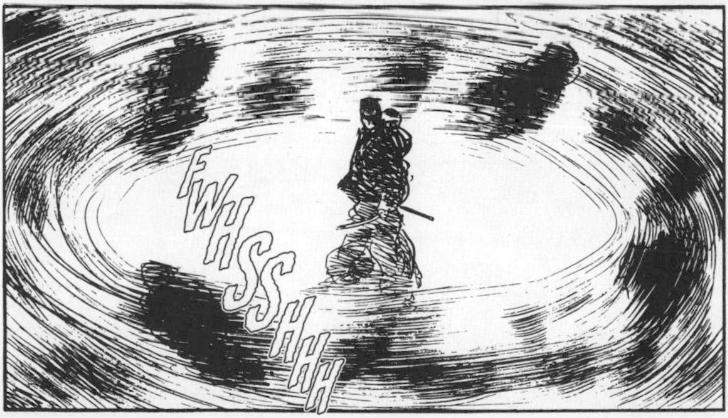
FWHSSHHH

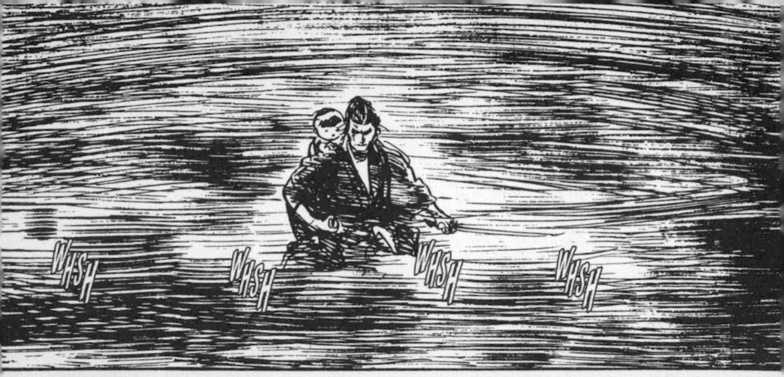
WHSH
WHSH
WHSH
WHSH
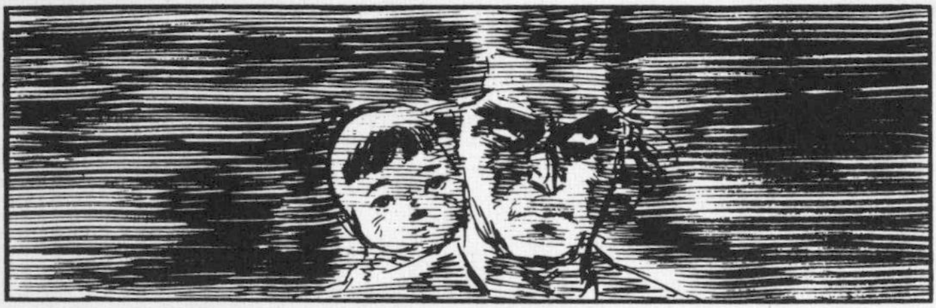
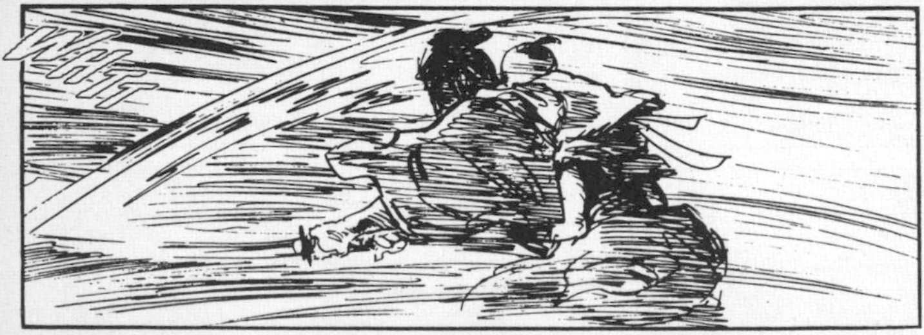
WHIT
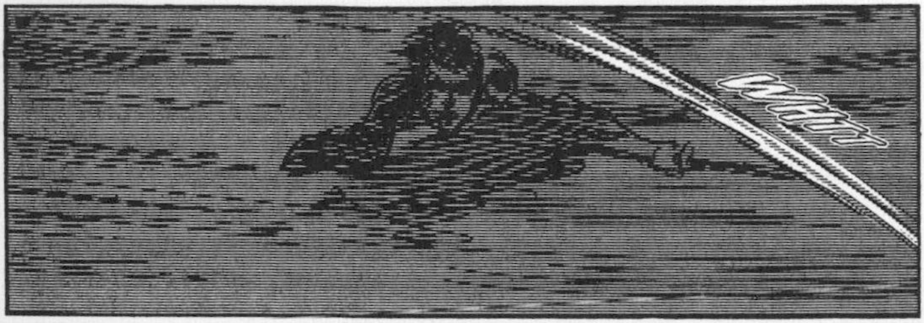

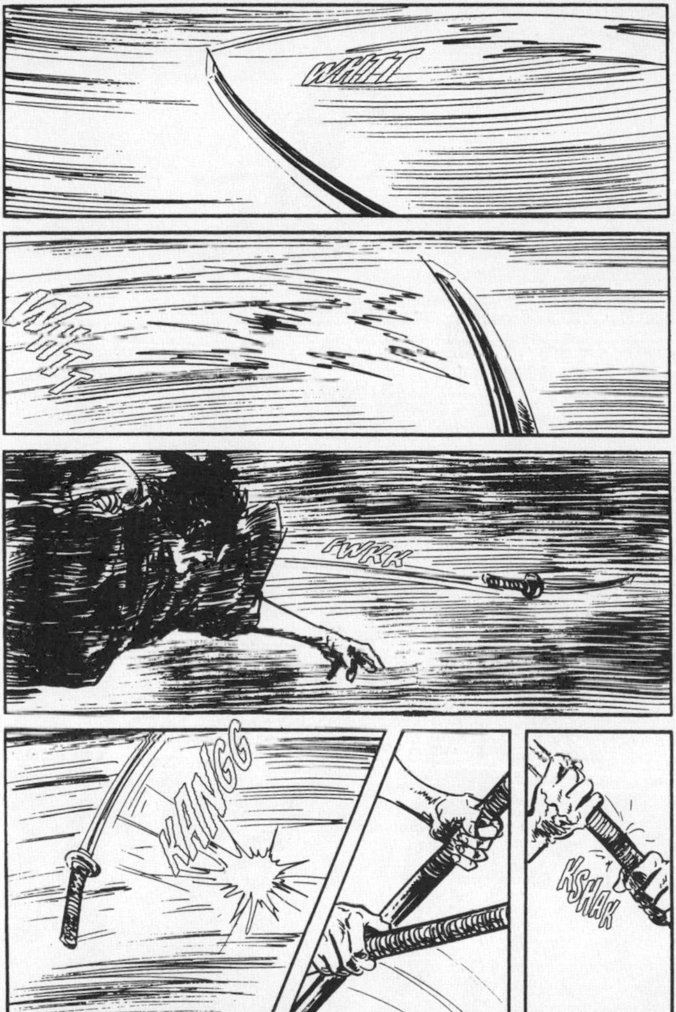
WHITT
WHITT
FWKK
KSHAK
KANGG

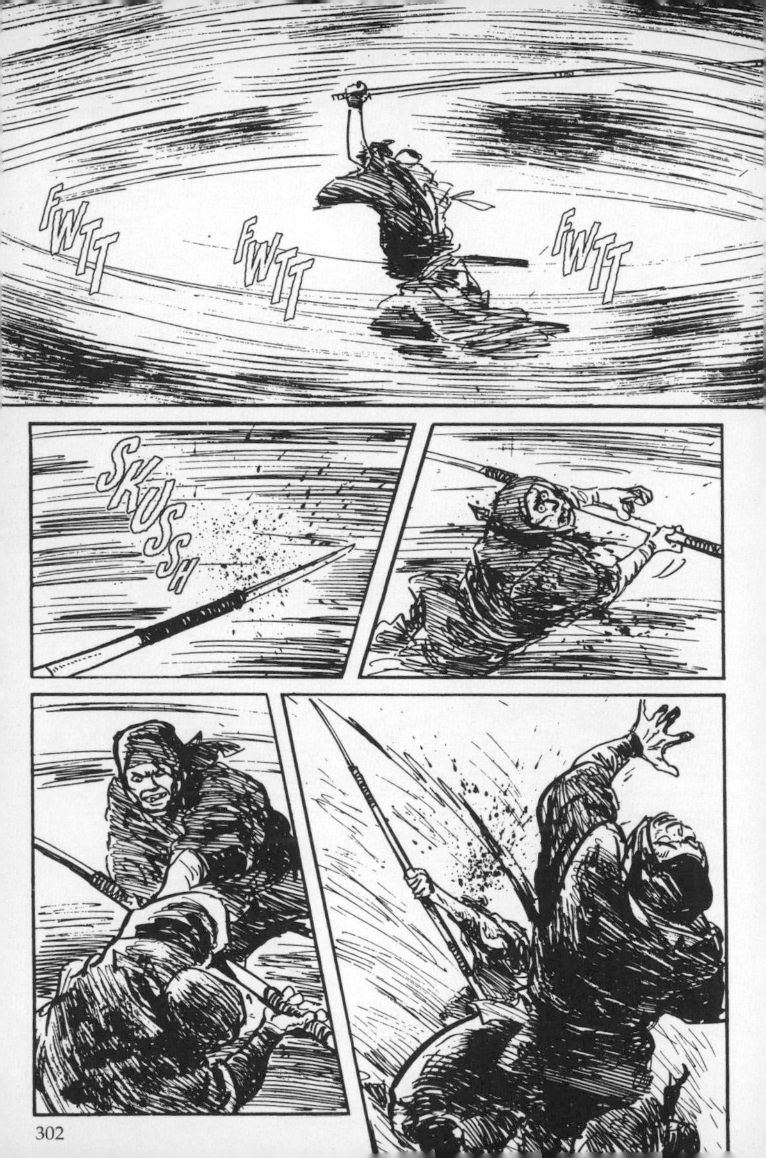
FWTT
FWTT
FWTT
SKUSSH

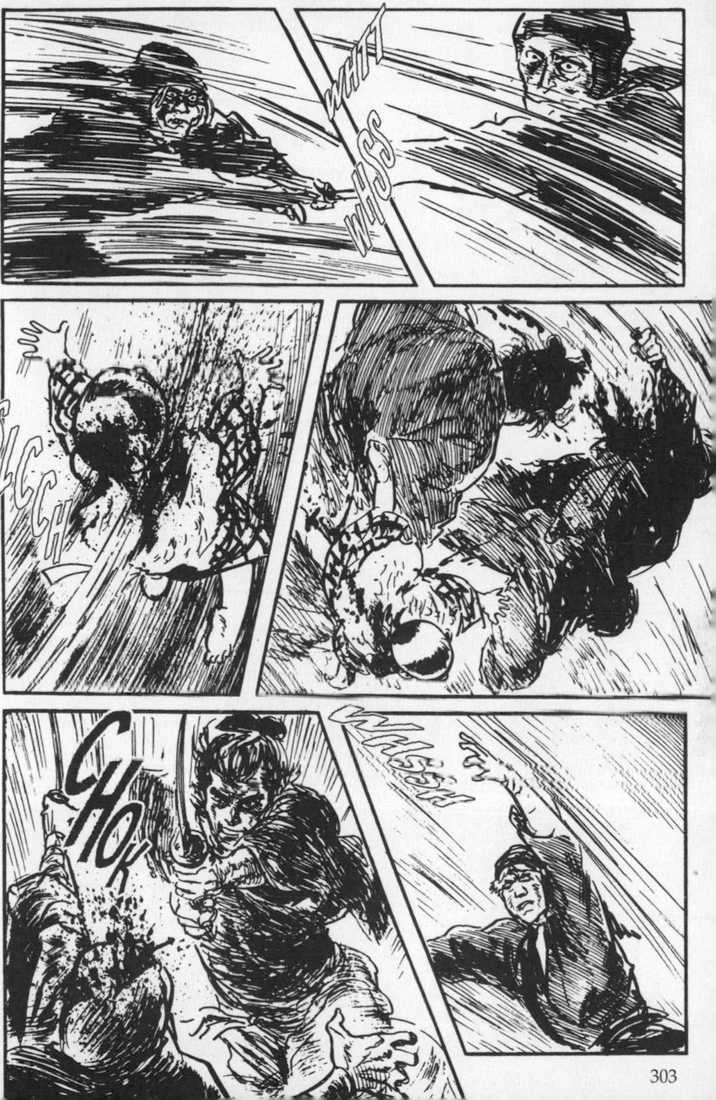
WHTT
WHSS
SLCCH
WHSSH
CHOK

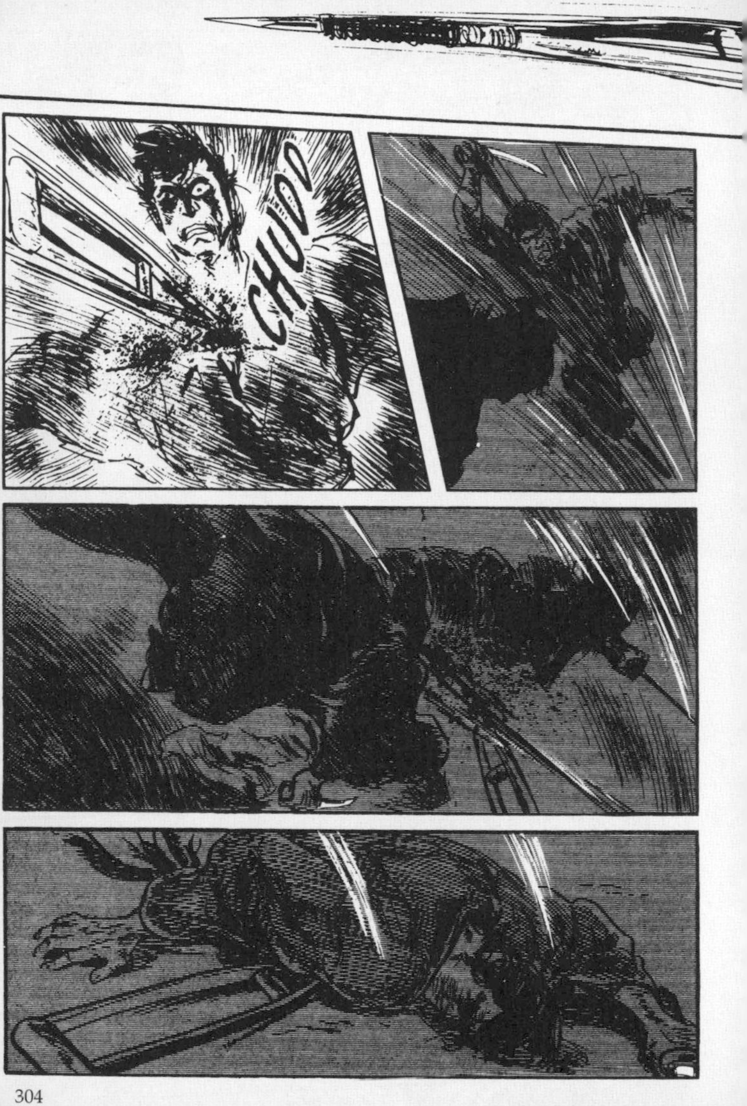
CHUDD

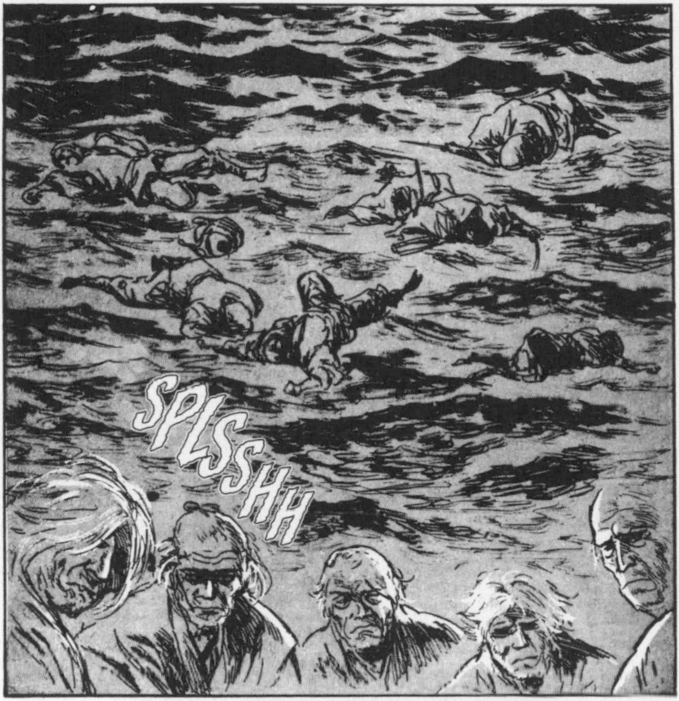
SPLSSHH

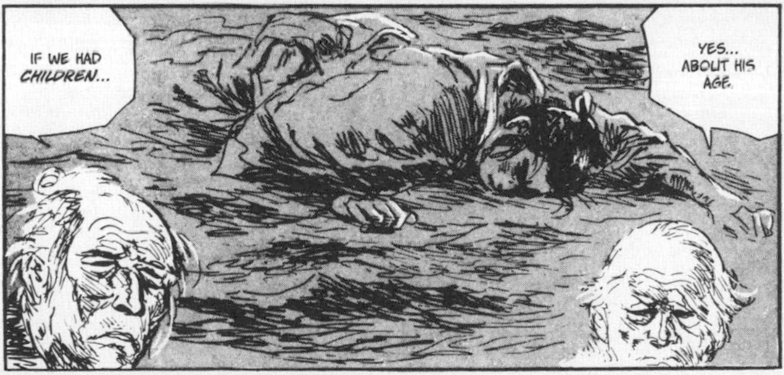
IF WE HAD CHILDREN...
YES... ABOUT HIS AGE.

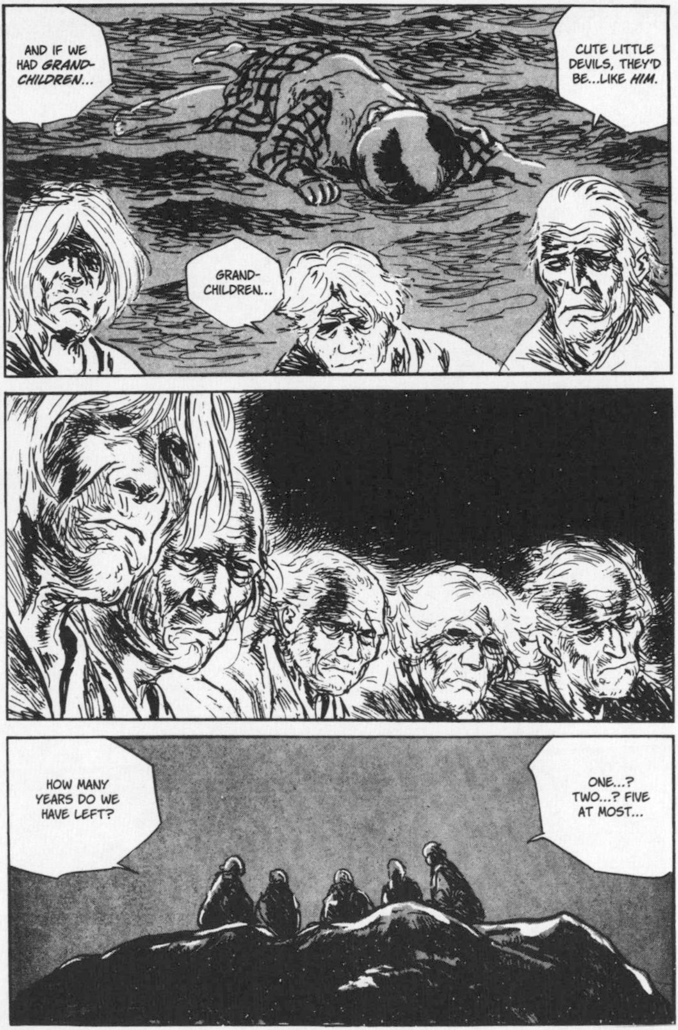
AND IF WE HAD *GRAND-CHILDREN*...
CUTE LITTLE DEVILS, THEY'D BE...LIKE *HIM*.
GRAND-CHILDREN...
HOW MANY YEARS DO WE HAVE LEFT?
ONE...? TWO...? FIVE AT MOST...

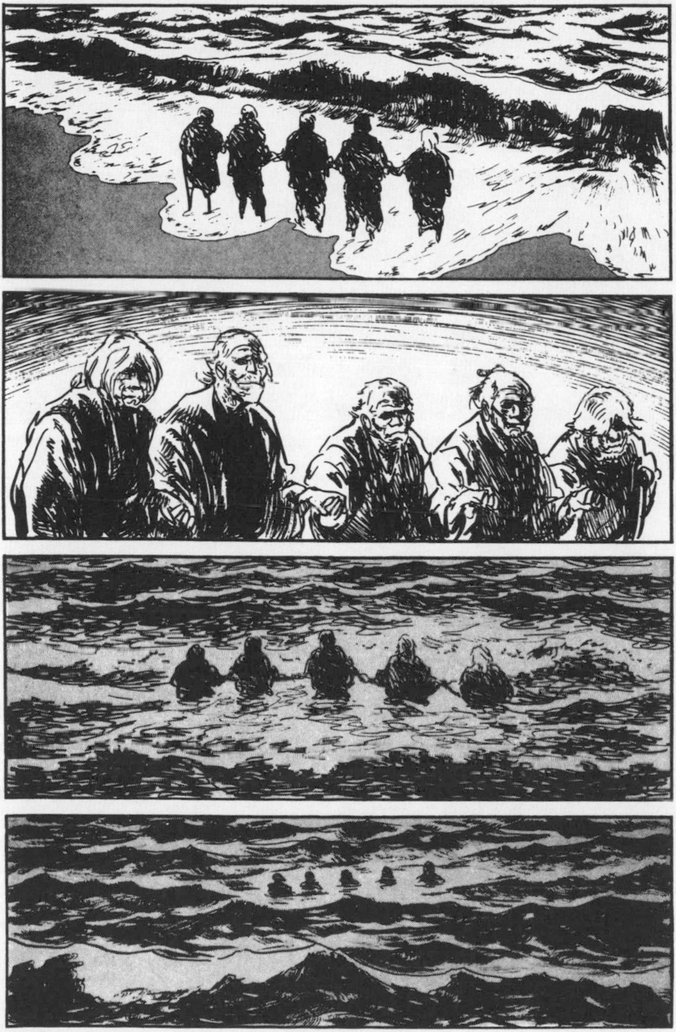

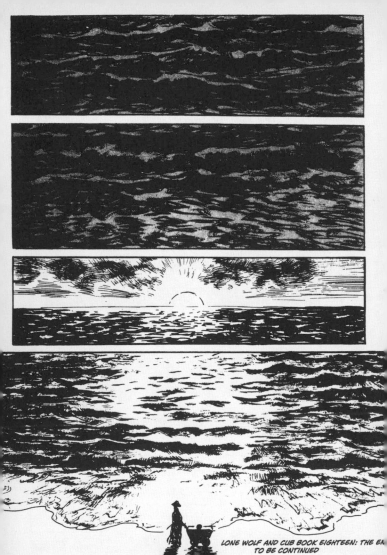

LONE WOLF AND CUB BOOK EIGHTEEN: THE EN
TO BE CONTINUED

GLOSSARY

ashigara
Lightly armed foot soldiers, the lowest ranks of the samurai caste.

buke
A samurai household.

bushi
A samurai. A member of the warrior class.

bushidō
The way of the warrior. Also known as *shidō*.

daikan
An official who collected taxes owed to Edo and oversaw public works, agriculture, and other projects administered by the central government.

daimyō
A feudal lord.

Edo
The capital of medieval Japan and the seat of the shōgunate. The site of modern-day Tokyo.

Fudai daimyō
The inner circle of clans pledging allegiance to the Tokugawa. The Fudai clans were Tokugawa allies even before Tokugawa Ieyasu's decisive victory of Sekigahara that launched the Tokugawa Shogunate.

go-shihai-sama
Master

han
A feudal domain.

nashigo
Ladder

hōgen
The second highest rank of Buddhist priest.

hōin
Hōin dai-wakō, the highest ranked Buddhist priests.

honorifics
Japan is a class and status society, and proper forms of address are critical. Common markers of respect are the prefixes *o* and *go*, and a wide range of suffixes. Some of the suffixes you will encounter in *Lone Wolf and Cub*:
dono – archaic; used for higher-ranked or highly respected figures.
sama – used for superiors.

jiji
Old man. Grandfather. Both intimate… and condescending.

jutsu
A martial arts skill, especially the techniques of the ninja.

kōgi kaishakunin
The shōgun's own second, who performed executions ordered by the shōgun.

koku
A bale of rice. The traditional measure of a *han's* wealth, a measure of its agricultural land and productivity.

kuzuyu
A gruel of arrowroot starch sweetened with sugar. A food of the very poor.

meifumadō
The Buddhist Hell. The way of demons and damnation.

nagamaki
A two-handed weapon taller than a man, with a long, curved blade.

ō-metsuke
Chief inspector. The supreme law-enforcement officer of the shōgunate.

rōnin
A masterless samurai. Literally, "one adrift on the waves." Members of the samurai caste who have lost their masters through the dissolution of *han*, expulsion for misbehavior, or other reasons. Prohibited from working as farmers or merchants under the strict Confucian caste system imposed by the Tokugawa shōgunate, many impoverished *rōnin* became "hired guns" for whom the code of the samurai was nothing but empty words.

ryō
A gold piece, worth 60 *monme*.

ryū
Often translated as "school." The many variations of swordsmanship and other martial arts were passed down from generation to generation to the offspring of the originator of the technique or set of techniques, and to any students that sought to learn from the master. The largest schools had their own *dōjō* training centers and scores of students. An effective swordsman had to study the different techniques of the various schools to know how to block them in combat. Many *ryū* also had a set of special, secret techniques that were only taught to school initiates.

sakibure-sōmetsuke
Advance runner. Metsuke inspector in charge of clearing the road for the shōgun.

sakki
The palpable desire to kill, directed at another person. Sometimes called blood lust. Based on the concept of *ki*, or energy, found in spiritual practices and Japanese martial arts like Aikido. These body energies can be felt beyond the physical self by the trained and self-aware.

sankyo sanke
The three sub-branches of the Tokugawa Clan. When there was no heir to the main Tokugawa line, one would be picked from two of these clans, while the fuku-shōgun (Vice-shōgun) always came from the third.

sayu
Unflavored hot water.

seppuku
The right to kill oneself with honor to atone for failure, or to follow one's master into death. Only the samurai class was allowed this glorious but excruciating death. The abdomen was cut horizontally, followed by an upward cut to spill out the intestines. When possible, a *kaishakunin* performed a beheading after the cut was made to shorten the agony.

Tozama daimyō
Daimyō who rallied to the Tokugawa side only after the Tokugawa victory at Sekigahara.

ukiyo
The floating world. The daily, and transient, world of man.

KAZUO KOIKE

Though widely respected as a powerful writer of graphic fiction, Kazuo Koike has spent a lifetime reaching beyond the bounds of the comics medium. Aside from co-creating and writing the successful *Lone Wolf and Cub* and *Crying Freeman* manga, Koike has hosted television programs; founded a golf magazine; produced movies; written popular fiction, poetry, and screenplays; and mentored some of Japan's best manga talent.

Lone Wolf and Cub was first serialized in Japan in 1970 (under the title *Kozure Okami*) in *Manga Action* magazine and continued its hugely popular run for many years, being collected as the stories were published, and reprinted worldwide. Koike collected numerous awards for his work on the series throughout the next decade. Starting in 1972, Koike adapted the popular manga into a series of six films, the *Baby Cart Assassin* saga, garnering widespread commercial success and critical acclaim for his screenwriting.

This wasn't Koike's only foray into film and video. In 1996, *Crying Freeman*, the manga Koike created with artist Ryoichi Ikegami, was produced in Hollywood and released to commercial success in Europe and is currently awaiting release in America.

And to give something back to the medium that gave him so much, Koike started the *Gekiga Sonjuku*, a college course aimed at helping talented writers and artists — such as *Ranma 1/2* creator Rumiko Takahashi — break into the comics field.

The driving focus of Koike's narrative is character development, and his commitment to character is clear: "Comics are carried by characters. If a character is well created, the comic becomes a hit." Kazuo Koike's continued success in comics and literature has proven this philosophy true.

GOSEKI KOJIMA

Goseki Kojima was born on November 3, 1928, the very same day as the godfather of Japanese comics, Osamu Tezuka. While just out of junior high school, the self-taught Kojima began painting advertising posters for movie theaters to pay his bills.

In 1950, Kojima moved to Tokyo, where the postwar devastation had given rise to special manga forms for audiences too poor to buy the new manga magazines. Kojima created art for *kami-shibai*, or "paper-play" narrators, who would use manga story sheets to present narrated street plays. Kojima moved on to creating works for the *kashi-bon* market, bookstores that rented out books, magazines, and manga to mostly low-income readers. He soon became highly popular among *kashi-bon* readers.

In 1967, Kojima broke into the magazine market with his series *Dojinki*. As the manga magazine market grew and diversified, he turned out a steady stream of popular series.

In 1970, in collaboration with Kazuo Koike, Kojima began the work that would seal his reputation, *Kozure Okami* (*Lone Wolf and Cub*). Before long the story had become a gigantic hit, eventually spinning off a television series, six motion pictures, and even theme song records. Koike and Kojima were soon dubbed the "golden duo" and produced success after success on their way to the pinnacle of the manga world.

When *Manga Japan* magazine was launched in 1994, Kojima was asked to serve as consultant, and he helped train the next generation of manga artists.

In his final years, Kojima turned to creating original graphic novels based on the movies of his favorite director, Akira Kurosawa. Kojima passed away on January 5, 2000 at the age of 71.